SOCIALIST
REGISTER
2 0 1 8

THE SOCIALIST REGISTER

Founded in 1964

To get online access to all Register volumes visit our website
http://www.socialistregister.com

SOCIALIST REGISTER 2018

RETHINKING DEMOCRACY

Edited by LEO PANITCH and GREG ALBO

THE MERLIN PRESS
MONTHLY REVIEW PRESS
FERNWOOD PUBLISHING

First published in 2017
by The Merlin Press Ltd.
Central Books Building
Freshwater Road
London
RM8 1RX

www.merlinpress.co.uk

British Library Cataloguing in Publication Data is available from the British
Library

ISSN. 0081-0606

Published in the UK by The Merlin Press
ISBN. 978-0-85036-733-1 Paperback
ISBN. 978-0-85036-732-4 Hardback

Published in the USA by Monthly Review Press
ISBN. 978-1-58367-671-4 Paperback

Published in Canada by Fernwood Publishing
ISBN. 978-1-77363-002-1 Paperback

Printed and bound in the UK on behalf of by Stanton Book Services

CONTENTS

Leo Panitch
Greg Albo
Preface ix

Denis Pilon
The struggle over actually existing democracy 1

Sheila Rowbotham
Women: linking lives with democracy 28

Martijn Konings
From Hayek to Trump:
the logic of neoliberal democracy 48

James Foley
Pete Ramand
In fear of populism:
referendums and neoliberal democracy 74

Adam Hilton
Organized for democracy?
Left challenges inside the Democratic Party 99

Natalie Fenton
Des Freedman
Fake democracy, bad news 130

Tom Mills
Democracy and public broadcasting 150

Nina Power
Digital democracy? 172

Ramon Ribera Fumaz
Greig Charnock
Barcelona en comú:
urban democracy and 'the common good' 188

Sharryn Kasmir
Cooperative democracy or competitiveness?
rethinking Mondragon 202

Leandro Vergara–Camus
Cristobal Kay
New agrarian democracies?
the pink tide's lost opportunity 224

Michelle Williams   Practising democratic communism:
                           the Kerala experience   244

Paul Raekstad   From democracy to socialism, then and now   263

Ian McKay   Challenging the common sense
                           of neoliberalism: Gramsci, Macpherson,
                           and the next left   275

Alex Demirović   Radical democracy and socialism   298

CONTRIBUTORS

Greig Charnock is a senior lecturer in international politics at the University of Manchester.

Alex Demirović teaches at the University of Frankfurt am Main and is a senior fellow at the Rosa Luxemburg Foundation in Berlin.

Natalie Fenton is a professor of media and communications studies at Goldsmiths, University of London.

James Foley recently completed his PhD on the politics of the Scottish economy at the University of Edinburgh, and is the co-author with Pete Ramand of the forthcoming *What is Scottish Independence For?*

Des Freedman is a professor of media and communications studies at Goldsmiths, University of London.

Ramon Ribera Fumaz is Director of the Urban Transformation and Global Change Laboratory at the Universitat Oberta de Catalunya.

Adam Hilton is a visiting lecturer in politics at Mount Holyoke College in Massachusetts.

Sharryn Kasmir is a professor of anthropology at Hofstra University in New York.

Cristobal Kay is a professor of development studies at the University of London School of Oriental and African Studies.

Martijn Konings is a senior lecturer in political economy at the University of Sydney.

Ian McKay is Chair of the Wilson Institute for Canadian History at McMaster University in Hamilton, Ontario.

Tom Mills is a lecturer in sociology at Aston University in Birmingham, England.

Dennis Pilon is an associate professor of politics at York University in Toronto.

Nina Power is a senior lecturer in philosophy at the University of Roehampton in London.

Paul Raekstad is a post-doctoral fellow in political science at the University of Amsterdam.

Pete Ramand is completing his PhD in sociology at the University of Wisconsin-Madison. He is co-editor of *Old Nations, Auld Enemies, New Times: Tom Nairn, Selected Works* (Luath, 2014).

Sheila Rowbotham's most recent book is *Rebel Crossings: New Women, Free Lovers, and Radicals in Britain and the United States* (Verso 2016). Her essay, 'Dear Dr. Marx: A Letter from a Socialist Feminist', appeared in the 1998 *Socialist Register*.

Leandro Vergara–Camus is a senior lecturer at the University of London School of Oriental and African Studies.

Michelle Williams is an associate professor of sociology and chair of the Global Labour Studies programme at the University of Witswatersrand, Johannesburg.

PREFACE

We have conceived this 54th volume of the *Socialist Register* on *Rethinking Democracy* as a companion volume to the 2017 volume on *Rethinking Revolution*. As we put it in the preface to that volume: 'The "political event" of gaining state power, whether by taking parliament or in a collapse of the existing political regime, has proven time and again to be less crucial than the social revolution of building capacities for self-government and the democratization and socialization of institutional resources ... The "event", in itself, ... will never be a sufficient condition for the exploited and oppressed to build their own capacities for establishing collective, rather than competitive, ways of living through developing socialist democracy.'

The Wilsonian rhetoric a hundred years ago of an essential opposition between revolution and democracy was reinforced for much of the twentieth century by the authoritarian cast of the Communist bloc countries; and by 1989, the triumph of capitalist liberal democracy was proclaimed as 'the end of history'. But as the contradictions of neoliberal capitalist globalization have thrown up ever more reactionary responses of the kind our 2016 volume on *The Politics of the Right* examined in close detail across a broad range of states, the antagonism between capitalism and democracy is increasingly visible. It becomes in this context all the more important to help lay some foundations for the new visions, organizations, practices, and institutions that will be required for the development of socialist democracy in the twenty-first century.

The essays with which this volume opens serve as a sharp reminder that the achievement of what is known as democracy today involved profound and protracted social struggles by working-class people, men *and* women, which were always resisted by those whose privileges and property were thereby challenged. The concept of post-democracy which has gained such currency in theoretical and political debate as a label for how neoliberal economic forces are 'undoing the demos' may be seen as neglecting how far the ideational and institutional traces of these resistances became embedded in 'actually existing liberal democracy'. And as the essays on 'neoliberal democracy' suggest, this laid the foundation for populist appeals in the name of defending 'our' democracy by so many reactionary and authoritarian forces. It is in this context that the deployment of referenda as useful instruments for restoring political credibility have suddenly turned into 'objects of fear' for the conventional state managers of globalized capitalism.

Their fear of 'populism' is, of course, also rooted in the accumulating evidence of the renewed electoral appeal of democratic socialist ideas and policies reflecting social struggles from below in the current conjuncture. At the same time, this poses sharp strategic challenges for the left today, as is addressed in the essay here that analyzes, in the wake of the Sanders insurgency, what it is about its organizational structures that makes the US Democratic Party so hard to change in anything like a socialist direction. The ascension of Jeremy Corbyn to the leadership of the British Labour Party – addressed by Hilary Wainwright in the 2017 *Socialist Register* – has even more acutely raised all the old questions associated with the limits and possibilities of democratizing the working-class parties through which social struggles from below have been traditionally channelled into the narrow framework of actually existing liberal democracy. It was surprising enough that Corbyn should have been elected as leader of the party in 2015; even more surprising was how far this came to be electorally validated in the general election of 8 June 2017, through securing the largest increase in the party's vote in any general election since 1945. While the timing of this just as we were in the final editing process of this volume constrained our ability to analyze this development more fully, in light of the *Register*'s extensive critical coverage of developments in the Labour Party since the first volume in 1964, some comments on this remarkable new development are in order here.

Corbyn's own early political formation amidst the protracted crisis of the postwar Keynesian state in the 1970s was deeply embedded in the last attempt to effect a radical democratic socialist transformation of the Labour Party, although this had already been defeated by the time Corbyn was first elected as an MP in 1983. The resurrection of this attempt today amidst the crisis of the neoliberal state inevitably raises the question of whether Ralph Miliband's sobering judgement in the 1976 Register still holds, i.e. 'the belief in the effective transformation of the Labour Party into an instrument of socialist policies is the most crippling of all illusions to which socialists in Britain have been prone'. But Miliband's no less sober observations at the time on the inability of the socialist left to create any effective 'organization of its own political formation, able to attract a substantial measure of support' also sadly continued to apply over the following decades – even as New Labour did its worst to bury any trace of socialist sentiment as well as completely stifle intra-party democracy.

Thus it perhaps should not have been quite so surprising that as the crisis of neoliberalism took New Labour with it after 2008, the prospect of transforming the Labour Party would once again eventually emerge as a plausible strategic option for the left in Britain. That the filmmaker Ken Loach, who in 2013 had stood at the forefront of Left Unity as yet another failed attempt to launch a serious socialist electoral alternative, should be found in 2017 making campaign videos for the Labour Party featuring a very broad range of working people demanding 'the full fruits of our labour' epitomizes the sudden reinvestment of considerable socialist hope, energy, and creativity in the party under Jeremy Corbyn's leadership. This may be taken as fully validating Andrew Murray's sharp critique of the Left Unity initiative in the 2014 *Socialist Register*, but he could hardly have imagined then that only three years later he would be seconded from his position as chief of staff of Britain's largest union, Unite, to the Labour leader's election campaign office.

Perhaps the most significant aspect of the June 2017 election was the greatly increased turnout by young people to vote for the Corbyn-led Labour Party. That this was achieved despite almost two years of constant denigration of Corbyn by his own members of parliament being amplified across the whole spectrum of the mainstream media, as well as against the drag of a central party machine more concerned with vetting than welcoming the new members attracted to the party, was in good part due to the actual momentum generated by Momentum, the organization specifically created to mobilize new members behind (and indeed in front of) Corbyn. With the greatest electoral support coming from working-class voters under 35, and especially from the semi-skilled, unskilled, and unemployed workers among them, this not only suddenly gave the Labour electorate a remarkably young cast, it also signalled a potentially very important shift in the party's class base.

It is worth noting that the last time anything like this happened was a full half century before in the two elections of the mid-1960s, when a new generation of working-class voters contradicted the widespread notion that class political differentiation was a thing of the past by voting Labour in such large numbers. It was only after the profoundly disappointing experience of a Labour government desperately attempting to manage the growing contradictions of the British 'mixed economy' and its 'special relationship' with the American empire that a great many of the young working-class voters turned away from the Labour Party by the time of the 1970 election. Of course, an explosion of activism also characterized this conjuncture. That the Labour Party was almost the last place to which these activists were attracted already points to one of the most important differences between the attempt to transform the party then, spearheaded by Corbyn's mentor Tony Benn, and the one spearheaded by Corbyn himself so many decades later, which has become the catalyst for drawing hundreds of thousands new members to the party.

The very nature of actually existing liberal democracy dictates that the issue of intra-party democracy immediately comes to the fore in this context. The reasons for this were well explained by Tony Benn himself in his essay in the 1989 *Socialist Register*:

> The British people are regularly told that they live in a democracy and that the Mother of Parliaments is respected all over the world as the model on which other democracies have based their own structures and practices. However, in reality, the institutions of Britain are far from democratic and the term democracy is almost always qualified by the adjective 'parliamentary' which may appear to be a minor change but, on close examination, turns out to be a major variation of the idea that the people are sovereign ...
>
> The failure of Labour governments in the past is that they have never told the people the truth, which is that Britain is not a democracy, that office and power are not the same, and in the absence of that knowledge people have never been encouraged to mount the counter-pressure that could shift the balance in favour of labour and against capital, and persuade the establishment that they have no choice but to concede to that pressure because of the strength which it commanded. Historically all social progress has always come from below, yet, almost by definition, those Labour leaders who sit in parliament, in cabinets, or in the higher counsels of the trade union movement, have won their own positions by climbing up a ladder called the 'status quo' and in doing so have escaped from many of the pressures and difficulties which are experienced by those they were elected to represent.

Any struggle to change this by working within the Labour Party is bound to be long and bitter, and its outcome very uncertain, even after important democratic victories in leadership selection and intra-party procedures. And as was indeed seen in the Campaign for Labour Party Democracy's decade long intra-party struggle through the 1970s and into the early 1980s, the strategic focus to initially concentrate the democratic impulse inward on the structures of the party has the perverse effect of projecting the intra-party divisions outward, blunting the very processes of democratic socialist persuasion, education and mobilization necessary not only for short-term electoral success but, in a longer term perspective, for the party to become an active agent of new working-class formation and capacity development.

Corbyn's remarkable electoral success in 2017, especially among young working-class people, is indicative of the very different political conditions produced by the crisis of neoliberalism, one marked by a common working-class revulsion against austerity which stands in sharp contrast to the divisions between public sector and industrial working-class militancy that so marked the 'winter of discontent' in the transition to Thatcherism. The concern of many Momentum activists to go beyond mobilizations for winning democratic constitutional changes at the annual party conference by investing the greater part of their energies and creativity into remaking local Labour Party branches into centres of working-class life is itself an important element in this new conjuncture. But what above all needs to be remembered about the defeat of the last socialist attempt to transform the Labour Party is that it was the union leadership that pulled the plug on it, including those from the left who had earlier supported it but done little to explain to their members what was really at stake. To credibly stress the possibilities rather than the limits of changing the Labour Party requires posing a fundamental challenge to the very way the party has been rooted in the working class through its links with the unions, reproducing a division of labour that has more often militated against rather than nourished new working-class formation and the development of democratic capacities. In this context, Andrew Murray's insightful admonition in his 2014 essay of the activist left for its lack of class-rootedness needs to be turned into a challenge to the pro-Corbyn unions themselves to validate their role in the current attempt to change the Labour Party by proving their capacity to change themselves.

The three essays in this volume that focus on the media in Britain demonstrate the role that public as well as private media play in fashioning the bad news that increasingly turns actually existing liberal democracy into a fake democracy. While the 2017 UK election showed that on-the-ground political campaigns alongside the creative deployment of social media can nevertheless be effective, these essays also demonstrate the need for reviving the type of radical reform agenda for democratizing the media that will require going well beyond what is envisioned either in Labour's *Digital Democracy Manifesto* or in its *Alternative Models of Ownership* report. Indeed, the latter's overwhelming stress on the democratic promise of cooperatives deserves to be critically assessed in light of the two following essays drawing on contemporary developments in Spain: the 'commons-based' models of public administration and social innovation now at work in the new urban democratic experience in Barcelona offer an inspiring contrast to the depressing incorporation of the Mondragon enterprises into the dynamics of neoliberal global markets. Still further negative as well as positive lessons may be learned from the two subsequent essays: the first on the frustration of the potential for rural democracy under Latin America's recent 'pink tide' governments of the left, the second looking to India to draw inspiration from the Communist Party in Kerala's ambitious state-led effort to build local institutions of participatory democratic governance.

The volume concludes with three wide-ranging essays that diversely engage with contemporary theoretical debates by drawing on the radical democratic legacy of Marxist theory. The *Register* has always tried to build on this legacy, as was so well captured by Hal Draper in his essay in the 1974 volume which defined Marx's programme as '*the complete democratization of society*, not merely of political forms .... For Marx, the fight for democratic forms of government – democratization in the state – was a leading edge of the socialist effort.' We hope that the essays in this volume which seek to further build on this to develop new visions of socialist democracy can serve as useful guides in the many more attempts that are surely still to come in the twenty-first century to transcend the limits of actually existing liberal democracy.

We want to thank all our contributors as well as Maciej Zurowski, the translator of the concluding essay, for all the hard work involved in producing essays of such a high calibre on such a challenging theme, and for being so cooperative with our editorial efforts to make them even better. These efforts would have been much more meagre but for the advice of so many members of the *Register*'s editorial collective, and especially the highly skilled and committed support of Steve Maher and Alan Zuege on our editorial team. And we are, as ever, very grateful for the way this has been brought to fruition by Adrian Howe and Tony Zurbrugg of Merlin Press, with yet another inspired cover designed by Louis McKay.

LP
GA
August 2017

THE STRUGGLE OVER
ACTUALLY EXISTING DEMOCRACY

DENNIS PILON

By many accounts the world is more democratic today than ever before. This is usually understood to mean that more countries observe the popularly accepted procedural norms of nation-based democratic practice, such as regular elections, parliamentary control of the executive, and the ability to organize politically, free from coercion by the state or forces within civil society. From a low of just nine democracies by this definition in 1943, the number had increased almost tenfold by 2010 to 87.[1] But as more and more of the world has embraced electoral democracy, public satisfaction with its workings in the countries with the longest experience of it has plummeted. American research reveals the starkest shift, from a 73 per cent approval rating of government in 1958 to just 19 per cent by 2015.[2] Other western countries report more modest increases in 'dissatisfied democrats' but the trends are clear.[3] The targets of public dissatisfaction are many, including political parties, the behaviour of specific politicians, the media, and the rather meagre openings for public input. Yet at the same time, public involvement in existing political opportunities – elections, political party membership, social movements – has declined precipitously. For a variety of pundits and political scientists, this increasing public disdain for and seeming indifference to politics, combined with the rising electoral support for populist anti-system parties from across the political spectrum, is indicative of a broader crisis in western electoral democracy. But just what the crisis is or what is causing it is less clear.

The failure to come to grips with the present democratic deficit in conventional public and academic discourse is not accidental but rooted in a fundamental misunderstanding of what democracy is and how it works. The most basic issue with western electoral democracies is that they are not – and never have been – terribly democratic, a problem that was masked for a time by the postwar economic boom. Political scientists and media commentators tend to miss this because they mistake ideal-type processes and institutions for democracy. But the achievement of what we call democracy – what we have dubbed here 'actually existing democracy' – was not merely about securing certain processes or institutions. It involved a broad *social struggle to install a kind of relationship amongst people for their own self-governance.* It was and remains a struggle because those who would prefer privilege and/or property to be the basis of governing decisions have resisted these attempts. To understand how and why our democracy works as it does, to develop a better explanation of its origins and reproduction, we need to examine the concrete struggles to gain and give shape to actually existing democracy, specifically in advanced capitalist countries.

It should be underlined that we are using the term 'democracy' in two senses. The first captures the relational ideal of a democracy where the great mass of people really does enjoy the power 'to do', to affect the decisions that shape their lives. But the second, actually existing democracy, gives a name to what has been produced through democratic struggle, a struggle that has involved both democratic and anti-democratic social forces, with results that are, not surprisingly, far from the democratic ideal. Struggles which were understood in the nineteenth century to promise/threaten to lead to a serious shift in social power have produced a host of institutional reforms that were not designed to create democratic institutions as much as new institutional spaces to continue contesting democracy and the depth of the democratic relationship. That they have failed to deliver on a substantive democratic experience should not be surprising then as their success in that area has depended on the strength of democratic pressure brought to bear on them, not any intrinsic democratic design or purpose. And the multiple forms of inequality produced or encouraged by capitalism have crucially affected the strength of democratic forces.

WHAT DEMOCRACY IS, AND IS NOT

Standard accounts of democracy suffer from a host of problems. With some, the problem is the predominance of theory. From political philosophy we learn that great men with big ideas have influenced the world because their thoughts have somehow trickled down to society – though evidence of just how this occurred is seldom supplied.[4] Or democracy is reduced to a mixture of different values – freedom, individualism, etc. – that when publicly adopted lead to a democratic breakthrough somehow. This is how defenders of liberal property relations like Locke get pressed into service as democratic theorists.[5] Probably the most common approach defines democracy according to its particular mix of processes and institutions i.e.

competitive elections, the possibility of alternation in government, the existence of non-government media, etc. Even when the stuff of democracy is up for debate, it is the structure of engagement that is often privileged, for instance, contrasting the small-scale citizen deliberation of ancient Greek democracy with the pragmatic large scale and indirect representative systems of today.[6] But all such accounts tend to empty democracy of social content, characterizing it as either a neutral decision-making device or relativistic concept that is whatever any group says it is.[7] Such anodyne approaches have contributed to a great deal of confusion, allowing a host of concepts to be added to the democratic canon – constitutionalism, separation of powers, checks and balances – that were actually once considered to be protections *against* democracy.[8]

To help sort through the different confused themes, we need to consider to what extent any of them help to answer the 'what' and 'when' questions of democracy. When scholars read back from our democratic present they tend to assume that somehow various things pushed us in the direction of democracy but they are seldom very specific about just when or how it happened. Sometimes we can easily point to a specific date, like the postwar restoration of electoral democracy in countries like Germany or Italy or the former Soviet bloc countries after 1989. By contrast, many western countries have unclear democratic starting points. Exactly when did the United States, United Kingdom or Canada turn into democracies? What is the threshold at which we can say each country definitively crossed from being not-democratic to democratic? Can countries be 'sort of' democratic? Or perhaps democracy is like pregnancy, it's not a 'sort of' condition. The former position is actually quite popular – scholars focusing on these countries often talk about a gradual evolution toward democracy or an emerging 'democratic element' within their broader governing systems.[9] But this is reading back from future events, making things that were often explicitly created to *not be* democracy into some kind of 'path towards democracy'.

There is embedded in the democratization discussion a confused assemblage of themes e.g. liberalism, parliamentarization, franchise extensions, elections, etc. Many scholars equate widening the franchise or holding regular elections with democracy. Yet this ignores countries like Germany where men got the vote early but could not really influence what the government did because the crown refused to surrender control of the state to parliament, hardly a democratic state of affairs.[10] Thus the extension of the vote to men in Germany was clearly not about advancing democracy, but something else. Reform was a common trope in nineteenth century Europe and had many competing purposes but one thing was consistent: it was usually mounted in opposition to democracy.[11] The point is, whether elections or franchise extensions are related to democracy depends on a host of other things that are going on, which can only be discovered by examining the struggles over such reforms historically.

Accounts of democratization which focus on how a particular combination of institutions – e.g. mass franchise, parliamentarization, free and fair elections – create the minimal conditions for democracy are definitely more useful.[12] Yet they too struggle with the 'when' question because fixing a definition of democracy on achieving a certain mix of institutions can lead to some seemingly bizarre results, like how racial exclusions would define America as undemocratic until 1965 or gender exclusions would have Switzerland only becoming democratic in 1972.[13] This difficulty with the 'when' of democracy leads back to problems with 'what'. Democracy as a mix of institutions avoids any substantive engagement with what people have thought democracy might do and, historically, it was the threat of what it might do that has made the idea of democracy simultaneously so inspiring and threatening to different groups of people.[14] Most academic accounts have such difficulty defining democracy because they tend to take its existence for granted. They accept at face value the claims of democracy amongst western countries and then note that there is no agreement on its precise limits. As a host of practices exist, and even critics within those countries offer competing ideas about democracy, it is relegated to the 'essentially contested concept' pile.[15] But this is a weak and historically uninformed position. It is also a dangerous one in our present climate, as it provides no basis to assess democratic claims or defend what little democracy may exist now.

Democracy is not that hard to define, actually. If it survived as a concept for over 2000 years in Europe after its brief historical existence in ancient Greece it is because it represented something concrete, not just anything. Put plainly, democracy means 'rule of the people', that is, a lot of people as opposed to traditional forms of rule involving just a small privileged group. More substantively, democracy is a state of affairs where people can participate in and influence the governing decisions that affect their own lives.[16] Of course, defining the 'people' and who is considered a citizen worthy of such participation has shifted amidst racial, ethnic, religious, class, and gender cleavages in different times and places. Critics often fault ancient Greek democracy for just this reason – its lack of inclusion. But this misses the larger point. Flawed as it might be from our contemporary perspective, the achievement of Greek democracy represented a significant shift in *social* power, in the relations amongst the people of the Greek city-states in terms of how governing was affected, authorized and carried out. That is why the privileged members of the Greek city states and their appointed scribes (e.g. Plato, Aristotle) had nothing but scorn for democracy – it represented a serious limit on their power to act. The distinctive thing about Greek democracy then was not merely the selection of governors by lot or that all citizens could participate in deliberations, but how it affected the social relations of Greek society. Thus to understand democracy we should not fetishize any particular institutions or processes or scale but conceive of democracy relationally. As Sheldon Wolin writes, 'Democracy is not about where the political is located but how it is experienced'.[17]

With this in mind we can see that institutions themselves are neither democratic nor undemocratic but only ever just potentially a means to democratic ends. What is important is the democratic substance they produce. Think of democracy as a relationship amongst people for their own collective self-governance. But the effort to introduce and sustain that relationship has always been contested by those who would prefer things to be organized in a different way (e.g. by status or wealth), as well as by the broader social relations of inequality – e.g. class, race, gender, etc. – that exist in any given locale. This is what we mean by 'democratic struggle': it is both the struggle to introduce democracy and then to maintain it, deepen it, defend it, etc. Dylan Riley captures this, drawing from Luciano Canfora's great work *Democracy in Europe: The History of an Ideology*, when he writes: 'The history of democracy therefore involves the study not of constitutional or political systems, but of moments of popular ascendancy, quickly absorbed by anti-democratic forces.'[18] Thus we judge democracy not by some fixed institutional standards, but by the extent to which it really does give the great mass of people some meaningful influence on the decisions that affect their own lives, to the extent it alters the broader relations of power in society. To do this, then, requires us to examine the struggles over actually existing democracies, conflicts that sometimes occur out in the open but also take place behind the scenes, particularly when we attend to the design of institutions meant to channel (or dampen) public demands.[19]

DEMOCRACY'S FALSE FRIENDS

With some sense of the 'what' of democracy we can turn more effectively to the question of 'when' actually existing democracy can be said to arrive. At present, a lot of things are credited with bringing about democracy that did not, or are equated with democracy when they were not. These 'false friends' then confuse the issue by crowding the field with allegedly democratic forces whose intentions were actually quite different. When we credit false friends with contributing to the achievement of democracy we overlook, misunderstand, or diminish the actual participants and events that should get the credit. The list of democracy's false friends could include the bourgeois revolutions of the eighteenth and nineteenth centuries, political campaigns to establish parliamentary control over the executive, reforms to elections, representation, voting rights, and a host of ideological interventions. Even the discourse of democracy itself turns out to be false friend at various historical junctures. Only by examining the struggles themselves can we identify if and when any of these battles actually did further a genuinely democratic agenda.

Attempts to link various bourgeois revolutions to democracy often amount to mistaking successful efforts to limit royal or arbitrary power with some more general victory of 'the people'. The English 'glorious revolution' of 1688 succeeded in strengthening parliament against the king but given the corrupt and narrow franchise the average person could hardly be said to have had much influence on either. Neither the American nor French revolutions of the late eighteenth century broke out for democratic reasons. Their leaders often clearly articulated their stark opposition to democracy. Still, it is common to read scholars who characterize the American Revolution as infused with a democratic ethos and the immediate post-revolutionary society as democratic.[20] But as Bernard Manin carefully recounts, the leading politicians of the era were primarily concerned to protect the rights of property owners, and described their newly designed republic as superior to democracy because it would assure that only the best people (read 'wealthy') would have influence.[21] The new United States also retained a fairly restrictive white male franchise both nationally and locally well into the nineteenth century, alongside more stark racial and gendered limits on voting.[22] An element of democratic discourse did emerge in the French case but it was largely a tactical and temporary concession. The forces that gave rise to the French Revolution initially sought to just rebalance power between the various estates in French society but amid a combination of factional infighting, military setbacks, and international pressure, things quickly spiralled out of control. In an attempt to consolidate power against both internal and external enemies, Robespierre's Jacobin faction introduced full male suffrage for all elections in 1793, but the broader conditions of 'the terror' were hardly conducive to open debate and democratic organizing. The revolutionary franchise reforms barely survived Robespierre's downfall in 1795.[23] Later the waves of revolutionary activity that swept across Europe in the 1820s, 1830s, and 1848 undoubtedly had popular support but their achievements only shifted power amongst elites, not away from them, and then only for a short time in most cases.

The bourgeois revolutions highlight the complexity of social struggle occurring from the late eighteenth to mid-nineteenth centuries across western countries. The primary political struggle was between monarchs and their conservative supporters on one side and everyone else on the other, with the latter category not merely limited to the bourgeoisie but also sometimes including elements of the aristocracy and the church. Aside from revolution, which was rare, such struggles tended to produce demands for institutional reform centring on parliament, elections, and/or the franchise. The struggles were about broadening the basis of elite rule to add more men of property to the governing ranks alongside more traditional rulers, not open the political system to mass influence. Here the use of elections as consultative or representative devices should not be mistaken as an opening to democracy because elections themselves had long been in use across Europe for various purposes, stretching back into the Middle Ages.[24] But as legislatures became sites for contesting executive power – effectively deciding who would control government – the rules for conducting them became a matter of political dispute.

The struggle followed two broad paths in continental Europe. In some countries, conservatives maintained executive power separate from legislative influence. In others conservatives ruled by dominating the legislative branch. In the former, liberals sought legislative control of executive decisions, while in the latter they generally contested a narrow franchise that limited their representation.[25] But in neither case did conservatives or liberals consider including the great mass of working people in the process. There were exceptions, like Germany, where conservatives had extended the vote to all adult men in 1871, but this was granted not as some embrace of democracy but to fend off liberal demands for parliamentary control of the executive. This is why Marx complained that the German legislature was a 'democratic swindle,' just a 'talking shop': the elected members could do little to affect government policy.[26] Great Britain represented a middle way between these two paths as a tenuous balance had been established between royal, aristocratic, and popular influence in Parliament by the early nineteenth century, with a restricted franchise to assure that the popular branch wouldn't be too popular. It is from this perspective that the various 'great' franchise reform acts of 1832, 1867 and 1884 should be understood. Far from being some gradualist 'steps toward democracy,' they represented one-off, negotiated expansions of elite influence over elected members and each was widely understood in their own time as the end of reform, not the beginning.[27] Their impact on increasing the class diversity of the electorate was weak and in many cases illusory, as a considerable number of working men who qualified to vote often found other regulations (like registration rules) would prevent them from participating. Indeed, the majority of working men in the UK would not be able to exercise a right to vote until after the First World War.[28]

Insofar as the spread of certain ideas so credited with bringing about democracy in the nineteenth century were indeed really important they reflected the impact of various strains of radicalism that placed social equality at the centre of their analysis, like British Chartism or continental socialism.[29] Yet the key ideological midwife to democracy is often held to be liberalism, an uneasy amalgam of different strains of nineteenth century thinking mostly rooted in the defence of (unequal) property rights. This unlikely marriage is possible only because today's democratic theorists tend to read liberalism backwards, projecting a clear set of contemporary and ideal liberal principles – freedom of speech, association, and assembly under the rule of law – into the past, where they act as a necessary precursor to democratic activity. But no such coherent form of liberalism actually existed at the time. Instead the strands of thought that would later be incorporated into liberalism – utilitarianism, whiggism, Lockean individualism – were primarily wielded to defend property and those who possessed it against arbitrary behaviour by conservative governments. The citizens discussed in such works, the possessors of various 'rights' and 'freedoms,' were understood to be men of property, not the great mass of people generally.[30] Meanwhile, notions about individual freedom, political rights, and the rule of law were hardly the singular innovations of would-be liberals; indeed most radicals of the period (the Chartists for instance) were far more committed to these goals.

The melding of liberalism with democracy in contemporary debate evinces a serious historical amnesia about the actual uses of liberal ideas in the nineteenth century, and the consistent opposition of nineteenth century liberals to democracy. As Domenico Losurdo recounts, liberal arguments were key to justifying the enclosure of common land, the use of workhouses for the poor, resistance to industrial regulation and a host of other social reforms, as well as imperialism, colonialism, and the dispossession of indigenous peoples elsewhere. The freedom of the individuals on the receiving end of these initiatives did not concern liberals.[31] The broader liberal vision for government was to establish what Ian McKay has called a 'liberal order,' one that would facilitate capitalist development free from traditional encumbrances or custom-driven social disorder.[32] Liberal thinking largely provided justifications for abandoning traditional community obligations in favour of contractually specific and limited ones. Not surprisingly then, liberals proved to be key critics and opponents of democracy, fearing that mass influence would allow the impoverished masses to oppress the wealthy few by reintroducing the community obligations liberals were trying to eliminate. Liberals would resist the shift to democracy at every turn, relenting only when the devastation of WWI suggested their whole liberal order might be swept away.[33] There is a reason that contemporary writers described the descent into the Great War as the 'failure of liberalism': its economics had led to great power brinkmanship while its politics had blocked all paths to a peaceful solution.

Though most of nineteenth century political struggle in the west involved establishing a liberal order, not democracy, more clever politicians often saw advantage in recasting essentially undemocratic processes as democratic ones precisely to weaken the rhetorical force of the term. Raymond Williams notes this shift occurring at different points in the late nineteenth century in a bid to displace traditional understandings of democracy as popular sovereignty in favour of democracy as particular processes.[34] In the United Kingdom, this occurred very gradually, as references to the British parliament slowly – almost imperceptibly – shifted from characterizing the House of Commons as the 'popular chamber' to being the 'democratic element' in the constitution as the nineteenth century neared its end, even though franchise reforms had hardly altered its composition. However, for others, like the Canadian fathers of Confederation, democracy remained an all-purpose put-down, something to lob at opponents in debates over franchise reforms and redistricting well into the twentieth century.[35]

CONTESTING ACTUALLY EXISTING DEMOCRACY

From the late nineteenth century to the present the struggle to establish and then shape the parameters of actually existing democracy has taken many forms. But in all cases the essential elements of conflict have required a combination of mass-scale public demonstrations for democracy, the creation of permanent organizations to mobilize democratic forces, and the development of a radically equalitarian agenda for social change. By contrast, anti-democratic forces have deployed a range of strategies to resist or limit the scope of what these actually existing democracies might do. These have included outright suppression of democratic forces by the state, organized public counter-mobilizations to intimidate and physically threaten democratic forces, the implementation of a variety of institutional reforms to limit or under-represent democratic organizations and political parties, and the use of considerable resources in an attempt to control and shape public discourse to discredit or just make invisible a genuinely democratic imaginary. As we shall see, the conditions of struggle have shifted decisively across this broad timeline, as the balance of political forces has altered via changes in their organizational and ideational strategies and the impact of historical events. But one thing has remained the same across time: the role of class. Struggles over democracy in capitalist societies have essentially pitted capitalism's winners and losers (i.e. capitalists and workers) against each other in an effort to use the state to either advance or redress capitalism's tendencies to enrich capitalists and exploit workers.

The role of class in the emergence of actually existing democracy is hardly disputed amongst democratization scholars but is seldom clearly explained. Most studies try to work out the relationship between long term structural changes in the economy and society and how this influenced demands for political reform. The changing class composition of society, the impact of capitalism on social reproduction, the various class disputes and alliances that resulted – all these factors are worked into an overarching explanation of where democracy comes from.[36] But such approaches fall short when it comes to the specifics of just how different locales transition from being 'not democracy' to democracy. It is one thing to say that various factors contributed to the result, it is another to show just when and how it occurred.

In this most studies offer little more than footnotes to Therborn's rightly acclaimed 1977 intervention on the 'The Rule of Capital and the Rise of Democracy'. There he argued that democracy was not so much a direct result of capitalism as an historical product of its contradictory tensions, particularly its embedded and necessarily antagonistic relationships amongst capitalists and between capitalists and workers. But, in all this, contingency was key. Capitalism, class structures, political alliances – these factors may have set the scene for social upheaval but they did not determine the outcome. As Therborn demonstrated – war, invasion, civil unrest – all these essentially unpredictable events proved to be crucial to most of the democratic transitions that emerged in the wake of the First World War.[37] Therborn spent less time on the factors that preceded the transitions, the institutional reforms that accompanied them, and the contestation that followed them. In other words, he paid less attention to the ongoing struggle over and reproduction of actually existing democracy. This is the *politics* of democratization in capitalist societies, one where anti-democratic forces tended to line up on the right and pro-democratic forces on the left. To understand this ongoing struggle we need to attend in more detail to the actual interactions of working-class politics with conventional elites in each period.

ESTABLISHING ACTUALLY EXISTING DEMOCRACY

As capitalism advanced across all western countries in the nineteenth century, various conservative and liberal political forces struggled to give shape to a political order that would protect or advance their interests. Struggles over the franchise or extending legislative influence over governing executives were initially about stabilizing property rights and the rules that would govern the new economy. Left to their own devices, the efforts of these political elites were producing a liberal order – a governing system based on the rule of law and power-sharing between traditional and propertied elites – not democracy. This only changed with the rise of working-class politics. From the mid to late nineteenth century working-class communities increasingly organized public protests, created organizations like unions and political parties to advocate on their behalf, and articulated a broad vision of a different society – socialism – that would use the state to democratize the economy.[38] Such efforts alone did not lead to any democratic breakthroughs but they did decisively alter the responses of traditional elites, particularly when it came to institutional reform. Suddenly, the stakes involved in political reform had risen appreciably.

Socialism may have been the spectre that haunted the nineteenth century west but with the rise of visibly organized working-class constituencies democracy was seen by conventional political elites as the more immediate threat, if only because they feared the latter would eventually deliver the former. The problem was this: both traditional conservative rulers and the new liberal bourgeoisie believed that when a full male franchise coincided with legislative control over executive power, the new working-class masses would outnumber everyone else and control of the state would fall into their hands, with dire economic consequences. Even as they fought amongst themselves, both conservative and liberal elites remained implacably opposed to democracy for this reason, and continued to be uneasy with the actually existing democracies established after the First World War throughout the interwar period. It was the threat of what democracy would do – how it might alter the balance of power between classes – that was at issue. The institutions themselves were judged by whether they might be a means to this end or a way of preventing this from coming to pass. Thus any given institutional reform – involving the franchise, legislative control of the executive, the secret ballot, voter registration, the voting system – may have been limited to a struggle for advantage between different elites or been part of a much broader social struggle over democracy. It all depended on the class dynamics in play at different times in different places.

Demands for a genuine and substantive democracy in the nineteenth century Western European and Anglo-American countries were primarily working-class demands. But to advance them required three different but complementary strategies. The first involved what might be called 'spectacles of opposition': marches, one day strikes, occupations, and creative challenges to the legitimacy of institutional power like the election of non-sanctioned 'peoples' parliaments'. Europe had a long history of institutional peasant 'rioting' and the moral uses of the crowd to enforce community norms against elite transgression.[39] But the events in this later period were qualitatively different, requiring new forms of organization. A second strategy spoke to this need with the creation of permanent organizations of and for the working class, most crucially trade unions and political parties. Finally, working-class demands only really gained stronger currency in this context when they were coupled with specific claims on the state, ones that would likely require the left to take state power.[40] The difficulty for existing political elites was gauging just what kind of threat these new working-class forces represented, which was in turn influenced by divisions within elite ranks themselves. Where conservatives and liberals could share power, the threat was minimized. Where conservatives retained control, liberals often found themselves in uneasy alliances with more radical forces. But in all cases, the rise of working-class politics forced the defenders of the political status quo to alter their strategy and tactics, sometimes through the use of force, sometimes via institutional reforms.

Pre-democratic western governments can be divided into roughly four regime types: executive conservative regimes, legislative conservative regimes, power-sharing regimes, and legislative liberal regimes. Executive conservative regimes would include Sweden, Finland, Norway, and Germany. Here the crown held on to executive power and legislatures were largely talking shops elected through restricted franchises (Germany being the exception with full male suffrage). In these regimes liberals were often calling for both an expansion of the franchise and legislative control of the executive, though the franchise issue would become muted somewhat once working-class forces came on scene. The classic example was Sweden where liberals had been championing both reforms since the 1880s. When a socialist party emerged in the 1890s liberals initially worked with them, but soon came to prioritize legislative control of the executive while socialists demanded full male suffrage. As more changes to the franchise occurred, this eventually allowed the socialists to surpass the liberals electorally.

Among the executive conservative regimes, the franchise was extended earlier in Germany. Conservatives saw this as a safe move because the crown retained all executive power. Meanwhile, giving all working men the vote effectively undercut liberal pressure to parliamentarize the executive for obvious reasons – such a move would deliver governing control to the working classes, something neither liberals nor conservatives would tolerate.

What conservatives didn't anticipate was how a legislative arena would give the left a focus for their organizing efforts. As Germany's Socialist Party developed its organizational power throughout the late nineteenth century – and its power was considerable, enrolling tens of thousands of members, creating social organizations, providing employment and health insurance, etc. – conservatives sought ways to limit their efforts. An outright ban on Socialist Party activities between 1878 and 1890 proved counter-productive, so conservatives tried more subtle institutional reforms. For instance, conservatives, with liberal support, introduced proportional voting wherever socialists dominated electoral representation (e.g. at the local or state level, on insurance or employment boards), primarily to weaken their position. Still, by the start of the First World War the socialists were the largest party in the national legislature.

Whereas France alternated between a conservative legislative and a kind of power-sharing regime from the post-revolutionary period to the First World War, the United Kingdom stood as the classic power-sharing regime, from roughly 1832 on. Residual royal power did continue to exist in the UK well into the reform era, and the threat of opposition from the hereditary House of Lords was significant right up to just before the First World War but, on the whole, a variety of conservative and liberal factions did effectively control government from a power base in the elected House of Commons throughout the nineteenth century, though on a narrow and uneven franchise.[41] Significant working-class organizations only emerged late in the nineteenth century, by which time a new party system had solidified around conservatives and liberals who had a lock on most of the elected representation. Working-class pressure did lead liberals to make electoral deals with the new Labour Party in the early twentieth century, but restrictive registration rules and a still restricted franchise limited their influence.

Legislative liberal regimes would include the USA, Canada, Australia, and New Zealand, where political competition for legislative influence was mostly defined by different liberal factions (usually divided over support for free trade versus tariffs) until the rise of left forces in the early twentieth century, though here too franchise restrictions were a point of conflict.[42] The United States was unique within this group having rid itself of conservatives as one result of its revolution in the eighteenth century. Property, race, and gender were initially the basis for the franchise, but with expansion to the west by the 1820s pressure mounted to include various ranks of white working men. Though commonly thought to have been achieved in the Jacksonian era, this franchise reform was actually rolled out in a very uneven manner, with white working-class men gaining the vote in rural areas at different times in the nineteenth century while the same voters in urban areas generally did not.[43] Additionally, American elections were widely seen to be corrupt, characterized by considerable violence (especially where voting was not secret), and subject to a host of electoral manipulations involving districting, voter registration, and vote counting well into the twentieth century. Populist and working-class political challenges were considerable in the 1890s and prior to the First World War but unable to break the duopoly of power represented by the two essentially dominant political parties. The separation of powers between the directly elected lower house and the indirectly elected Senate (up to 1918) and President also weakened the ability of working-class challengers to threaten the conventional politicians' power base.

What we see in common across western countries is how the rise of an organized working-class politics forced responses from conventional political elites, whatever the mix of conservative and liberal factions in any given locale. But the nature of the governing regime, the structure of governing power, and balance of competing forces within and outside it decisively influenced the responses. Working-class demonstrations were public examples of potential working-class support and power, which gained salience whenever a whiff of revolution was in the air. Working-class organizations strengthened the mobilization of the working class and allowed working-class parties to eventually outpoll liberal forces in electoral contests. And working-class political ideas about how society could be reorganized more broadly, along with specific policy promises around employment and services, upset the consensus ideologies that legitimized conservative and liberal rule. When it became clear that suppression of working-class politics would be too costly, conventional political elites responded with a slew of institutional reforms designed to weaken them. The tricky bit was moving on such reforms without giving undue ground to other elite opponents.

In all locales conventional elites had held on to some kind of significant veto power before the First World War, depending on what had already been conceded. It might have been accomplished with a narrow franchise or by limiting legislative oversight of the executive, or it could be secured via an upper house or imperial oversight, or through the use of plural votes, indirect voting, or districting that favoured traditional elites. The surrender of these final veto points was the moment of transition from 'not democracy' to 'actually existing democracy' in the west. Contra liberal platitudes, the break only came with violence, or the threat of violence, rather than some incremental, liberal-led process of change. Prior to the First World War it was clear that neither conservatives nor liberals were prepared to open up political competition in a way where working-class voters and their parties could vie for power. Only the privations of wartime shifted this consensus, primarily because the conditions of waging war – a total war like no other in human history – increased the collective capacities of the working class. Elites still feared that with a mass franchise working-class voters would comprise a majority of the electorate and overwhelm them, so many in this context turned to institutional reforms in an attempt to limit working-class influence. The key reform was a shift to proportional voting systems, which would limit the over-representation typical of the traditional plurality and majority voting systems in use everywhere and possibly allow for divisions in working-class politics to emerge. This strategic response would prove popular and was eventually adopted in all countries of mainland Western Europe after the First World War and was considered seriously in most of the Anglo-commonwealth countries as well.

The end of war saw the other countries fall in line with this version of actually existing democracy, though conservative regimes like Germany and Sweden held out to the very end of the war when defeat and revolution seemed both likely results. As Geoff Eley points out, revolution was a key factor in brokering the actually existing democracy deal, given elite fears at a time when the Russian Revolution of 1917 was a very real possibility everywhere.[44] Proximity to the war zone itself and Russia's new revolutionary regime were both clearly important factors in these differing elite responses. Continental European countries faced a degree of social upheaval that motivated fairly rapid elite concessions. Elites elsewhere had more time to work out just how much or how little need be conceded.

STABILIZING ACTUALLY EXISTING DEMOCRACY

Nineteenth century conservative and liberal fears that a 'democratic tyranny' would result from the electoral empowerment of the working class did not come to pass with the achievement of the actually existing democracies after the First World War. Instead, the working-class electorate proved to be much less homogenous in their voting patterns than previously enfranchised groups. At the same time, working-class organizations proved unable to maintain their wartime and immediate postwar mobilizing efforts into the 1920s. In countries that had adopted proportional voting systems, working-class parties found themselves shut out of office or unable to do much even when they did gain office. Everywhere the parameters of the new actually existing democracies remained contested. In some cases, like Sweden, Norway, Australia, and New Zealand, the advent of the Great Depression helped remobilize working-class organizations and led to a breakthrough for the left. But in others, like Italy, Germany, Austria, and Spain, reactionary forces were successful in bringing the democratic experiment to an end. However, in most western locales, the interwar period represented a kind of standoff over actually existing democracy, with the left unable to advance while traditional elites refused to cede much more than the appearance of democratic process.[45]

1919 proved to be the culmination and peak of left democratization pressure. General strikes broke out across the western world and workers took over the direct administration of cities as far afield as Turin, Seattle, and Winnipeg. A host of left political parties did register gains at the ballot box. And public opinion more generally reflected a strong desire to see governments shape the world differently in the postwar world. Institutional reforms touted as 'democratic' were quickly introduced by nervous elites wherever the left appeared to have the upper hand. But appearances would prove to be deceiving. Advancing into the uneven economic times of the 1920s, left mobilizing faltered while left electoral politics split between those committed to revolution and those prepared to work through existing state institutions. In Western Europe, the combined electoral strength of communist and socialist parties rarely exceeded 40 per cent of the popular vote at best. The left did gain office in some locales in the 1920s in coalitions or as minority governments (e.g. Germany, Sweden, UK) but found their legislative programmes blocked by bourgeois parties. Left aspirants for political office were unable to seize power at the level of state. Meanwhile, direct action did not fare much better. The 1926 general strike in Britain ended in failure, exposing the weakness of organized labour to force its agenda onto conventional politics. Anti-democratic forces were proving successful at using new institutions to marginalize the left and democratic supporters.

This led to some re-evaluation on the left of their traditional commitment to reforms like proportional representation. Historically most left parties supported it as a matter of common sense fairness – that every vote should count and count equally – but, given the hostility of bourgeois parties to working with the left or their agenda in the interwar period, various parties in Europe and beyond started to have doubts. Critics in the Scandinavian countries were now seeing how the votes were not adding up their way, and opponents across various bourgeois parties – formerly rivals amongst themselves – were now pretty much united against the left and its social and economic agenda. In the UK, the British Labour Party was one of the first left parties to repudiate PR, arguing that given the implacable opposition of other parties, the media, and the social elites, only the exaggerated majorities associated with the first-past-the-post voting system would give a Labour government the breathing room to pass its policies and have the public experience them before judging them at the polls. The British influence on such matters soon spread to left forces in Canada and New Zealand who similarly dropped their previous commitment to PR.[46]

The cataclysmic decline of capitalist economies in the 1930s created new opportunities for the left to press for a more democratic society, reanimating the three-pronged strategy of demonstrations, renewed organizational capacities, and a clear counter discourse to the status quo both politically and economically. Surprisingly, one of the strongest responses came in the US, a country without a left party in the Western European or Anglo-commonwealth sense, where populist forces were able to shift the Democratic Party to the left to sponsor a significant public works programme in the depths of Depression.[47] In Canada, public marches of the unemployed drew considerable public sympathy and contributed to the breakdown of the party system just before 1935 federal election. Though a new left party and other populist forces proved electorally popular, the first-past-the-post voting system delivered a victory to the centre-right Liberal Party, which declined to respond to the economic crisis.[48] In the largest countries in Western Europe the forces of left and right fought each other to a standstill (France) or civil war (Spain) or a coup (Germany) or a reactionary party realignment (UK). Only in the larger Scandinavian countries (e.g. Norway, Sweden) and distant British Commonwealth countries (e.g. Australia, New Zealand) were forces of the left able to exploit divisions on the centre-right to advance some modest democratic and economic reforms. But on the whole the interwar period appeared to confirm left fears about the incompatibility of capitalism and democracy. These new actually existing democracies tended to survive only where they remained weak and shallow. Signs of potential democratic strength or substance led to confrontation, instability, and some kind of neutralization of the democratic threat by the political right.

It would take another world war and another round of institutional reforms (with particular attention to proportionality in election outcomes in continental Europe) to force some substance into actually existing democracies in the West. The conditions aiding a working-class push for greater democracy were very different in 1945 than in 1919. As with the First World War, the war had helped mobilize working people both organizationally and ideologically. Left demands for strong government action to create a new, fairer society after the war proved electorally popular, at least initially. From 1945 to 1947 the left dominated politics across Western Europe, winning elections and quickly implementing a policy mix that included a substantial nationalization of the economy alongside the introduction of a broad social welfare regime.[49] Commentators would eventually characterize these reforms as transforming capitalism into a 'mixed economy' with both public and private dimensions, a result emerging from a 'postwar consensus' for change. But consensus did not merely 'emerge', it was produced through active political struggle. In 1945 the political right in most Western countries remained opposed to interventionist economic policies and the welfare state, and actively campaigned against them. The precise character of the postwar consensus differed across countries, depending on the balance of class forces in play.

A key factor in the struggle over actually existing democracy in the postwar period was the role of American imperial power in shaping and, for a time, stabilizing the postwar international order. Largely untouched by the physical devastation of the war, the US used its economic muscle to discipline Western countries and bring them into line with American foreign policy objectives. As one of the occupying powers in Germany and Italy, the US counselled delay in holding elections, primarily to give time to the discredited, collaborationist forces of the right to reinvent themselves as Christian Democrats. Particular attention was paid to institutional rules to ensure that the centre-right of the political spectrum could maximize its representation against the perceived rising popularity of the left – and this meant the US insisted on proportional representation for elections in both countries. However, when the right appeared ascendant by the 1950s American opinion quickly shifted to support some form of majority voting to marginalize the left. The US leveraged access to Marshall Plan economic aid to divide the left as well, contributing to a breakdown in left unity between communists and socialists at both the party and trade union level across Europe, particularly in France and Italy. This was aided by the broader campaign against the left in the guise of the Cold War, where loyalty to the trumped up threat of Soviet aggression became a mark of national identity and a powerful means of discrediting left actors (most of whom were not actually communists) and progressive projects throughout civil society.[50]

American political elites were free to campaign against the left internationally in part because they faced no significant left political force at home. Cold War hysteria and McCarthyite witch-hunts destroyed what was left of the organized political left outside of the Democratic Party. Attempts by left forces to burrow within the Democratic Party to gain influence were usually weakened by the party's southern voting bloc and the influence of American business. Class issues in the US often had to be cast in other terms, like race, and suffered the limits that such political organizing entailed. The

American civil rights movement created impressive spectacles of resistance to the entrenched racism and poverty African-Americans faced, particularly in the 1960s. But their cross-ideological appeal – support stretched from the libertarian right to liberal left and further – blunted the economic aspects of the structural racism. Some class elements emerged with Johnson's 'Great Society' welfare reforms of 1965-66 but compared to other western countries the US had the weakest welfare state by far.[51] It would be a problem faced by all of the so-called 'identity politics' movements of the 1960s and 1970s.

But to the extent that the left remained mobilized organizationally, there were limits on just how far US influence and right-wing forces could push anti-democratic initiatives. Across Europe millions of people continued to vote for parties associated with socialism and communism while in most Anglo-commonwealth countries some kind of left/labour party was a potential governing force at the national and/or subnational level. And these parties, unlike the right, remained mass parties with thousands of active members and often millions of non-active supporters. This meant that each society had anywhere from a third to half of their voters (and more non-voters) committed to a counter or at least non-hegemonic democratic politics, backed by trade unions which reached peak levels of organization and membership in the decades immediately following the Second World War. Indeed, despite a wall of negative media coverage of the left throughout the postwar period, support for such parties remained strong.[52] At the same time, the left was obviously influenced by the sense of what was possible, given continued organized resistance from the right. To that end, the electoral left made its peace with the limits of a form of economic democracy existing within the confines of capitalism, increasingly identifying nationalization and the welfare state as 'socialism' in the context of a US-managed international trade system.

The politically-managed postwar standoff between left and right came under increasing strain in the 1970s. Various social movements emerged in the mid to late 1960s, adding to an increasing militancy amongst workers, to contest the narrow confines of actually existing democracy. Protests of various kinds – anti-war, women's liberation, ecological – mushroomed, and work days lost to strikes spiralled upward. This spilled over into left parties with serious efforts to improve their internal democracy in terms of candidate selection and policy development.[53] Even progressives within the US Democratic Party made gains in the 1970s, opening up the smoke-filled back rooms that traditionally controlled decision-making.[54] At the same time, the economic expansion of the postwar period appeared to stall. In various locales the left debated whether it was time to move beyond the

Keynesian welfare state compromise with capital. The left in the UK Labour Party crafted an Alternative Economic Strategy that would have seen a Labour government make economic investment decisions more democratic by nationalizing the banks, among other proposals. In Sweden, the long governing socialists introduced the Meidner Plan in an attempt to bring more democratic influence to bear on economic decision-making. In Canada the left in the New Democratic Party put forward a Waffle Manifesto to limit American influence on Canadian economic decisions. But in each case the party of the left lost its nerve, opting to simply defend the Keynesian status quo for as long as possible.[55]

The challenge for the left from the 1970s on was that key pillars of its support were decaying from the inside. Peter Mair suggests a process of 'hollowing out' of formerly mass parties of the left was occurring. As women joined the workforce and the welfare state ameliorated some of the most egregious aspects of capitalism, membership in left parties began to decline and then plummet rapidly. Parties of all stripes turned to the state for financing, weakening their connection to civil society and fuelling a mediated form of politics (largely via expensive television advertising) rather than more direct approaches like door-to-door campaigning.[56] Additionally, starting in the 1960s, left parties went through a process of what Gerassimos Moschonas has called 'middle-classization', where formerly working-class leadership cadres and candidates were slowly replaced by members of the middle class.[57] And then, from the late 1970s, the generation shaped by the working-class conditions and politics of the Depression and the Second World War were retiring, losing influence in the day-to-day politics of left, and from the 1980s on dying off. Organizationally, unions proved better able to sustain their membership numbers going into the 1980s, but the right's counter-offensive in attacking public services and government ownership of key industries and utilities would eventually undermine the union movement as well, given that union density rates have been sustained largely by the expansion of unionized public services since the 1970s.

If the left had forced the right to abandon the key tenets that had defined 'sound finance' in the interwar period – balanced budgets, low social spending, and low taxes – after the Second World War, then the right's counter-offensive beginning in the 1970s marked a creative return to such nineteenth century economic thinking: neoliberalism. The project, eventually adopted across the political spectrum, sought to return all aspects of life to market regulation via privatizing and reducing public services, while shifting the tax burden away from the wealthy and business. Neoliberalism represented a clear attack on the actually existing democracy established in the postwar period, as its goal was nothing less than to strip from governments the ability to respond to the social and economic needs of their working classes. Indeed, right wing think-tanks like the Fraser Institute and the Heritage Foundation openly promoted neoliberal policies like free trade precisely to limit the ability of governments to respond to democratic demands from their own people.

As neoliberalism solidified as the new economic common sense in the 1980s and 1990s, the left stubbornly defended the postwar Keynesian economic orthodoxy of a mixed economy of public and private investment, at least at first. But attempts to defend such policies in government became increasingly difficult. Though left parties remained popular and came to power in a host of locales in the 1990s and into the new century, they came under increasingly vicious and orchestrated media attacks highlighting allegedly wasteful government programmes, widespread cheating in social programmes (e.g. welfare fraud), and a hyped-up government debt hysteria. The claims were not backed up by serious facts but it didn't matter – they were repeated ad nauseum.[58] In the past, left forces had been able to defend themselves against such tactics because they had so many party members and their own channels of communications, and they could count on a working-class culture that helped make voters somewhat resilient to the self-serving claims of the hegemonic media. But the decline of working-class organizations, particularly those run by working-class people themselves, had contributed to a radical demobilization of the working class and the erasure of working-class experience from view, particularly in popular culture (except as figures of ridicule, like TV's Archie Bunker from *All in the Family* or the various lumpen-proletariat characters from the sketch comedy show *Little Britain*). This has contributed to serious declines in voter turnout amongst the working class, specifically youth.[59]

Deserted by the working class at the polls, unrecognizable as working-class parties in terms of their spokespeople or policies, left parties increasingly embraced neoliberalism (or 'progressive competitiveness' as Greg Albo has put it) in a bid to gain a greater share of the middle-class electorate.[60] As twenty-first century capitalism continues to squeeze more profits from working people by pushing down real wages and living standards, working people have tried to resist, and this has led to a return to attempts at institutional fixes to either revive the substance of actually existing democracy or strip it further of its weak democratic output. Voting system reform became one scene in the struggle, where neoliberal proponents in countries like Japan and Italy tried to introduce new voting systems to help the break the political deadlock preventing the introduction of neoliberal policies.

They were only partially successful. But in other places voting system reform became a strategy of resistance to neoliberalism. In New Zealand, where neoliberal advocates had captured the leadership of both right and left parties, an outraged electorate drove a populist anti-politician grassroots campaign that ultimately replaced the country's unrepresentative first-past-the-post voting system with proportional representation. Similar campaigns have been launched for similar reasons in the United Kingdom, Canada and the United States.[61] Ironically, a reform once seen as key to weakening the democratic relationship after both world wars now appears to be crucial in strengthening it, given the present balance of class forces.

Yet institutional changes like voting system reform remained unusual in the postwar period. For the most part political elites supported by the economically powerful discovered that they did not necessarily need institutional devices to keep the democratic relationship weak. They could manage the outcomes via other means: advertising, agenda setting, polling, and so forth.[62] Over time they have been aided in their efforts by the decline of working-class organizations, a development that has contributed to the widespread demobilization of the working class as well as evisceration of working-class identity as a basis for collective action. This is one reason that more contemporary 'spectacles of opposition' like Occupy have proven unable to capitalize on their success in delegitimizing existing economic arrangements – they have lacked both the organizational resources to mobilize mass support and the ability to articulate a broad alternative vision of an economically democratic society to the masses. This organizational weakness has also allowed the electoral right to go on the offensive, engaging in a series of voter suppression tactics aimed at keeping working-class voters from the polls while sponsoring myriad ideological alt-news web sites to misinform and confuse voters.[63] At the same time a host of right-wing friendly liberal intellectuals have begun to muse openly about the impracticality and irrationality of democracy.[64] Thus, as we can see, in the struggle over actually existing democracy throughout the twentieth century both left and right sought out and developed both ideas and concrete strategies to empower themselves and disempower their enemies.

ACTUALLY EXISTING DEMOCRACY IN THE TWENTY-FIRST CENTURY

A variety of progressive scholars have declared our contemporary moment to be one of 'post-democracy'; one where neoliberal economic forces are 'undoing the demos'.[65] But such claims grant too much to the allegedly democratic substance of actually existing democracies, which were never terribly democratic to begin with. Given their contested origins and the conflicting political aims they embraced, this should not be surprising. Actually existing democracies were born of struggle between democratic and anti-democratic forces, and their institutional super-structures were never designed to be democratic but rather represented often desperate compromises achieved in times of crisis between competing social forces unsure of their own power or that of their opponents. The institutional edifices they produced were their best guess about how to continue their struggle over democracy, to either strengthen a democratic relationship amongst people for their collective self-governance or to weaken it. Historically, working-class politics was key to the achievement and increasing depth of actually existing democracies, primarily due to its ability to mobilize the working class as a political force, as we have seen from tracking the actual transitions and changes in Western countries. Securing some kind of actually existing democracy after the First World War, defending it during the interwar period, expanding it after the Second World War, and defending it again amid neoliberal pressures more recently – all these campaigns have required political action anchored in mobilized working-class communities. The weakness of working-class politics today is the single greatest threat to maintaining what little democracy remains in actually existing democracies.

There have been signs of a recent revival of working-class politics – Bernie Sanders in the US, Jeremy Corbyn in the UK, various new left parties in Europe – but what is required to further such a project is still unclear. Sanders near-victory in the Democratic primary against the heavily favoured Hilary Clinton in 2016, and Jeremy Corbyn's stunning Labour result in the June 2017 British election highlight the value of some traditional left tactics: door-to-door campaigning, personal contact between potential working-class voters and the left party seeking their support, a clear message of hope and class politics that focuses public attention on inequality and the actors – the system – responsible for it. And yet the job of fighting over actually existing democracy today also involves new conditions and a reinvention of critical and innovative democratic strategies, a challenge Geoff Eley noted has faced the left in every generation. What hasn't changed is the need to mobilize the great mass of people who need democracy into the struggle to achieve it, because it is only with such a mobilized force that broader social relations of power can be altered. Democracy is a relationship amongst people for their own self-governance, but the inequalities created by capitalist social relations arm democracy's opponents to work at continually weakening the relationship. Only collective action to achieve and defend democracy can resist this, and the resistance must be material, organizational, programmatic, and aimed at transforming power at the level of the state.

NOTES

1   Max Roser, 'Democracy', *Our World in Data*, Oxford: Ourworldindata.org, 2016.

2   Pew Research Center, *Beyond Distrust: How Americans View Their Government*, Washington D.C.: Pew Research Center, November 2015, p. 5.

3   Roberto Stefan Foa and Yascha Mounk, 'The Danger of Deconsolidation: The Democratic Disconnect', *Journal of Democracy* 27(3), 2016, pp. 5-17.

4   For an example of this approach, see J. Roland Pennock, *Democratic Political Theory*, Princeton: Princeton University Press, 1971. For a treatment that does connect philosophical ideas with actual events, see Jan-Werner Muller, *Contesting Democracy: Political Ideas in Twentieth Century Europe*, New Haven: Yale University Press, 2011.

5   For an example of this approach, see Boris Dewiel, *Democracy: A History of Ideas*, Vancouver: UBC Press, 2000.

6   A great deal of the participatory democracy literature makes this mistake. For a recent example, see Dario Azzellini and Marina Sitrin, *They Can't Represent Us! Reinventing Democracy from Greece to Occupy*, London: Verso, 2014.

7   For examples, see Robert A. Dahl, Ian Shapiro, and Jose Antonio Cheibub. eds, *The Democracy Sourcebook*, Cambridge: MIT Press, 2003.

8   Sheldon Wolin takes up these themes in 'Norm and Form: the Constitutionalizing of Democracy', in J.P Euben, J.R. Wallach, and J. Ober, eds, *Athenian Political Thought and the Reconstruction of American Democracy*, Ithica: Cornell University Press, 1994, pp. 29-58; and 'Fugitive Democracy', *Constellations* 1(1), 1994, pp. 11-25.

9   For examples of this approach, see Ruth Berins Collier, *Paths Toward Democracy: The Working Class and Elites in Western Europe and South America*, Cambridge: Cambridge University Press, 1999; and John Markoff, 'Where and When Was Democracy Invented', *Comparative Studies in Society and History* 41(4), 1999.

10   On the struggle to parliamentarize the executive across Western countries, see Klaus von Beyme, *Parliamentary Democracy: Democratization, Destabilization, Reconsolidation, 1789-1999*, Houndsmill: Palgrave Macmillan, 2000.

11   For examples of how electoral reforms were used to frustrate democratic demands, see Dennis Pilon, *Wrestling with Democracy: Voting Systems as Politics in the Twentieth Century West*, Toronto: University of Toronto Press, 2013.

12   See Deitrich Rueschemyer, Evelyne Huber Stephens, and John D. Stephens, *Capitalist Development and Democracy*, Chicago: University of Chicago Press, 1992.

13   Goran Therborn wrestles with this very difficulty in his 'The Rule of Capital and the Rise of Democracy', *New Left Review* 103(May-June 1977), pp. 16-17.

14   See C.B. Macpherson, *The Real World of Democracy*, Toronto: House of Anansi Press, 1992, pp. 1-2.

15   See Phillip Green, 'Democracy as a Contested Idea', in P. Green, ed., *Democracy*, New Jersey: Humanities, 1993, pp. 2-18; and Laurence Whitehead, 'The Vexed Issue of the Meaning of Democracy', *Journal of Political Ideologies* 2(2), 1997, pp. 121-35.

16   As Josiah Ober argues, Greek democracy was less about processes and the scale of interaction and more about the 'capacity to do things' i.e. the power to do, to have impact, to influence what was going on. See J. Ober, 'The Original Meaning of "Democracy": Capacity to Do Things, Not Majority Rule,' *Constellations* 15(1), 2008, pp. 3–9. Nor is ancient Greece the only non-modern example of people living under a broadly democratic form of governance. Anthropologists and indigenous scholars

highlight how throughout history there were many examples of small-scale societies operating in ways we would recognize as democratic. See Julia Paley, 'Toward an Anthropology of Democracy', Annual Review of Anthropology 31(1), 2002, p. 476.

17 See Wolin, "Fugitive Democracy," p. 18.

18 See Dylan Riley, 'Freedom's Triumph: The Defeat of Democracy in Luciano Canfora', New Left Review 56(March-April 2009), p. 48. For the original insights, see Luciano Canfora, Democracy in Europe: A History of an Ideology, Oxford: Blackwell, 2006.

19 The theme that institutional channels for popular participation were designed primarily to constrain that participation is developed in Benjamin Ginsberg, The Consequences of Consent: Elections, Citizen Control and Popular Acquiescence, Reading, Mass.: Addison-Wesley, 1982; and given ample illustration in Pilon, Wrestling with Democracy.

20 See John Dunn, Democracy: A History, Toronto: Penguin, 2006; and John Roper, Democracy and Its Critics, London: Unwin Hyman, 1989. Even Marxists make this mistake; see Brian S. Roper, The History of Democracy, A Marxist Interpretation, London: Pluto, 2013, who characterizes the English, American, and French revolutions as democratic.

21 See Bernard Manin, The Principles of Representative Government, Cambridge: Cambridge University Press, 1997, pp. 2–4.

22 See Alexander Keyssar, The Right to Vote: The Contested History of Democracy in the United States, New York: Basic Books, 2000.

23 See Malcolm Crook, Elections in the French Revolution, Cambridge: Cambridge University Press, 1996.

24 A.R. Myers, Parliaments and Estates in Europe to 1789, London: Thames and Hudson, 1975, pp. 24–8.

25 This process is sketched out in von Beyme, Parliamentary Democracy.

26 See Hal Draper, 'Marx on Democratic Forms of Government', in Ralph Miliband and John Saville, eds, The Socialist Register 1974, London: Merlin Press, 1974, p. 118.

27 For elite attitudes to the 1832 reforms, see Michael Levin, The Spectre of Democracy: The Rise of Modern Democracy as Seen by Its Critics, New York: New York University Press, 1992, p. 28. For elite attitudes to later reform acts, see Robert Saunders, 'The Politics of Reform and the Making of the Second Reform Act, 1848–1867', Historical Journal 50(3), 2007, pp. 571–91.

28 See Neal Blewett, 'The Franchise in the United Kingdom 1885–1918', Past and Present 32(1), 1965; and H. Matthew, R. McKibbon, and J. Kay, 'The Franchise Factor in the Rise of the Labour Party', English Historical Review 91(July), 1976, pp. 723-52.

29 See Owen Ashton, Robert Fyson, and Stephen Roberts, eds, The Chartist Legacy, London: Merlin Press, 1999; and Geoff Eley, Forging Democracy: The History of the Left in Europe, 1850-2000, Oxford: Oxford University Press, 2002.

30 For a critical investigation of nineteenth liberalism, see Domenico Losurdo, Liberalism, A Counter-History, London: Verso, 2014. For evidence of how 'Liberal' emerged as coherent political identity from its roots in whiggism and various strands of radicalism in the UK only in the 1860s, see Angus Hawkins, Parliament, Party and the Art of Politics in Britain, 1855-59, Houndsmill: Palgrave Macmillan, 1987.

31 Recounted in detail in Losurdo, Liberalism, A Counter-History.

32 See Ian McKay, 'The Liberal Order Framework: A Prospectus for a Reconnaissance of Canadian History', Canadian Historical Review 81(4), 2000, pp. 616-45.

33   Losurdo notes that 'it should not be forgotten that not only did the classics of the liberal tradition refer to democracy with coldness, hostility and sometimes frank contempt, but regarded its advent as an unlawful, intolerable, rupture of the social contract and hence as a legitimate cause for the "appeal to Heaven" (in Locke's words) or to arms.' He reminds us how often violence was necessary to overcome liberalism's 'exclusion clauses', for example, the American Civil War, the twentieth century World Wars, etc. See Losurdo, *Liberalism, A Counter-History*, 341.

34   See Raymond Williams, *Keywords*, Glasgow: Fontana, 1976, pp. 85-6.

35   See Dennis Pilon, 'The Contested Roots of Canadian Democracy', *Studies in Political Economy*, 98:2(2017) pp. 105-23.

36   This literature is reviewed in Jean Grugel, *Democratization: A Critical Introduction*, Houndsmill: Palgrave Macmillan, 2002.

37   See Therborn, 'The Rule of Capital and the Rise of Democracy'.

38   For detail on these developments, see Eley, *Forging Democracy*; and E.J. Hobsbawm, 'The Making of the Working Class', *Uncommon People: Resistance, Rebellion and Jazz*, 1984; London: Weidenfeld, 1998.

39   For an exploration of this pre-modern, collective enforcement of customary rights see E.P. Thompson, *Customs in Common*, New York: New Press, 1991.

40   This is set out in detail in Eley, *Forging Democracy*.

41   For a detailed treatment of this period and the changes, see H.J. Hanham, *The Nineteenth Century Constitution, 1815-1914*, Cambridge: Cambridge University Press, 1969.

42   The source for the following section on reforms to western elections, voting rules, and legislative control of the executive is Pilon, *Wrestling with Democracy*, particularly chapters 2 to 5.

43   See Keyssar, *The Right to Vote*, 170.

44   See Geoff Eley, 'What Produces Democracy? Revolutionary Crises, Popular Politics and Democratic Gains in Twentieth Century Europe', in Mike Haynes and Jim Wolfreys, eds, *History and Revolution: Refuting Revisionism*, London: Verso, 2007, pp. 172-201.

45   This next section draws from Donald Sassoon, *One Hundred Years of Socialism*, New York: New Press, 1996; Eley, *Forging Democracy*; and Stefano Bartolini, *The Political Mobilization of the European Left, 1860-1980: The Class Cleavage*, Cambridge: Cambridge University Press, 2000.

46   See Dennis Pilon, 'Labour and the Politics of Voting System Reform', in S. Ross and L. Savage, eds, *Rethinking the Politics of Labour in Canada*, Halifax: Fernwood, 2012, pp. 93-4.

47   See Adam Hilton, 'Party Reform and Political Alignment: The New Politics Movement in the Democratic Party', York University: PhD dissertation, 2016.

48   See James Naylor, *The Fate of Labour Socialism*, Toronto: University of Toronto Press, 2016.

49   See Eley, *Forging Democracy*, 287-316.

50   See Pilon, *Wrestling with Democracy*, chapter 6.

51   See Hilton, 'Party Reform and Political Alignment: The New Politics Movement in the Democratic Party'.

52   See Gerassimos Moschonas, *In the Name of Social Democracy*, London: Verso, 2002.

53   See Leo Panitch and Colin Leys, *The End of Parliamentary Socialism*, London: Verso, 1997, chapter 7.

54   See Hilton, 'Party Reform and Political Alignment'.

55   See Panitch and Leys, *The End of Parliamentary Socialism*, pp. 118-24; and Sassoon, *One Hundred Years of Socialism*, pp. 534-71, 706-13.

56   See Peter Mair, *Ruling the Void: The Hollowing Out of Western Democracy*, London: Verso, 2013.

57   See Moschonas, *In the Name of Social Democracy*, chapter 8.

58   See Donald Gutstein, *Not a Conspiracy Theory: How Corporate Media is Hijacking Democracy*, Toronto: Key Porter Books, 2009.

59   For how this occurs, see Dennis Pilon, 'Voter Turnout and the Electoral Subaltern: Utilizing "Class" as Identity', *Studies in Political Economy* 96(2015), pp. 69-91.

60   See Greg Albo, 'A World Market of Opportunities? Capitalist Obstacles and Left Economic Policy', *Socialist Register 1997*, London: Merlin Press, 1997; and Alan Zuege, 'The Chimera of the Third Way', *Socialist Register 2000*, London: Merlin, 2000.

61   This is dealt with in detail in Pilon, *Wrestling with Democracy*, chapter 7. More recently, conservative forces in Eastern Europe have struck upon the adoption of single member, first past the post voting systems as means of weakening their democratic opponents.

62   For more on this, see Jeffrey C. Isaac, *Democracy in Dark Times*, Ithaca: Cornell University Press, 1998.

63   On voter suppression tactics, see Tova Andrea Wang, *The Politics of Voter Suppression*, Ithaca: Cornell University Press, 2017.

64   For examples of anti-democratic liberalism, see Bryan Caplan, *The Myth of Rational Voter*, Princeton: Princeton University Press, 2007; and Jason Brennan, *Against Democracy*, Princeton, Princeton University Press, 2016.

65   See Colin Crouch, *Post-Democracy*, Cambridge: Polity, 2004; and Wendy Brown, *Undoing the Demos*, Cambridge: MIT Press, 2015.

WOMEN: LINKING LIVES WITH DEMOCRACY

SHEILA ROWBOTHAM

In Paris during May 1968, students protesting against their conditions were joined by young workers. As the rebellion erupted, posters were plastered on the walls. This was among them:

> Student
> who questions everything
> the relations of the worker to the employer
> the relations of the pupil to the teacher
> have you questioned
> the relations of man to woman?[1]

Over the course of the year the questioning spread internationally. Apparently spontaneously, women in this 'new left' were beginning to envision a democratic revolution that redefined the scope of politics. In September 1968, a young German student, Helke Sander, exploded at a left conference in Frankfurt: 'Comrades your meetings are unbearable'. Women, she asserted, wanted more democratic forms of communication, the recognition of the links between personal, sexual life and public political participation, because the aim was the transformation of daily life. She described how men in the revolutionary student movement regarded these as 'frontier trespasses'.[2]

Later that autumn I wrote an article 'Women: A Call to Revolt' for the British left paper *Black Dwarf*. It was published in January 1969, and in the same year grew into the pamphlet *Women's Liberation and the New Politics*. In it, I sought to understand why women and other oppressed groups appeared to acquiesce. I was preoccupied with silence and how it could be broken.[3]

I

Encouraged by the beginnings of the women's liberation movement, I started looking at how women had resisted in the context of past revolutions, struggles for reforms, and movements for national liberation. Women petitioning Parliament in 1651 during the English Revolution protested, 'We have for many years chattered like Cranes and mourned like Doves'.[4] While in 1739, Mary Collier, the washerwoman and poet, declared in 'The Woman's Labour', 'No Learning ever was bestowed on me'.[5] Born in the late seventeenth century, Collier never attended a school, but was taught to read by her mother. She read on amid a life of labour, writing graphically from experience. For seventeenth and eighteenth century women in Europe, access to education, though restricted to relatively privileged women, was a vital means of finding a way to articulate discontents. Even for the relatively fortunate, the space was confined; the poet and literary critic Anna Laeticia Barbauld warned of the need to operate surreptitiously when embarking on 'thefts of knowledge'.[6] In many other countries, from India to Indonesia, education was later to prove a crucial first step towards wider emancipation.[7]

The outbreak of the French Revolution in 1789 led small groups of women to challenge their predicament *as women*. It also provided a framework for connecting grievances to a wider critique of existing society, and to visions of what might be. 'Woman, wake up' commanded the butcher's daughter Olympe de Gouges in 1791, 'the tocsin of reason is being heard throughout the whole universe; discover your rights'.[8] These rights were asserted in Britain the following year by the teacher and writer. Mary Wollstonecraft's *Vindication of the Rights of Woman and Strictures on Political and Moral Subjects* (1792) defended women's claims and defied the censure that silenced revolt. It sprang from the ferment of debate among radical Dissenters in London, who were influenced by events in France. Written at speed over the autumn of 1791, it expressed the passion of a woman who was sexually and economically on the edge. Loathed by reactionaries, the book transmitted filaments of subversion through the generations.[9]

Out of the grim realities of the French Revolution other voices emerged. Turmoil forced uncustomary understandings. On 2 March 1793 poor women demonstrated at the National Convention. Bread was scarce and soap so expensive laundresses could not ply their trade. When the Convention was adjourned they were heard in the corridors exclaiming angrily, 'When our children ask us for milk, we don't adjourn them until the day after tomorrow'.[10] Their responsibilities to their families legitimated untoward action. In Lyon in September 1792, women raided shops, distributing goods at prices fixed by a 'tribunal féminin' and enforcing their 'taxation' armed with pikes.[11] They sought to impose a moral economy in which the prices of basic goods should be fair and just.

The poor in Britain were left with great hardship after the long war with

France ended in 1815. Female Reform Societies began to form in the hope that by extending manhood suffrage the sufferings of their families would cease. Several hundred women proudly took part in a demonstration in St Peter's Fields, Manchester in 1819. When the yeomanry charged, many women were among the wounded, and two were killed. It was known ever afterwards as 'Peterloo', the workers' Waterloo.[12]

The rights of women as women were not forgotten. Anna Wheeler, unhappily married to a drunken Irish landowner, found inspiration in Mary Wollstonecraft's *Vindication*. Leaving her husband, she became involved in radical networks in Britain and France, collaborating with the enlightened William Thompson on *An Appeal of One Half the Human Race, Women, Against the Pretensions of the Other Half, Men, to Retain them in Political and thence in Civil and Domestic Slavery* (1825). While recognizing the immediate need for rights, this argued that the full emancipation of women required a cooperative society. In his introduction, Thompson affirmed their shared vision:

> You look forward to a better aspect of society, where the principle of benevolence shall supersede that of fear, where restless and anxious individual competition shall give place to mutual co-operation and joint possession, where individuals in large numbers, male and female forming voluntary associations, shall become a mutual guarantee to each other for the supply of all useful wants and … where perfect freedom of opinion and perfect equality will reign.[13]

Thompson and Wheeler were both influenced by the movement for the emancipation of the slaves, and though the *Appeal* distinguished the manner in which slaves and women were constrained, it pointed to a similarity. Like the slave-owners, men assumed the cultural power of defining women's 'nature' and how they should be, think, and act.[14] 'He has a system of domineering hypocrisy which he calls morals,' wrote Thompson.[15]

II

From the 1830s, ideas of a cooperative alternative to capitalism – Robert Owen's 'New Moral World' took hold. Amid the debates on how to achieve it differing strategies were advocated, education, co-operative communities, trade unionism and political rights. The Owenite Grand National Consolidated Trades Union included Female Lodges; and the union paper, *The Pioneer*, edited by James and Frances Morrison, praised the ideas of Mary Wollstonecraft, opposed 'the insolent despotism of man', and argued for equal pay.[16] During 1834, when the strawbonnet makers became involved in a conflict with men who were taking over what had been a women's trade, the women are warned, 'Let no man laugh you out of your claims to liberty; nor let flattery deter you from the hope you have now of gaining your freedom'.[17] Not only was democracy acquiring economic and social dimensions, it combined with an awareness of the personal power relations of gender.

The late 1830s saw the mass mobilization of women in the Northern factory areas against a punitive new Poor Law that divided impoverished families in the workhouses. Women resisted not with a new moral world in mind, but because the state was impinging on what they saw as their legitimate sphere, the home. In 1839 members of the Female Political Union of Newcastle-upon-Tyne announced:

Our husbands are over wrought, our houses half-furnished, our families ill-fed and our children uneducated – the fear of want hangs over our heads; the scorn of the rich is pointed towards us; the brand of slavery is on our kindred, and we feel the degradation. We are a despised caste, our oppressors are not content with despising our feelings, but demand the control of our thoughts and wants![18]

The extremity of their predicament hurtled them towards the uncustomary: 'We have been told that the province of women is in the home, and that the field of politics should be left to men; this we deny, the nature of things renders it impossible.'[19]

The emerging working-class Chartist movement was concerned with restoring lost circumstances and relations, while at the same time pressing for new political, economic and social rights. Women participated in demonstrations and meetings as well as the new cultural forms generated by the movement, from the naming of babies to education. Most Chartist women assumed the extension of the male franchise would secure better economic and social conditions for the working class.[20] But in 1851, when the movement was faltering, a Women's Rights Association was formed in Sheffield. Once again women were claiming a space in which to be heard: 'the voice of woman is not sufficiently heard, and not sufficiently respected, in this country'.[21] A middle class Chartist, Anne Knight, upbraided the men for not acknowledging that 'the rights of all human beings are equal'. She wanted women to be included in the demand for suffrage.[22]

Networks of radical women crossed boundaries. Flora Tristan, a French engraver influenced by Mary Wollstonecraft, met Anna Wheeler and

Chartists on her visits to London. In 1843 she proposed an international organization, the Universal Union of Working Men and Women. Tristan believed that class combination, rather than suffrage, was the way to emancipate men and women alike.[23] However, during the 1848 revolution in France women detailed their specific wrongs, setting up their own clubs, co-operative associations and papers such as *La Voix des Femmes* and *La Politique des Femmes*. They agitated for education, legal rights, child care, and cooperative workshops under workers' control, and sought to build up the confidence of working-class women by stressing the tacit knowledge they had acquired in running their households as a basis for thinking about economic issues.[24]

After the defeat of the revolution key activists were arrested. While in prison, the self-educated seamstress Jeanne Deroin, and a teacher, Pauline Roland, heard about the Sheffield Women's Rights group and an exciting new women's movement in America. In 1851 they sent a message of support to the American Women's Rights Convention from their prison cell: 'Only by the power of association based on solidarity – by the union of the working class of both sexes to organize labour – can be acquired ... the civil and political equality of women and the social right for all.'[25]

The American women's movement arose from the movement against slavery. Lucretia Mott, a Quaker, and her fellow campaigner Elizabeth Cady Stanton, along with a handful of other white women, called the first women's convention for equal rights at Seneca Falls in 1848, where the former slave turned abolitionist Frederick Douglass spoke passionately in favor of women's suffrage. Black women, including the former slave Sojourner Truth and the poet Frances Ellen Harper, later became involved, but faced prejudice from some white women equal rights supporters as well as from abolitionists, including some black men. [26]

The British liberal thinker John Stuart Mill had long been convinced of the importance of women's rights. He and Harriet Taylor had been close for many years, and after learning of the American women's movement's meetings in 1850 he encouraged her to write an article, on the 'Enfranchisement of Women', for the *Westminster Review*. Recognizing the significance of the movement in America and taking hope from the Sheffield women's petition for the franchise, it asserted 'What is wanted for women is equal rights, equal admission to all social privileges; not a position apart, a sort of sentimental priesthood.'[27] Taylor and Mill optimistically imagined change was about to come. The article appeared in 1851, the year that he and Harriet were finally able to marry. She died in 1858.

During the 1850s and 1860s small groups of British women campaigned for access to higher education and employment, as well as suffrage. On the whole they were scrupulously careful to rest their case on respectability, and the memory of writers like Wollstonecraft, Thompson, and Owen was confined to clusters of secularists and radicals. Just occasionally traces of sedition slipped through to a new generation of suffrage activists. Barbara Leigh Smith (later Bodichon), who was wealthy and well educated but illegitimate, was given the *Vindication* by a forward-thinking aunt. She went on to help found *The English Woman's Journal* and Girton College, Cambridge.[28]

Mill, unsuccessful in his attempt to amend the 1867 Reform Bill to include 'persons' rather than simply 'men', made the case for women's suffrage on the same terms as men in *The Subjection of Women* (1869). This was not universal suffrage, as the poorer sections of the male working class still remained disenfranchised. Nevertheless the implications of the book were far-reaching. Mill's insistence that women's interests could not be included within the rights of men challenged the legal subordination of one sex upon the other and asserted the individual's right to freedom and equality.[29] Moreover, opposing fixed ideas of femininity, he argued 'the nature of women is an eminently artificial thing'.[30]

The Subjection of Women received a critical reception in Britain from women as well as men. Yet it travelled around the world, going immediately to the United States, Australia, New Zealand, and was later translated into French, German, Swedish, Danish, Polish, Russian and Italian. It influenced Finnish, Japanese and Indian women to name but a few.

Mill had come to the conclusion that it was politic to focus on one reform at a time. However the movements influenced by individual rights did not necessarily develop in ways he approved. He was alarmed by the campaign against the Contagious Diseases Acts that began in 1869. These Acts allowed for the forcible search of women suspected of being likely to spread venereal disease to the armed forces. Josephine Butler and her fellow campaigners regarded the Acts as invading women's persons; as one opponent of the CD Acts put it, 'espionage of enslaved wombs'.[31] As working-class women were the ones in danger of being seized and examined, the women's cause gained support from groups of radical working-class men.

Mill had spoken passionately against domestic violence, but he feared that by engaging with issues such as VD and prostitution, other reforms would be imperiled. He told Butler that while he supported the campaign, strategically the key to change was 'political enfranchisement'.[32] Ironically, the opponents of the CD Acts were able to secure the repeal of the Acts in

1886 (though the laws remained in colonial India). British women were not to be fully enfranchised until 1928.

Also, regardless of Taylor and Mill's strictures against woman's distinct mission, the 'sentimental priesthood' evinced considerable emotive power through calls for social purity. These could assert conservative or exclusive forms of female power, but could also be radically subversive in demanding equal sexual standards for men and women. The American woman doctor Mary Walker became president of the National Dress Reform Association in 1866, alarming her fellow campaigners for women's suffrage by dressing in male clothes. Dismissive of sexual pleasure, she advocated intercourse solely for the purposes of procreation, endorsing sexual self-sovereignty for all women. Condemning the rape of a Native American woman, Walker insisted on the *woman always having supreme control of her person, as regards invasion by men*'.[33]

Social purity's emphasis upon woman as a superior moral force resulted in powerful temperance movements, which would later contribute to suffrage victories in some American states as well as Australia and New Zealand. A defiant minority of women transposed concepts of individual rights into the tabooed zone of sexuality. Small groups of free lovers differed over whether free love meant a monogamous relationship based on honesty, equality, and personal harmony, or whether it encompassed a variety of lovers. The iconoclastic American rebel Victoria Woodhall gave individual rights and bodily control a personal twist in 1871, insisting 'I have an inalienable constitutional and natural right to love whom I may, to love as long, or as short a period as I can, to change that love every day I please'.[34]

The American free lovers Josephine and Flora Tilton distributed advice on contraception in the 1870s.[35] However, others were opposed to artificial forms of preventing procreation, favouring instead changes in sexual practices. Elmina Slenker argued for 'Dianaism', a non-penetrative sexuality she believed would enable women to 'have none but wished for children'.[36] Economic inequality, lack of effective contraception, and cultural prejudices made free love a far more dangerous choice for women than for men. Nevertheless new women who were claiming emancipation also asserted autonomous personhood. In 1888 the British novelist Mona Caird referred to 'the obvious right of the woman to *possess herself* body and soul'.[37]

III

Karl Marx deplored the influence of Woodhull upon the New York section of the First International, expressing his impatience 'of follies and CROCHETS, such as ... false emancipation of women and the like'.[38]

Nevertheless in his early writings Marx had not only adopted Charles Fourier's claim that a society could be measured by the extent of women's emancipation as an abstract concept,[39] he added significant material and social dimensions. *The German Ideology* posits: 'The production of life, both of one's own in labour and of fresh life in procreation, now appears as a double relationship; on the one hand as a natural, on the other as a social relationship'.[40]

In the first volume of *Das Kapital,* published in 1867, Marx, having observed many defeated uprisings, searched for the key to human emancipation in the 'historical development of the antagonisms, immanent in a given form of production'.[41] He detailed the working conditions of seamstresses, silk workers, bleachers, and straw-plaiters, along with the devastating impact of the factory on the bodies and minds of working-class people and predicted that the disintegratory tendencies of capitalism would pull women beyond the domestic sphere, dissolving existing forms of the family.[42] Marx's preoccupation with labour in his later writings tended to subsume the more diffuse insights of his earlier writing.

Engels later elaborated on the dual character of the reproduction of life in his *Origin of the Family, Private Property and the State* (1884). Procreation, domestic activity, and caring in the family could, he saw, be regarded as integrally interconnected with economic, political and social relationships as a whole.[43] This approach made it possible to demonstrate that personal and public aspects of gender relations could be subject to change. However, the implications were left hanging, as neither he nor Marx were concerned with *how* women's *active* agency might arise from their analysis. Instead women's emancipation was assumed to follow from the emancipation of the proletariat as a whole.

Marx and Engels' influence contributed to the rise of socialist groups, including the German Social Democratic Party, and in 1879 its leader Auguste Bebel published the book *Die Frau und die Sozialism.* Bebel wrote with passionate indignation about women's working conditions, including those of prostitutes, and he proposed that women's domestic labour could be eased if life in the community were socialized. Eleanor Marx and her partner Edward Aveling reviewed the English translation of Bebel's book in 1885 with enthusiasm: 'Women are the creatures of an organized tyranny of men, as the workers are the creatures of an organized tyranny of the idlers.'[44] This assertion of women's distinct oppression was to hover unsettlingly in the heterodox outskirts of what came to be called 'Marxism'.

Amended and extended, editions of Bebel's work later reached large numbers of women internationally. In the late nineteenth century socialists and social reformers in many countries did indeed struggle to reclaim resources controlled by the national and local state for working-class women and children. Some socialists also recognized that because women's subordination arose from entangled roots it required a range of approaches. During the early 1880s in Lille, the French textile area, the Marxist Parti ouvrier français (POF) directed their propaganda at women as workers whose class interests were the same as men's, while accepting that women also experienced special forms of oppression. Hence some meetings were for women only to discuss grievances and to encourage women to participate in politics. They also addressed women as members of working-class families by encouraging food cooperatives, mutual savings and insurance schemes, and urging them to elect socialists to municipal and national office. At the same time, they stressed that fathers as well as mothers had an interest in communal projects and social provision, which could ease the conditions of domestic living, and that women should not be bounded by the home.[45]

An obvious hurdle for those who saw organizing at work as the key to social transformation was that female factory workers were in the minority. Domestic service, small 'sweat shops', and 'outworking' were more typical forms of employment for women often forced to the bottom of the labour market. As Anna Julia Cooper noted in 1892 in her *A View From the South*, even when lecturers in the Northern States of America referred to 'our working girls', they only meant 'white working girls'. She asked:

> How many have ever given a thought to the pinched and down-trodden colored women bending over wash-tubs and ironing boards – with children to feed and house rent to pay, wood to buy, soap and starch to furnish – lugging home weekly great baskets of clothes for families who pay them for a month's laundering barely enough to purchase a substantial pair of shoes.[46]

Cooper was well placed to critique discriminatory perspectives. A black American intellectual and campaigner whose mother had been a slave, she had won a scholarship through the church, resolutely transcending the narrow scope of the vocational training offered to her. *A View From the South* acutely articulates how race, gender, and class intertwine, It also challenges the hegemonic disregard for black women's experiences which could be expressed by white women and black men alike.

Experiencing multiple forms of oppression could overwhelm individuals' ability to resist. So African American women reformers sought to provide mutual aid and encouragement while campaigning for change. Organizers of working-class women adopted similar approaches in many different contexts.

A subjective awareness of several forms of discrimination could also be a potential strength, for it could activate understandings and empathy with others. In 1891, Frances Ellen Harper, the African American veteran of the anti-slavery, temperance and women's suffrage movements, linked both racism and anti-Semitism with imperialism and the class system: 'Among English speaking races we have weaker races victimized, a discontented Ireland and a darkest England.'[47] Two years later, speaking at the World's Congress of Representative Women in Chicago, Harper called for 'a society that was not dominated by the greed of gold and the lust for power'.[48]

IV

In Britain, working-class women began to take up the demand for suffrage in the belief that this would improve working and living conditions. Among them was Sarah Reddish, who had begun her working life aged eleven as a silk winder in the North of England. Active in the Women's Co-operative Guild, which provided social and cultural sustenance in struggle, in 1894 Reddish argued that just as it was assumed that men should participate in the 'science of government' through the 'larger family' of the co-operative store, the municipality, and the state, 'women as citizens should take their share in this work also'.[49] She also disputed the undervaluing of women's contribution in the home, criticizing confining stereotypes of wives and mothers *and* the occlusion of men's roles in the family as husbands and fathers. Reddish was demanding not simply entry into the masculine public sphere, but refuting the gendered demarcations through which politics and domestic life were conceived and constituted.

During the 1890s, a few women were also beginning to cut through the theoretical divide between individual and social perspectives on womens' emancipation. In 1891 Harriot Stanton Blatch, socialist daughter of the American radical feminist Elizabeth Cady Stanton, related the idea of 'Voluntary Motherhood', or control over conception and child rearing, to access to a good education and financial independence.[50] In 1897 the British ethical socialist Enid Stacy connected women's 'right to their own persons' with political citizenship and demands for state provision for mothers. Her imagined future combined the full development of all with service to one another.[51]

Others simply took quiet forms of personal direct action in the here and now. Two confident literary scholars, Charlotte Porter and Helen Archibald Clarke, who were followers of the poet Walt Whitman, considered that woman-to-woman love was superior to the love of husbands. They lived happily together in 1890s Boston, their relationship marked by the ceremonial exchange of rings. Porter's opposition to the rule of 'plutocrats' inclined her to socialism, but she argued space must be secured for individualism to prevent authoritarianism.[52]

The new century saw mass movements of women for suffrage, in which rebellions converged and political democracy fused with social and personal liberation. In Finland, amid the Nationalist revolt against the Russian Czar, a militant working-class movement developed in which women demanded the vote. Agitation spanned the cities and the villages. After the Great Strike of 1905, some working women threatened another strike, which was to extend to cooking and demands for men to care for children so they could go to meetings. They won universal suffrage in 1906.[53]

In India during the early twentieth century, women resisting British colonialism linked women's rights with nationalism and applied the demand for self-determination to their own freedom and equality as women.[54] In 1911 Chinese women participated in the successful uprising against the Manchu Dynasty. The Chinese Suffragette Society then demanded education; the abolition of foot binding; prohibition of concubinage, child marriages, and prostitution; the establishment of social services for women in industry, improved rights in marriage, the family and politics. They adopted the tactics of violent direct action used by the militant Women's Social and Political Union in Britain as a means of struggling for reform.[55]

On 4 May 1919 a Chinese student movement mobilized against foreign domination. Workers and even schoolgirls joined students in urging shoppers to buy Chinese goods. The young Mao was profoundly influenced by their activism.[56] In the continuing tumult of the 1920s, startling connections appeared in Chinese cities between political and social revolt and personal sexual rebellion. Birth control groups formed; free marriage, celibacy and divorce were debated. Several women writers radicalized by the May Fourth movement wrote about love between women.[57] Same sex relations between men also surfaced in novels, portrayed as either a positive aspect of cultural reform or negatively as the mark of a crisis in masculinity.[58]

A series of revolts converged early in 1917, when Russian women textile workers in Petrograd went on strike and, using neighbourhood networks, collected support among women from the markets and food queues. War had caused prices to rise in other countries where women took direct action over consumption. But in Russia men joined the women, the army mutinied against the Czar, and constitutional reform was followed by the rise of the Bolsheviks to power.[59]

The impact of the Russian revolution not only encouraged direct action at work and in communities, but in relation to the body. Margaret Sanger in America, influenced by the anarcho-syndicalist emphasis upon workers' control, had already coined the term 'birth control' in 1914, and in 1922 her friend, the Canadian Stella Browne, announced in a letter to the British journal *The Communist*, 'Birth control is woman's crucial effort at self-determination and at control of her own person and her own environment'.[60]

The American socialist feminist Crystal Eastman took a broader tack, defining 'the problem of women's freedom' as being 'how to arrange the world so that women can be human beings, with a chance to exercise their infinitely varied gifts in infinitely varied ways'.[61] Crucial starting points for Eastman were reproductive choice, economic independence, and access to resources from the state to help with the raising of children. However such reforms remained remote and utopian for many women, even in rich countries. African American women, for example, continued to resort to mutual self-help. In Richmond, Virginia, Maggie Lena Walker set up a friendly society, a department store to provide better jobs for black women, and a Penny Savings Bank. From the early 1900s through to the early thirties her motto was, 'First by practice and then by precept'. The result was a cluster of social and economic innovations that provided a base for a stand against lynching and segregation well before the Civil Rights movement.[62]

These creative, adventurous women were not to know that Depression and the rise of fascism, supported by women as well as men, was to be followed by war. Women did, of course, participate in movements *against* fascism, and continued to agitate for social and economic reforms, but forced on to the defensive, the scope of possibilities narrowed. Writing *Three Guineas* in 1938, an apprehensive Virginia Woolf accentuated the need to remember 'the public and the private, the material and the spiritual'.[63]

Post-war France was still reeling from war and occupation when Simone de Beauvoir proclaimed, 'no biological, psychological or economic fate determines the figure that the human female presents in society'.[64] Her call to revolt in *The Second Sex* (1949) resounded when the American women's liberation movement emerged two decades later. 'I am a woman giving birth to myself' announced an early slogan.[65]

Women's liberation birthed me into diverse histories as I began discovering more and more rebel women resisting the silencing, disregard, inequality, coercion and control which marked their lives. I also came to see that not simply a yearning for individual freedom, but loving connection to kin could ignite rebellion. Such practical struggles – to change how things were and to reconfigure how things might be – arose from immediate dissatisfactions, yet they intimated a broader remaking of the everyday. I marvelled at how some women subjected to differing forms of oppression could empathize with others, men as well as women.

Because women's subordination crossed over customary categories, so too did the claims for social change. I was to realize that contesting the boundaries of personal and public spheres, shifting bits about and subverting definitions of what belonged where, in culture and in material existence, had not been invented in 1968. Many earlier periods of turmoil had evoked an awareness of the *interconnections* between inner and outer bondages. Nevertheless, the confident aspirations of 1960s social movements enabled a new recognition of their significance.

V

The possible was shape-shifting in the early days of women's liberation. Gaining courage through questioning everything, mounting innumerable forays and raids against male citadels, we learned about politics through doing. We experienced the power of trusting one another, swopping skills, sharing ideas and comprehending differences. We developed theories from pooling experiences in small groups, took them to our conferences, and turned them into grassroots campaigns. The impact of these spiralled outwards, influencing women and men in unions and radical and social democratic parties. Some have shaped new realities and profound shifts in culture.

Remarkably, regardless of differing circumstances, women's groups sprang up in many countries in Latin America, India, Sri Lanka, Pakistan, South Korea, Taiwan, Japan, the Philippines, Turkey, Egypt, and even in Iran, China and the former Soviet Union. Many histories of rebellion and interlinking influences, not just from West to East, were to be uncovered. As Kamla Bhasin from India and Nighat Said Khan from Pakistan reflected, 'an idea cannot be confined within national or geographic boundaries'. They saw 'feminism' as 'a transformational process' and pointed to its long history in South Asia.[66]

Moreover, as globalization disrupted the customary survival strategies of poor women in many countries in Latin America, Asia, and Africa, differing forms of women's movements arose around livelihood and rights. Housing, sanitation, prices, and working conditions mobilized women. So did access to water, to firewood, to space in the cities to vend their goods, or to credit to buy materials. Women defied aggression from local vested interests, and domestic violence from their own men. They have also asserted their reproductive rights against both state policies and the interests of multinationals.[67]

Such movements expressed both collective and individual empowerment. In the summer of 1987 five thousand women street vendors marched through the streets of Ahmedabad, India demanding 'Dignity and Daily Bread'.[68] As a Brazilian woman worker put it 'A woman who participates is the owner of her own nose'.[69] They inspired a rethinking of being and existence. Gita Sen and Caren Grown envisaged a new feminism in 1987, explaining that 'Our vision of feminism has at its very core a process of economic and social development geared to human needs through wider control over and access to economic and political power'. [70]

In Britain, however, Margaret Thatcher's government had arrived in 1979. The same year saw our last socialist feminist conference and the publication of two thousand copies of *Beyond the Fragments* in which Hilary Wainwright, Lynne Segal, and myself argued that feminist experiences and understandings were vital for remaking socialism. Without idealizing movements from below, we wanted them to be resources for renewal.

By this time the hopeful utopianism of the early 1970s had buckled; division and acrimony marked the British women's liberation movement. We had set out to encourage democratic participation and to eliminate all forms of hierarchy and learned the hard way just how difficult this is in practice, especially when deep political divisions appeared. For those of us who were socialist feminists, gender subordination was linked to class, race, and ethnicity. We were in and against capitalism, with and against men.

By the early 1980s many socialist feminists turned outwards, joining the vigorous resistance to cuts in welfare and privatization in the public sector that affected many women. There were strikes, notably in the mining industry, where working-class women and men adopted innovative tactics by linking work and communities. However the trade union movement suffered many defeats and socialist feminists, like the rest of the left, were increasingly forced on the defensive. I do not think many of us realized then that capitalism had changed gear.

In Britain it proved hard to maintain a multifaceted politics, especially as the right became ascendant during the 1980s. Saying simply that men caused women's oppression or that equal opportunities were needed within capitalism could be more easily encapsulated, and were the themes that prevailed in the British media. Attempts to contest these polarities invariably were just cut out. During the 1990s being a socialist feminist in Britain came to seem an archaic eccentricity. When I visited countries such as Brazil, Canada, France, Holland and India, where this was not then the case, I found it hard to explain what had happened to us.

Looking back now I suggest that the existence of a powerful current of socialist feminism depends upon activist socialist *and* feminist movements which are perceived to be making changes. In combination these disrupt the cultural spaces where otherwise conservative and liberal ideas dominate; they also provide vital ballast that can secure ground for reflection and complexity in political thinking.

As for what can or cannot be achieved in practice, social movements themselves are shaped by the specific circumstances in which they arise. The gains that they can make are also affected by the contours of differing kinds of capitalist society. For instance, in the US considerably more 'give' was evident in response to self-affirmation and to assertions of individual rights than to the basic social protections through welfare that, before the spread of neoliberalism, were characteristic of social democratic regimes. It proved easier in the US (and eventually in Britain) to push some women individually up a few notches under the banner of equal opportunities than to argue that we needed to extend opportunities for equality for all.

In Britain, though both the new left utopianism of early women's liberation and the socialist feminism of the 1970s were subsumed, I believe their creative self- expression, innovative collectivity, and awareness of the significance of community control in relation to the state are still crucial. Though women culturally are certainly more visible now, it is sobering to see how the broader strategic implications of women's endeavours to combine the democratization of politics, daily life, and personal relating over the last few decades have been marginalized, not only in mainstream culture but also on the left. Because of such elisions I suspect there will always need to be autonomous mobilizations of women, supported by men, challenging the material and cultural axes of male power.

And indeed the anti-capitalist movements resisting the impact of neoliberal capitalism globally from the 1990s have contributed to a new wave of feminist activism linked with environmental and anarchist movements. More diffusely, a feminist awareness among young women has engaged with both alternative and mainstream culture. The mood has been far more personally confident, even though the political context has been harsh, and counter-hegemonic visions assailed.

Yet again women have disagreed over whether women's freedom can be pursued in isolation or needs to be linked to other forms of subordination, and once again the commitment to democracy and equality has proved harder in practice than in theory. Questions of whether feminism can be combined with reinterpreting aspects of religious beliefs hostile to women, or whether it is necessarily secular in outlook, have also come increasingly to the fore. More recently, the issue of whether gender identity is fluid or fixed has proved particularly contentious.

Nevertheless, amid these debates in Britain a revival within the left of the Labour Party in response to the open approach to leadership of Jeremy Corbyn has, regardless of the horror of the right wing, brought socialism back on the agenda and the term 'socialist feminism' has started to reappear.[71]

VI

Neither women's nor human emancipation can be guaranteed. Sadly, intensifying insecurity, fear, and humiliation can enhance the appeal of a rhetoric of freedom and inner fulfillment through submission to authoritarian power. Some women, like some men, can be susceptible to religious or secular versions of this illusory promise. Some – but certainly not all. Women in the Middle East and Asia have risked ostracism, persecution, and even death in defending basic rights to education, personal liberty, and political participation. While in January 2017 opposition to Donald Trump overcame all the festering differences between women's groups, rooted out feminist pensioners, inspired young women at school, and brought out around two million women and men around the world, many of whom had never demonstrated before. Slogans declared, 'Have Sex. Hate Sexism', 'Bridges not Walls', and 'Love Trumps Hate'.[72] Once again, when times got bad, women took the initiative in raising hope aloft. But holding it up there is going to require a whole lot of exposing, opposing, transforming. For, while an emancipatory future knows no bounds, the powerful are adept and ruthless at stacking the odds against it being realized.

The blunt truth is that the extreme right does not mess about making fine distinctions. Hence it is a good time to stress that socialist feminism has historically appeared in both reformist and revolutionary guises, that in certain periods liberal and socialist feminists have had shared goals, even if at others they have been at odds. The immediate imperative politically is to reach out to all those women who remain hostile to feminism and to insist that human emancipation belongs to all, women and men alike.

Linking democracy to living has proved a rather longer job than many of us envisaged fifty years ago.

NOTES

1   Quoted in Helke Sander, 'Action Committee for the Liberation of Women', SDS Conference, Frankfurt, September 1968. Typed manuscript, translated by Jon Birtwhistle, in Papers of Sheila Rowbotham, London School of Economics, The Women's Library.

2   Sander, 'Action Committee for the Liberation of Women'.

3   See Sheila Rowbotham, 'Women a Call to Revolt', *Black Dwarf*, January 1969, in Tariq Ali and Susan Watkins, eds, *Marching in the Streets*, London: Bloomsbury, 1998, pp. 2009-2010; Sheila Rowbotham, *Women's Liberation and the New Politics*, May Day Manifesto, London: 1969, reprinted in Sheila Rowbotham, *Dreams and Dilemmas*, London: Virago, 1983, pp. 5-32.

4   Petition against the law on debt, 1651, quoted in Ellen MacArthur, 'Women Petitioners and the Long Parliament', *English Historical Review* 24(96), October 1909, pp. 708-709.

5   Mary Collier, 'The Woman's Labour', in E.P. Thompson, ed., *The Thresher's Labour by Stephen Duck and the Woman's Labour by Mary Collier*, London: Merlin Press, 1989, p. 15. On Collier, see Thompson, ed., 'Introduction', pp. ix-xii; Donna Landry, *The Muses of Resistance: Laboring-Class Women's Poetry in Britain, 1739-1796*, Cambridge: Cambridge University Press, 1990, pp. 56-77.

6   Mrs Barbauld, 1775, quoted in W. Lyon Blease, *The Emancipation of English Women*, London: David Nutty, 1913, pp. 77-78.

7   See Kumari Jayawardena, *Feminism and Nationalism in the Third World in the 19th and 20th Centuries*, London: Verso, 2016.

8   Olympe de Gouges, 'Declaration of the Rights of Woman', 1791, in Darline Gay Levy, Harriet Branson Applewhite and Mary Durham Johnson, eds, *Women in Revolutionary Paris 1789-1795*, Urbana: University of Illinois Press, 1979, p. 92.

9   Mary Wollstonecraft, *A Vindication of the Rights of Woman* (1792), London: Verso, 2010. On its impact see Sheila Rowbotham, 'The Reputation of Mary Wollstonecraft', *Labour Heritage, Women's Research Committee, Bulletin No. 4*, (Summer) 1993, pp. 3-6; Eileen Janes Yeo, ed., *Mary Wollstonecraft and 200 Years of Feminisms*, London: Rivers Oram Press, 1997; Barbara Taylor, *Mary Wollstonecraft and the Feminist Imagination*, Cambridge: Cambridge University Press, 2003.

10   'The Women of Paris Respond to the Delaying Tactics of the National Convention', February 25, 1793, in Levy et al, ed., *Women in Revolutionary Paris*, p. 132.

11   W.D. Edmonds, *Jacobinism and the Revolt of Lyon 1789-1793*, Oxford: Clarendon Press, 1990, pp. 124-27.

12   See Ruth and Edmond Frow, eds, *Political Women 1800-1850*, London: Pluto Press, 1989, pp. 16-20.

13   William Thompson, *Appeal of One half the Human Race, Women, Against the Pretensions of the Other Half, Men to Retain them in Political and Thence in Civil and Domestic Slavery* (1825), London: Virago, 1983, p. xxvi.

14   Thompson, *An Appeal*, pp. 155-64.

15   Thompson, *An Appeal*, p. 189

16   *The Pioneer*, 2 June 1834, 26 October 1833, 5 April 1834, in Frows, ed., *Political Women*, pp. 138, 158, 174.

17   P.A.S., 'Straw-Bonnet Workers Organise', *The Pioneer*, 24 May 1834, in Frows, ed., *Political Women*, p. 177.

18   'Address of the Female Political Union of Newcastle upon Tyne to their Fellow Countrywomen', *Northern Star*, 2 February1839, in Dorothy Thompson, ed., *The Early Chartists*, London: Macmillan, 1971, p. 128.

19   'Address', Thompson, *The Early Chartists*, p. 128.

20   See Dorothy Thompson, *The Chartists*, London: Maurice Temple Smith, 1984, pp. 120-51.

21   'Women's Rights Association', 17 December 1851, Sheffield: Frows, ed., *Political Women*, p. 201.

22   Anne Knight, 'Friend of the People', 8 March 1851, in Frows ed., *Political Women*, p. 202.

23 See Máire Cross and Tim Gray, *The Feminism of Flora Tristan*, Oxford: Berg, 1992, pp. 57-58; Sandra Dijkstra, *Flora Tristan: Feminism in the Age of George Sand*, London: Pluto, pp. 160-68; *The London Journal of Flora Tristan, 1842*, translated by Jean Hawkes, London: Virago, 1982, pp. 36-56.

24 See Sheila Rowbotham, 'A New Vision of Society: Women Clothing Workers and the Revolution of 1848 in France', in Juliet Ash and Elizabeth Wilson, eds, *Chic Thrills: A Fashion Reader*, London: Pandora, 1992, pp. 189-99; Evelyne Sullerot, 'Journaux Féminin et Lutte Ouvrière 1848-1849', in Jacques Godechot, ed., *La Presse Ouvrière*, Bures-sur-Yvette, Essons, Société d'Histoire Bibliothèque de la Révolution de 1848, 1966, pp. 97-98; Maria Mies, 'Utopian Socialism and Women's Emancipation', in Maria Mies and Kumari Jayawardena, eds, *Feminism in Europe: Liberal and Socialist Strategies 1789-1919*, The Hague, Institute of Social Studies, 1981, pp. 53-59, 76-77.

25 Jeanne Deroin and Pauline Roland quoted in June Hannam, *Isabella Ford*, Oxford: Basil Blackwell, 1989, p. 121.

26 Paula Giddings, *When and Where I Enter: The Impact of Black Women on Race and Sex in America*, New York: Bantam Books, 1984, pp. 54-71; Temma Kaplan, *Democracy: A World History*, Oxford: Oxford University Press, 2015, pp. 52-55.

27 Harriet Taylor Mill, *Enfranchisement of Women* (1851), London: Virago, 1983, p. 42; on their collaboration, see Richard Reeves, *John Stuart Mill: Victorian Firebrand*, London: Atlantic Books, 2007, p. 204-61.

28 Gillian Gill, *Nightingales: Florence and her Family*, London: Hodder and Stoughton, 2004, p. 85; Pam Hirsh, *Barbara Leigh Smith Bodichon, Feminist Artist and Rebel*, London: Chatto and Windus, 1998, p. 85.

29 See John Stuart Mill, *The Subjection of Women* (1869), Virago: London, 1983, pp. 57-72.

30 Mill, *The Subjection of Women*, p. 38.

31 Mary Hume-Rother, quoted in Judith R. Walkowitz, *Prostitution and Victorian Society: Women, Class and the State*, Cambridge: Cambridge University Press, 1980, p. 130.

32 Reeves, John Stuart Mill, p. 431.

33 Mary Walker quoted in Jonathan Katz, *Gay American History: Lesbians and Gay Men in the U.S.A*, New York: Thomas Y. Crowell, 1976, p. 248.

34 Victoria Woodhull quoted in Arlene Kisner, *The Lives and Writings of Notorious Victoria Woodhull and her Sister Tennessee Claflin*, Washington: Times Change Press, 1972, p. 28. On individual rights and the body see Rosalind Petchevsky, *Abortion and Women's Choice: The State, Sexuality and Reproductive Freedom*, New York: Longman, 1984.

35 Wendy McElroy, *Individualist Feminism of the Nineteenth Century*, Jefferson NC: McFarland and Company, 2001, pp. 19-47, 78-82.

36 Elmina Slenker, 'Dianaism', *Lucifer* 1(15), 14 April 1897, p. 117, quoted in Sheila Rowbotham, *Dreamers of a New Day*, London: Verso, 2010, p. 85.

37 Mona Caird, 'Marriage', *Westminster Review*, August 1888, quoted in Lucy Bland, *Banishing the Beast: English Feminism and Sexual Morality 1885-1914*, London: Penguin Books, 1995, p. 129.

38 Karl Marx to Friedrich Bolte, 23 November 1871, Letter 165 & 1870 – 73, *Marx and Engels Collected Works* Vol. 44, London: Lawrence and Wishart, 2010, p. 252. Marx, who suspected the influence of followers of the former Chartist Bronterre O'Brien, later described Woodhull as 'a banker's woman, free-lover, and general humbug'. Karl Marx, 'Notes on the "American Split",' 28 May, 1872.

39 T. B. Bottomore, ed., *Karl Marx Early Writings*, New York: McGraw Hill, 1964, p. 154.

40 Karl Marx and Frederick Engels, *The German Ideology* Vol.1, London: Lawrence and Wishart, 1965, p. 41. See Sheila Rowbotham, *Women, Resistance and Revolution*, London: Verso, 2014, pp. 60-77.

41   Karl Marx, *Capital, A Critical Analysis of Capitalist Production* Vol. 1, London: George Allen and Unwin, 1957, p. 494.

42   Marx, *Capital* Vol.1, p. 496.

43   Frederick Engels, *The Origins of the Family, Private Property and the State,* Preface to the First Edition (1884), London: Lawrence and Wishart, 1972, p. 71.

44   Eleanor Marx and Edward Aveling, 'The Woman Question: A Socialist Point of View,' *The Westminster Review* VI(25) 1885, p. 211. On the amended versions of Bebel's work, see Richard J. Evans, *The Feminists,* London: Croom Helm, 1979, pp. 156-157. In the 1890s anarchist-communist women in Argentina took up the dual character of women's oppression. See Maxine Molyneux, *Women's Movements in International Perspective: Latin America and Beyond,* London: Palgrave, 2001, pp. 13-37.

45   Patricia Holden, *Working Women and Socialist Politics in France 1880-1914: A Regional Study,* Oxford: Clarendon Press, 1986, pp. 183-7.

46   Anna Julia Cooper, *A View From the South,* Oxford: Oxford University Press, 1988, p. 254.

47   Frances Ellen Harper, 'Duty to Dependent Races', *Transactions of the National Council of Women in the United States,* Philadelphia: J.B. Lippincott, 1891, no page numbers, n8748, Library of Congress.

48   Frances Ellen Harper speaking at the World's Congress of Representative Women, 1893, quoted in Hazel Carby, *Reconstructing Womanhood: The Emergence of the Afro-American Woman Novelist,* New York: Oxford University Press, 1987, p. 70.

49   Sarah Reddish, 1894, quoted in Gillian Scott, *Feminism and the Politics of Working Women: The Women's Co-operative Guild 1880s to the Second World War,* London: UCL Press, 1998, p. 77. For a wider conceptual framework see Ruth Lister, *Citizenship: Feminist Perspectives,* London: Palgrave Macmillan, 2003.

50   Harriot Stanton Blatch quoted in Ellen Carol Dubois, *Harriot Stanton Blatch and the Winning of Woman Suffrage,* New Haven: Yale University Press, 1997, pp. 66-67.

51   Enid Stacy, 'A Century of Women's Rights', in Edward Carpenter, ed., *Forecasts of the Coming Century,* Manchester: The Labour Press, 1897, pp. 100-101.

52   Sheila Rowbotham, *Rebel Crossings: New Women, Free Lovers, and Radicals in Britain and the United States,* London: Verso, 2016, pp. 170-171.

53   Evans, *The Feminists,* p. 86-89, 217-218; Eric Blanc, 'Finland 1906: The Revolutionary Roots of Women's Suffrage: An International Women's Day Tribute,' *JohnRiddell.com,* 4 March 2015.

54   Radha Kumar, *A History of Doing: An Illustrated History of the Women's Movement in India,* New Delhi: Kali for Women, 1991, pp. 58-60.

55   Elizabeth Croll, *Feminism and Socialism in China,* London: Routledge and Kegan Paul, 1978, pp. 63-68.

56   Jayawardena, *Feminism and Nationalism in the Third World,* pp. 183-9.

57   Leila J. Rupp, 'Loving Women in the Modern World', in Robert Aldrich ed., *Gay Life and Culture: A World History,* London: Thames and Hudson, 2006, pp. 244-5.

58   Wenqing Kang, *Obsession: Male Same-Sex Relations in China 1900-1950,* Hong Kong: Hong Kong University Press, 2009, pp. 63-94.

59   Temma Kaplan, 'Women and Communal Strikes in the Crisis of 1917-1922', Renate Bridenthal, Claudia Koonz, and Susan Stuard, eds, *Becoming Visible – Women in European History* Second Edition, Boston: Houghton Mifflin, 1987, pp. 432-46. On earlier traditions of women workers and community resistance see Martha A. Ackelsberg, *Free Women of Spain: Anarchism and the Struggle for the Emancipation of Women,* Oakland: AK Press, 2005, pp. 73-77.

60   Sheila Rowbotham, *Dreamers of a New Day,* p. 92; Stella Browne, Letter, *The Communist,* 19 August 1922, p. 8. See also Stephen Brooke, 'The Body and Socialism: Dora Russell in the 1920s', *Past and Present* 189(November), 2005, pp. 147-77.

61   Crystal Eastman, 'Now We Can Begin', *The Liberator* (December), 1920; Blanche Wiesen Cook, ed., *Crystal Eastman: On Women and Revolution*, Oxford: Oxford University Press, 1998, pp. 53-54.

62   Elsa Barkley Brown, 'Womanist Consciousness: Maggie Lena Walker and the Independent Order of Saint Luke', in Ellen Carol DuBois and Vicki L.Ruiz, eds, *Unequal Sisters: A Multi-Cultural Reader in U.S. Women's History,* New York: Routledge, 1990, pp. 208-23.

63   Virginia Woolf, *A Room of One's Own and Three Guineas,* London: Chatto and Windus, 1984, p. 267.

64   Simone de Beauvoir, *The Second Sex*, translated by Constance Borde and Sheila Malovany-Chevallier, London: Jonathan Cape, 2009, p. 293.

65   Quoted in Sheila Rowbotham, *Women in Movement: Feminism and Social Action,* New York: Routledge, 2013, p. 271.

66   Kamla Bhasin and Nighat Said Khan, *Some Questions on Feminism and Its Relevance in South Asia* (pamphlet), New Delhi: ali for Women, no date, p. 4.

67   There is a vast literature on these movements. For brief summaries see Rowbotham, *Women in Movement*, pp. 293-307 and Sheila Rowbotham and Stephanie Linkogle, eds, *Women Resist Globalization: Mobilizing for Livelihood and Rights,* London: Zed Books, 2001, pp. 96-117.

68   Sheila Rowbotham and Swasti Mitter, eds, 'Introduction', *Dignity and Daily Bread: New Forms of Economic Organising Among Poor Women in the Third World and the First,* London: Routledge, 1994, p. 1.

69   Quoted in Sonia E. Alvarez, 'Women's Movements and Gender Politics in the Brazilian Transition', in Jane S. Jaquette, ed., *The Women's Movement in Latin America: Feminism and the Transition to Democracy,* Boston: Unwin Hyman,1989, p. 32.

70   Gita Sen and Caren Grown, *Development Crises and Alternative Visions*, London: Earthscan, 1987, p. 20.

71   For a discussion of the British experience see the revised edition of Sheila Rowbotham, Lynne Segal, and Hilary Wainwright, *Beyond the Fragments: Feminism and the Making of Socialism* (1979), London: Merlin Press, 2013, pp. 7-106. On the wider context see Amrita Basu, ed., *The Challenge of Local Feminisms: Women's Movements in Global Perspective,* Boulder: Westview Press, 1995; and Nancy Holstrom, ed., *The Socialist Feminist Project,* New York: Monthly Review Press, 2002. On more recent developments see Nancy Fraser, 'Feminism, Capitalism and the Cunning of History', *New Left Review* 56(March/ April), 2009, pp. 116-117; Johanna Brenner and Nancy Holmstrom, 'Socialist-Feminist Strategy Today'; and Joan Sangster and Meg Luxton, 'Feminism, Co-optation and the Problems of Amnesia: A Response to Nancy Fraser' in Leo Panitch, Greg Albo and Vivek Chibber, eds, *Socialist Register 2013: The Question of Strategy,* London: Merlin Press, 2012; Bryan D. Palmer and Joan Sangster, 'The Distinctive Heritage of 1917: Resuscitating Revolution's Longue Durée', *Socialist Register 2017 Rethinking Revolution,* London: Merlin Press, 2016. For a statement from anti-capitalist feminists see the web site of Feminist Fightback, http://www.feministfightback.org.uk. Though the term 'intersectionality' has become widely used by feminists to link gender, race and class, I prefer to continue using 'socialist feminism' because this makes it possible to see women as *active* agents in actual historical movements.

72   Amanda Hess, 'How a Fractious Women's Movement Came to Lead the Left', *The New York Times Magazine*, 7 February 2017; thanks to Helen Taylor and Bristol protesters for 'Love Trumps Hate'.

FROM HAYEK TO TRUMP:
THE LOGIC OF NEOLIBERAL DEMOCRACY

MARTIJN KONINGS

The motivating force, ethical appeal, and emotional purchase of the neoliberal image of the market have all too often eluded progressive critics. To the extent that they have recognized the affective aspects of neoliberal politics, they have tended to focus on its alliances with neoconservative philosophies and to view these as instrumental and external. According to such accounts, neoconservatives have legitimated laissez-faire economics and private enrichment through appeals to conservative religious values, and large sections of the American public have been curiously unable to see through this obvious hypocrisy – giving rise to the kind of despair at the people's irrationality that is expressed in the title of Thomas Frank's book *What's the Matter with Kansas?*[1] Such approaches conceive of the legitimating spirit of neoliberalism as an external ideological moment, portraying populists' loyalty to neoliberal discourses as a kind of cognitive impairment or moral failure.

This style of explanation has been stretched to new limits with the rise of Trump, a phenomenon that has become truly incomprehensible, operating in ways that are beyond the perceptual register of the progressive worldview. Throughout the two-year election process itself, many dismissed his strong showings in early polls and confidently asserted that he would drop out of the primary race soon enough. As Trump's candidacy proved more resilient than expected, such predictions gave way to grudging acknowledgements that Trump enjoyed more appeal than initially expected but the latter were quickly replaced with predictions that he would never be able to capture the nomination. After Trump did win the nomination by a wide margin, the second half of 2016 was dominated by claims that he had done so much to alienate key constituencies that his election had become a mathematical impossibility. For much of the campaign, the *New York Times* webpage showed an electoral barometer indicating a very high likelihood that Clinton would win the election. Manifesting the culture of data analysis and claims to technical expertise that progressive media outlets like to associate themselves with, it always seemed like a digital-era talisman meant to stave off impending doom. On Election Day, the dial flipped over to a decisive Trump victory in just a few hours, as Trump took the lead in several key states, revealing unsuspected resentment beneath measured political opinion.

All this reflected above all the inability to see Trump's victory as a real historical possibility. Progressives have taken their own sense of utter disbelief as reflecting the cognitive limitations and moral deficiencies of those supporting the Trump enterprise. Notions that we have entered a post-truth era that is qualitatively different from the traditional workings of ideology, or that there is something uniquely sadistic or punitive about Trump's politics, serve more as discussion material for the commentariat than as meaningful contributions to political theory. As explanations of recent developments, they are outdone by Steve Bannon's conviction that Trump is a modern-day Andrew Jackson, working to restore the republican promise of the American polity with a single-minded commitment to the ruthless subordination and eradication of those standing in the way of its realization. Progressives' focus on Trump's lack of basic policy expertise and personal incivility only served to reinforce the popular impression that he would and could take on the webs of Washington collusion that protected political and corporate elites alike and prevented any significant action on putting special interests back in their place.

The inability to discern this ethical core at the heart of neoliberal political projects leads to the dilemmas that are so familiar to progressives. To take two examples, historian Mark Lilla (2016) singled out the Democratic preoccupation with diversity and 'identity politics' as the main cause behind Trump's victory. Hillary Clinton, he argued, made the 'strategic mistake' of 'calling out explicitly to African-American, Latino, L.G.B.T. and women voters at every stop';[2] this rubbed the white working classes the wrong way, and they voted for Trump in droves. Lilla would be one of those progressive commentators that long-time *Critical Inquiry* editor W.J.T. Mitchell (2016) has in mind when he writes 'Can I just say that I am sick and tired of hearing liberals and leftists beating their breasts about how they failed to empathize sufficiently with the white working class in this country?' And he adds: '[P]lease, all you liberals, leftists, hipsters, intellectuals, progressives, school teachers, and people who read something besides Twitter feeds, and watch something besides Fox News, stop apologizing for losing this election. ... Before you assemble in a circular firing squad to put the blame on yourselves, take a moment to assign the blame where it belongs: on the idiots who voted for this man.'[3] Lilla and Mitchell voice what are fairly common sentiments on the left, and the logic of progressive politics leads to this standoff as a very real strategic dilemma. At work here is a kind of political blackmail, which asks us either to legitimate the exclusions and oppressions of neoliberalism in hopes of blunting their sharpest edges for some; or to turn a blind eye to the ethical force of the neoliberal image of the market that drives this exclusionary politics, leaving us to view its supporters as simple idiots, unthinking hostages of false consciousness.

The limitations of prevailing progressive perspectives are particularly evident in the credulity-straining ways in which the Bush administration, previously accused of all manner of authoritarian and even fascist tendencies, has been reframed as representing a brand of moderate conservatism, at some distance from the racism, nativism and misogyny embraced by Trump.[4] To be sure, the concern with fascism is hardly inappropriate – the problem is precisely that such readings make the situation seem exceptional, painting it as a deviation from a more normal course of historical development and therefore not amenable to explanation and intervention. On the one hand this entails a tendency to dramatize the immediacy of the danger and to overstate the ease with executive powers can abrogate the powers of democratic institutions. On the other hand, it diverts attention from the ugliness that neoliberal democracy is capable of producing even when its key institutions are still fully intact and functional.

To understand this properly, we need to attend carefully to what has sustained the legitimacy of neoliberalism. A key point of reference here is of course the financial crisis of 2007-2008, which was widely seen as heralding the end of neoliberalism. Explanations for why neoliberalism is at present still operational have tended to focus on the ability of financial elites to capture public discourses and institutions. But capture explanations are intellectually defensive, framed to provide a more or less plausible reason for something that was expected to occur yet has not rather than to explain what in fact happened. The question that needs answering is precisely how elites could continue to access such tremendous material, institutional, symbolic, and other resources even in a context where discontent with key neoliberal institutions was at an all-time high and the political air was thick with contempt and distrust towards bankers.[5] This essay argues that the paradoxical political dynamics that ensued following the crisis of 2007-2008 reflect a more basic logic at the heart of neoliberal governance. There is of course always a possibility that instability will result in simple breakdown, failure pure and simple; but one of the distinctive features of the neoliberal age is nonetheless that crises have often served to reactivate and intensify subjects' attachments to the very norms and conventions that have been malfunctioning. The point here is by no means to belittle or denigrate the significance of the often highly creative and important forms of resistance that have emerged since the financial crisis. Rather, the aim is to bring into sharper focus what those movements are up against – neoliberalism's distinctive sources of legitimacy.

AGAINST EXCEPTIONALISM:
THE LEGITIMACY OF NEOLIBERALISM

By and large, progressive assessments of the significance of the financial crisis have been problematic and misleading. Immediately after the crisis, progressive commentary was pervaded by a sense of profound optimism about the return of the protective state and Keynesian interventionism as the pillars of a new social compromise. Many declared the end of the neoliberal policy regime and its replacement with a regime committed to the re-regulation of financial capital. The crisis was taken as a turning point in the 'Polanyian' logic of double movements, a model of the dynamics of capitalist society that has found tremendous traction among critical scholars in recent decades. According to the Polanyian conceptual schema, periodic 'disembedding' movements, when the speculative logic of the market becomes unmoored from its social foundations and expands beyond its natural province, will be followed by 're-embedding' movements, when society intervenes to re-subordinate markets by re-imposing limits and restoring foundations.[6]

The Polanyian model is of interest not so much in its own right but rather because it formalizes some of the key assumptions of contemporary progressive thought. The latter sees the capitalist economy and the democratic polity as governed by logics that are different but in principle compatible – as evidenced by the widely celebrated combination of political stability and economic prosperity that characterized the early postwar period. But it insists that we cannot take this harmony for granted: with a certain cyclical regularity, the expansionary logic of the market will rear its head to upset the balance between economic freedom and political community. At such moments, imperatives of economic growth and accumulation come into conflict with the sovereignty and community organized through public and civic institutions. This is where contemporary progressive liberalism differs from classic social democracy (in the tradition of Bernstein and Crosland) and earlier forms of progressive liberalism (for instance, Fabianism and early twentieth century American Progressivism), which tended to imagine a more linear path of secular progress, with a gradually expanding edifice of social and political rights being built on top of a base of civic and economic rights.

The anticipated re-embedding movement has conspicuously failed to materialize. Expectations of a return to a more Keynesian policy consensus were initially buoyed when Western governments effectively nationalized failing financial institutions and announced wide-ranging fiscal stimulus packages, but hopes for a renewal of the commitment to public protection were disappointed before too long. The Obama administration managed to pass the American Recovery and Reinvestment Act and the Dodd–Frank Wall Street Reform and Consumer Protection Act, but already by that time concerns were widespread that it did relatively little to constrain Wall Street, not enough to help Main Street, and for all intents and purposes served to normalize the regime of too-big-to-fail expectations. Hopes for progressive legislation took a further hit when the Democrats lost the 2010 midterm elections, which emboldened Republicans to sabotage any Democratic attempts to rein in the financial sector. For instance, the Consumer Financial Protection Bureau has had to fight for its life practically from the moment it was conceived, and has remained fairly powerless. But not only did these developments dash hopes for a Polanyian countermovement, they were part of a positive restoration of neoliberal policies that was particularly evident in the precipitous rise to political prominence of austerity discourses, which targeted public debt as a key problem. What many declared would be a post-neoliberal era has ended up very much like a neoliberalism reloaded.

And yet, this has not done much to prompt a significant reorientation of progressive thought, which is back in the business of denouncing out-of-control market dynamics, confidently asserting that the next crisis will force the much-needed political change that failed to materialize last time.[7] They take the fact that neoliberal policies are alive and well as only so much more evidence of the irrationality of neoliberalism's naïve faith in market self-regulation and its essential inability to function as a coherent principle of governance. Such perspectives see neoliberalism as incapable of appreciating the role of communal deliberation and of engendering consensus and stability, and consequently as principally unable to generate its own sources of legitimacy. The resilience and survival of neoliberalism is seen to be exceptional – not grounded in an organically functioning support system of coherent norms and practices but dependent on ad hoc tricks and nefarious political schemes. According to the idea of institutional capture, politicians and policymakers have been unable to pursue reforms or to learn from the crisis because of financial capital's tight hold on public institutions and discourses.

But such explanations are incomplete at best and misleading at worst. Of course, the role of elites has been an important factor in preventing popular grievances from translating into politically effective messages, and in preventing any change at the level of institutional politics that did occur from translating into durable policy changes. How true this was could be seen in the US, where even common sense proposals met with enormous resistance right from the start. The proposal for a rule regulating proprietary trading (which would have imposed some restrictions on banks' ability to mix up their own money with that of their clients, not unlike the New Deal's Glass-Steagall separation of commercial and investment banking), proposed by Paul Volcker, the man who had played such a crucial role in the neoliberalization of finance yet had come to feel that things may have got out of hand, was quickly painted as the idea of an inexpert crank and never stood a real chance. A version of it did get passed, but was so watered-down and riddled with exemptions that in practice it has imposed few constraints on the practices of banks. A reading of Sheila Bair's account of her years at the Federal Deposit Insurance Corporation bears this point out quite concretely: her willingness to take on entrenched interests was actively fought by other (often more powerful) regulatory actors such as Treasury Secretary Tim Geithner, who, in their wish to get the system back on track, were generally hostile to any initiatives that might challenge the ability of key financial actors to resume operations and so disrupt the workings of the system.[8] However, the idea of institutional capture cannot stand on its own as an explanation for the failure of neoliberalism to expire. The power of elites is itself a function of the continued viability of neoliberal institutions and discourses, and to simply say that their power prevented the demise of neoliberalism therefore runs the risk of being somewhat tautological or uninformative. It does not account for the structural conditions that have permitted neoliberalism to escape what appeared to be an inevitable fate.

Progressive capture accounts are part of a wider trend of explanation that follows a 'Schmittian' logic. Carl Schmitt, a German political and legal theorist associated with the Nazi regime, considered the idea that that authority could ever be fully consensual or legitimate to be naively idealist. Authority in the end was always exceptional, not derived from democratic norms but rooted in the power of pure decision. His work has been revived in recent times, initially and most prominently through Agamben's work on the 'state of exception',[9] but it has now also found significant traction among political economy scholars.[10] On such readings, crisis creates an exceptional state of disarray that permits elites to bypass the normal procedures of parliamentary democracy and public accountability and to seize control of key institutions. Whereas the Polanyian schema sees the uncertainty of a crisis as something that democratic forces can use to their advantage, Schmittian explanations follow the opposite logic, viewing moments of systemic instability as occasions when the normal rules of liberal democracy are rendered powerless and developments come to be governed by unaccountable elite decisions and unlegitimated control. In the progressive critique of neoliberalism, the Schmittian line of argument has become the excuse story for the failure of the Polanyian line of argument. Both perspectives are insufficiently attuned to the specific ways in which neoliberalism has made crises productive, disposing us to respond to them in ways that restore the specific dynamics through which its logic operates.

BEYOND THE CRITIQUE OF ECONOMISM

The Polanyian perspective is typically framed as a pluralist critique of the 'economistic fallacy'[11] – the tendency, seen as common to Marxist political economy and orthodox economics, to essentialize the economy, to imagine that it is an autonomous, self-reproducing system that has no need for external inputs, limits, or foundations. According to this argument, economistic approaches are fooled by the fantasy of market self-regulation and so fail to recognize the forces of instability unleashed by, and ultimately the essential impossibility of, endless market disembedding. Polanyi's work, by contrast, underscores the crucial importance of the embeddedness of the market in the substance of human life – social bonds, political community and moral values.

Polanyian scholarship, however, has by no means escaped the problem of essentialism, economic or otherwise. To understand why this is the case, we need to take a closer look at what is entailed by the critique of market disembedding. The main reason why market expansion is considered unsustainable over the longer term is that it involves the proliferation of fictitious tokens that are not grounded in economic realities. Speculation, the key mechanism of market disembedding, is viewed as generating financial claims that are not grounded in the production of real value. It is seen to result in the periodic build-up of unsustainable, top-heavy structures of fictitious claims – a dynamic that must sooner or later always come to a halt, when foundational values reassert themselves and overleveraged financial structures begin to unravel. The conceptual logic here of course is deeply indebted to a materialist essentialism, which sees 'real value' as bound up with a structure of industrial production, and speculation as an unwarranted transgression of the limits of that structure.

In the meantime, the expansionary tendencies and systemic properties of capital are explained entirely in negative terms, as the inability of economic actors to recognize foundations and limits and to attribute reality to fictions. If disembedding is said to be unsustainable, a phenomenon that is only viable as long as the basic laws of economic gravity are suspended, we get no plausible explanation for why this dysfunctional phenomenon occurs in the first place. Polanyian thought thus revolves around a systemic, self-expansionary dynamic that it is unable to theorize in a positive way. Moreover, this materialist essentialism is allied to an idealist essentialism. The disembedding dynamics of capital are seen to be disruptive to the balance of capital and democracy that prevailed during the post-New Deal period. We find here an assumption that there exists an essential congruence between the circumstances that permit the production of true economic values and the norms of democracy and community. The Polanyian model does not so much advance a new, non-economistic understanding of the economy but rather tries to balance an economistic conception of the economy with an idealist understanding of society and the state.

What has maintained the plausibility of these Polanyian critiques is the Marxist commitment to the idea of an ontologically situated economic logic that is specific to capital.[12] This essay rather works from the idea that the question of capital's expansionary, self-valorizing nature only becomes manageable if is *not* couched in such essentializing terms and if it is instead considered in the context of the modern subject's intuitive awareness of the necessity of contingency. The expansionary dynamics of capital are driven by the recognition that secular risk is the only game in town and an awareness that there is no safety in a stationary state. In other words, capital's characteristic self-expansionary dynamic is prompted by the *absence* of pre-existing, foundational values. A substantivist conception of value is precisely an obstacle to a plausible account of capitalism's systemic properties – including the ways in which the logic of capital penetrates into other spheres of human life. On this reading, speculation is not a dysfunctional deviation from basic structures but the driving force behind the totalizing logic of capital, its constant tendency to penetrate into new areas of life and to subject everything it encounters to a logic of valorization. This entails the need to recognize speculation as a potentially productive move: a dynamic of fictitious projection and subsequent valorization is at the heart of capital's operation. The operation of that double movement pre-empts the relevance of any Polanyian double movement between economics and politics. The real double movement obtains not between an economistically conceived economy and an equally essentialized political sphere, but is internal to the logic of capital.[13]

The progressive model of what constitutes a coherent social order very quickly gives rise to exceptionalist modes of explanation: developments are not explained in their own right but rather as deviations from a normative logic that dictates the need for judicious combinations of capitalism and democracy. The dynamics of the post-crisis context have consequently remained largely illegible from a progressive standpoint. The ways in which resurgent forms of democratic engagement have boosted above all the right rather than the left have been incomprehensible. Treatments, for instance, of Tea Party populism and its demand for fiscal austerity have had a highly dismissive tone: it has been treated as an irrational fringe phenomenon that is at odds with the real values and dynamics of American democracy.[14] Nor have progressive perspectives been able to offer penetrating readings of the ways in which authoritarian tendencies have fed off the revival of popular engagement with questions of finance and debt. Defining such impulses strictly in opposition to democratic governance, progressive approaches turn a blind eye to their increasingly visible symbiosis.

Of course, Polanyian scholarship has paid considerable attention to questions of authoritarianism and fascism. But it theorizes such phenomena specifically as the result of a breakdown or self-implosion of liberal democracy, that is, as an outcome of the *failure* of the Polanyian double movement. It can only think of authoritarianism as *reaction against* the failure of the double movement – rather than as the dynamic of the double movement itself, internal to the logic of neoliberalism. That is in some ways a plausible way to model the rise of fascism during the interwar period, when capitalism came close to literally breaking down as a principle of socialization. But its applicability at the present moment is far more limited: declarations of the imminent collapse of capitalist order have been proved wrong repeatedly, and capital has been able to revitalize itself time and again by pushing its speculative logic into new areas of human life. Certainly that revitalization has at times had a decidedly vampiric character, but we should probably be more interested in accounting for capital's paradoxical life than simply insisting on the fact that it is really dead.

How to move beyond the bifurcation of politics and economics that underlies this inability to address key aspects of the present moment? That is of course to raise a question that has long been at the heart of Marxist state theory: how is the economic present in the political? Existing theories have tended to emphasize either an instrumentalist model or a structuralist model (or some combination thereof), the former emphasizing the ways in which corporate and financial elites are able to use personal influence to shape the choices made by public policymakers, and the latter viewing the operations of the state as structurally bound to the functional requirements of capital.[15] Both have an obvious relevance, but both also suffer from distinctive and well-known problems: the first shares the conspiratorial valences associated with capture theory, and the latter too often reproduces the economic determinism characteristic of an orthodox base-superstructure model. As a consequence, even many Marxist theories nowadays shy away from the very idea that contemporary politics is at its core shaped by the logic of capital, choosing instead to emphasize the principal institutional autonomy of the political[16] – even when the growing imbrication of economy and polity is one of the most pronounced trends of the present.

Instead of trying to account for relationships of causal determination, this essay asks how politics becomes infused with a capitalist risk rationality and what that means. What exactly is it that inflects the logic of democratic interaction so persistently around the expanded reproduction of capital? Not everywhere and not always, but often enough that it frequently bedevils those who put a great deal of faith in the emancipatory power of modern democratic politics. Key here is to insist on the materiality of ideology. Of course many Marxist theorists have made that point, but it has at times been difficult to make this idea concrete and to attenuate its connection to a base-superstructure model, or more generally a 'spatial' model of capitalism as involving different regions that 'interact'.[17] Such approaches have great difficulty understanding how ideology is present within other spheres of human life and the concrete ways in which it affects and shapes their operations. To speak of the materiality of ideology is to say that it often does not work at a primarily cognitive or discursive level, but operates in more machinic and embodied ways. Ideology does not work primarily through (mis)representations but more fundamentally through modulations situated at the level of emotional affinities, habitual dispositions, and affective attachments – a structure that can certainly be activated through such (mis)representations.[18]

RE-ASSESSING NEOLIBERALISM

At this point it is helpful to reflect on what the term 'neoliberalism' refers to. The Polanyian schema relies on a rather literal interpretation of the 'neo' in 'neoliberal': it sees neoliberalism as a simple revival of or return to classic laissez-faire liberalism, marked above all by the subordination of public institutions to market criteria. As a result, it is often unclear in what qualitative respects liberalism can be seen to be 'new' – it seems we are just dealing with a re-run of classic liberalism. Neoliberalism is accordingly criticized as representing a naïve faith in market self-regulation that is oblivious to the ways in which speculative dynamics undermine the foundations of social order. And the expansion of finance that has occurred under present-day neoliberalism is seen as necessarily leading to the kind of economic and political collapse that occurred in the 1930s.

Debates in recent years have paid more attention to the specific ideological and institutional sources of the rise of neoliberalism. One prominent line of thinking has tended to conceive of it as a discrete project advanced by specific elites, actors and ideas who seek to bypass the ordinary mechanisms of political decisionmaking to impose neoliberal policy templates.[19] But this reproduces some of the problems discussed in the above. In Mirowski's account, neoliberalism is an exceptionalist, Schmittian project: a form of government that works by paralyzing or bypassing the normal rules of democracy. For Klein, crises are crucial here: the widespread disarray that they create offers opportunities for neoliberal elites to pursue reform agendas that would never have been tolerated if the populace was paying full attention. More recent scholarship has pursued this path of enquiry by turning to the concept of authoritarian neoliberalism.[20]

There can be little doubt that shock, awe, and capture have been key modalities of neoliberalism. But it is not clear that such an emphasis is useful for understanding all aspects of its operation, especially in the Western world, where neoliberal programmes have often come to power by mobilizing a great deal of political support. Stuart Hall observed the popular traction of Thatcherism and proposed the idea of 'authoritarian populism' to capture the paradoxical dynamics at work.[21] But even this is perhaps not sufficiently attuned to the ability of neoliberal discourses to capture the imagination of contemporary citizens: it isn't just that elites are capable of manipulating the sentiments of the populace, but also that the discourses and images of neoliberalism have an actual *sui generis* appeal. The affective charge of neoliberalism has not simply involved the production of consent for a project that has already been formulated, but rather the ways in which democratic processes have themselves been actively involved in the production of a neoliberal mode of rule.

The power of neoliberalism has never been reducible to the top-down imposition of a pro-capital regime: it has been rooted in a broader field of beliefs, practices and institutions. Recent contributions have relied on Foucault's lectures on neoliberalism in the *Birth of Biopolitics* to reflect on the contours of 'neoliberal reason' or 'neoliberal rationality', so steering the analysis of neoliberalism away from exaggerated concern with the actions of small circles of elites.[22] To view neoliberalism through this lens is to argue that it has not been simply a naïve faith in the virtues of utilitarian logics but instead a more or less coherent governance philosophy and that its practical operations have been sustained by governmentalities – subjectively rooted dispositions, inclinations and affinities.

Foucault cautions against the tendency to view neoliberalism simply as a return to classical liberalism. Whereas classic liberalism had always made strong claims about the natural legitimacy or self-evident efficiency of the market in managing risk, neoliberalism was driven by an awareness that this solution was too simple and that the continued viability of capitalism required more than faith in the natural efficiency of markets. Whereas classical liberalism saw its task as removing institutional obstacles to the utilitarian logic of the market, neoliberalism has been characterized by an awareness that the order it envisages needs to be actively constructed institutionally, discursively and politically. For Foucault, then, neoliberalism needs to be understood as an engagement with the limitations of classical liberalism as these had manifested themselves amidst the social and economic instability of the early twentieth century.

We should remind ourselves here that neoliberal ideas were first formulated during the interwar period, when capitalism experienced a crisis whose intensity may be difficult to imagine for those who have come of age during the neoliberal era. This was a major factor in precipitating the collapse of the international liberal world order and the turn to economic nationalism. Under these circumstances, capitalism had lost much of its legitimacy, and capitalist elites' fear of the power of labour movements and the danger of Communism can hardly be overestimated. As Plehwe reports, the word neoliberalism was used first in the 1920s by authors who were specifically minded to rescue liberal principles in the face of advancing socialist forces.[23] Plehwe also observes that interwar Vienna served as something of an intellectual training ground for the neoliberal movement:[24] there, Ludwig von Mises and Friedrich Hayek entered into debates with proponents of socialist policies that would eventually take the form of the socialist calculation debate.[25] Both realized acutely that, if neoclassical economics was correct, the case for capitalism and against socialism was on shaky grounds. Their defence of capitalism was less concerned with the ideal efficiency of markets and rather emphasized the practical limitations of human knowledge about the future and the way this undermines socialist ambitions for the transparent shaping of the future in line with collectivist principles.

Neoliberal thought could thus be viewed as an attempt to reformulate the principles of classical liberalism in a context where the latter had lost much of their legitimacy. This involved a recognition of the limits of liberalism and an awareness that a revitalization of capitalism could not simply be a reactionary project seeking a return to earlier times. In that sense, neoliberalism has always been rooted in an appreciation of the problems associated with the liberal market utopia that Polanyi was so critical of. The contemporary Polanyian critique of neoliberalism as a critique of disembedding fails to acknowledge that neoliberals themselves already grappled with very similar issues and proposed particular solutions to make capitalism viable again. To say that neoliberalism involved a reflexive engagement with the limits of classical liberalism, rather than simply being an attempt to restore that dystopia, means that we need to recognize the ways in which the neoliberal project has been minded to produce its own sources of legitimacy – it has at times succeeded and at other times failed to do so, but it has never been uninterested in this question.[26]

CONTOURS OF NEOLIBERAL REASON

In Foucault's account, the distinctive characteristic of neoliberalism is the emergence of a more purposeful and proactive relationship to the secular condition of inescapable risk. He views liberalism and neoliberalism as distinctive rationalities of governance that cannot be grasped through essentializing oppositions of economic and politics or markets and states – only through an engagement with the broader question of how humans engage their world in a context where traditional metaphysical certainties and theological justifications of authority have lost much of their force.

Premodern sources of social order were political and religious, grounded in the claims of rulers to divine appointment and the ways in which such claims were supported and legitimated by the church. This always prominently included a critique of the proliferation of commercial relations: activities oriented primarily to money-making were condemned as corrosive and disruptive, as attempts to appropriate and trade in what belonged to God – time.[27] In the context of the Scottish Enlightenment, as it became increasingly difficult to believe literally that human history was orchestrated by an outside force, the mechanisms whereby contingency is transformed into order were increasingly viewed as situated at the level of the secular itself. What became thinkable was the idea of secular self-organization, as expressed in Adam Smith's notion of the 'invisible hand'.[28] What Smith's work on the social division of labour and the role of the market amounted to was an argument that the speculative engagement of the future could under certain conditions be legitimate. Direct control or intervention by political authorities was not always necessary and indeed potentially harmful. Through the workings of the invisible hand, commercial and financial activities could advance order, supporting rather than undermining governance.

Money now appeared no longer as an irrational, corrupting force but rather as a harmless facilitator of economic interaction – it was 'neutral', as David Hume was the first to argue, a mere means of coordination and commensuration.[29] In neoclassical economics the neutrality tenet has come to refer specifically to allocative efficiency, but in the context of the Scottish Enlightenment it was deeply embedded in a republican mode of thought that viewed the self-organizing rationality of the market as a bulwark against illegitimate concentrations of authority and monarchical tyranny. Compared to the arbitrariness of sovereign interventions, money was a far more just adjudicator, and enforcing the logic of the market would provide a constraint on the latter. The neutrality postulate therefore had a clear political dimension: far from being differentiated in the way they are nowadays in political theory, republican and liberal discourses were closely intertwined.[30] The liberal-republican image of the market is therefore imbued with a moral and political significance that contemporary critics of unbridled capitalism tend to miss.

Of course, the distinction between the appropriate and inappropriate uses of money goes back to at least antiquity. But neither Aristotle nor the medieval theologians following him could have said is that money was *in principle* neutral: they viewed the danger of unnatural chrematistics as an ever-present one, acutely present already in the appropriate use of money. In modern life, this changes: even as specific financial forms continue to attract charges of irrationality, the idea of money as a social institution becomes immune from that critique. It is no longer seen as a corrupting force but instead as a principally innocuous symbol that can *itself* become corrupted. Whereas in the past political and religious ordering principles had needed to be safeguarded from the corrupting influence of commerce, in the modern conception it is precisely the market itself that needs to be protected from heteronomous influences.

To say that the modern economic imaginary pivots on the idea of market neutrality is to underscore that at the very same time as the modern subject comes to intuit the inevitability of risk, it becomes deeply invested in the prospect of security: as it becomes aware that the future is not determined by an outside authority, it becomes concerned with the possibility of controlling that future and making it predictable. Foucault understood this well, and he saw discourses of political economy and discourses of security as arising hand in hand in order to shape the experience of modern life.[31] He viewed modernity as engendering a distinctive 'apparatus (*dispositif*) of security'.[32] The rationality of liberal governance is thus shaped by the productive tension between the ever-present need to engage risk and the need to achieve immunity from contingency. The notion of market neutrality should therefore be seen as the ideological expression of a distinctly secular rationality: together with the emerging legitimacy of secular time and the awareness of self-organizing mechanisms arises the idea that the future can be rationally controlled. As such it is an image of the economic that modulates the politics of capitalism – a regulative fantasy that attends capitalist expansion.

Neoclassical economics fully sanitized the liberal imaginary. Conceptualizing money as a technical one-off solution to the problem of coordination, it took time and uncertainty out of risk and so obscured the paradoxical affective structure embedded in the liberal conception of the market. Hayek understood well that in this way it had abandoned important political ground – evident in the ease with which the methods of neoclassical economics could be adopted by the enemies of liberalism. In the socialist calculation debate, he took on the ways in which neoclassical assumptions regarding knowledge and the future had made socialist planning seem like a viable option of social organization. And he viewed progressivism and social democracy as premised on a very similar epistemological naivety.

Foucault considered Hayek's work as holding important clues to the logic of neoliberalism even though he was not able to pursue this connection in much detail.[33] Whereas neoclassical theory suppresses the ongoing role of uncertainty and speculation in economic life, Hayek's work thematizes it. Hayek was deeply indebted to Smith's work and the way it intuited the principles of spontaneous economic ordering,[34] but he nonetheless felt that the notion of an 'invisible hand' still retained too many theological affinities – it still smacked too much of a belief in divine trickery. Hayek's more thoroughly secularized mind categorically denies the possibility of outside interventions or steering and views the emergence of economic order as driven by nothing but trial and error, uncertainty and discovery. Whereas Smith advanced his famous metaphor in order to address the question of how order might still be possible in a secularizing world that can no longer see itself as governed by a divine mind, Hayek proposed his understanding of spontaneous self-organization not to address a concern about the limitations of secular reason but precisely in response to its 'conceit':[35] the faith in rationalist constructivism that he saw as the defining characteristic of twentieth-century socialism and progressivism. In other words, his claim was not just that acting without certainty was acceptable but that it was necessary and imperative, that there is no source of order other than the interaction of speculative positions. 'Catallaxy' was not simply a principle of 'economic' organization that needed to be respected by political authorities, but the only game in town.

This implies a different relationship to risk. Whereas classical liberalism was primarily concerned to discount the uncertainty of the future, neoliberalism is interested in the outer edges of calculability, the incalculable and unpredictable.[36] In a Hayekian logic, failure is itself a productive event, an indispensable aspect of the discovery processes that generate order. This means that neoliberal reason is characterized by a concern with time and the future that remains suppressed in classic economic liberalism (and is entirely absent in neoclassical economics). It is accordingly more interested in financialization than commodification,[37] more taken with the promises and prospects of investment than the immediate utility of consumption, more engaged with the generative role of speculation than the stasis of general equilibrium.[38] Whereas classic liberalism is steeped in the logic of controllable and predictable risk, neoliberalism intuits the limits and paradoxes of that logic. It views the speculative engagement of uncertainty as a productive impulse.

Crucially, however, these insights only ever served as a renewed justification of the tenet of market neutrality. Even as Hayek's understanding of self-organization incorporated influences from twentieth-century systems theory, it often seems as if his work was written at a time before it became customary to distinguish republicanism from liberalism, imagining the market above all as a source of protection against cumulative inequalities or structural power differentials.[39] In Hayek's work market neutrality comes to serve more and more as a regulatory horizon, permanently out of reach, forever receding and demanding an intensified commitment to the uncertainties of the market. In a radicalization of the counterfactual logic that liberalism had instituted, the fact that risk and uncertainty never result in equilibrium conditions only serves to heighten the importance of the active engagement of the uncertainty that is the only source of order. Neoliberal reason has thus recovered the liberal-republican imaginary of market neutrality and recharged the productive tensions of the risk-security axis, turning the security dispositif fully into an imperative for risk engagement.

This forcefield has been held together by an obstinate willingness to attribute the widely observed and experienced non-neutrality of actually existing capitalism to external sources of corruption, actors who seek exemption from the rigorously neutral dictates of the market. The fact that capitalist life is often so patently at odds with the republican image of the market has often not occasioned a revision of that image but has rather heightened the felt importance of ensuring its realization. The progressive understanding of neoliberalism's persistence in terms of its affiliation with Schmittian exceptionalism is therefore not simply misleading but also suffers from a massive blind spot: it fails to see that neoliberal reason *itself* already contains a critique of exceptionalism and institutional capture. The way in which it has directed that critique precisely at the progressive political project has been central to its rhetorical traction and political success. The unreflexive moment here is thrown into even sharper relief when it is recalled that capture theory is *literally* a neoliberal theory, pioneered by George Stigler,[40] one of the founding members of the Mont Pelerin society. From a neoliberal perspective, nothing has done more to undermine the neutral operation of capitalism's institutions than progressive elites' conceited claims to expertise and the way in which this has supported those who seek bailouts and handouts.

In the context of the 1970s, where economic conditions were increasingly seen as being undermined by the ways in which the state shielded sections of the population from the consequences of their actions, the prospect of institutional purification through the willing embrace of self-reliance struck a particular chord. The neoliberal subject works to be resilient, not simply safe – it seeks to achieve security not through avoiding risk but by embracing it. At work here is a logic of pre-emption, a paradoxical orientation that blurs the distinction between prevention and activation, defensive and offensive moves, security and risk. Pre-emptive reason can be understood as an operationalization of the dispositif that Hayek insisted was the only possible way to produce order through contingency: it is characterized by a willingness to move beyond a naïve doctrine of prevention and to proactively engage the future. It intuits the importance of acting in the absence of certainty and appreciates the power of provocation. The notion of pre-emption has been exploited by critical security scholars (Massumi 2007, de Goede 2008),[41] but here I would like to suggest it also provides a useful lens for looking at questions of political economy.

The Bush administration demanded vigilance and preparedness in the name of security, while simultaneously declaring that the war on terror would have no end. Similarly, neoliberalism forever demands a commitment to the speculative logic of risk in the name of a future security that it simultaneously announces will never materialize. In this way it amplifies the paradoxes of the modern security dispositif: even as it presents itself as eliminating threats and obstacles to economic security, its modus operandi is predicated on the possibility of activating and engaging new sources of contingency, proactively enforcing adjustment by allowing crises and instability to play a productive role. Neoliberalism goes beyond the concern to make the future predictable to embrace an orientation to the pragmatic uses of instability, uncertainty and crisis.[42]

THE LOGIC OF NEOLIBERAL GOVERNANCE

Neoliberal policies have often been oriented not to the prevention of failure but rather to its pre-emption – in the dual sense of the word, both activating it and forestalling its potentially most serious consequences. Here we should remind ourselves that, for all the attention that has in recent years been lavished on the ideological sources of neoliberalism, it was really the pragmatically driven shift of monetary policy initiated by Paul Volcker that restructured the institutional landscape of the American political economy.[43] Volcker saw the American financial system heading for decline, and he acted on this awareness pre-emptively by triggering a potentially productive crisis. The turn to monetarism was meant to provoke, motivated not by a clear perception of the outcome of this move but by an intuition of its productive, ordering potential.

The Volcker shock was offensively speculative, creating new sources of uncertainty in hopes of stabilizing the financial system. What was not in itself surprising, then, was the dramatic expansion of financial activity that followed the policy turn; that was precisely why in the past the Federal Reserve had held back from contractionary policies or quickly reversed them. The Volcker speculation consisted precisely in the wager that the instability caused by the Fed's persistence with those policies would set in motion wider processes of adjustment. The extent to which the success of the monetarist turn was contingent on such wider adjustments was illustrated by Volcker's own admission that the Reagan administration's confrontation with organized labour had been crucial to the conquest of inflation.[44] And that was only one element in a wide-ranging set of policies that accelerated the destruction of the secure employment contracts of Fordism. The resulting precarity and contingency for the bulk of the American population offered a wealth of investment opportunities and have served as important sources of capitalist revitalization.[45]

The neoliberal era has seen a dramatic growth of personal and household debt, much of it extended in ways and for purposes that earlier generations would have considered absurdly speculative. What has been termed 'the capitalization of almost everything'[46] finds its fullest expression in the rise of 'human capital.' The tendency to think of neoliberalism as involving a recommodification of labour (as opposed to its partial decommodification effected during the era of Fordism) is problematic insofar as one of the key results of neoliberal restructuring is precisely the decrease in opportunities for straightforwardly exchanging one's labour for a wage.[47] The neoliberal subject is a speculative actor, an 'entrepreneur of himself' who aims to explore and activate the productive potential of its capacities and affinities and to realize this in monetary terms.[48] Foucault considered the notion of human capital to be one of neoliberalism's main innovations:[49] he viewed it as containing an implicit critique of the way neoclassical economics had reduced labour to a generic technical parameter.[50] Anticipating notions of immaterial, cognitive, and affective labour that have been developed by autonomist scholars, the notion of human capital brings into view a broader, post-Fordist understanding of production that is more in tune with the speculative dimension of economic value.[51] Time and again, neoliberal capitalism has upset assumptions of objective limits and managed to push the logic of capitalization into new areas of human life.

Even as neoliberal restructuring brought down inflation and alleviated external pressure on the dollar, these developments were accompanied by significant financial volatility and the 1980s saw a series of bailouts of systemically important ('too big to fail') institutions, which fostered expectations regarding the way the American state would handle such events in the future.[52] This new institutional configuration facilitated a reorientation of financial governance: the new approach that emerged recognized that crises were likely to continue to occur periodically, that the use of bailouts could not be ruled out, and that the aim should be to manage their application and minimize their undesirable side effects. Panitch and Gindin capture this development in terms of a shift of concern from 'failure prevention' to 'failure containment'.[53] Among Federal Reserve insiders this became known as the 'mop up after' strategy.[54]

It is crucial here to recognize that, as Ewald emphasizes, the transition to pre-emptive modes of governance should not be understood as a clean replacement of one principle with another: the speculative orientation of neoliberal governance always articulates with the continued operation of principles of insurance and forces of normalization.[55] The neoliberal concern to provoke the future has always been complemented by a reactionary moment that manifests itself fully when uncertainty threatens to tip over into failure. At such times, acute uncertainty tends to create its own kind of certainty − not an ability to act on accurate knowledge of the future, but a definite certainty as to what needs to be done in the absence of such knowledge. At such times, society has no option but to fortify the historically generated nodal points of financial interconnectedness − that is, to bail out the banks. The logic of pre-emption now manifests itself in yet a third sense, as a foreclosure on the future. This reactionary moment too has a prominent presence in Hayek's work, which insists on the need to respect norms handed down from the past, even if we are unable to rationally justify such adherence (e.g. his dismissal of the very concept of social justice).[56]

What happens in such moments does not follow a Polanyian logic. Of course, the sense of dire necessity that accompanies bank bailouts works to intensify the moral indignation they elicit. But the motivating force of this works in paradoxical ways. The crises of neoliberalism do not represent moments of political openness, when a sudden absence of structural determinations could facilitate the emergence of a countermovement. Neoliberal reason faces uncertainty not as an external condition but as something that it works to incorporate into its mode of operation. Although it enjoys no guarantees in this respect, it is nonetheless one step ahead of the post-Keynesian critics who think that the capitalist logic of risk finds an objective limit in 'true uncertainty'. Progressive talk of a double movement has all too often been pre-empted by the operation of capital's own double movement, which is supervened by an imaginary of neutrality that connects much more readily with the neoliberal experience of injury and betrayal.[57]

Rarely does the normative image of the market as a flat, decentralized structure acting as a constraint on accumulations of power enjoy more traction than at times when it has been betrayed in the most spectacular way. The past decades have seen numerous crises, and the resulting popular anger and discontent have above all generated widespread calls for the restoration of a truly republican economy.[58] Nor is this simply an issue of political legitimation understood in a traditional sense: blurring the distinction between political legitimation and economic value, neoliberal governance techniques have not simply provided after-the-fact rationalizations but rather invited productive responses, active participation in its logic of pre-emption. There is of course an ideological dimension at work here, a politically relevant discrepancy between the logic and image of capital. But precisely because this discrepancy is so dramatic that it is obvious, criticizing it as a sort of cognitive mistake or diversion is largely beside the point. Populists are only too aware that their ideals have been betrayed – that is exactly what they are responding to.

Austerity discourses sit at the heart of the generative tensions of neoliberal reason: they represent a paradoxical combination of reactionary and forward-looking sentiments, enjoining us to repay the debts inherited from the past in order to secure the future. The austerity turn has been widely interpreted in terms of the ability of financial elites to block the Polanyian countermovement. Austerity policies are seen as producing short-term benefits for 'rentier interests' that come at the expense of the production of real value: pursuing austerity instead of Keynesian demand stimulation, financial and political elites are seen to deepen the recession and to undermine the preconditions of economic growth.[59] Although it is certainly true that the austerity turn has promoted precarity and accelerated the shift away from a world of consistent employment and steady paychecks, it is far from clear that this has undercut rather than promoted the valorization of capital. From the view of the double movement suggested in this essay, austerity policies should not be seen as a continuation of the 'disembedding' movement. Instead, the austerity drive is the movement whereby capital secures its speculative investments and valorizes its fictions.

Austerity was capable of eliciting popular support because of the way it manifested itself as the aim to restore a republican market that functions as a bulwark against unearned privilege and concentrations of power. Austerity has not only or primarily been associated with dire necessity and the dreary idea that there is simply no alternative: it appears as a means to undo capture and drive out special interests. The popular traction that this has given austerity discourses was on full display when it became a rallying cry for the Tea Party movement. That movement's central aim was to restore an earlier, less decadent America founded on republican values, where the undeserving are not pampered with bailouts financed by taxes on hardworking citizens and where economic security is achieved not through welfare and handouts but through self-reliance and risk engagement.

CONCLUSION

It is important to underscore the extent to which this neoliberal imaginary has only held because of the way in which it is able to contrast its moral commitments to the progressive philosophy that it views as rejecting or threatening such republican values. This means that the legitimacy of neoliberalism has to a high degree been sustained by the willingness of contemporary progressives to play their part in a public morality play – namely, the part of the out-of-touch patrician whose politics is driven by feelings of moral superiority rather than a genuine concern to ensure the basic fairness and neutrality of society's institutions. But here we should remind ourselves that this disconnect between the republican imaginary and progressive politics is very much a product of the postwar era. Early twentieth century progressivism saw itself as continuing the political commitments of the republican tradition, seeking forms of authority and community that would not be imposed on, but instead would exist in organic interaction with, the dynamics of an economic system organized around individual property. Such political impulses were still prominently evident in the making of the New Deal, and it was only during the postwar era that progressive elites became fully invested in the promise of top-down social engineering and lost touch with key concerns of the popular mindset.

Among recent political developments, the Bernie Sanders campaign stands out for the way in which it managed to recover some of these connections and for how, in doing so, it came very close to successfully challenging Hillary Clinton for the Democratic presidential nomination. Sanders represents a politics that remains within the ideological parameters of liberalism, but nonetheless recognizes the systemic sources of capitalism's oppressions and refuses to foment or exploit divisions among the lower classes. It now seems that the Sanders movement, far from having petered out following his loss in the presidential primaries, has continued to gather momentum. In this way it has become the closest thing to a believable source of opposition to the logic of neoliberalism. This is of course precisely why it elicited such intense and concerted resistance from the Democratic party establishment, which did not fight Sanders with all its might because they thought that his political ideas were too far out of the mainstream to be credible (the official line of the Clinton campaign), but precisely because they understood that his anti-neoliberal politics could find far more traction than progressive managerialism.

This is not to say that there exist no consequential differences between Clinton-style neoliberalism and Trump-style neoliberalism. One can point to any number of policy areas where Trump has already inflicted damage that would not have occurred under a Clinton administration. Where progressive neoliberalism goes wrong is in believing that it is possible to embed the expansionary dynamics of capitalism in a durable manner and that it can offer a stable alternative to the more virulent approaches to neoliberal restructuring. It is telling that even though during the 1990s Bill Clinton's administration implemented some of the most significant neoliberal reforms, it still ended up as the target of the kind of vitriolic hatred associated with Fox News that did so much to invigorate the politics of the Bush era.

This essay has focused on the US both because of the importance of that case in its own right but also because it offers the clearest manifestation of the paradoxical logic of neoliberal legitimation. Things certainly look different in the European context, where the austerity idea has not been carried by a popular movement and where capture explanations might seem to have more applicability. Indeed, authors like Streeck and Bonefeld have in recent years argued that European integration is fundamentally a Schmittian project, designed to insulate executive power and economic policy from the pressures of democracy.[60] But this is certainly still too one-sided. The turn to austerity policies in the post-crisis eurozone could never have been effective if it had not been for the remarkable speed and flexibility with which the focus of Western European public opinion was redirected from almost visceral disgust with financial elites to a general acceptance of key tenets of austerity policy – that budgets need balancing and debts need to be paid. The consequences of austerity have been real enough, but they have primarily served to add fuel to a resurgent nationalism that is above all concerned to keep out the foreigners who are unwilling to stay put and suffer its consequences in their own country. That is not to say that there are no inspiring initiatives on the left of the political spectrum, but at least in Western Europe it often seems that, to the extent that such movements have been capable of shifting the institutional makeup of the political landscape, the result has been to push labour parties closer to a culturalist nationalism that co-exists comfortably with anti-territorism discourses and islamophobia.

The rise of Jeremy Corbyn as leader of the British Labour Party and his recent electoral success may seem to indicate a possible break with this logic. In some respects Corbyn's position is analogous to that of Sanders, but the former's chances of actually heading a government are much more realistic. But the legacy of British Labourism and European social democracy is such that it is difficult to imagine a Corbyn government that would not very quickly become embroiled in the trade-offs of progressive politics. That could of course also be the case for a Sanders-style US president, but the very fact that the road to executive power is so much harder and longer in the US case means that, if such were to materialize in the next decade or so, it will have been on the strength of a popular movement that has been able to effect major transformations in the institutional and ideological structures of the Democratic Party and the US political system at large. Sanders' electoral success – much more so than Corbyn's – has been closely associated with the repoliticization of questions of debt, finance, and banking since the financial crisis. Of course there are plenty of reasons to think that the deck is heavily stacked against an effective left-wing reappropriation of republican radicalism – but this is nonetheless where, it seems to me, the battle is to be found and fought, at least for the foreseeable future. Even if Trump gets rid of some hard-won citizenship rights, it is far less likely that this battle will be lost because of a lack of democratic freedom than because of the failure to exercise such freedoms and put them to productive use to penetrate and subvert from within the logic of the neoliberal imaginary.

NOTES

1   Thomas Frank, *What's the Matter with Kansas?: How Conservatives Won the Heart of America*, New York: Holt, 2005.

2   Mark Lilla, 'The End of Identity Liberalism', *New York Times*, 18 November 2016.

3   W.J.T. Mitchell, 'Further Night Thoughts on the Trump Election', https://critinq. wordpress.com/2016/11/16/further-night-thoughts-on-the-trump-election.

4   For instance, Rick Perlstein, 'I Thought I Understood the American Right. Trump Proved Me Wrong', *New York Times*, 11 April 2017.

5   Cf. Nicholas Kiersey, 'Everyday Neoliberalism and the Subjectivity of Crisis: Post-Political Control in an Era of Financial Turmoil', *Journal of Critical Globalisation Studies* 4, 2011, p. 5.

6   Wolfgang Streeck, 'How to Study Contemporary Capitalism?', *European Journal of Sociology* 53(1), 2012; Nancy Fraser, 'A Triple Movement? Parsing the Politics of Crisis After Polanyi', *New Left Review* 81(May-June), 2013; Fred Block and Margaret R. Somers, *The Power of Market Fundamentalism: Karl Polanyi's Critique*, Cambridge, MA: Harvard University Press, 2014.

7   Thomas I. Palley, *Financialization: The Economics of Finance Capital Domination*, New York: Palgrave Macmillan, 2013; Costas Lapavitsas, *Profiting Without Producing: How Finance Exploits Us All*, New York: Verso, 2014; Wolfgang Streeck, *Buying Time: The Delayed Crisis of Democratic Capitalism*, New York: Verso, 2014; Steve Keen, *Can We Avoid Another Financial Crisis?*, Cambridge: Polity, 2017.

8   Sheila Bair, *Bull By the Horns: Fighting to Save Main Street From Wall Street and Wall Street From Itself*, New York: Free Press, 2013.

9   Giorgio Agamben, *State of Exception*, Chicago: University of Chicago Press, 2005.

10   Philip Mirowski, *Never Let a Serious Crisis Go to Waste: How Neoliberalism Survived the Financial Meltdown*, New York: Verso, 2013; Wolfgang Streeck, 'Heller, Schmitt and the Euro', *European Law Journal* 21(3), 2015.

11   Block and Somers, *The Power of Market Fundamentalism*, p. 44.

12   Moishe Postone, *Time, Labor, and Social Domination: A Reinterpretation of Marx's Critical Theory*, Cambridge: Cambridge University Press, 1993; David Harvey, *The Limits to Capital*, London: Verso, 2007.

13   Angela Mitropoulos, *Contract and Contagion: From Biopolitics to Oikonomia*, Minor Compositions, 2012; Martijn Konings, *Capital and Time: For a New Critique of Neoliberal Reason*, Stanford: Stanford University Press, 2018.

14   Theda Skocpol and Vanessa Williamson, *The Tea Party and the Remaking of Republican Conservatism*, Oxford: Oxford University Press, 2012.

15   Clyde W. Barrow, *Critical Theories of the State*, Madison, WI: University of Wisconsin Press, 1993.

16   For instance, Bob Jessop, *The State: Past, Present, Future*, Cambridge: Polity, 2015.

17   Nicos Poulantzas, *State, Power, Socialism*, London: Verso, 1980.

18   Maurizio Lazzarato, *Signs and Machines: Capitalism and the Production of Subjectivity*, Los Angeles, CA: Semiotext(e), 2014.

19   David Harvey, *A Brief History of Neoliberalism*, Oxford: Oxford University Press, 2005; Naomi Klein, *The Shock Doctrine: The Rise of Disaster Capitalism*, New York: Picador, 2008; Philip Mirowski, *Never Let a Serious Crisis Go to Waste*.

20   Ian Bruff, 'The Rise of Authoritarian Neoliberalism', *Rethinking Marxism* 26(1), 2014.

21   Hall, Stuart, 'The Great Moving Right Show', *Marxism Today*, January 1979, p. 15.

22   Michel Foucault, *The Birth of Biopolitics*, New York: Palgrave, 2008 [1979]; Wendy Brown, *Undoing the Demos: Neoliberalism's Stealth Revolution*, New York: Zone Books, 2015; Pierre Dardot and Christian Laval, *The New Way of the World: On Neoliberal Society*, New York: Verso, 2014.

23   Dieter Plehwe, 'Introduction', in Philip Mirowski and Dieter Plehwe, eds., *The Road from Mont Pèlerin*, Cambridge, MA: Harvard University Press, 2009, p. 10.

24   Plehwe, 'Introduction,' p. 11.

25   See Friedrich Hayek, *Individualism and Economic Order*, London: Routledge & Kegan Paul, 1949.

26   Damien Cahill and Martijn Konings, *Neoliberalism*, Cambridge: Polity, 2017.

27   Jacques Le Goff, *Your Money or Your Life*, New York: Zone Books, 1988.

28   Jonathan Sheehan and Dror Wahrman, *Invisible Hands: Self-Organization and the Eighteenth Century*, Chicago: University of Chicago Press, 2015.

29   David Hume, 'Of Money', in Eugene F. Miller, ed., *Essays: Moral, Political, and Literary*, Indianapolis: Liberty Fund, 1985 [1752].

30   Andreas Kalyvas and Ira Katznelson, *Liberal Beginnings: Making a Republic for the Moderns*, Cambridge: Cambridge University Press, 2008.

31   Foucault, *Birth of Biopolitics*; Michel Foucault, *Security, Territory, Population*, New York: Palgrave Macmillan, 2007 [1978].

32   Foucault, *Security, Territory, Population*, p. 6.

33   Nicholas Gane, 'The Emergence of Neoliberalism: Thinking Through and Beyond Michel Foucault's Lectures on Biopolitics', *Theory, Culture & Society* 31(4), 2014.

34   Christina Petsoulas, *Hayek's Liberalism and Its Origins: His Idea of Spontaneous Order and the Scottish Enlightenment*, Abingdon: Routledge, 2001.

35   Friedrich Hayek, *The Fatal Conceit: The Errors of Socialism*, London: Routledge, 1988.

36   Melinda Cooper, 'Complexity Theory after the Financial Crisis', *Journal of Cultural Economy* 4(4), 2011.

37   Melinda Cooper, *Life as Surplus: Biotechnology and Capitalism in the Neoliberal Era*, Seattle: University of Washington Press, 2008, p. 10.

38   Cf. Joseph Vogl, *The Specter of Capital*, Stanford: Stanford University Press, 2015, p. 57.

39   Miguel Vatter, 'Foucault and Hayek: Republican Law and Liberal Civil Society', in Vanessa Lemm and Miguel Vatter, eds, *The Government of Life. Foucault, Biopolitics, and Neoliberalism*, New York: Fordham University Press, 2014.

40   George Stigler, 'The Theory of Economic Regulation', *Bell Journal of Economics and Management Science* 2(1), 1971.

41   Brian Massumi, 'Potential Politics and the Primacy of Preemption', *Theory and Event* 10(2), 2007; Marieke de Goede, 'The Politics of Preemption and the War on Terror in Europe', *European Journal of International Relations* 14(1), 2008.

42   Francois Ewald, 'The Return of Descartes's Malicious Demon: An Outline of a Philosophy of Precaution', in Tom Baker and Jonathan Simon, eds., *Embracing Risk: The Changing Culture of Insurance and Responsibility*, Chicago: University of Chicago Press, 2002, p. 294.

43   Leo Panitch and Sam Gindin, *The Making of Global Capitalism: The Political Economy of American Empire*, New York: Verso, 2013.

44   Paul Volcker, Interview, Commanding Heights, PBS, 26 September https://www.pbs.org/wgbh/commandingheights/shared/minitext/int_paulvolcker.html.

45   Randy Martin, *Financialization of Daily Life*, Philadelphia: Temple University Press, 2002; Maurizio Lazzarato, 'Neoliberalism in Action: Inequality, Insecurity and the Reconstitution of the Social', *Theory, Culture & Society* 26(6), 2009.

46   Andrew Leyshon and Nigel Thrift, 'The Capitalization of Almost Everything. The Future of Finance and Capitalism', *Theory, Culture & Society* 24(7-8), 2007.

47 Lisa Adkins, 'Out of Work or Out of Time? Rethinking Labor After the Financial Crisis', *South Atlantic Quarterly* 111(4), 2012; Melinda Cooper, 'Shadow Money and the Shadow Workforce: Rethinking Labor and Liquidity', *South Atlantic Quarterly* 114(2), 2015.

48 Foucault, *Birth of Biopolitics*, p. 226.

49 Foucault, *Birth of Biopolitics*, pp. 219-33.

50 Foucault, *Birth of Biopolitics*, pp. 220-21.

51 Foucault, *Birth of Biopolitics*, p. 232.

52 Gary H. Stern and Ron J. Feldman, *Too Big to Fail: The Hazards of Bank Bailouts*, Washington, D.C.: Brookings Institution Press, 2004.

53 Panitch and Gindin, *The Making of Global Capitalism*, p. 266.

54 Alan S. Blinder and Ricardo Reis, 'Understanding the Greenspan Standard', in *The Greenspan Era: Lessons for the Future*, Kansas City: Federal Reserve Bank of Kansas City, 2005.

55 Ewald, 'The Return of Descartes's Malicious Demon', p. 285.

56 Friedrich Hayek, *Law, Legislation and Liberty, Volume 2: The Mirage of Social Justice*, Chicago: University of Chicago Press, 1976, pp. 62-85.

57 Martijn Konings, *The Emotional Logic of Capitalism: What Progressives Have Missed*, Stanford: Stanford University Press, 2015.

58 Martijn Konings and Leo Panitch, 'US Financial Power in Crisis', *Historical Materialism* 16(4), 2008.

59 Mark Blyth, *Austerity: The History of a Dangerous Idea*, Oxford: Oxford University Press, 2013; Andrew Gamble, *Crisis Without End?: The Unravelling of Western Prosperity*, New York: Palgrave Macmillan, 2014.

60 Streeck, 'Heller, Schmitt and the Euro'; Werner Bonefeld, 'Authoritarian Liberalism: From Schmitt Via Ordoliberalism to the Euro', *Critical Sociology*, 2016, online first, https://doi.org/10.1177/0896920516662695.

IN FEAR OF POPULISM:
REFERENDUMS AND NEOLIBERAL DEMOCRACY

JAMES FOLEY AND PETE RAMAND

Referendums have grown sharply in Europe. While in the 1970s they ran at a rate of three per year, the annual figure is now eight, excluding countries like Switzerland where direct democracy is a regular part of government. Lying behind this increase is the question of European integration. There have been forty referendums on this question alone since 2000, compared to ten in the 1990s and only three in the 1980s.[1] In earlier decades, liberal intellectuals often celebrated such popular votes as pacifying, nation-building devices that helped to build effective bridges between people and parliaments, but increasingly critics view them as at best a nuisance and at worst an open invitation for irresponsible charlatans to manipulate reckless, ignorant voters prone to the most odious excesses of nationalism. 'Direct democracy is fine for things that don't matter, such as the Eurovision song contest,' claims *The Economist*, 'But it is no way to run a country, let alone a continent.'[2] Until Donald Trump came along, referendums were perhaps the most frequent reference point for liberal panic about populism, a term recently referring to any public or political opposition that falls outside of the settled terms of the political 'centre'. For Martin Kettle of the *Guardian*, 'the referendum is now the weapon of choice for populist parties of left and right'.[3] Elsewhere, the *Guardian* calls them 'a demagogue's dream, allowing populists free rein to fan fears, distort realities and appeal to emotions'.[4]

Several recent referendums have indeed been focuses for 'anti-establishment' backlash. Examples include the Italian constitutional poll (2017) and Greece's *oxi* (2015), both of which allowed anger at the bank bailouts and cuts programmes to coalesce and in turn inspire gloomy meditations on the dangers of unchecked popular participation. However, perhaps the biggest source of unease has been the two interconnected referendums in the United Kingdom, on Scottish independence (2014) and leaving the European Union (2016). Although the Scottish vote was lost, support for independence surged in the campaign's closing weeks and the possible breakup of Britain incited much angst and even panicked interventions from the top of American government. Brexit has raised even deeper questions about the future of neoliberalism, European capitalism and US hegemony. Like the Scottish case, it concerns the fate of the United Kingdom, the state that, since 1979, has often gone furthest in supporting American power and neoliberal economics, with Labour, Britain's historic party of social democracy, pioneering the European turn to 'Third Way' neoliberalism. While the outcome of negotiations remains unclear, Brexit could mean the decline of Britain as a strong, stable enforcer of America's will in Europe; alternatively, it could foreshadow the final collapse of the European Union. Moreover, since Scotland voted to remain in the EU, a second independence poll was officially proposed by its Parliament, and while this has been postponed indefinitely, it remains the dominant issue in Scottish politics and one dimension of the UK constitutional crisis. These cases highlight a shift where the referendum is now the preferred means of engineering a significant regime change. Other European states may choose to follow this lead, hence the fear of 'contagion' spreading from Britain. While left-wing forces formally led neither campaign, both have come to epitomize fears about the underlying weakness of the neoliberal order.

Sadly, there are few precedents for a socialist analysis of referendums. Gramsci wrote of why they were inferior to their preferred Soviet model of workplace delegation: 'Communists are on principle opposed to the referendum, since they place the most advantaged and active workers on the same plane as the lazy, ignorant and idle workers ... the delegates' assembly is an assembly performing the function of a referendum'.[5] The British Labour Party in its social democratic period was also strongly against referendums and favoured parliament as the means for solving all conflicts.[6] Labour's early suspicions were perhaps well founded, since the Conservatives had glorified plebiscites in Britain as a reactionary device to divide the working class over issues like Ireland. Hitler and Franco famously preferred the plebiscite to parliament, and there is a tradition of such illiberal manoeuvres in European modernity going back to Napoleon.[7] Nonetheless, experiments with 'direct democracy' have also been central to the more emancipatory ends of socialist history. Even recently, in the years following 2008, anti-establishment protests centred on demands for 'real democracy'. The recurring problem, though, for critics of parliamentarism is that, as Norberto Bobbio expresses it, the referendum 'is the only mechanism of direct democracy which can be applied concretely and effectively in most advanced democracies'.[8] Referendums are the actually-existing form that direct democracy takes in capitalist nation states. We consider them not as utopian alternatives to parliamentary democracy, but as measures of the strengths and weaknesses of its dominant forces. The question we wish to answer is whether intervention on these terms is worthwhile in building an anti-systemic left.

Today, the problem is redoubled because there are no workers' councils or parties of politically advanced workers to contrast to actually-existing parliamentary capitalism. Gramsci's views are informed by the live and active potential of direct rule from factories, a historical force with no real contemporary parallels. The same point, of course, would apply to any thinker of that era. Socialist thinking on referendums must be *conjunctural*, and today it should focus on what they express about the dual crises of capitalist democracy and of anti-systemic left-wing politics. In our view, referendums typify some of the strategic dilemmas radical leftists will face in countries where capitalist authority figures have limited legitimacy but where our forces are a small, divided minority. They are theatres for political distrust, for what Peter Mair calls 'ruling the void'[9] in a world where elites no longer fear the organized power of workers or the prospect of expropriation by socialist governments.

Our focus is primarily on (non-Swiss) European referendums that tend to focus on constitutional and sovereignty issues. We are aware that referendums in the USA are substantially different, focusing on local state-level policy issues and having a high degree of control by big business.[10] Latin American referendums have a unique history, with much more exciting lessons for the left. However, some of the arguments we make here will still be applicable to all cases of 'actually-existing' direct democracy under capitalism.

We believe that, in all cases, socialists must take a stance on referendums that distinguishes our approach from knee-jerk liberal unease about a populist backlash. Liberals undoubtedly have some well-founded concerns about racism, and while such concerns can be abused – Nick Clegg was one of many liberals who liken Scottish nationalism, which favours increased immigration, with UKIP's actively racist goals[11] – they should not be ignored. But although many populist movements are indeed racist, simply crowding in behind liberals is problematic. We risk legitimising the neoliberal consensus of previous decades (which has its own brand of racism) and becoming intellectually complicit with a failing parliamentary system in capitalist states. Most worrying of all, we risk handing the banner of democratic renewal to the radical right. Here, we aim to develop the beginnings of a class analysis of what referendums mean for capitalist democracy, and what class forces they are bringing into being in the post-2008 context with special reference to Scotland and Brexit. We will consider the historical development where, after the defeat of communism, referendums went from being instruments of harmony to being new grounds for fear of the masses. We then consider whether 'populism' can be a theoretically useful explanation, either for descriptive purposes or for explaining the tactical success of 'outsider' movements. Last, we look at working-class voting patterns in the recent British referendums; at the use of populist rhetoric in both; and at the implications for socialist strategy.

THE PECULIARTITY OF REFERENDUMS

Why do governments take the risk of referring difficult and potentially damaging questions to the random factor of a public vote? Some referendums are ordered by the constitution or by civic campaigns and are thus forced on governments against their will. However, these cases are comparatively rare. Until recently, a more general answer was that governments called referendums expecting that they would win them and shore up their power while also reinforcing the authority of dominant institutions. In practice, most referendums are won from the top down: on European integration, voters endorse the government position in 73 per cent of instances,[12] and naturally where these votes register a win for the government they pass unnoticed with no musings on the perils of direct democracy. Before 2008 parliamentary elites mostly assumed that the enjoyment of a consumer lifestyle, cheap credit, and imported goods would ensure the conformity, or at least non-rebellion, of most of the population. Referendums thus acted as surrogates for passive entry into globalization. But there was equally a *nationalist* side to them: by calling and winning them, leaders hoped to extract concessions from Brussels for their particular national interests. This brokerage could prove highly successful. When Sweden, Austria, and Finland held referendums on the Maastricht Treaty and European membership in 1993 and 1994, they gained important opt-outs. As Matt Qvortrup notes, 'The Swedes ... were able to opt out of the single currency as a result of their referendum brinkmanship, and Finland and Austria were able to get concessions in foreign-policy areas that guaranteed their neutrality in international affairs'.[13] In calling European referendums, governments expected that a coalition of opinion-formers would come together around the benefits of globalization and make sure the motion passed. However, in doing so they also sought to increase the bargaining power of nation states inside European institutions. In this sense, they could be a 'win-win' for national governments.

Between the final years of the Cold War and the crisis of 2008, much writing on referendums therefore saw them as instruments of social harmony. In perhaps the most prestigious account of referendums in Britain, Vernon

Bogdanor considers their use as a 'conservative device' designed as 'an instrument of protection not change'.[14] Since parliament sets the agenda, 'the urge towards popular participation or self-government has not played a very important part in its advocacy'. In Bogdanor's view, they encourage the 'search for consensus' and 'all party agreement' and thus have the function of building the strength of parliament as an institution independent of the parties that compose it. Referendums are thus formally designed to be *pro-systemic*, to build up consensus and to shore up necessary myths of consent and popular sovereignty.

Post-1989, pointing to the referendums in post-Soviet Eastern European states, Jürgen Habermas wrote optimistically of restoring a principle of responsible citizenship and building a harmonious link between public and parliament. Referendums here are 'a way of proceeding which permitted a broader discussion and opinion formation as well as a more extensive – and, above all, better prepared – participation,' giving voters 'the eventual responsibility for the process'.[15] Thus, they ensure that the population are integrated into a decision, and then, if it fails, stability remains because 'it would have been the people's own mistake that they would have had to cope with'.

These positions reflect the confidence of that era – the assumption that populations would embrace an assumed historical path, whether towards the disintegration of the Soviet systems or towards the surrender of national economic controls in return for free trade and high-level influence, and that contrary cases would gradually recede in time. However, the few cases where referendums took an anti-systemic position and (briefly) halted the inevitable assume greater significance in the context of recent events. The French and Dutch referendums on the European Constitution and the Irish votes on the Nice and Lisbon Treaties are three such examples.

The reception that greeted these polls suggests deeper roots to the current elite fixation with populism. Jacques Ranciere's *The Hatred of Democracy*, which claims that official respect for democracy is combined with a growing elite contempt for it, is partly inspired by the events surrounding the European Constitution vote. 'The principle surprise of the referendum was this,' he notes, 'A majority of voters … judged that the question was a real question, not a matter for calling for the simple adherence of the population but one for the sovereignty of the people, and so a matter to which this latter could respond no as well as yes'.[16] Ranciere observes that the only explanation that elites could find for such behaviour was the evil of populism:

The oligarchs, their experts and ideologues managed to find the explanation for this misfortune, in fact the same one they find for every disruption to the consensus: if science did not impress its legitimacy upon the people, it is because the people is [sic] ignorant. If progress does not progress, it is because of the backward. One word that all clerics incessantly chanted captures this explanation: 'populism'... Populism is the convenient name under which is dissimulated the exacerbated contradiction between popular legitimacy and expert legitimacy, that is, the difficulty the government of science has in adapting itself to manifestations of democracy and even to the mixed form of representative system.[17]

Ranciere traces this anti-populism to a longstanding dilemma in the intellectual roots of the Cold War victory of Western-style democracy and neoliberalism. On the one hand, the victory of liberalism offered a superficial intellectual respect for all things democratic. In France, and beyond, this took the form of an anti-totalitarian discourse that offered a bridge out of Marxism for post-1968 radicals, expressing the nightmare of a society crushed and controlled by the state. For thinkers burned by radical experiments with Maoism, democracy acquired a new sacredness. However, crucially, to remain clean of demagogic temptations, they insisted that liberal democracy must always remain *formal democracy*. Any attempt to imagine a deeper democracy, however well meaning, would inevitably lead back to the lure of totalitarianism. Alongside this discourse, and apparently opposed to it, sat another branch of neoliberalism. In the writings of Americans like Daniel Bell, Samuel Huntington and Christopher Lasch emerged a critique of the consumer culture and narcissistic individualism that sees 'democratic man' as a dangerous enemy who represents the breakdown of a privileged sphere of political expertise. The demon, here, is formally the opposite: a hedonistic, irresponsible society devouring the state. However, the two discourses work in tandem to defend a space for expert political management, and, without an organized socialist threat, the common enemy of both positions is populism.

When the Lisbon Treaty reappeared in 2008, most countries chose not to give their population a vote after the French and Dutch votes halted the Constitution railroad. Officials drafted a barely revised version of the Treaty, although this time the public would have no say except in Ireland, where an amendment to the Irish Constitution forced a poll on all changes to Ireland's sovereignty within Europe. When the Irish unexpectedly voted no and held up the treaty's implementation, the whole continental establishment turned on the country. As Kristin Ross remarks, the reaction was like the French vote, but with the added element of racism towards a peripheral country considered 'ungrateful' for voting the wrong way after it had received European aid. Indeed, many French liberal intellectuals – figures like Bernard Kouchner and Daniel Cohn-Bendit – organized the hatchet job, as Ross notes:

> The referendum was supposed to be nothing more than an exercise in rubber-stamping the experts' text. But the Irish decided to treat the vote as a real vote … It was purposefully drafted … to communicate to voters through its very form that it was best to leave such complex matters of governance up to the experts, the technocracy. EU officials were quick to blame 'populism' for the defeat. The Irish, they insisted, must be made to revote, presumably until the correct result could be reached. Valery Giscard d'Estaing and Nicolas Sarkozy immediately called for a new vote.[18]

Before 2008, the discourse on referendums reflected the tensions of a triumphalist era. Both democratic and undemocratic alternatives to capitalism and parliament had been pushed to the extreme margins, and elites installed trading rules in the manner of scientific detachment. Successful referendums seemed to testify to mass acceptance of these norms. However, the period saw a chilling of relations between parliaments and the governed, represented in declining turnout at elections and a measurable growth in contempt for politicians and political institutions.[19] This was rarely if ever treated as a crisis. Unlike the working-class strikes of the 1970s, voter 'apathy' did not threaten to make the West 'ungovernable' and posed no security threat. It seldom disrupted the process of global economic expansion. Even when anger at the political consensus resulted in mass civil disobedience, as with the Iraq War, there was little question of protest movements delaying the outcome. But it did occasionally prompt uncertainty about the *meaning* of 'apathy'. Was it a sign of a sated, consumerist population? Or was it an omen of lurking discontent? Although the referendums in France, Ireland and the Netherlands only delayed Europe's fate, they testified to doubts about whether disrespect for political authority could become a dangerous political force.

Referendums, then, have functions that help increase the legitimacy of dominant institutions and manufacture a consensus in their interest. However, they contain a dual nature. Since they usually, by their nature, involve the deliberate imagining of a general agreement that crosses the top representatives of parties, businesses, and classes, they open the door to the mass rejection of all established political authority. This explains why they can quickly turn from useful instruments for restoring political credibility into objects of fear. It also suggests why the story of a failed referendum is always the same: 'ignorance' allied to 'populism'.

REFERENDUMS AND RULING CLASS STRATEGY

Given what we have said above, it is easy to overestimate the extent to which referendums reflect a coherent 'strategy' of capitalist politics. Often, their emergence testifies to the messiness of parliamentary decision making, as leaders misjudge public trust in their authority or stick to failed formulas long after they have proved ineffective. Both the 2014 and 2016 referendums in Britain started from significant misjudgements. In the Scottish case, the nationalists had preferred a referendum focused on three choices: a) the constitutional status quo; b) full Scottish independence; or c) so-called 'devolution max', i.e. transferring most fiscal powers from London to the Scottish parliament. The Conservative-Liberal government forced a two-option referendum on the SNP, aiming to expose the distance between the SNP's model of outright independence and moderate Scottish opinion. Both rival governments, Scottish and British, aimed to define a question narrow enough to ensure a decisive victory and a boost for their forces. The British government won. However, their gambit nearly proved disastrous for the British state, considered as a 'unionist' bloc, when support for independence surged amid worries about the coalition government's austerity package. In the 2016 case, the cosmopolitan David Cameron proposed an EU referendum to win over sceptical right-wing voters who might be tempted to vote for UKIP. He based this on three misjudgements: first, an excessive assessment of the threat of Ed Miliband's Labour; second, an assumption that they could enter another coalition with the Liberal Democrats, who would quash a referendum; and third, a belief that even if the European poll went ahead it would result in a guaranteed 'Remain' victory once Westminster gained 'concessions' from Brussels over immigration. In both referendums, the main UK parties presented a 'united front' of their own leaders added to top businesspeople, economists and policy experts, thinking that this would ensure a decisive, historic victory. In both cases, they underestimated the 'void' between this ruling bloc and public opinion.

In believing that he could neutralize racist sentiment by appeasing it, Cameron was committing an error that ruling parties in Europe have made for decades. This miscalculation is a key reason for the rise of right-wing populism. Since the 1980s, European parties of the centre have sought to win over disenchanted voters from the far right by offering a watered-down version of anti-immigrant populism. They expected that, by speaking this language, they would nullify the threat of anti-establishment racism through co-optation and steal a march on their centrist rivals. Instead, in every case, precisely the opposite happened. Adopting anti-immigrant rhetoric simply confirmed the respectable role of racism in politics. Long term, this did nothing for the legitimacy of mainstream politicians, but it certainly added to the mainstream credibility of right-wing outsiders.

In theory, by portraying a cross-party alliance with strong business, academic and celebrity support, referendums should work as an instrument for effectively engineering consent. However, by presenting customary authority speaking as one voice, a referendum can also channel the various sources of anger at the establishment. This is doubly likely when other channels for protest, like trade unionism or left-wing politics, have been closed off; referendums can then become potential focuses for a generalized legitimacy crisis. Indeed, where the influence of political 'insiders' has weakened, any referendum throws open the debate to popular movements and, equally, to unscrupulous outcasts from the ruling elite. Although they formally aim to strengthen parliament by reaching a social consensus on divisive issues, referendums also threaten instability as professional politicians sacrifice full control of the decision.

Where a ruling bloc can successfully stage a referendum without significant challenge, it suggests their strength in orchestrating at least passive support. Where, on the contrary, a united front of the ruling elite comes under significant challenge, it suggests their weakness. Between 1989 and 2008, mainstream politics was defined by a set of norms, powers, and widely-defended hypocrisies that defined a 'centre-ground', a gravitational force that applied in most countries. Of the many referendums in this period, only a few presented real opportunities for forces opposed to capitalist globalization. Since 2008, even the strongest supporters of neoliberalism are pessimistic about its prospects to provide growing living standards for most of society. The votes for centre-left parties that strongly associated themselves with the consensus have often collapsed or weakened substantially. Parties like the Scottish National Party (SNP), the Front National, and UKIP have grown in influence, and, in some cases, new parties like Syriza, Podemos, and the Five Star Movement have become serious political forces. Elsewhere, mainstream parties have been less able to police their members. Outsiders like Jeremy Corbyn, Bernie Sanders, and Donald Trump have emerged within the most established centre-left and centre-right parties of the neoliberal era. In this context, political authority has no clear location. A new hegemonic capitalist project has yet to emerge. Referendums here can quickly catalyze instability, but the decision to call them is increasingly falling out of government hands.

THE QUESTION OF POPULISM AND ANTI-POPULISM

Critics invariably link referendums to populism, which without a socialist threat has increasingly become the commonest construction of the elite fear of mass democracy. However, the infamous vagueness of the term 'populism' hinders scientific attempts at identifying, classifying, and categorising the forces described by it. The subject implied by the word – the people – is empty as a fixed sociological category, and few political parties have embraced a populist label, which is usually intended as a slight, insinuating that while a movement may have numbers it nonetheless lacks intellectual credibility. Those left-wing thinkers who do adopt it have suggested that populism should be defined as a political tactic or as discursive framing rather than an expression of a social category, a 'demarcation strategy between "us" and "them"', in the words of Raquel Garrido of France Insoumise.[20] Populism, Reyes observes, is 'a particular species of [an] antagonistic relation that pits "the people" against "the elite"'; but, equally, 'populism is the dimension of the political which constructs and gives meaning to "the people"'.[21] The same point, the author notes, also applies to the question of 'elites'. This explains why left wing, right wing and centrist movements can use a formally similar discourse to express radically different points. The enemy of right wing populism might be the 'liberal elite' who impose an alien political correctness; for leftists, the business elite; for a centrist force like the Scottish National Party, the Westminster elite or the 'unionist' elite. In describing these enemies, they constitute their own potential forces as the unorganized, isolated mass of people finally entering a stage of revolt. Populism, then, is the discourse of those who see themselves as outsiders from mainstream politics but who nonetheless claim to represent a strong strand of unrepresented public opinion.

While we find this approach to populism useful, we would add some qualifications. First, we should note that, while the term 'elite' has diverse uses, we should not allow this to disguise the real existence of hierarchies of power and structures of class in society. Although elite can mean many different things, unlike 'the people' it does have some correspondence to actual social categories. Indeed, a phrase like 'liberal elite', notwithstanding its many abuses, can still express something about the way in which the professional upper middle class turn their knowledge, cultural power, and minority activism into advantages under neoliberalism. For those of us who defend a Marxist class analysis, it is important to qualify a tendency in left-populist thinking that can exaggerate the autonomy of politics. Even Podemos leader Pablo Iglesias has expressed qualifications about Ernesto Laclau's[22] way of (dis)solving the link between structure and superstructure, suggesting that populist theory is a 'very useful tool … for the practical interpretation of the autonomy of politics' while rejecting its anti-foundationalist theoretical conclusions.[23] The influence of Laclau on Podemos is arguably clearest in the studied vagueness of the terms they use to designate their enemy – *la casta* – and thus their new subject-position, *la gente*. As Perry Anderson observes, the advantage of such vagueness is that it promotes the process of gathering together around a new position from outside of established politics. But its downside is also clear: it makes identifying the 'objective conditions for a such a "populist rupture"' obscure, meaning – among other problems – that where successes occur they are difficult to replicate in other countries.[24] This may explain Iglesias' reticence to fully defend Laclau's ontology. In any case, Podemos is also vulnerable to the charge of achieving rhetorical and organizational success at the expense of analytical weakness.

Second, we should note that *anti-populism* involves a similar process of 'Othering' designed to define its own forces. In naming populism as the enemy, their opponents define a moderate centre-ground who are above populism's influence and who thus represent the rational defence of existing institutions. The dangers of such anti-populism are perhaps clearest in the Hillary Clinton campaign, as Jodi Dean observes:

> [L]iberals will continue to amplify identity, consolidating into the single figure of Trump the histories and structures of racism, sexism, and homophobia. This Trump-washing will make regular Republicans look reasonable and Democrats look like champions of equality and diversity. The hatred the Trump candidacy legitimized will take on a liberal form of hatred for working-class white people, in the name of a multiculturalism that erases the fact of a multiracial working class. Communicative capitalism will provide the field of response – the circulation of outrage and righteousness, individualized statements of fear and alliance.[25]

'Moderate' Republicans, like the Bush family, are welcomed into a progressive alliance against the common enemy of divisiveness. A similar labelling process happens even against the least dangerous populisms, and indeed is used to dismiss centre-or-left populisms by association with the right. Liberal commentators in Britain regularly condemn the SNP, a pro-immigration, moderately pro-business party, as a bewildered, xenophobic herd victoriously trampling over enlightened values. For Phillip Stephens of the *Financial Times*, the Scottish referendum 'had reawakened the allegiance of the tribe'.[26] Will Hutton described the same vote as auguring 'the death of the liberal enlightenment before the atavistic forces of nationalism and ethnicity'.[27] Such comments naturally take little notice of how both British mainstream parties frequently used jingoistic rhetoric of blood and soil to justify routine invasions of Muslim countries. Populism, regarded as a tactic, is real, and political outsiders increasingly identify referendums as a site for building their forces. However, an equally pervasive force is anti-populism, whose goal is to defend what Tariq Ali characterizes as the 'extreme centre'.[28]

THE WORKING CLASS IN THE UK REFERENDUMS

For decades, New Labour, Conservatives and establishment commentators have been denying the role of class in British politics. However, the dual fears of referendums and populism have brought a fashionable obsession with the working class as a significant political force. *The Economist* typifies this trend when it paints a picture of 'a sharply polarized country, with a metropolitan elite that likes globalization and an angry working class that does not.'[29] Unfortunately, this rhetoric, which essentializes the working class as a set of uneducated white males who have been 'left behind', moves in the opposite direction than many of us wanted. Given the staggering rise in inequalities since the 1970s, the radical left has sought to renew class analysis by incorporating the diversity of actual workplaces into a new political subject.[30] The current discourse on working-class voters does the opposite: it *depoliticizes* working life and turns poor communities into throwbacks. However, better examples do exist. The Scottish independence referendum was equally populist and inspired fresh thinking on working-class identity, but this movement was clearly – whatever its faults – pro-immigration and strongly influenced by anti-war politics. Even though the result of rising Scottish nationalism has weakened the historic forces of social democracy in Scotland, and Scotland's discourse of class remains rooted in romanticized, backward-looking cultural stereotypes rather than the contemporary world of work,[31] nonetheless the contrast between the two shows that similar processes can be negotiated and framed in radically different ways. In both referendums, the traditional Scottish nationalist and Eurosceptic votes received an influx of working-class protest votes that may traditionally have gone to Labour. However, one took an anti-immigrant, radical right direction; the other took an anti-Tory populist direction.

Does the thesis of a working-class populism explain the surge behind these referendums? Much depends on which sociological definitions we choose. Using a mainstream occupational account of class, 53.6 per cent of working-class people voted for Scottish independence, significantly stronger than the official rate for middle-class voters (41.7 per cent).[32] This looks decisive, but the picture is more complicated than these superficial categories suggest, which we can show by looking at income groups: over 56 per cent of bottom quartile income earners voted yes, but only about 42 per cent of the next lowest quartile did so. Support was thus strongest among the very poor with 'little to lose'. Home ownership therefore proved a crucial variable, with a critical divide between owner-occupiers – vigorously against independence – and social renters, who were fiercely in favour.[33] This reflects the two biggest areas of support for independence: those who rely on benefits and have no mortgages; and young voters who tend to rent accommodation.

Our provisional analysis using Erik Olin Wright's neo-Marxist categories tends to confirm this view. Support for independence appears strikingly low among skilled workers (24 per cent), and is far higher among non-skilled workers (42 per cent).[34] However, the strongest groups are those not measured in the occupational approach to class: 61 per cent of the sick and disabled backed Scottish independence, as did 53 per cent of the work-seeking unemployed. The Scottish Radical Independence Campaign, reflecting this, tended to imagine class as being a *community of deprivation*. This reveals a longstanding trend in Scottish socialist culture that has its origins in the mass unemployment of the 1980s and the successful anti-Poll Tax campaign of the early 1990s. Noticeably, these 'welfare' groups championed by populists in Scotland are precisely those often racialized and targeted by the right wing in England. This testifies to a *pluralism* and *inclusiveness* in Scotland that draws from the historical roots of the campaign's left-populist streak. However, it also suggests the failure of leftists in Scotland to reach workplaces and the organized working class.

Using other categories, we at first get a similar and even more polarized view of Brexit, which was supported by nearly two thirds of C2, D, E occupational groups across the UK.[35] On most conventional definitions of 'working class', therefore, there was a majority for Leave. For example, 59 per cent of those who perceive themselves as working class backed Leave, as did 66 per cent of those with an income of under £1,200 per month, and 57 per cent of those earning between £1,200 and £2,200 per month.[36] Notably, academically defined left-right differences played little role. According to NatCen, 50 per cent of left-wing voters backed Brexit, not noticeably different than the figure for right-wing voters (53 per cent); a deeper divide is between authoritarians (66 per cent pro-Brexit) and libertarians (18 per cent). While the Scottish independence vote was strongly associated with a welfare-based idea of the working class, the opposite was the case with Brexit: 75 per cent of anti-welfare voters backed Leave, compared to 30 per cent of pro-welfare voters. To dig down into these confusing figures, the National Centre for Social Research used 'latent class analysis', an inductive quantitative method, which identified five distinctive groups in the population. Middle-class liberals, making up a quarter of Britain, were most opposed to Brexit, with only 8 per cent backing it. Another group, classified as young working-class Labour voters, a further quarter of the population, was also quite opposed, with just 39 per cent backing Brexit. By contrast, affluent Eurosceptics, the older working-class and economically-deprived anti-immigrant voters were big support bases for leaving the EU.

With Brexit, a final, crucial distinction is the question of 'race'. There is undoubtedly a strong link, although the issue is perhaps less clear cut than many imagine. According to the British Election Study, 51 per cent of 'white British' people voted to leave, which is higher than 'other white' (34 per cent), mixed (37 per cent), Asian (32 per cent), Black (29 per cent) and others (43 per cent).[37] This suggests an unambiguous division, although perhaps a weaker divide than between authoritarian and liberal voters. However, two things are clear: first, that immigration was one of the most important issues for Leave voters, albeit, according to official polling, less important than a vaguer sense of national sovereignty; and, second, that an emerging, and worrying, idea of the forgotten 'white working class' has grown out of the referendum.[38] By contrast, Scotland's nationalist, populist referendum campaign was disproportionately backed by poorer minorities, including the Irish population who are Scotland's largest immigrant group.

THE SCOTTISH REFERENDUM AND BREXIT

The Scottish referendum campaigns combined contradictory aspects of left populism. They united around a common hatred for 'Westminster' and, more broadly, the centralization of power in London. Given mass alienation from career politicians, this was, in some ways, tacitly astute and ensured unity across the movement. For the left-wing campaign, Westminster stood for routine wars, for dumping nuclear weapons on Scotland, for servility to America, for cross-party support for austerity and for all the failings of Tony Blair's 'Third Way' rebranding of Labour. Mainstream Scottish Nationalism gave space for such expression and sometimes embraced it as part of its rhetoric. Indeed, the SNP had been a regular – if not always consistent – critic of British foreign policy and capitalized on Labour's legitimacy problems after Iraq. However, their leaders took an inconsistent stance on economics: they argued for a 'caring' Scandinavian state that would wipe out poverty and protect public services, contrasting this with the cruelties of Conservative austerity, but they also proposed lower corporation taxes on Laffer Curve grounds. Right wing nationalists could share with leftists a common enemy in Westminster, since they believed that London control over corporation tax, immigration and labour policy was thwarting Scotland's ability to 'catch up' through greater competitiveness. This contradictory message was targeted at different groups. To traditional Labour voters in

Scotland's working-class heartlands it sounded firmly social democratic: the SNP offered the only hope for Old Labour values. Meanwhile, to business leaders, they presented themselves as the party of low taxes and deregulation.

Nonetheless, the scale and temporary success of Scotland's radical movement should be emphasized. It proves that a working-class populist revolt against a centre-left complicit in neoliberalism does not always lead to chauvinism. The radical fringe that escaped official control by the mainstream Nationalist party was not simply confined to cosmopolitan elites in the cities. During the referendum, Scotland experienced arguably the largest grassroots insurgency in the country's history. The depth of community involvement in Scotland remains extraordinary. At one stage, dozens of talks, debates and rallies were happening in village halls, pubs, cafes and churches every day of the week, often in Scotland's poorest and most remote communities. Although many meetings contained standard signs of Scottish nationalism, like the Saltire flag, they rarely if ever featured racist sentiment.

However, the referendum's aftermath has clearly benefited the liberal centre and Conservatives at the left's expense. The Scottish National Party has grown enormously from 29,000 members in early 2014 to a high of more than 120,000,[39] but the influx of radicalized, working-class and left-wing members has barely shifted its neoliberal policies. Indeed, the Brexit referendum has built a new solidity to its centrism, as 'progressive' Scotland unites around the common enemy of Westminster 'extremism'. The Scottish Green Party has, if anything, been noticeably keener on the European Union and more fearful of Brexit than the SNP, reflecting its base among middle class, professional and petty bourgeois voters. They style themselves as a loyal opposition and, philosophically, take a pro-systemic approach. Leftist forces have not expanded, and trade union politics of the centrist variety is weakened by the ongoing collapse of the Labour Party in Scotland, which has been only partially slowed by the rise of Corbyn.

This problem shows the potential pitfalls of left populism: Laclau and Mouffe never address how new left discourse translates into new left forces. Even if radical ideas gain serious currency in mainstream debate, there is no automatic translation into socialist infrastructure. The Radical Independence Campaign mobilized thousands of activists across the country and made socialist politics more relevant in the referendum than it had been in a long time. Radical ideas were earnestly considered as activists pondered the challenges of founding a new country during a severe crisis of capitalism. But socialist activists assumed that exposure to left wing ideas would lead away from mainstream politics; instead, they legitimized it. By uniting around the shared common enemy of Westminster, the Scottish left created the illusion that Britain's problems derived solely from the political decisions of the UK Parliament rather than from the failings of the present phase of capitalism. Populist thinkers argue that the crucial task is to give new meaning to the enemy and to worn-out ideas like democracy. Scottish socialists did this with some success, painting Westminster as the repository of all the failings of neoliberalism and thus gaining a large audience that took these evils seriously. But, despite this, the left failed to turn active support in the referendum into a permanent left infrastructure.

The Scottish left, like the English left, has been traumatized by the question of the European Union. The independence movement took a broadly liberal line, supporting free movement of people and free movement of capital simultaneously, reflecting the movement's determination that 'Westminster' was the enemy, that Westminster's extreme right fringe was an expression of the true character of the whole institution, and that any stance against this must be justified. The SNP's leader, Nicola Sturgeon, outlined this philosophy in a speech at Stanford:

> The EU referendum also posed a challenge for those of us who support free trade, who welcome immigration and who believe that the benefits of globalization, if they are properly managed – and that's an important caveat to stress – these benefits should outweigh the costs. It demonstrated that we can only sustain support for a dynamic and open economy if we do more to build a fairer and inclusive society.[40]

Explicitly, Sturgeon favours the 'German economic model developed after the war', the *ordoliberal* ideal of strong government and consensus built around the market.[41] The European Union question has thus been the mediator between a centrist movement with an influential left-populist fringe, and the 'realism' of building a nation state around a firm, competitive market system setting itself against the 'chaos' of Westminster populism, a term increasingly used in Scotland to encompass both Brexit and Jeremy Corbyn's Momentum. The Scottish independence movement, having started as a populist rebuke to the neoliberal establishment, is now squarely part of the operation to revive that consensus. Scotland's radical left, having briefly gained significant legitimacy during the 2014 campaign, suffered by failing to define its enemy broadly enough to include the behaviour of the European Union.

In some ways, the English Brexit vote was more clearly defined by class differences than the Scottish vote. However, other factors intruded to make this referendum – in practice – even more difficult for the left. In marked contrast to the Scottish independence movement, Brexit voting was marked by elderliness, whiteness, and authoritarianism. English working-class communities evidently favoured Brexit over the status quo, but there was little activism behind this, and certainly nothing approached the popular assembly model seen in Scotland and Southern Europe.

In recognising a significant working-class majority for Brexit, we do not endorse the view that 'blames' the 'white working class' for the recent populist turn in politics. Brexit, like the movement around Trump, was a cross-class movement with strong roots in reactionary sections of the middle class, England's so-called 'gin and Jag belt'. However, the relevant point is the break between politically correct, liberal attitudes and the traditional voting patterns of working-class communities that brought centre-left governments to power in the past. Working-class communities alone did not cause Brexit. However, we have lost the automatic expectation that working-class communities will obediently follow the leadership of the Labour Party, or that a breakdown in Labour loyalty in the working class would benefit a more radical left project.

To win government power, traditional social democratic parties had to articulate a set of values together: left wing, pro-minority, working class, urban, pro-welfare. In retrospect, what glued these distinct elements into a united bond of solidarity was a strong, universalist public sector and welfare state. Decades of privatization, a weakening of social security and a turn to individual solutions like consumer credit left widespread insecurity without the promise of centre-left reforms to build a stable future. Both independence voters and Brexit voters are concerned about the decline of the public sector. Indeed, much of the most right-wing sentiment surrounding Brexit concerns issues of 'overcrowding' in schools and hospitals, and the Leave campaign's main commitment was to spend more on the National Health Service. Noticeably, a significant majority of UKIP voters favoured government action to redistribute income from rich to poor. Although UKIP began as a project defined by a very London-oriented economic liberalism, its appeal subtly shifted under Nigel Farage and the party grew among disenchanted, anti-metropolitan voters. Anti-immigrant politics promised what social democracy once offered: more jobs, better public services, quick reforms to improve living standards for the 'common man' organized from the top down by politicians with the common touch.

Interestingly, Corbyn's undoubted success with a radical left message in the 2017 election only marginally affected the breakdown between Labour and its working-class base. Corbyn scored Labour's highest percentage vote among (officially-defined) *middle-class* voters since 1979; by contrast, Theresa

May achieved the largest *working-class* Conservative vote since the same year.[42] As with the Scottish referendum, age proved decisive to Corbyn's progressive appeal: Labour's 'swing' was primarily among under 44-year-olds, and much of it came from 25-34s, while the Conservatives gained among over 55s. Labour also proved overwhelmingly more popular among black and ethnic minority voters. These various complications make it difficult to justify the hard conclusion presented by some analysts that Labour was unpopular among the working class. The problem partly lies with the categories used in official market research. For example, Conservatives were nearly twice as popular as Labour among homeowners, and Labour was twice as popular as the Conservatives among people in social housing. Labour also unexpectedly picked up crucial votes from Leave and UKIP supporters, suggesting that Corbyn was tactically astute in pitching his appeal around improving public services rather than re-running the Brexit referendum. The Remain parties most associated with calls for a second referendum – SNP, the Liberal Democrats and the Greens – all performed worse than expected. Corbyn performed extremely well among the most educated voters, and showed that a radical left message can gain a serious base in Britain; however, Labour still lost ground to the Conservatives in many working-class areas. The Scottish Yes campaign succeeded in radicalizing and drawing out two groups who normally do not vote: young people and the poorest sections of the working class. Corbyn enjoyed substantial success with young people, but has yet to experience a similar upsurge among the poorest workers. Thus, the Yes campaign still holds potential lessons for his project of radicalizing the Labour Party.

LESSONS FOR SOCIALIST STRATEGY

Referendums are examples of the strategic dilemma socialists might face in coming years. Previously, they acted as measures of the strength of consensus. Today, they typify an era in which, first, mainstream politics has limited legitimacy; second, capitalist economies offer little hope for fast improvements in living standards; and, third, the organized left is weak as an independent force, as witnessed by a continued decline of numbers and agency in trade unions, a lasting crisis of moral purpose in historic social democratic parties, and the failure of radical left forces to cohere into a mass force. If these trends continue, random, anti-establishment, anti-system outbursts of a national-popular type are likely to grow. A 2016 report for the European Council on Foreign Relations estimates that 'outsider parties' have plans for referendums on thirty-four issues. 'Across Europe, traditional political elites are being challenged by newer, smaller, and leaner parties from both left and right,' they note. 'Their weapon of choice is undoubtedly the referendum, used to whip up popular support for their pet issues'.[43] Constitutional referendums present themselves as probable areas for such disturbances for two reasons: because they offer alienated voters a 'quick fix'; and because they force the establishment to present a united front, heightening the possibility for anti-establishment forces to fuse.

Of course, having seen the chaos of the British state in dealing with Brexit and Scottish independence, official politicians elsewhere will be unlikely to agree to similar referendums in their own countries. However, discontented elements of the establishment and new political forces will look towards Britain for examples. The collapsing legitimacy of the European Union, and continued support for it by the traditional centre-left, offers a huge opportunity to far-right parties to campaign for their own referendums in many European countries. Meanwhile, nationalists in Northern Ireland, the Basque country and Catalonia are already looking to Scotland and will push for their own polls. The call for referendums is increasingly falling outside of the control filters and agenda setting of mainstream politics and is the 'weapon of choice' against consensus.

How do socialists respond to such a situation? In some countries, left-populism has become a genuine force: thirteen of the forty-five parties that the European Council on Foreign Relations list as 'populist' belong to the left and centre-left, even if many of those listed are simply holding onto gains made long before 2008.[44] However, elsewhere, in Britain for example, the experience has sometimes been divisive and unhappy. Although the referendums highlighted here have created renewed interest in class, they have proved extremely challenging for the traditional forces of social democracy and socialism. The Scottish independence referendum brought about an epochal collapse in Labour support without the corresponding growth of a radical working-class alternative. The EU referendum nearly proved disastrous for Jeremy Corbyn's worthy experiment in democratising the Labour Party, inciting a (thoroughly undemocratic) centrist-liberal coup against him. While he fended off the coup, and while his middle-ground tactics proved highly effective in bringing a huge Labour vote in 2017, the EU-fixated centrists who still control most Labour party seats in parliament were, until recently, determined to force him from power. Indeed, immediately after he achieved the highest Labour vote since 2001, a group of more than 30 MPs tried to use the question of the Single Market to divide the Labour Party against Corbyn's leadership.[45] And even where the left has resoundingly succeeded, they have suffered from their victories. When Greece's new Syriza government still felt compelled to renege on its mass mandate to oppose the Troika's demand for spending cuts, even after winning its *oxi* referendum, this split the party and led to a major loss of members.

Since 2008, despite the obvious problems of capitalism, leftist anti-systemic movements have lacked the forces to make a breakthrough. The European right has been building its own case and its own personnel for decades, by drawing together the issues of Brussels, immigration and Islam, and their ideas have mainstream legitimacy thanks to decades of political appeasement and daily doses of tabloid rhetoric. In many countries, radical conservatives have thus responded more effectively than the left. Socialist forces have been weakened by the neoliberalization of social democratic parties and in some countries by the organized left's reluctance to overcome division and challenge for power. Underlying both troubles is the weakness of trade unions and working-class organization. Clearly, the major task for the left is the difficult one: rebuilding our own scattered forces.

However, divisions within mainstream politics will continue to offer socialists the opportunity to influence national debates, which could quicken the process of rebuilding forces. Referendums are precisely the sort of strategic area where such intervention is possible. Here, we wish to indicate what we consider as general strategic points.

First, referendums are attractive sites for presenting grievances that parliamentary politics offers no mechanism for debating. Although they will mostly emerge from inter-elite debates, and elites will always have the formal power to set the agenda, referendums are potentially more 'open' to outsider politics than parliaments. When an urgent need for left wing alternatives emerges, as in 2008, social movements of the left can find themselves shut out of political discussion. There are significant barriers to entry caused by the path-dependence of the parliamentary system. This limits the left's ability to present 'realistic' goals, which reduces even marginally leftist movements to an intellectual and activist core. Often, even the most modestly phrased socialist or social democratic goals find no room for mainstream expression. While radical right demands have been appeased, the opposite applies to social democratic policies, even where they might seem hugely popular, like rail renationalization in Britain. An organized left with limited numbers, prospects of government, or even representation in parliament can still influence the debate by putting forward issues that expose the unrepresentative nature of mainstream politics.

Second, we should ask, why do referendums prove so effective for populism? It is worth remembering Lenin and Gramsci's classic complaint that referendums dissolve party organization. This happens, of course, in capitalist political alliances too, which has various effects. In some cases, like the Scottish referendum and most European referendums, it encourages the dominant parties to behave as a united front and to downplay all differences between them. In others, like the Brexit case, the ruling party may split between loyalists and opportunists. Either situation presents opportunities for leftist critique. Often, mainstream parties are also divided between the duties of stable government and the need to lead a populist argument. This offers outsiders the opportunity to become the most vigorous spokespeople for a point of view that escapes the safety-first banalities of the official line in electoral politics.

Third, referendums will expose the preparedness and organization of the left regardless of whether we choose to engage with them. For decades, the English left had tried to ignore the question of the European Union, seeing it as a right-wing question that socialists should avoid, a position that reflects the economism of the old left and the liberalism of the left's younger cohort. Therefore, little work went into debating the issue internally. When the referendum arrived, it exposed a damaging divide between millennial leftists strongly influenced by American-style identity politics, and older sections that based their analysis on the question of controlling capital.[46] In the age of social media, such divisions are harder to suppress. These tensions remain unresolved inside the Labour Party: Corbyn has largely accepted Brexit and promoted public service investment and controls on larger businesses, but the appeal of his 'new politics' lies among professionals and young people, while Labour has yet to fully recover in working-class areas. In Scotland, by contrast, the socialist left had done years or even decades of ideological preparation to unite its forces. Traditionally, leftists had opposed 'nationalism' and supported the 'united British working class'. However, a generation of debate had ensured that, although the Scottish left was still distorted by division, it could present a unified argument for independence. A caveat here is that preparation and unity can lead to the wrong answers. In Scotland, as we argued above, the argument focused far too heavily on the enemy of Westminster at the expense of a broader anti-neoliberal populism, which led to immediate results but also to liberal conclusions on the European Union. However, overall this point shows that the left is best when it ideologically prepares simple answers for the thorny problems that will genuinely divide mass opinion and create active debate, rather than endlessly debating the intricacies of issues it feels most comfortable discussing.

Fourth, referendums have a definite timeline and offer a quick opportunity to win a victory that has easily imaginable results that affect mainstream politics in unusually marked ways. By throwing up a campaign, the left can quite easily and quickly build influence locally, as the Radical Independence Campaign in Scotland proves. RIC also proves that temporary forces do not translate into permanent socialist infrastructure. Nonetheless, we would argue that the left's involvement in the Scottish question on broadly national-popular lines has been to our long-term advantage. It has ensured that working-class identity in Scotland has not taken a 'white working class' form, and instead remains a possible site for anti-racist, anti-war politics.

Fifth, and crucially, although referendums have escaped the *discursive* control filters of capitalist politics, the result is not always a triumph for democracy over elite interests. Here, we can point to the illiberal, majoritarian nature of many populist campaigns. But there is perhaps a more important issue to mention: simply winning a popular vote does not guarantee that its spirit will be honoured, even where the numbers prove decisive. The case of Syriza's *oxi* victory highlights the problem. A victory must be imposed not only over parliament, but also over the transnational agencies, financial interests, and corporations that oversee and control parliament's behaviour. Democracy's limits are not just the elite consensus of parliament. They also reflect the current phase of capitalism, or, often, failings intrinsic to capitalism in any phase. The same, of course, applies to right-populist campaigns for a complete moratorium on borders, promises that are largely built on fantasies. Unlike the 1930s, capitalism today is not threatened by socialism and therefore its leaders do not see populists as fruitful allies but rather as nuisances.

Referendums are useful tools for any outsider movement seeking to expose the divide between established, controlled, 'tactical' political speech and mass opinion. Strategically, that is crucial, but that is also their limit. Until the left has forces strong enough to challenge the interests that also control parliamentary politics, democracy will only emerge in outbursts of rage.

In many places the left lacks the forces to succeed in presenting its own radical democratic experiments. The momentum of Occupy, the *indignados*, and other experiments has fizzled out. Nevertheless, in Southern Europe, the left has enough social power to influence debates to its advantage, and may continue to challenge for government. Elsewhere in the global north, even in the most unpromising circumstances, the left can still effectively intervene, as the campagins for Corbyn and Sanders proved. However, both campaigns raise the question of whether left-wing leaders can permanently take control of parties locked by their alliances into habitual centrism. Despite Corbyn's success in 2017, it remains entirely possible that the normal routines of 'capitalist democracy' will eventually incorporate or expel these leadership experiments. Most Labour MPs remain committed to a centrist project, and much of their new voting base is committed to anti-populist moderation.

Given a tightly packed centrist consensus, referendums should be taken seriously as sites of socialist intervention. Today they act as theatres for a crisis of democratic meaning. Although traditionally referendums were meant to ratify an elite consensus and parade the legitimacy of parliament, recently they have had the opposite effect. Rather than live in fear of the divisive majoritarianism, the best strategy is to engage in full knowledge of the contradictions that a national-popular discourse will bring about. Jeremy Corbyn, bridging between appeasing his youthful supporters' fear of anti-immigrant populism and addressing populist discontent in Labour's heartlands, illustrates the problems that arise from failing to articulate decisive left-populist leadership. However, Scotland's radical left proves that, where left-populism lacks a clearly defined enemy, even the best organized radical campaign can be a bridge into mainstream neoliberal politics.

The debates that emerge in referendums are never debates on the left's terms unless a left-popular government comes to power, which remains unlikely outside of a few countries. However, recent examples show that these terms are not necessarily fully under elite control either. Where referendums emerge, the left must avoid the liberal temptation to cower in fear of populism. Demanding referendums has proved to be an effective tactic for problematizing issues that have been 'sacred' for the political centre, and if we harness that logic they may provide one avenue for reinvigorating our forces. In a moment of historical weakness for the working class as an emancipatory historical agent, ignoring it is not an option.

NOTES

We would like to thank Lili Chan and Erik Olin Wright for commenting on an early draft of this paper.

1   Matt Qvortrup, 'Europe Has a Referendum Addiction: How Direct Democracy Went From the Rarest of All Political Procedures to Europeans' Bargaining Chip of Choice', *Foreign Policy*, 21 June 2016.

2   'Referendumania', *Economist*, 19 May 2016.

3   Martin Kettle, 'If Referendums Are the Answer, We're Asking the Wrong Question', *Guardian*, 23 June 2016.

4   Jon Henley, 'Why Referendums Are Problematic – Yet More Popular Than Ever', *Guardian*, 6 October 2016.

5   Antonio Gramsci, *Selections From Political Writings 1921-1926*, translated by Quintin Hoare, New York: International Publishers, 1978, p. 50.

6   Matt Qvortrup, *Referendums Around the World: The Continued Growth of Direct Democracy*, Basingstoke: Palgrave MacMillan, 2014, pp. 4-6.

7   Qvortrup, *Referendums Around the World*, pp. 4, 7-10.

8   Norberto Bobbio, *The Future of Democracy: A Defence of the Rules of the Game*, Minneapolis: University of Minnesota Press, 1987, p. 54.

9   This term comes from Peter Mair, *Ruling the Void: The Hollowing of Western Democracy*, London: Verso, 2013.

10   There have been some attempts in North America to deepen the quality of referendum democracy through the use of randomly selected citizens assemblies. For a discussion of these experiments see John Gastil and Robert Richards, 'Making Direct Democracy Deliberative through Random Assemblies', *Politics and Society* 41(2), 2013.

11   Paul Gilbride, 'Nick Clegg: SNP and Ukip Share the Same Divisive Impulse', *Express*, 29 March 2014

12   Qvortrup, 'Europe Has a Referendum Addiction'.

13   Qvortrup, 'Europe Has a Referendum Addiction'.

14   Vernon Bogdanor, *The People and the Party System: The Referendum and Electoral Reform in British Politics*, Cambridge: Cambridge University Press, 1981, p. 69.

15   Jürgen Habermas, 'National Unification and Popular Sovereignty', *New Left Review* 219(September/October), 1996, p. 12.

16   Jacques Rancière, *Hatred of Democracy*, translated by Steve Corcoran, London: Verso, 2009, p. 79.

17   Rancière, *Hatred of Democracy*, pp. 79-80.

18   Kristin Ross, 'Democracy for Sale' in Giorgio Agamben et al., *Democracy in What State?*, translated by William McCaib, New York: Columbia University Press, 2011, p. 84.

19   Mair, *Ruling the Void*.

20   Raquel Garrido, 'France Rebels', *Jacobin*, 12 April 2017.

21   Oscar Reyes, 'Skinhead Conservatism: A Failed Populist Project', in Francisco Panizza, ed., *Populism and the Mirror of Democracy*, London: Verso, 2005, pp. 105-6.

22   Ernesto Laclau, *On Populist Reason*, London: Verso: 2002.

23   Pablo Iglesias, 'Spain on Edge', *New Left Review* 93(May/June), 2015.

24   Perry Anderson, 'The Heirs of Gramsci' *New Left Review* 100(July/August), 2016.

25   Jodi Dean, 'Not Us, Me', *Verso Blog*, 26 November 2016.

26   Philip Stephens, 'The World is Saying No to Scottish Separation', *Financial Times*, 11 September 2014.

27   Will Hutton quoted in Neil Davidson, 'A Scottish Watershed', *New Left Review* 89(September/October), 2014.

28   Tariq Ali, *The Extreme Center: A Warning*, London: Verso, 2015.

29   'After the Vote, Chaos', *Economist*, 25 June 2016.

30   Leo Panitch, 'Reflections on Strategy for Labour', in Leo Panitch, Colin Leys, Greg Albo, and David Coates, eds, *Socialist Register 2001: Working Classes, Global Realities*, London: Merlin Press, 2000.

31   Davidson, 'A Scottish Watershed'.

32   Ailsa Henderson and James Mitchell, 'The Scottish Question, Six Months On', Transatlantic Seminar Series, 27 March 2015.

33   Henderson and Mitchell, 'The Scottish Question, Six Months On'.

34   This analysis was conducted using data from the 2013 and 2014 Scottish Social Attitudes Surveys (SSA), an annual survey of nationally representative samples of adults in Scotland conducted by Scotcen Social Research on behalf of the UK Economic and Social Research Council. ONS operational categories in the SSA were adapted

to operationalize Erik Olin Wright's '12-location class matrix'. Wright specifies two dimensions within employment: relations to authority within the production process and levels of skill and expertise. On the dimension of authority Wright distinguishes between managers, who are involved in strategic and organizational planning in the workplace, supervisors, who possess some degree of power over other workers but who are not involved in organizational decision making, and those with no authority over others. On the skill dimension, Wright differentiates between expert occupations that ordinarily need an advanced degree, skilled occupations that require a lower level of specialised training, and occupations that do not necessitate significant training. This produces a class map of 'contradictory locations within class relations', 'privileged appropriation locations within exploitation relations' and 'polarized locations within capitalist property relations'. See Erik Olin Wright, *Class Counts*, London: Verso, 1997, pp. 19-26.

35   These are NRS social grades, a demographic classification system popular with market researchers. The grades are: A – upper middle class (higher managerial, administrative or professional); B – middle class (intermediate managerial, administrative or professional); C1 – lower middle class (supervisory or clerical and junior managerial, administrative or professional); C2 – skilled working class (skilled manual workers); D – working class (semi-skilled and unskilled manual workers); E – non working (casual or lowest grade workers, pensioners, and others who depend on the welfare state for their income). Market researchers often group these into ABC1 and C2DE, which are taken to designate the 'middle' and 'working class'.

36   Kirby Swales, 'Understanding the Leave Vote', NatCen Social Research, December 2016.

37   Swales, 'Understanding the Leave Vote'.

38   Susan Watkins, 'Casting Off', *New Left Review* 100(July/August), 2016.

39   Bridget Morris, '120,000: SNP Membership Hits Record Level After Post-Brexit Surge', *National*, 22 July 2016.

40   Michael Fry, 'Stanford Treated to a Side of Sturgeon Rarely Glimpsed: Nicola, Capitalist', *National*, 10 April 2017.

41   Fry, 'Stanford Treated to a Side of Sturgeon Rarely Glimpsed: Nicola, Capitalist.'

42   'How Britain Voted in the 2017 Election', *Ipsos Mori*, 20 June 2017.

43   Susi Dennison, 'Brexit and Europe's New Insurgent Parties', *European Council on Foreign Relations*, 24 June 2016.

44   Dennison, 'Brexit and Europe's New Insurgent Parties'.

45   Rob Merrick, 'Brexit: Labour MPs Demand Jeremy Corbyn Fights to Stay in Single Market', *Independent*, 21 June 2017.

46   Watkins, 'Casting Off'.

ORGANIZED FOR DEMOCRACY? LEFT CHALLENGES INSIDE THE DEMOCRATIC PARTY

ADAM HILTON

Socialists make their own history, but not under conditions they choose. American socialists were starkly reminded of how the nightmarish weight of the past continues to haunt the present during the 2016 presidential nomination contest between independent, democratic socialist Senator Bernie Sanders and former First Lady, Senator, and Secretary of State Hillary Clinton. On the one hand, Sanders' decision to forego a third party campaign and run as a Democrat provided him with a national audience, an opportunity to introduce democratic socialism to a new generation, and a mass-based fundraising vehicle that collected millions in small donations. On the other hand, running as a Democrat against the standard bearer of the party establishment seemed almost to guarantee that he would lose. And while he came closer than many expected, the outcome only appeared to confirm that when it comes to the Democratic Party, the left simply cannot win.

Unlike all other advanced capitalist democracies, the United States never produced a labour-based political party. As labour and social democratic parties emerged elsewhere during the late nineteenth century, American trade unionists debated whether or not to launch an independent party or join an existing coalition, ultimately opting for a nonpartisan strategy of 'pure and simple unionism' for fear of violent repression, partisan conflict in the union rank and file, and the off-putting sectarianism of many American socialists.[1] Almost a half-century later, amidst the Great Depression, the Democratic Party under Franklin Roosevelt's New Deal successfully integrated insurgent farmer and labour groups, after which independent third-party vote shares in US elections declined and never recovered.[2] Since the 1930s, state laws regulating political parties have served to strengthen the two-party duopoly, legislating comparatively high thresholds for third party ballot access.[3]

The familiar conundrum of the American left in party politics was rehashed in a flurry of post-Sanders assessments. Many on the left were quick to disabuse Sanders supporters of misplacing their hope in a lost cause. While the Sanders campaign had improved the standing of democratic socialism as a legitimate political position in the US, a 'capitalist party' like the Democrats was nevertheless beholden to wealthy donors and corporate lobbyists, having moved irretrievably from its New Deal–Great Society traditions to embrace neoliberalism with a human face.[4]

This essay examines the relationship between the left and the Democrats by playing on the double meaning of the term 'challenges' employed in its title. It seeks to undertake a strategic assessment of the 'challenges' facing left political power in the Democratic Party by drawing insights from the mixed results of various 'challenges' the left has presented inside the party historically. That strategic assessment must be based, I argue, on an institutional understanding of the Democratic Party as an organization, requiring the development of more sophisticated analytic tools than those typically employed by Marxists and others on the left. The fundamental point to be drawn from this analysis is that while a robust, well-organized left can *conceivably* exercise power inside the Democratic Party, that power is unlikely to serve socialist ends of building the collective power of the working class due to the way the party is organized. Past efforts to transform the party organization into a party of different type, culminating in the New Politics movement of the late 1960s and early 1970s, demonstrate the difficultly of overcoming this problem. Coupled with the unlikelihood of producing the labour-based third party that has eluded the American left for well over a century, the analysis presented here suggests that rather than dismissing the Democrats and pinning our hopes on a third party, the American left must rethink which kinds of goals can be accomplished in the realm of American party politics, and which cannot. The first step is to come to terms with the nature of American political parties, and specifically, the Democratic Party.

WHAT KIND OF ORGANIZATION IS THE DEMOCRATIC PARTY?

A 'bourgeois' party?

When Marxists are asked about the nature of the Democratic Party, it is often said that the party is a 'bourgeois party'. While varying shades of this view are widely held, it is more often used in the pub or at a political meeting than put down and defended in print. And while it makes for good agitprop, its analytic foundations are more problematic.

The concept of 'bourgeois party' can be developed in two different ways:

one, as an analogy with the bourgeois state; the other, as an analogy with a working-class party – neither of which is very satisfying. On the one hand, stretching from the writings of Marx, Engels and Lenin to the 1970s debate between Ralph Miliband and Nicos Poulantzas, the state in capitalism is said to be a capitalist state due to its structural dependence on privately controlled capital accumulation for its own reproduction. This structural dependence exerts pressure on state actors to conduct public policy in ways that promote investor confidence. It may well be true that government officeholders hail from the same social class as investors, attended the same elite schools, or were trained by their economics professors to think like *homo economicus*. But even if these contingent qualities of state actors are assumed away – replaced, say, by leftist members of working-class parties – the state's structural location in the political economy would still exert pressure on policymakers to govern on behalf of capital.

Just as in the state debate itself, several causal mechanisms have been suggested to be at work in making a party bourgeois. Continuing the power structure approach of C. Wright Mills, G. William Domhoff, for instance, places his emphasis on the qualities of the personnel of the party leadership and its social roots within the capitalist class.[5] In contrast, Lance Selfa suggests that the connections linking the party to capital 'are not ideological' in nature.[6] Rather, the bourgeois nature of the party is due to the personnel's concern with 'the staffing of the government but not with altering the state'.[7] In addition, Thomas Ferguson's 'investment theory of political parties' sees the major American parties as blocs of wealthy investors rather than coalitions of voters or interest groups.[8] To secure the funds necessary for electoral success, party officials and candidates must orient their appeals to large donors found among the nation's corporate elite, who expect to reap returns on their investments in the form of favourable public policy.

These perspectives draw valuable connections between political and corporate elites, who, in the US especially, are often the same people. However, these explanations tend to muddle rather than distinguish what is contingent and therefore changeable from what is structural and enduring. The difference is important to consider, not only because it helps us understand the past, but because it holds implications for strategy in the present. To take Ferguson as an example of a structural perspective, it is at times rather ambiguous if a party's policy agenda reflects the interests of its major investors in a direct, unmediated sense, or if investors' preferences themselves reflect their strategic accommodation with competing partisan groups' interests and demands.[9] While it is undeniably important how parties raise their resources, investors' preferences may be shaped as much by the class struggle inside the party, which determines what they can achieve politically, as by their specific position in the political economy alone. Adjudicating this ambiguity requires opening the black box of the bourgeois party and paying adequate attention to the determinants of the intraparty balance of forces, such as its institutional structure, its mechanisms of governance, and the organization of other non-bourgeois forces inside it.

This brings us to the other way of conceiving a bourgeois party, drawn in contrast to a working-class party. For most Marxists, working-class parties are those that 'transform the proletariat into a class' by building the collective capacities of working people to think, organize and act as a cohesive social force, and also translate that power into votes, and votes into seats in government. Working-class parties may develop robust subcultures of proletarian community life or link more indirectly to trade union federations. But in any and all cases, working-class parties enjoy solid electoral support from a majority of working-class voters.

From this perspective, the Democratic Party is something less than a working-class party but more than its bourgeois counterpart. Even though, as will be developed below, Democratic Party organs have rarely served as centres of community life, the party apparatus did develop structural links with trade unions in most large industrial states in the 1930s as well as at the national level in the process of presidential nomination and campaigning. In some states, such as Michigan, these institutional linkages of elite brokerage fused into tightly integrated party-union relationships. In other states, through the Congress of Industrial Organizations' political action committee (CIO-PAC) and, later, the AFL-CIO's Committee on Political Education (COPE), organized labour engaged in voter registration, door-to-door canvassing, literature distribution and get-out-the-vote drives for unionists and non-unionists alike. In terms of the electorate, the Democratic Party had already become home to most low-income and poor voters prior to the New Deal, which only deepened the trend. Contrary to oft-heard claims concerning reactionary white workers voting for Republicans since the time of Nixon, patterns of voting behaviour between low and high-income white voters have continued to *diverge* since the late 1970s, as those in the bottom third of the income distribution have cast ballots for Democratic presidential candidates at significantly higher rates than affluent whites.[10] Moreover, while never approximating European social democracy, Democratic presidents have a fairly consistent pattern of governance that, on average, has produced less income inequality than during Republican administrations.[11]

None of this is to suggest that the Democratic Party transforms working-class voters into a class. It does not, and, as I will argue below, it probably cannot. (Nor should it be omitted that more straightforwardly working-class parties experience difficulty doing this too.) But the organized presence of workers in the party, whether through their trade unions or as voters, does have important consequences. Conceptually, then, the notion of a 'bourgeois party' fails to bring sufficient analytic clarity to the nature of power in the Democratic Party, leaving its allegedly capitalist foundations underdetermined. If it stems from its personnel, the personnel can be changed. If it is a matter of money, there appear to be conditions under which this can be mitigated. What is most problematic is the concept's tendency to cut off more probing questions concerning how ruling parties actually work and how the left should strategically orient itself in response. Given the obstacles to a viable third party in the United States, such questions are imperative.

Openness without entry: The puzzle of Democratic Party organization

Going beyond simplistic labels requires a direct engagement with the organizational structure of the Democratic Party and the strategic options it presents. The overall pattern of American party development has been shaped by the institutional environment in which the parties are embedded. US presidentialism, the separation of executive and legislative powers, and the federal division between national and subnational levels of government have all stamped American parties with distinctive and enduring features. This is especially so because political parties in the US have no constitutionally prescribed form or rules. The federal Constitution makes no mention of them, and some of its most important framers denounced the 'mischief of factions' thought to act as 'sores on the body politic'.[12] Nevertheless, sharpening disputes within the first and second Congresses over the extent of federal power in the new republic caused some of those same framers to rethink their hostility to parties. Durable legislative coalitions formed to ensure majority rule in the House of Representatives. To ensure full agenda control, these parties-in-government coordinated their partisan politicking with members of state legislatures, who selected senators, and over the selection of state electors, who elected the president and vice president. The spread of white male suffrage in presidential elections in the 1830s and 1840s gave rise to the first mass parties in the world – the Democrats and the Whigs – as each organized faction of the political class mobilized blocs of voters in support of their party's slate of candidates for elective office.

This pattern of American party development contrasts sharply with the emergence of mass parties in Western Europe, which spread like a 'contagion from the left' as disenfranchised working-class parties organized large dues-paying memberships and complex, bureaucratic leadership structures, while existing elite parties-in-government responded in kind.[13] Rather than emerging from civil society and storming their way into a resistant state, American mass parties were an improvised invention of the party-in-government, which then spiraled outward from the state to mobilize parties-in-the-electorate for the purpose of winning elections at all levels of government.[14] Partisanship was cultivated by elite appeals to voters' affective social group attachments, politicizing social cleavages along ethnoreligious lines, geography and through the use of revolutionary martial imagery.[15] American parties had no formal memberships in the European sense, and partisan mobilization ebbed and flowed with the rhythms of the electoral cycle.

The American form of party development had distinctive effects on the kinds of organizations produced to accomplish state-led party building. When then-Senator Martin Van Buren, presidential candidate Andrew Jackson, and other political entrepreneurs built the national Democratic Party to facilitate Jackson's election in 1828, they minimized start-up costs by inviting existing state and local party organizations to affiliate under a unified Democratic label. However, state and local organizations already had in place their own leaders, platforms, and governing reputations. To entice incorporation, the national organization granted subnational party units significant autonomy in the design and operation of state and local party activity. While the subnational parties were expected to support the national party's presidential candidate, they were free to pick and choose their own platforms, candidates, and policies.[16] All levels of the party would enjoy the collective benefits of the spoils of national office, such as jobs, contracts, and infrastructure building. But rather than functioning as branch offices of a centralized, hierarchical national bureaucratic organization, state and local parties were knit together in a patchwork of organizations, factions, cliques, and classes, with no formal process to formulate intraparty cohesion or even adjudicate intraparty conflicts. For the vast majority of their existence, American political parties have been, structurally speaking, parties of states' rights.

To be sure, the national parties developed coherent formal structures that vested nominally supreme authority in the quadrennial national conventions, their interim national committees and chairs, and the congressional campaign committees. However, to speak of 'national political parties' in the American context is something of a misnomer. For much of their near two-century existence, the national parties have been little more than loose confederations of state and local organizations. Indeed, the national party as a governing body has been so consistently weak, ineffective, and nearly invisible in relation to its state and local counterparts that one prominent party scholar referred to it as 'the ghost party'.[17] And while there have been some recent trends to the contrary, it remains the case that American political parties are some of the most decentralized organizations in the democratic world.[18] As E. E. Schattschneider once observed: 'Decentralization of power is by all odds the most important single characteristic of the American major party. ... Indeed, once this truth is understood, nearly everything else about American parties is greatly illuminated.'[19]

However, rather than illuminating nearly everything about them, the decentralized structure of American parties poses a puzzle for those inclined to dismiss them as simply bourgeois institutions. Why should this structure be so systematically inclined toward capitalist interests? After all, such a loose confederation of relatively autonomous state and local organizations implies fairly low barriers to entry and influence than if the party had the oligarchical bureaucracies of the kind Roberto Michels examined in the German Social Democratic Party.[20] There were, of course, important analogues to oligarchical parties in the US, specifically the urban machines found in many large northern cities in the post-bellum period, as well as the authoritarian enclaves built in the southern states during Jim Crow.[21] However, these examples only underscore the degree of autonomy local and state organizations enjoy in the context of American federalism. Northern machines and southern party-states could coexist within the same national party alongside comparatively open organizations in other locations.

The puzzle is only compounded when state and local party organizations are examined in detail. Outside the two exceptions mentioned above, most subnational parties continue to be very thinly institutionalized entities, meaning that while they may have a complete set of officers and by-laws in place – and this is a relatively *recent* development – they may lack paid full or part-time staff, a year-round office, or even a formal budget.[22] Because of their proximity to the grassroots, local organizations are chiefly concerned with undertaking labour-intensive activities, such as voter registration, door-to-door canvassing, and get-out-the-vote mobilization. However, due to lack of funds, most local organizations are dependent on raising armies of volunteers to perform this work. Local parties usually fail to accomplish this, playing a supplemental role to candidate organizations. In fact, as of 2017, up to half of all local committee positions were vacant, not due to barriers to entry but because of lack of community interest.[23]

What is more, the introduction of the direct primary and civil service reform around the turn of the twentieth century further limited the control that party organization leaders could exert over the nomination process (however, these reforms also more firmly institutionalized the Democratic-Republican two-party system).[24] Party nominations were now conducted under state laws, using state-printed ballots, and giving self-declared partisans (and sometimes independents or even just anyone) the opportunity to cast a ballot for their preferred candidate before the general election. As will be shown below, this did not rule out the ability for organized subterfuge and manipulation, especially of the presidential nominating process. But it did constitute a significant watershed in American party development that rendered 'boss rule' mostly a thing of the past.[25]

All this is to say that, contrary to what a notion like 'bourgeois party' would lead us to expect when we examine Democratic Party structure, the party organization's entrance appears to be standing relatively ajar. The strategic options this party structure opens up can be seen, for instance, in the course of the mid-twentieth century civil rights movement. As Eric Schickler has recently shown, what has long been understood as an elite-driven, top-down realignment of the Democratic Party in the mid-1960s was, in fact, the culmination of a quarter-century-long struggle within the New Deal coalition to bring civil rights to the top of the national agenda.[26] Beginning in 1936, labour-liberals in the Democratic Party and labour activists within the Congress of Industrial Organizations (CIO) broadened the meaning of New Deal liberalism by fusing concerns with economic and racial inequality into a programmatic agenda built around fair employment practices, anti-lynching legislation, collective bargaining, and voting rights. The electoral activity of the CIO-PAC, lobbying efforts by liberal organizations such as Americans for Democratic Action (ADA), and the conversion of northern African American voters from the party of Lincoln to the party of Roosevelt shifted public opinion on civil rights, and pressured local and mid-level Democratic officeholders to endorse pro-civil rights planks in state party platforms and to bring civil rights legislation to state legislatures and Congress long before national party leaders responded. While the new conventional wisdom has pointed to party federalism and the role of the South in limiting the liberalism of the New Deal era, the decentralized party structure actually cut both ways, providing well-organized groups and movements with a power base from which to reshape the national party.[27] By the time President Lyndon Johnson overcame the southern filibuster of the Civil Rights Act in 1964, the majority of the non-southern Democrats were already on board.

Clearly, when the left has a widespread, organized social base capable of affecting public opinion and the behaviour of voters, party actors have incentives to respond. Precisely because there is no 'party line' to toe, officeholders and office seekers can be pressured to shift their own positions on issues via lobbying, public criticism, or tight nomination challenges without it resulting in them being 'purged' or denied the party label. With very few exceptions, no such disciplinary capacity exists in American parties. The porousness that flows from their decentralized structure, as well as the history of the left in the party, suggests that they are open to leverage. What matters most is who is best organized to take advantage of this openness.

So the puzzle remains: if there are few barriers to entry that keep the left out of the Democratic Party and, as we have seen, the left could, under specific circumstances, exert influence in the party, why is there so little entry? Part of the reason may stem from the nature of the party organizations themselves, which continue to be shaped by the legacy of their top-down, inside-out origins. Because US party organizations were developed by parties-in-government to develop a voter base in civil society, those organizations have been more oriented toward helping candidates win elections than in building the political capacities of their social base. Because American parties are not funded by dues structures, they do not build mass memberships through community-oriented organizations, activities, and citizen education. Because subnational units under the same party label are relatively autonomous from each other as well as the national organization, heterogeneous and even outright antagonistic social forces may be grouped into the same coalition, rendering partisan majorities less meaningful, more difficult to hold accountable, and often skewed toward small, powerfully positioned blocs.

These campaign-oriented party structures have the effect of inverting the classic model of party-building activity: rather than building the social base to enlist growing numbers of loyal voters, American parties direct their most sustained activism toward cultivating partisan loyalty within the business community, from whom they raise most of their money, and conduct their campaign activity through top-down, data-driven strategies of identifying and 'activating' pluralities of likely partisan voters in swing districts. The same party structures that are so passive at the base are vigorously active at the top, seeking out and persuading potential donors to contribute, listening to their concerns, and developing a shared sense of consciousness and purpose in the public sphere.

In short, there is an important – in fact, crucial – distinction to make between organizational openness (lack of barriers to entry) and democratic effectiveness (meaningful participation) inside the Democratic Party. Formally, Democratic Party organizations are quite democratic: whoever shows up can participate. But substantively, getting to cast a vote to approve a new budget at the annual meeting of the local Democratic Party does not amount to much, and thus fails to draw substantial citizen interest. The lack of internal deliberation concerning major policy issues of the day and alternative political visions for society functions as a significant disincentive for widespread grassroots participation.[28] Relatively low levels of party-oriented activism between elections have been an enduring feature of American politics that cannot be explained as generational or cultural failures. Historically, Americans have been a nation of joiners.[29] Voluntary civic associations, however, offer what American party organizations do not: large, economically diverse memberships; social and community bonds of solidarity; and geographically rooted, yet federated, networks that share in a perceived moral purpose. Participatory organizations such as these did not simply bring together likeminded individuals (as, say, a party primary might), but provided forums in which shared identities and preferences were forged. Leadership roles were regularly rotated, spreading civic capacities among the rank and file, and pooling membership dues often financed group activities.

Civic organizations, however, are no substitute for parties. Often formally apolitical or nonpartisan organizations, voluntary associations focus mostly on mutual aid for members and cannot nominate people for public office. The point, however, is to show the nature and purpose of an institution may have as much influence as its structure in promoting internal participatory democracy. American political parties were not created for such a purpose, nor have they come to play that role as mass-membership civic associations have themselves declined in recent decades.[30] They are fundamentally electoral devices for the aid of party candidates and officeholders. The question, however, is whether they can *only* be that.

IS A DIFFERENT DEMOCRATIC PARTY POSSIBLE?

In a reflective moment following the end of the Sanders insurgency, Seth Ackerman outlined an ambitious blueprint for a new party of the left in *Jacobin* magazine, listing several key structural criteria that a truly democratic party would need to include:

> In a genuinely democratic party, the organization's membership, program, and leadership are bound together tightly by a powerful, mutually reinforcing connection. The party's *members* are its sovereign power; they come together through a sense of shared interest or principle. Through deliberation, the members establish a *program* to advance those interests. The party educates the public around the program, and it serves, in effect, as the lodestar by which the party is guided. Finally, the members choose a party *leadership* – including electoral candidates – who are accountable to the membership and bound by the program.[31]

While Ackerman is correct to point out that 'the Democratic Party has none' of these features, he is not the first to make such an observation. Back in the 1940s and 1950s, a group of political scientists organized a special task force under the auspices of the American Political Science Association to study the consequences of what they considered to be lack of 'responsible parties' in the American polity. Chief among their complaints was the 'ambiguity of membership,' the absence of any 'central figure or organ which could claim authority to take up party problems, policies and strategy,' as well as the 'excessive measure of internal separatism' made possible by the parties' federal structure.[32] By contrast, a responsible party system required nothing less than 'parties [that] are able to bring forth programs to which they commit themselves ... possess sufficient internal cohesion to carry out these programs. ...[and] which cannot be brought about without party procedures that give a large body of people an opportunity to share in the development of the party program'.[33]

Just as Ackerman's analysis has been prompted by a poignant display of Democratic Party deficiencies in the 2016 primary campaign, the Committee on Political Parties undertook their critique of the American party system in the shadow of the infamous Dixiecrat revolt at the 1948 Democratic National Convention. After the CIO, ADA and other labour-liberals had fought successfully for the inclusion of a strongly worded civil rights plank in the party platform, delegates from Mississippi and South Carolina walked out in protest to launch the rival States' Rights Party. While their immediate goal of denying President Harry Truman a majority in the electoral college failed, the aftermath of the revolt displayed the ability of state parties to discipline the national organization: Truman only temporarily withheld patronage from several Dixiecrat supporters in Congress, and the national leadership spent the 1950s walking back its commitment to civil rights.[34]

As these instances display, party procedure and organization are likely to become objects of scrutiny in the context of larger political battles inside the party. It should be no surprise then that the most far-reaching attempt to reform the Democratic Party in light of its perceived organizational deficiencies came in the wake of the party crisis of 1968. The post-1968 party reforms were driven by the New Politics movement operating within and outside the Democratic Party's official Commission on Party Structure and Delegate Selection (known as the McGovern-Fraser Commission for its two chairmen). Hailing from segments of the civil rights, student, antiwar, and feminist movements, as well as the labour-left, New Politics activists viewed party reform as the opportunity to assert greater membership control and officeholder accountability, and thereby change the fundamental dynamics of American politics.

Their reform agenda was shaped in part by the many instances of abuse, chicanery, and even outright exclusion antiwar activists had experienced in the 1968 battle for the Democratic nomination. The campaigns of senators Eugene McCarthy and Robert Kennedy had forced President Johnson out of the race, but Vice President Hubert Humphrey had taken his place as the party's standard bearer. Unlike the gradual persistence of the civil rights movement moving up through the party structure, the nature of the antiwar cause and its sense of urgency, as well as its countercultural flair and its antagonism to longstanding Cold War policy, created a near ubiquitous backlash from low and mid-level party officials. Throughout the nominating process, McCarthy and Kennedy supporters were frustrated by undisclosed caucus meeting locations, arbitrary rulings from committee chairs, abusive uses of proxy voting, locked doors, massive filing fees, and nonbinding primary results. While the insurgents had collectively wrapped up the majority of primary victories, Humphrey had a majority of convention votes without having contested a single primary contest. As the reform commission concluded in its official report in 1970: 'meaningful participation of Democratic voters in the choice of their [1968] presidential nominee was often difficult or costly, sometimes completely illusory, and, in not a few instances, impossible.'[35]

In the wake of the disastrous Democratic National Convention in Chicago and the narrow loss in the November election, the McGovern-Fraser reform commission issued binding guidelines to ensure that no candidate would again achieve the party's presidential nomination in the way Humphrey did. State parties were obliged to comply with a set of 'reasonable standards' meant to ensure all rank-and-file Democratic activists and voters had a 'full, meaningful, and timely opportunity to participate' in the selection of the party's nominee. These included codifying transparent rules regarding procedure and holding open meetings at publicized times and locations. More controversially, the guidelines also banned proxy voting, closed slate making, and ex officio or automatic delegate status for party officials and officeholders, meaning that all aspiring delegates – whether movement newcomers or sitting members of Congress – had to run in their home districts and publicly pledge their support for a presidential candidate. Furthermore, convention delegates were to be allocated proportionally according to candidates' state-levels of support rather than in winner-take-all contests. Slates of delegates were bound to cast their first ballot for their candidate, curtailing the opportunity for party leaders to broker over the nominees in the infamous smoke-filled rooms at the back of the convention hall.

Ironically, though the American New Left is remembered for its emphasis on the virtues of decentralization, the New Politics project required a significant *centralization* of party power in the national convention, the national committee, and the reform commission they created. It was precisely the decentralized structure of party federalism that had enabled local and state committee chairs to improvise rules and procedures to exclude insurgents. To ensure that insurgent voices were heard, the nominally supreme power of the national 'ghost party' had to be actualized. Decisions made at the national level regarding the conduct of party governance, including the installation of very strong affirmative action provisions, were imposed on all fifty state parties. If they failed to comply, as did Chicago Mayor Richard Daley's defiant Illinois delegation at the 1972 convention, they were stripped of their credentials and ejected from the convention.

Crucially, New Politics reformers understood that removing the barriers to participation that kept the insurgents out in 1968 would not be sufficient to transform the party going forward. At the heart of the reform commission's work emerged a perspective critical not just of the technical specifics of the presidential nomination process, but of political parties' role in linking society and the state. As one internal report put it:

> These hearings [have] revealed that reform goes much further than simply reforming internal structures. Making the party 'open' is only a first step … for even if the doors of the party are opened wider to the grass roots, it is not at all certain that the grass roots will rush in to seize the opportunity. …It is not enough to 'democratize' party procedures if large numbers of people are not interested in participation.[36]

Participation, some argued, had to go beyond 'just ratifying someone else's choice' of party candidates.[37] There had to be positive incentives for meaningful citizen participation, incentives that were compromised by the structure and operation of the party, which threw together racial egalitarians and Jim Crow proponents, as well as peace activists and cold warriors, into the same partisan coalition. The party would be unable to draw in popular participation without some way of forging a significant degree of ideological coherence and policy cohesion. A more programmatic party therefore required 'losing some of the allegiances' of the past (e.g. southern conservatives), who received the benefits of majority party status but were 'allowed to scab on us at the ballot box and in Congress'.[38] The party would have to develop some policymaking capacity if platforms were to be more than just a 'hodgepodge of platitudes' from which officeholders felt free to distances themselves between elections.[39] Indeed, the electoral focus could no longer be the exclusive concern of the party, which 'must serve the people between election years'. What was needed, they said, was 'a new kind of political service organization' that was 'activist' in orientation.[40]

Thus, beyond merely 'opening the party' to new entrants in the presidential nominating process, as significant as that was, the New Politics movement pressed ahead in the years after the 1968 crisis with a comprehensive blueprint for building a different Democratic Party. The plan, its authors hoped, would 'discard the frustrating weaknesses of the present system … and usher in a new and vastly strengthened structure, based on grassroots support'.[41] The proposed Democratic Party Charter not only institutionalized the new nominating process in the party's first-ever constitution, but also sought to transform the loose confederation of state and local parties into a national, mass-based, participatory organization. This was to be accomplished by introducing a new set of regional party organizations to interface between the state and national levels, expanding the national committee and creating an executive council, which would include congressional party leaders, and implementing a mass-member dues system to alleviate the party's fundraising reliance on wealthy contributors. Regional and national party organizations would convene midterm policy conferences so that party officials, officeholders, and rank-and-file party members could formulate a platform without the added pressure of nominating a presidential candidate. These 'mini-conventions,' it was imagined, would act as 'a transmission belt between movement politics and party politics'.[42]

However, a different Democratic Party never fully materialized. The prospects for transformation diminished as the party leadership deserted the 1972 Democratic National Convention in droves, even as new entrants of women, African Americans, and people under thirty soared. The most critical defection came from the AFL-CIO leadership, who, in addition to their open distaste for the counterculture and their 'softness' on communism, also promoted a narrative that cast the New Politics movement as 'elitist' and 'anti-working class' in nature. In fact, these accusations were belied by the United Auto Workers' financial support and active participation in the reform process from the outset, as well as the dozens of AFL-CIO unions and locals that openly defied federation president George Meany's policy of neutrality in the presidential election and endorsed antiwar candidate and New Politics spokesperson George McGovern. Moreover, the proportion of working-class people and unionists serving as convention delegates increased significantly in 1972, which, along with the entrance of more women, young people, and people of colour, made the event 'more representative' than the 1968 Chicago convention.[43]

Beyond Cold War ideology or cultural differences between the old left and the new, many labour leaders saw the reforms as a threat to their primary source of power in the selection of presidential nominees, which had relied on deals brokered in the smoke-filled rooms that the reformers were in the process of dismantling. Many unions' longstanding pattern of elite brokerage with party leaders appeared unable to adapt to new participatory institutions that would require unions to invest significant resources in the political education of their own rank and file. Other unions however, especially those historically subordinated within the AFL-CIO hierarchy, saw party reform as an opportunity to refashion the labour–liberal alliance at a moment when the power of conservative southern Democrats was waning. Indeed, their enthusiasm for a different Democratic Party helped resurrect 'a guaranteed job for all' in the 1972 party platform for the first time since Roosevelt introduced it in 1944.

However, as the party charter was being rolled out amidst the nomination of McGovern, counter-reformers began laying the groundwork for subverting the reform project. McGovern's landslide defeat in November provided the rationale the anti-New Politics forces needed to argue that the reformers and their project for transforming the party was reckless, and that their effort to 'Europeanize' the Democratic Party would continue to result in electoral disaster.[44]

Branding themselves as the Coalition for a Democratic Majority (CDM), counter-reformers of various stripes (southern Democrats, conservative labour leaders, cold warriors, elected officials and neoconservative intellectuals) made a well-publicized case that it was 'unrealistic to talk of the desirability – even the possibility – of a united, liberal "national" party driving out the impure and arousing new converts by trumpeting a sweeping national program'.[45] In contrast to the blueprint for a wholly new party, they argued, Democrats 'should continue to build along the lines of a federative, pluralistic party, in keeping with the character of American politics,' especially 'the peculiarly limited roles and duties of an American-style national political party'.[46]

The CDM's internal party lobbying campaign successfully unseated McGovern's choice for chair of the Democratic National Committee (DNC), weakened the New Politics' affirmative action provisions, and revised the party charter into a vehicle for institutionalizing the old order. As mandated by the 1972 McGovern convention, the party held its first-ever midterm policy conference in 1974, only to have its agenda limited by the DNC chair to approving the new constitution, which was rammed through in a single session with no allowance for amendments or motions to adjourn.

The result was, as some supporters observed, 'a piece of paper that, in effect, codifies the existing system – a loose coalition of state parties and interest groups,' which stood as 'testimony ... to the primacy of candidates over structure' in American politics.[47]

Skirmishes between reformers and their opponents continued to flare sporadically within the Democratic Party throughout the 1970s, especially around the fight to implement the 1972 platform resolution for guaranteed full employment.[48] But the New Politics movement had decisively lost the initiative with McGovern's devastating defeat and the dissipation of social movement activity outside the party. The structure of party federalism had imposed an all-or-nothing scenario on reformers. Failure to win the presidency prevented them from consolidating their victories and continuing the project of party transformation. While counter-reformers lacked the ability to fully roll back the clock on most of the reforms to presidential nominations, they weakened the guidelines for affirmative action, scrapped the mass membership scheme, and eventually restored automatic delegate status for top Democratic officials and officeholders under the guise of 'superdelegates' who were guaranteed a voice as unpledged voting delegates at national conventions. The upshot was that while reformers had permanently altered the process of presidential nomination, their larger vision for an 'activist' party organization was left unrealized.

THE SANDERS INSURGENCY AND 'OUR REVOLUTION'

The next phase of Democratic Party development is well known: amidst staggering landslide defeats in the presidential elections of 1980, 1984, and 1988, moderate and conservative Democrats grouped within the Democratic Leadership Council (DLC) waged a concerted campaign to move the party away from what they considered to be 'special interest groups' and toward the political centre, all in the name of 'saving' the party from its 'headlong dash into social democracy'.[49] In language reminiscent of the CDM during the previous decade, DLC leaders warned their fellow Democrats that 'we cannot afford to become a liberal party; our message must attract moderates and conservatives, as well'.[50] The DLC's neoliberal 'Third Way' placed the party's ideological emphasis on equality of opportunity, personal responsibility, and private sector initiative. This reorientation was evident in the governing strategy of the DLC's Bill Clinton as well as the presidential candidacy of Al Gore. Indeed, so effective was *this* transformation of the party that midway through President Barack Obama's first term, the DLC officially closed its office doors, declaring 'we had accomplished our mission'.[51]

The socialist surprise

The apparent hegemony of the Third Way in the Democratic Party made it all the more surprising that an independent senator and self-described socialist from Vermont could so effectively rattle the almost preordained status of Hillary Clinton as the party's standard bearer in the 2016 nomination contest. Beginning with only 4 per cent support among Democratic primary voters in March 2015, less than a year later Bernie Sanders had achieved near victories in the early Iowa and Nevada caucuses and scored a commanding 22-point win in the New Hampshire primary. These were followed with victories in ten other caucus states as well as nine primaries, including Wisconsin, Indiana, West Virginia and Michigan, the last of which the pollsters at *FiveThirtyEight* called 'one of the greatest upsets in modern political history' (and one that foreshadowed Clinton's rust belt difficulties in the general election).[52] All this occurred despite Clinton's advantage in fundraising (though Sanders raised money from more people), her near solid support from party establishment superdelegates, as well as DNC chair Debbie Wasserman Schultz's efforts to shield Clinton from criticism by scheduling originally only six debates (down from twenty in 2008) during weekends and other inconspicuous times. While probably not decisive, the anti-Sanders sentiment within the DNC (as illustrated in staff emails disclosed by Wikileaks) did not help Sanders either, except by forcing Wasserman Schultz's resignation.

In addition to the institutional disadvantages he largely overcame, Sanders' socialist moniker – a non-starter in the US politics since the first Red Scare after the First World War – also failed to spoil his candidacy. While his brand of democratic socialism amounted to little more than Scandinavian social democracy, his tenacious defence of an avowedly redistributionist agenda was a significant and positive departure in the context of bipartisan neoliberalism. By championing universal healthcare, a livable minimum wage, business regulation, and progressive taxation, Sanders returned to and expanded on Franklin Roosevelt's unrealized 'Second Bill of Rights' – often explicitly – positioning himself as both an outsider capable of breaking elite control over Washington as well as a legitimate successor to a venerable, if now marginal, Democratic tradition.[53]

The reasons underlying Sanders' surprising success are difficult to pin down definitively, and in any case probably do not reduce to a simple explanation. Structural and conjunctural factors include decades of rising material inequality, the lingering effects of the Great Recession, the impact of Occupy Wall Street, and the disappoints of the Obama administration as well as the near dynastic coronation of Clinton despite a decimation of

Democratic officeholders over the course of the Obama presidency.[54] While few saw Sanders coming, his message found a significant amount of traction that sent shockwaves through activist circles, the news media, trade unions and, particularly, the Clinton campaign organization.[55]

However, narratives that cast the nomination contest as a battle for the ideological soul of the Democratic Party are not clearly borne out by the primary entrance and exit polling data. While self-described conservative and moderate Democrats preferred Clinton by a ratio of 61 to 36 per cent, liberal Democrats still preferred Clinton, if by a far narrower margin of 53 to 46 per cent. What's more, voters who identified as 'very liberal' split their support evenly between the candidates: 50 per cent for Sanders; 49 per cent for Clinton. Evidently, while accepting the limits of plotting ideology along a unidimensional scale, increasing liberalism among Democratic voters did not correlate with candidate preference as well as one might have expected. And it is worth emphasizing that the first figure reported above indicates that more than a third of self-described moderate and conservative primary voters cast ballots for Bernie.[56]

More than ideology, income, education, or any other single factor, support in the Sanders-Clinton contest split along partisan lines. At the aggregate level, Sanders did particularly well among young, white voters who identified as independent and prioritized income inequality as a top issue. Accordingly, Sanders did best in contests where state laws allowed independents to participate or easily register as Democrats, but came up short in states where independent voters were excluded or found registration processes restrictive, such as Pennsylvania and New York. In 2016, however, independents made up only 22 per cent of the Democratic primary voters, the vast majority of whom were diehard Democratic partisans, two-thirds of which supported Clinton.[57] It is not very surprising, then, that Sanders did relatively poorly among older voters of colour, whose degree of Democratic partisanship far outstrips their rate of ideological self-identification as liberal.[58] To be sure, aggregates can obscure important underlying trends, such as the fact that within the millennial age cohort, support for Sanders was higher among Latino/a, Asian American, and African American voters than among whites.[59] But for all the commentary about the purported favourability of millennials toward socialism, a Harvard Institute of Politics youth poll conducted in the spring of 2016 found that, despite Sanders being their most popular presidential candidate, a majority of 18- to 29-year-olds reject both capitalism *and* socialism, with capitalism getting the plurality of support.[60]

These figures serve two important purposes. On the one hand, they serve as an antidote to the longstanding article of faith among data-driven political analysts that demography is destiny, and the complacent view of politics that optimistically looks to generational change as the guarantor of a brighter political future.[61] While rooted in history and political economy, political identities are constructed through political, social, and cultural processes and the institutions and narratives elites, social groups, and everyday people create to try to deal with them. They are not simple reflections of 'objective' conditions. Additionally, demographic change does not automatically translate into increasing numbers of voters, as those groups projected to be growing fastest are the most likely to encounter structural and circumstantial barriers to voting.

On the other hand, the figures serve to refute the commonplace assumption that Sanders' appeal was limited by the hegemony of Democrats' liberal ideology, which brooks no dissent, especially from an avowedly socialist perspective. On the contrary, it is more productive to interpret the data as evidence of the party's lack of ideological coherence. In an era where concern is growing about polarized partisanship, it has become all too easy to project a mirror-image relationship between the parties as the Republicans, by all measures, have shifted *dramatically* to the right and Democrats have moved only modestly to the left since the 1970s (due mostly to the decline of its southern conservative wing).[62] Whether examining the mass electorate, activist and donor networks, or elite officeholders, Republicans display much greater consistency in identifying as ideologically conservative and viewing politics in terms of clashing political principles, whereas Democrats display a much greater array of perspectives, ranging from very liberal to conservative (with a plurality of moderates), and see politics as a means of securing concrete benefits for target populations.[63]

The absence of a unifying liberal vision in the Democratic Party was perhaps best exemplified in Clinton's attempt to paint Sanders as a single-issue candidate. As she addressed one campaign rally:

> If we broke up the big banks tomorrow … would that end racism? Would that end sexism? Would that end discrimination against the LGBT community? Would that make people feel more welcoming to immigrants overnight?[64]

Clinton's disingenuousness notwithstanding, her statement is indicative of the group dynamics of the Democratic coalition, as well as the limitations of group coalitional politics when united by party rather than worldview. While the laundry list of Democratic issue items has expanded (for good reason) and become more internally compatible over time, it has not been articulated within a new vision of society where most, if not all, these agenda items might be realized. Instead, groups' discrete demands are left to compete against each other for recognition and influence within a diverse field of separate identities.

The absence of any animating, unifying liberal ideology in the Democratic Party is nothing new, of course. As we have seen, it is an outcome that has been produced deliberately by sets of historical actors, including preventing the creation of internal party forums that could ostensibly forge such a partisan ideology. The Sanders insurgency did not so much represent a clash between competing worldviews within the Democratic Party than an attempt to inject a coherent, class-based worldview into an environment that has traditionally been hostile to all-encompassing perspectives. Party federalism and the Democratic group-interest coalition militate against such a unified movement. Whether or not a partisan clash between insiders and outsiders can be elaborated into an ideological contest over the kind of society we want to build, this is a project that requires sustained organization spanning more than one electoral cycle.

Continuing 'the political revolution' by 'transforming the party'

Clinton's narrow loss of the presidency to Donald Trump spurred widespread speculation that the Democratic Party had nominated the wrong candidate. It is impossible to know what would have happened had Sanders prevailed in the nomination fight. However, Clinton's defeat certainly did open greater space for Sanders Democrats to make the case that the 'millions of people who voted for Mr. Trump did so because they are sick and tired of the economic, political and media status quo'.[65] Accordingly, Sanders and his post-campaign successor organization, Our Revolution, have launched an ambitious project meant to continue the 'political revolution' galvanized by his candidacy, and to eventually 'transform the Democratic Party'.

Rolling out Our Revolution in a webcast to many thousands of supporters, Sanders dedicated the organization to aid progressive candidates 'fighting at the grassroots level for changes in their local school boards, in their city councils, in their state legislatures and in their representation in Washington'.[66] Formally established as a 501(c)(4) non-profit social welfare organization, Our Revolution functions as a candidate-oriented fundraising vehicle. It is allowed to raise unlimited amounts of money from undisclosed recipients (though its Board of Directors has made it a policy to disclose the names of donors contributing more than $250 on its website), but it is not allowed to engage in partisan political activity as its 'major purpose'. This means that while the organization can endorse candidates for office and raise and use resources for their election, Our Revolution cannot coordinate its activities with candidate organizations directly. This has led some to criticize Our Revolution's status as a non-profit rather than a traditional political action committee, especially after the defeat of Tim Canova in a high-profile primary challenge against former DNC chair Wasserman Schultz in the summer of 2016. Due to the inability to strategically coordinate with Canova's campaign, Our Revolution invested itself in redundant phone banking and failed to schedule an expected appearance from Sanders, who only listed Canova in a string of sixty personal endorsements.[67] The organization also came under fire from a number of young staffers who resigned in protest after the leadership appointment went to Sanders' campaign manager Jeff Weaver, whose decision to file the organization's designation as a non-profit appeared to jeopardize its mission.[68] Normally, 501(c)(4)s have functioned as 'dark money' channels for large, multimillion dollar corporate funds to be used for issue and candidate advertisements. However, Our Revolution's website boasts 140,000 individual donations during its first six months of operation, with a $22 dollar average contribution.

Notwithstanding this rocky start, Our Revolution has persisted and stabilized with a board of directors composed of civil rights, human rights, and labour leaders, as well as environmental activists. The organization has had a modest success rate of candidate endorsements, backing winning candidates in just over half of more than one hundred contests in 2016, and a third of winning candidates in 2017 contests as of this writing (June), mostly at city and state levels.[69]

The continuation of the Sanders movement in the post-election period also spilled over into what was easily the most contested fight for control of the DNC chair, a position few usually pay close attention to outside party officialdom. Keith Ellison's stated intention to 'transform the party' from the grassroots level up, as well as his embrace by leading Senate Democrats, rattled many officeholders and DNC members, triggering frantic behind-the-scenes efforts from within the Obama White House to offer up attractive candidates to counter the influence of the Sanders wing of the party, which they feared would push the party in too liberal a direction.[70] While Obama's pick for DNC chair, former Labor Secretary Tom Perez, narrowly prevailed, Perez's creation of a new deputy chair position for Ellison suggests that the new chair may see the path to party unity and electoral success as requiring some recognition, rather than suppression, of the party left. Perez's own partnership with Sanders in a 'come together and fight back' tour around the country seems to confirm this. It is also worth noting in this context that the radical reform agenda of the New Politics movement received the pragmatic acquiesce of, rather than principled support from, then DNC chair Lawrence O'Brien. Chairpersons' actions as well as their inactions can be of enormous importance to the internal balance of party forces.

However, for the Sanders movement, 'transforming the party' evidently does not mean the same thing it did for reform activists who invoked the same rallying cry in the past. In contrast to the New Politics movement, few Sanders Democrats have suggest a wholesale restructuring of the party apparatus to facilitate new forms of grassroots engagement or community organization, or that new party mechanisms must be put in place to hold Democratic officeholders accountable to principles determined democratically and prioritized in the party platform.[71] In fact, in his post-campaign book, *Our Revolution*, Sanders makes no mention of Democratic Party organization in his blueprint for a transformative agenda.[72]

True enough, Sanders supporters' ire for the party's superdelegates and the artificially inflated lead they gave Clinton in the nomination contest resulted in the formation of a new internal party 'unity commission' to explore possible rule changes for future conventions. But it is more likely that the commission will tinker with primary rules than produce game-changing reforms on the scale of its McGovern-Fraser predecessor in the 1970s. For all the surface level similarity between 1968 and 2016 – when the chosen successor of a sitting Democratic president, preferred by party insiders over a left-leaning candidate, loses in a close election – the experience of the Sanders supporters through the campaign and convention was quite unlike that experienced by antiwar activists nearly fifty years ago. Due in part to the lasting legacy of the reforms engineered by their New Politics predecessors, Sanders supporters fought on a playing field that, while certainly tilted against an independent insurgent, was not literally closed off to them, as it was in 1968. While a fanciful scenario, it is difficult to imagine that had Sanders swept the primaries and racked up more delegates than Clinton, the superdelegates would have dared to cast their votes as a bloc to swing the nomination to Clinton. Such a manoeuvre would have plunged the party into crisis, assisting Trump's path to victory and exiling the Democrats to the electoral wilderness. Had Sanders' delegate lead exceeded the 15 per cent margin of superdelegate votes at the national convention, even this last ditch effort would have failed to deny him the nomination.

Rather than transform the party by reforming its structure, the Sanders movement has emphasized shifting the internal balance of power in government by filling local, state and federal offices with progressives, whether under the Democratic label or not, united by a common policy agenda. This is an implicit acknowledgement that what the left must do now is organize a widespread power base inside and outside the state, not get bound up in complex negotiations over delegate selection devices in which it lacks the requisite influence to prevail. What remains to be seen is how far a candidate-oriented fundraising vehicle such as Our Revolution can carry forward the momentum of the Sanders insurgency. Its chances will be improved if movement forces and partisan forces continue to push in the same direction in opposition to the Trump administration. However, the true test of left power in the Democratic coalition will only come when Democrats inevitably retake control of the federal government, when movement and partisan forces are more likely to diverge.[73]

CONCLUSION

Given the preceding analysis, it is theoretically conceivable that a widespread, well-organized left movement could penetrate the Democratic Party, exerting significant influence within state and local organizations, and perhaps even having an important presence in national nominating contests. Such a hypothetical scenario, while straining the party's financial dependence on capital, might result in important changes in the Democratic Party brand, its programme, and perhaps even public policy. History has shown that the permeable structure of the party can be leveraged by well-organized political groups, especially during moments of sharp party crisis, whether they work through the party from below or take advantage of momentary openings at the top. Both strategies have their risks and downsides, to be sure. But it seems unjustifiable to dismiss the possibility out of hand with a reference to the Democrats' unchanging nature as a 'bourgeois party'. While the Democratic Party is a complex organization that cannot be transformed into a working-class socialist party, it is not necessary impenetrable to such forces should they organize outside it and enter. The party may court the bourgeoisie, but it cannot close the door on uninvited guests.

However, even if left power could be achieved in the Democratic Party – and that is a big if – it will not in and of itself serve the purposes of the socialist project of strengthening the class capacities of everyday working people. Ironically, it is precisely the thinness of Democratic Party organization that makes it so penetrable on the one hand, and renders it so unsuitable for democratizing purposes on the other. The party, from the local to the national level, is not built for participatory democracy. The experience of the New Politics reform movement suggests the practical limits to transforming the party organization in ways that facilitate community engagement, capacity building, and internal party democracy. This means that while a strong left might make effective use of the Democratic Party for winning seats in government, the Democratic Party cannot be used to build the left.

Nor is this participatory, organizational dimension merely a superfluous addendum, something that need not bother those who understand left political power as primarily about advancing a better policy agenda. Those who today espouse a 'Tea Party of the left' fundamentally misunderstand the asymmetry between left and right-wing movements and the incommensurability between the foundations of right and left-wing political power.[74] The Tea Party played an important role in the sweeping Republican gains in the 2010 congressional elections, as well as shifting the ideological centre of House Republican members – freshmen and incumbents alike – far to the right. But once the uprising of angry white Republican activists had been effectively put to use by Fox News and DC-based, free market PACs, the hundreds of genuine grassroots Tea Party organizations that had sprouted up across the country in the wake of Obama's election were left to atrophy. The uprising was 'successful' because it aligned with the goals of well-funded ideologues intent on transforming the GOP, who in turn posed as spokespersons of a mass movement. But these self-selected leaders were unaccountable to the leagues of activists for whom they claimed to speak, nor were their priorities – privatizing Social Security and eliminating Medicare – even compatible with the desires of the mostly older civic activists who composed the Tea Party rank and file.[75] While the sentiment of rolling back the horrendous Republican Party and stopping the Trump agenda in its tracks is understandable, it speaks volumes about the elite orientation of the American left that such a proposal is going viral as 'model' for progressive activists during the Trump era. While such a project could deliver Democratic electoral victories, it is unlikely to be accompanied by any political empowerment for constituents themselves. And without a new politics, new policies are likely to remain elusive.

Given the present insurmountable odds facing any third party project in the US, this leaves the left in a difficult spot. Strategies to deal with this dilemma are beyond the scope of this essay – indeed, any one essay. But one productive development that is implicit in much of the post-Sanders activism is for the left to divorce the twin tasks traditionally assigned to the working-class party, separating the organization of the proletariat into a class from the imperative to win governmental power. Both are indispensable activities that cannot proceed in isolation from each other: organizing workers as voters does not in itself build class capacities; class power that fails to become state power also fails to change the world. For third party advocates, these twin tasks would be married in a labour-based socialist party. In the context of the really existing USA, however, this is not a viable option.

In the post-Sanders moment, what is needed is for the left to begin to build a working-class party surrogate: a geographically rooted network of mass-member civic organizations, oriented toward building a base within working-class communities and labour unions that can also act as an effective independent pressure group on the Democratic Party. Social movements, while invaluable forms of social power, are no substitute for mass-based organizations and inevitably decline. Such an organizational network must focus its activities around concrete demands that are responsive to working-class needs such as expanding public institutions and decommodified access to basic resources, which challenge the logic of neoliberal social and economic policy. Precisely because this effort is not premised on exiting the Democratic Party to launch of third-party alternative, it would avoid the pitfalls experienced by the 1990s Labor Party project of expending precious resources in negotiating state ballot access and the spoiler problem that can result in Republican victories.[76] It would also provide space for dissident voices inside unions, many of whom vocally protested their leaderships' undemocratic endorsement of Clinton over Sanders in the 2016 primaries. Moreover, the permanent existence of this structure would provide a year-round centre for working-class community life rather than the typical American party organization that is reanimated only with the coming of campaign season. Its focus on educating and developing its constituents would empower them to act collectively, which would include engaging in the electoral process, but would not be limited to it.

Most importantly, such an organization would break from the illusory notion underpinning Green Party strategy and other third-party perspectives that presumes that a left constituency and electoral potential already exists in a dormant state in American society, awaiting only activation by a sufficiently progressive platform or candidate.[77] If the left is ever to enjoy widespread popularity, a broad-based left constituency must be created. The second annual People's Summit, which drew some 4,000 activists to Chicago in June 2017, including many from the swelling ranks of Democratic Socialists of America, is a very positive development and serves the vital purpose of galvanizing a collective sense of purpose, strength and enthusiasm. But when dispersed across the half-million political jurisdictions that exist in the US, that cadre, however essential, remains a minority incapable of shifting the balance of social and political power on its own, however militant it may be. Victories that may occur in the San Francisco Bay Area or in New York City are significant and can figure as important showcases that educate and inspire movement groups elsewhere. But as the history of the postwar labour-left shows us, gaining only regional footholds in a federated polity mitigates the ability to translate hard-won electoral successes into lasting policy achievements that institutionalize a more favourable basis for future struggles nationwide.

To avoid repeating the past, the American left has to build *extensive* power across the country, especially in places where it lacks pre-existing enthusiasts. This strategy entails shifting from what Jane McAlevey has astutely distinguished as the difference between mobilizing and organizing, and necessarily requires resurrecting the lost art of political persuasion – a technique that has atrophied with the rise of data-driven activation email blasts, paper membership organizations, and the moralizing tactics of the left's online outrage industry.[78] While the extent of Trump's working-class base has been exaggerated, Sanders has himself demonstrated in post-election televised town hall events that scapegoating perspectives found amongst alienated midwestern workers are convertible into class-based grievances. Such an enterprise requires going beyond fundraising organizations, non-profits, and media-based PACs. How such an organizing project could be undertaken on a mass scale without the institutional resources of a new labour movement is admittedly difficult to envisage. But beginning from a perspective that accepts the need to build the base will minimize misplaced hopes in Trump's own self-destruction, the 2018 elections, or finding the next Bernie Sanders.

This working-class organizational network implies that the left break from understanding political parties as vehicles emergent from civil society for the conquest of government. This theory of party fuels the perspective that the major parties fail to perform this task in a democratic and representative way, and thus should be supplemented or displaced by a different kind of party, organized from below. The truth of the matter is that American parties are products of state actors, invented for the purposes of facilitating officeholders' legitimacy to advance their preferred agenda and cultivating a base for reelection. Their age, endurance, flexibility, and legal status make them akin to organs of the state itself, straddling a semi-private, semi-public boundary that renders them more similar to 'public utilities' than civil society organizations.[79] Their hollow structures and campaign operations help organize the bourgeoisie and disorganize the working class. Yet, their nebulous status between civil society and the state make their internal politics rather sensitive to changes in the societal balance of power and prone to contradiction. Historically, the terrain of American parties – beset by competing group demands, factional conflict, and no shortage of palace intrigue – has been a flood land of insurgent movements. Rarely in the vanguard, American parties have nonetheless been at the centre of past transformative political projects – emancipatory and reactionary – that have shifted the fundamental dynamics of the political economy.

Accordingly, from a strategic point of view, the existing major political parties in the US should be considered as sites of class struggle, just as the rest of the governing apparatus has been conceptualized for many on the left since the days of the 1970s state debate. While it is true that we lack the kind of party capable of playing the lead role in organizing the working class, our response must be to invent extra-party organizations that compensate for this deficiency, which develop people's potential to think, strategize, and act collectively, and can engage strategically and effectively inside the Democratic Party.

The burden of the American left is to build the power of the working class without the assistance of the working-class party. When it comes to translating that power into votes, and votes into seats in government, which is necessarily part of the struggle, we have very few options. The party we need is not the party we have. That will continue to be a constraint under which we labour to make our own history.

NOTES

1   Robin Archer, *Why Is There No Labor Party in the United States?* Princeton: Princeton University Press, 2007. See also, Seymour Martin Lipset and Gary Marks, *It Didn't Happen Here: Why Socialism Failed in the United States*, New York: W. W. Norton, 2000.

2   Barry Eidlin, 'Why Is There No Labor Party in the United States? Political Articulation and the Canadian Comparison, 1932 to 1948', *American Sociological Review* 81(3), 2016.

3   John F. Bibby and L. Sandy Maisel, *Two Parties – Or More? The American Party System*, Second Edition, Boulder: Westview Press, 2003, pp. 70-2.

4   See Kim Moody, 'From Realignment to Reinforcement', *Jacobin*, 25 January 2017, available at www.jacobinmag.com. Cf, the special issue, 'The Party We Need', *Jacobin* 23(Fall), 2016.

5   G. William Domhoff, *Who Rules America? The Triumph of the Corporate Rich*, Seventh Edition, New York: McGraw-Hill, 2010.

6   Lance Selfa, *The Democrats: A Critical History*, Chicago: Haymarket Press, 2008, p. 18.

7   Selfa, *The Democrats*, p. 18.

8   Thomas Ferguson, *Golden Rule: The Investment Theory of Party Competition and the Logic of Money-Driven Political Systems*, Chicago: The University of Chicago Press, 1995, pp. 17-110.

9   See Jacob S. Hacker and Paul Pierson, 'Business Power and Social Policy: Employers and the Formation of the American Welfare State', *Politics & Society* 30(2), 2002.

10   Larry M. Bartels, *Unequal Democracy: The Political Economy of the New Gilded Age*, Princeton: Princeton University Press, 2008, p. 73, Figure 3.2; Nicholas Carnes and Noam Lupu, 'It's time to bust the myth: Most Trump voters were not working class', *Washington Post*, 6 June 2017.

11   Larry M. Bartels, *Unequal Democracy: The Political Economy of the New Gilded Age*, Second Edition, Princeton: Princeton University Press, 2016, ch. 2.

12   James Madison, *Federalist 10*, available at www.avalon.law.yale.edu; Richard Hofstadter, *The Idea of a Party System: The Rise of Legitimate Opposition in the United States*, Berkeley: University of California Press, 1969, p. 2.

13   Maurice Duverger, *Political Parties: Their Organization and Activity in the Modern State*, Translated by Barbara and Robert North, London: Methuen, 1964, p. xxvii.

14   John H. Aldrich, *Why Parties? A Second Look*, Chicago: The University of Chicago Press, 2011; Martin Shefter, *Political Parties and the State: The American Historical Experience*, Princeton: Princeton University Press, 1994, pp. 4-6; Leon D. Epstein, *Political Parties in Western Democracies*, New Brunswick: Transaction Publishers, 1980 [1967].

15   Cedric de Leon, 'Vicarious Revolutionaries: Martial Discourse and the Origins of Mass Party Competition in the United States, 1789-1848', *Studies in American Political Development* 24(1), 2010.

16   Aldrich, *Why Parties?* pp. 120, 128.

17   E. E. Schattschneider, *Party Government*, New Brunswick: Transaction Publishers, 2004 [1942], p. 164.

18   Robert Harmel, Matthew Giebert, and Kenneth Janda, *American Parties in Context: Comparative and Historical Analysis*, New York: Routledge, 2016.

19   Schattschneider, *Party Government*, p. 129.

20   Roberto Michels, *Political Parties: A Sociological Study of the Oligarchical Tendencies of Modern Democracy*, Translated by Eden and Cedar Paul, New York: The Free Press, 1962.

21   Leon Epstein, *Political Parties in the American Mold*, Madison: The University of Wisconsin Press, 1986; Robert Mickey, *Paths Out of Dixie: The Democratization of Authoritarian Enclaves in America's Deep South, 1944-1972*, Princeton: Princeton University Press, 2015.

22   Douglas D. Roscoe and Shannon Jenkins, *Local Party Organizations in the Twenty-First Century*, Albany: State University of New York Press, 2016, p. 52.

23   Marjorie Randon Hershey, *Party Politics in America*, Seventeenth Edition, New York: Routledge, 2017, p. 59.

24   Epstein, *Political Parties in the American Mold*; Alan Ware, *The American Direct Primary: Party Institutionalization and Transformation in the North*, Cambridge: Cambridge University Press, 2002; John F. Reynolds, *The Demise of the American Convention System, 1880-1911*, New York: Cambridge University Press, 2006.

25   David Karol, 'Political Parties in American Political Development', in Richard M. Valelly, Suzanne Mettler and Robert C. Lieberman, eds, *The Oxford Handbook of American Political Development*, Oxford: Oxford University Press, 2016, pp. 473-91.

26   Eric Schickler, *Racial Realignment: The Transformation of American Liberalism, 1932-1965*, Princeton: Princeton University Press, 2016. See also, David Karol, *Party Position Change in American Politics: Coalition Management*, New York: Cambridge University Press, 2009, pp. 102-33.

27   Ira Katznelson, *Fear Itself: The New Deal and the Origins of Our Time*, New York: Liveright, 2013, especially pp. 133-224.

28   Carlo Invernizzi-Accetti and Fabio Wolkenstein, 'The Crisis of Party Democracy, Cognitive Mobilization, and the Case for Making Parties More Deliberative', *American Political Science Review* (11)1, 2017.

29   Theda Skocpol, *Diminished Democracy: From Membership to Management in American Civic Life*, Norman: The University of Oklahoma Press, 2003.

30   Skocpol, *Diminished Democracy*; Robert D. Putnam, *Bowling Alone: The Collapse and Revival of American Community*, New York: Simon & Schuster, 2000.

31   Seth Ackerman, 'A Blueprint for a New Party', *Jacobin* 23(Fall), 2016, p. 109.

32   Committee on Political Parties, *Toward a More Responsible Two-Party System*, New York: Reinhart, 1950, p. 3.

33   Committee on Political Parties, *Toward a Responsible Two-Party System*, p. 1.

34   Sean J. Savage, 'To Purge or Not to Purge: Hamlet Harry and the Dixiecrats, 1948–1952', *Presidential Studies Quarterly* 27(4), 1997.

35   Commission on Party Structure and Delegate Selection, *Mandate for Reform*, Box 157, Folder: Mandate for Reform, Papers of George S. McGovern, Seely G. Mudd Manuscript Library, Princeton University, Princeton, New Jersey.

36   Report of the Grass Roots Participation Subcommittee, 22 August 1969, Box 149.C.12.3B, Folder: Democratic Party Reform, 1969, Donald M. Fraser Papers, Minnesota History Center, Saint Paul, Minnesota.

37   Testimony of Stephen Jelin, Box 13, Folder: 4A Detroit Hearing 4/26/69, Democratic National Committee Records, National Archives, Washington, DC.

38   Keynote Address of Harold Hughes, Box 3, Folder: National Committee Reform, DNC Records; Testimony of Paul Schrade, Box 16, Folder: LA Hearings 6/21/69, DNC Records.

39   Testimony of Theodore Sorensen, Box 13, Folder: 3A New York Hearing 5/3/69, DNC Records.

40   Testimony of Robert Toal, Box 13, Folder: 4A Detroit Hearing 4/26/69, DNC Records.

41   Letter from James O'Hara and Donald Fraser to undisclosed recipients, Box 44, Folder: Democratic Party, O'Hara Rules Commission, Formation of Commission, Finances, James O'Hara Collection, Bentley Library, University of Michigan, Ann Arbor, Michigan.

42   Thomas E. Cronin, 'On the American Presidency: A Conversation with James MacGregor Burns', *Presidential Studies Quarterly* 16(3), 1986, p. 536.

43   John W. Soule and Wilma E. McGrath, 'A Comparative Study of Presidential Nomination Conventions: The Democrats 1968 and 1972', *American Journal of Political Science* 19(3), 1975, p. 502.

44   Coalition for a Democratic Majority, 'Resolution on Charter', Box 47, Folder: Democratic Party Charter Commission, Drafts and Background Material 2, O'Hara Collection.

45   Coalition for a Democratic Majority, 'An Analysis of the Draft Charter for the Democratic Party', Box 48, Folder: Democratic Party, Coalition for a Democratic Majority, Correspondence, October 1973–November 1974, O'Hara Collection.

46   CDM, 'Analysis of the Draft Charter'; Ben Wattenberg, quoted in Penn Kemble and Josh Muravchik, 'Balancing the Democrats', *The New Leader*, 20 January 1975, Box 48, Folder: Coalition for a Democratic Majority, Affirmative Action 1, O'Hara Collection.

47   Robert S. Boyd, 'Charter Nails Down Reforms But Is Short of Dems' Goals', *Detroit Free Press*, 9 December 1974; Christopher Lydon, 'The Democrats and Reform', *New York Times*, 1 December 1974.

48   See Paul Heideman, 'It's Their Party', *Jacobin*, 4 February 2016; and Adam Hilton, 'Searching for New Politics', *Jacobin*, 16 February 2016.

49   Al From, *The New Democrats and the Return to Power*, New York: Palgrave Macmillan, 2013, p. 173.

50   From, *The New Democrats*, pp. 50-1.

51   From, *The New Democrats*, p. 255. See also, Curtis Atkins, 'Forging a New Democratic Party: The Politics of the Third Way from Clinton to Obama', PhD diss., York University, 2015.

52   Harry Enten, 'What the Stunning Bernie Sanders Win in Michigan Means', *FiveThirtyEight*, 9 March 2016, available at www.fivethirtyeight.com.

53   Bernie Sanders, 'On Democratic Socialism in the United States', 19 November 2015, available at www.berniesanders.com.

54   Between 2008 and 2016, Democrats lost 63 members of the House of Representatives, 11 senators, 13 governors, and 947 state legislative seats. While it is typical to see a two-term president's party lose seats down ballot, Obama's losses are greater than any modern predecessor. See Edward-Isaac Dovere, 'Democrats in the Wilderness', *Politico*, January/February 2017.

55   Jonathan Allen and Amie Parnes, *Shattered: Inside Hillary Clinton's Doomed Campaign*, New York: Crown, 2017.

56   David A. Hopkins, 'Party Asymmetry in the 2016 Presidential Nomination Contest', Paper presented at Annual Meeting of the American Political Science Association, Philadelphia, PA, September 1-4, 2016.

57   See William G. Mayer, 'The Nominations: The Road to a Much-Disliked General Election', in Michael Nelson, ed., *The Elections of 2016*, Thousand Oaks: CQ Press, 2017, pp. 44-5, Table 2.6.

58   As Grossman and Hopkins report, 'According to media exit polls, 95 percent of African Americans supported Obama in the 2008 presidential election, even as only 28 percent of black voters identified as liberal. Similarly, just 25 percent of Latino voters in 2008 considered themselves to be liberal, while 67 percent voted for Obama'. Matt Grossman and David A. Hopkins, *Asymmetric Politics: Ideological Republicans and Group Interest Democrats*, New York: Oxford University Press, 2016, p. 45.

59   Farai Chideya, 'Unlike Their Parents, Black Millennials Aren't A Lock For Clinton', *FiveThirtyEight*, 20 September 2016.

60   Harvard Institute of Politics, *Spring 2016 Poll*, 25 April 2016, available at iop.harvard.edu.

61   Barry Eidlin, 'Demographics Are Not Destiny', *Jacobin*, 14 December 2016.

62   See, for instance, Nolan McCarty, Keith T. Poole, and Howard Rosenthal, *Polarized America: The Dance of Ideology and Unequal Riches*, Second Edition, Cambridge: MIT Press, 2016.

63   Grossman and Hopkins, *Asymmetric Politics*, p. 29, Figure 2-2.

64   Clinton, quoted in Amanda Marcotte and Moe Tkacik, 'Hillary Clinton Suggested Breaking Up the Banks Won't End Racism and Sexism. Is She Right?' *In These Times*, 11 March 2016, available at www.inthesetimes.com.

65   Bernie Sanders, 'Where the Democrats Go From Here', *New York Times*, 11 November 2016.

66   Sanders, quoted in Eliza Newlin Carney, 'Nonprofit Structure Backfires on "Our Revolution"', *The American Prospect*, 1 September 2016.

67   Clare Foran, 'How the Political Revolution Failed Tim Canova', *The Atlantic*, 30 August 2016.

68   Alan Rappeport and Yamiche Alcindor, 'Bernie Sanders's New Political Group Is Met by Staff Revolt', *New York Times*, 24 August 2016.

69   See www.ourrevolution.org.

70   Jonathan Martin and Maggie Haberman, 'Democrats' Leadership Fight Pits West Wing Against Left Wing', *New York Times*, 22 November 2016.

71   However, the Massachusetts chapter of Our Revolution did recently propose at the state Democratic Party convention that party resources be withheld from candidates who failed to govern in accordance with the state's progressive platform. The proposal was ruled out of order. See Theo Anderson, 'Sanders Backers Plant Left-Wing Flag in Massachusetts Democratic Party', *In These Times*, 6 June 2017.

72   Bernie Sanders, *Our Revolution: A Future to Believe In*, New York: Thomas Dunne Books, 2016.

73   See Michael T. Heaney and Fabio Rojas, *Party in the Street: The Antiwar Movement and the Democratic Party after 9/11*, New York: Cambridge University Press, 2015.

74   Ezra Levin, Leah Greenberg, and Angel Padilla, 'To Stop Trump, Democrats Can Learn From the Tea Party', *New York Times*, 2 January 2017; Indivisible Guide, available at www.indivisibleguide.com.

75   Theda Skocpol and Vanessa Williamson, *The Tea Party and the Remaking of Republican Conservatism*, New York: Oxford University Press, 2016.

76   Mark Dudzic and Adolph Reed Jr, 'The Crisis of Labour and the Left in the United States', *Socialist Register 2015: Transforming Classes*, London: Merlin Press, 2014.

77   Dudzic and Reed, 'The Crisis of Labour and Left', p. 359.

78   Jane McAlevey, *No Shortcuts: Organizing for Power in the New Gilded Age*, New York: Oxford University Press, 2016.

79   This idea is elaborated in Epstein, *Political Parties in the American Mold*, pp. 155-99.

FAKE DEMOCRACY, BAD NEWS

NATALIE FENTON AND DES FREEDMAN

Media and democracy, like Cagney and Lacey or Starsky and Hutch, are inseparable. You just can't have one without the other. The free exchange of ideas, information, and symbols that nourish citizens and replenish the system as a whole have long been seen as a central foundation of democratic societies. Indeed a complex normative paraphernalia has emerged to describe the key responsibilities placed on media in the emergence and sustenance of democracy: as an independent watchdog and monitor of unchecked power, a tribune of the people, a defender of minorities, a fourth estate, and a public sphere. Free media are said to provide the oxygen, the lubrication or indeed the sinews of a fully functioning and robust democracy.[1]

Yet in those liberal democracies of the west where this vocabulary is most deeply entrenched, we are seeing quite the opposite: a media that all too often preys on the vulnerable and bows down before the powerful; a media whose noble crusade for truth and justice has been replaced by a carnival of gossip and spectacle; a media that demonstrates a commitment to consumer, rather than popular, sovereignty; a media that is no longer an outlier but a constitutive part of class rule; a media that has adopted the mantras of the free market rather than the difficult practices involved in ensuring free expression, political participation and democratic renewal. The result has been a growing loss of authority and legitimacy. In Europe, the only media sector that is trusted by a majority of the population is radio, while the trust of ordinary Americans in the media has fallen from 53 per cent of citizens in 1997 to only 32 per cent in 2016.[2] In 2017, the Edelman Trust Barometer reported that the media was distrusted in 82 per cent of the 28 countries they surveyed, and it had dropped to an all-time low in 17 of those countries. Traditional media showed the steepest decline.[3]

This collapse in trust is far from unique, and is related to the same backlash against entrenched interests that has also eaten into the credibility of neoliberal political parties and politicians. While politicians and the media often fight it out for the last place in the trust stakes, business and NGOs are also tarred by the same brush. Given that the mainstream media are seen to be ever more closely entangled with elite power, so are they also implicated in the same mire of corruption and scandal.

This is part of a wider narrative about the degeneration of the liberal 'centre' and its failure both to stand up to, and to distinguish itself from, the market forces that have eviscerated, evacuated, hollowed out, reined in, commodified, trivialized and generally contaminated those spaces with which democracy has been traditionally associated. Of course, it is neoliberal forces, rather than liberal democracy more generally, that are most frequently associated with this degeneration. For millions of people, it is the icy calculation of neoliberal logic and the narrow instrumentalism of allegedly self-correcting markets that has ridden roughshod over permanent jobs, organic communities, egalitarian structures, and democratic aspirations. The emphasis on economic efficiency has depoliticized much government decision-making, transforming social, political, and moral dilemmas into technical and managerial problems, leaving little room for public participation.

With the veneer of liberal watchdog now stretched perilously thin across the mainstream media, it should come as no surprise that neoliberal rationality has been so successful in occupying the terrain of the liberal centre. Rather than the 2008 global financial crisis spurring the questioning of the logic of global capitalism, we saw its logic extend. Austerity policies became a normalized solution to the crisis wherein, as Blyth says:

> … those at the bottom are expected to pay disproportionately for a problem created by those at the top, and when those at the top actively eschew any responsibility for that problem by blaming the state for their mistakes, not only will squeezing the bottom not produce enough revenue to fix things, it will produce an even more polarized and politicized society in which the conditions for a sustainable politics of dealing with more debt and less growth are undermined. Populism, nationalism and calls for the return of 'God and gold' in equal doses are what unequal austerity generates …[4]

Unemployment, high levels of personal debt, extreme poverty, and inequality feature heavily in this particular post-crash moment. As governments seek to manage their deficits, the protective mechanisms of welfare that remain shrouded by the spectre of democracy too often end up excluding, rather than supporting, those in need. In England between June 2010 and March 2016, welfare reforms enacted deductions of £26 billion in UK social security and tax credits spending with 'deficit reduction' being the primary goal of government.[5] Local authorities in England are currently dealing with a scheduled 40 per cent cut in core funding from central government. In response, councils and other public agencies seek to further outsource and share services as a means of reducing costs, detaching these services from democratic processes and depoliticizing decisions about public welfare and the public good.

The impact of the crisis has been especially marked for the poor and minority communities as well as for young people whose experiences (in the UK at least) are also inflected by the 'war on terror', student fees, housing inflation, and urban riots.[6] Not surprisingly, we have seen people's overall confidence in established systems of governance start to crumble:

> Only a third of the public think the system by which Britain is governed works well (33%) with those living furthest from Westminster most likely to be dissatisfied. Just 35% believe that when people like themselves get involved in politics they can change the way the country is run. Only 13% feel they have some influence over decision-making nationally although 41% would like to be involved in decision-making. More people (46%) would like to be involved in local decisions but just 25% currently feel they have some influence at the local level.[7]

These are the conditions in which a series of political 'earthquakes' have taken place: the decision taken by UK voters in 2016 to leave the European Union, the election of Donald Trump in the United States, the collapse of the main parties in the French presidential elections of 2017, and the resurgence of the anti-austerity politics of Jeremy Corbyn. These events have brought to the fore the economic dislocation that has taken place since the 1980s, revealing deep class, as well as generational and ethnic, divisions. Marginalized voices have kicked back against a post-war party system that has failed them and a professional political elite that has largely ignored them. These were also the circumstances in which the media's democratic credentials were to be sorely tested.

THE DEMOCRATIC MEDIA SWINDLE

The central issue for us is not that we are suddenly surrounded by what is described as 'fake news' but that we have been living with fake democracy. This takes the form of a democratic facade that promises much but delivers little, leaving its citizens confronted by what Raymond Williams described as 'the coexistence of political representation and participation with an economic system which admits no such rights, procedures or claims'.[8]

Colin Crouch has described the closure of alternatives under neoliberalism as a situation of 'post-democracy' in which 'politics and government are increasingly slipping back into the control of privileged elites in the manner characteristic of pre-democratic times'.[9] For Crouch, it is a paradox of contemporary democracy that despite the surfeit of apparently democratic-sounding developments – the collapse of deference, increases in transparency and literacy, and more opportunities formally to engage in democracy – we nevertheless have to be persuaded to vote and to exercise 'civic responsibility'. The media themselves are partly to blame: their attachments to power and their use of sensationalism and soundbites 'degrade the quality of political discussion and reduce the competence of citizens'.[10] This sham sovereignty is not incidental to, but intertwined with, the liberal capitalism of which our mainstream media industries are very much a part.[11] The real problem isn't the Macedonian cottage industry churning out pro-Trump messages, but the fact that in equating liberal democracy (and a liberal media) with meaningful control of our collective lives, we have been *swindled*.

Actually existing democracy (rather than its utopian ideal) – both in its rhetoric and its political routines – has very successfully used discourses of equality and autonomy to commodify individualism and constrain freedom. It has promised popular rule and self-governance through market exchanges and constitutional guarantees, but instead we have a shrink-wrapped democracy that celebrates only the most pallid forms of participation and engagement with all political nutrients removed. Citizens have been recast as consumers and collective decisions transformed into questions of individual need and choice. And in doing so, it has given us nothing more than the illusion of democratic communications: a media where editors and top politicians dine at the same tables, are educated at the same institutions, and share many of the same corporate values and ideological agendas; a media that is disaggregated in theory but centralized in practice; a media where the tools may be open source but where the most powerful networks remain closed. This is a media marked by commerce, complicity, and caution rather than critique, creativity, and a journalism of conscience.

Media institutions are massively implicated in fake democracy as both subject and object of a socio-economic restructuring that favours the upward transfer and concentration of property and wealth.[12] Mainstream media outlets have failed to use their symbolic power to challenge this shift to offer alternative visions and truly representative narratives, serving up instead an anaemic diet of stories that are frequently shallow, decontextualised, misleading, or downright biased – for example the economics journalism that assumes the 'expertise' of financial commentators and the legitimacy of austerity policies,[13] the reporting of 'terror' that marginalizes geopolitical tensions and inequalities,[14] the negative coverage of progressive movements and leaders,[15] and the popular representations of welfare claimants as 'revolting subjects'[16] that seek to mobilize a sense of disgust towards the 'unproductive' and 'undeserving poor' in the contemporary world.

In posing these questions about the relationship between media and democracy, we are drawing on Marx's famous invocation of liberal democracy as an enormous swindle in which superficially democratic forms of constitutional government were employed to undermine the possibility of a fully functioning democracy based on equality and popular control. Speaking of the United States as 'the archetype of democratic humbug',[17] Marx, according to Hal Draper, insisted that it 'had to develop to its highest point the art of keeping the expression of popular opinion within channels satisfactory to its class interests'.[18]

Mainstream media have long played this essential role – framing debate and identifying controversies but always seeking 'to strictly limit the spectrum on acceptable opinion'[19] whether this relates to issues concerning the economy, immigration, or foreign intervention. We are now facing a new democratic swindle in which elite media institutions – from the BBC and the *New York Times* to Google and Facebook – are using the crisis posed by the growth of anti-establishment politics to argue that only they are capable of sustaining a consensual, rational, and credible information ecology that can expose 'fake news' and protect 'established truths'. The problem is that they intend to achieve this by relying on the same personnel, the same evangelical belief in algorithms (even if the algorithms themselves may be forced to change), and the same agendas that failed dismally in their democratic responsibilities and that are intimately connected to the neoliberal order that has so alienated millions of people.

BAD NEWS

Convergent shifts in cultural production, journalism, political communication, marketing, and data mining have contributed to the emergence of a mediated regime facilitated by deregulated, commodified, affective and ever faster forms of what Jodi Dean calls 'communicative capitalism'.[20] Political discourse is commandeered by the stuff of entertainment, while the news all too often traffics in trivialities and repackaged public relations material[21] and occupies an increasingly fragile and narrow centre ground. This determination, traceable across the last forty years, to subjugate *all* areas of mediated activity to market logic and competition through ever-more commercialization, privatization, and restructuring has prepared the way for what Will Davies has referred to as 'post-truth politics' based on an over-supply of 'facts' and an under-provision of meaningful analysis.[22] We now have a mainstream journalism that fails to perform what is assumed to be the central role of media in a liberal democracy: to interrogate the power relations that shape our world. This is partly because of the quick-fix, rapid-fire, clickbait-focused strategies that don't allow for critical reflections, but also because media organizations themselves are increasingly implicated in power relations that they have little reason to illuminate or challenge. Add to this the refusal by the entire mainstream UK press to comply with a system of independent self-regulation recommended by Lord Justice Leveson after an 18 month inquiry into the ethics and standards of the press that was agreed by all parties in Parliament, supported by the vast majority of the population, and designed to hold the press to account for misrepresentation, distortion, and illegal behaviour,[23] and we have a confluence of processes that have hollowed out those remaining democratic spaces in our most popular news media outlets.

Of course, while democracy is about far more than an accountable press or a truly social media, the sheer scale of the largest media organizations compounds the problems of 'fake democracy'. Despite Rupert Murdoch's claim that 'no one controls the media or will ever again',[24] markets in both 'new' and 'old' media sectors are heavily concentrated and skewed towards wealth creation, effectively suffocating any notion of the public interest. Media landscapes – from the analogue world of the print title to the global digital monopolies of Google and Facebook – are increasingly monopolistic in nature, resistant to traditional forms of regulation, and out of reach of democratically organized political will-formation. The UK, for example, has a supposedly competitive national newspaper market but just five companies – largely presided over by tax exiles and media moguls – control 90 per cent of daily circulation (albeit one that is shrinking), and help to set the agenda for the rest of the news media. For all the rhetoric about a 'paradigm shift' from traditional to social media that works to the advantage of both the populist left and right, it is not the case that that legacy media have lost the ability to influence conversation and conduct. Research on the agenda-setting influence of right-wing newspapers on broadcast coverage of the 2015 general election,[25] together with the domination of those same voices of coverage of the referendum on membership of the European Union,[26] points to the continuing ability of established voices to distort conversations about contemporary politics and to delegitimize progressive arguments.

The situation is actually worse when it comes to the increasingly profitable digital world. While there may be thousands of digital start-ups, Apple and Spotify alone account for 63 per cent of the global streaming market and Facebook is fast becoming the dominant digital platform for news. Meanwhile Google has some 90 per cent of global desktop searches, and Google and Facebook together account for around two-thirds of all digital advertising in the US. According to the *Financial Times*, 85 cents of every dollar spent on digital advertising in America went to those two companies in the first quarter of 2016, evidence of 'a concentration of market power in two companies that not only own the playing field but are able to set the rules of the game as well'.[27]

What we are witnessing now is not the total eclipse of the 'old' by the 'new', but instead a rather strange and unpredictable dance between two sectors that are heavily interconnected. Both sets of players – digital intermediaries and more traditional content providers – are battling to command and monetize public attention. The bewildering market power wielded by the likes of Google and Facebook has not come at the expense of the influence of mainstream press and broadcasters. Google, Facebook and Twitter are, if anything, *reinforcing* the agenda-setting power of the mainstream news brands by facilitating their increased circulation. For some time now, Google has been ranking news providers in relation to what it considers to be the most reliable indicators of news quality. But it turns out that algorithms are not much better at assessing news values and ensuring a diverse flow of sources than human beings. According to Schlosberg, while this means that they may be less prone to editorial intervention of the sort that we are used to, it also means 'they rely on quantitative measures of quality, which produces their own bias in favour of large-scale and mainstream providers'.[28] Schlosberg goes on to note that:

> ... the most contentious metric is one that purports to measure what Google calls 'importance' by comparing the volume of a site's output on any given topic to the total output on that topic across the web. In a single measure, this promotes both concentration at the level of provider (by favouring organisations with volume and scale), as well as concentration at the level of output (by favouring organisations that produce more on topics that are widely covered elsewhere). In other words, it is a measure that single-handedly reinforces both an aggregate news 'agenda', as well as the agenda-setting power of a relatively small number of publishers.[29]

The gatekeeping power of Google and Facebook works, therefore, *in tandem* with that of mainstream news providers, mutually reinforcing each other around what they consider to be real, legitimate, and authoritative news. Only in much of the popular press, in the UK at least, this press is riddled with distortions, misrepresentations, and illegitimate news. When even Wikipedia decides that the UK tabloid newspaper the *Daily Mail* is not a trusted source of information you know something is amiss.[30] But Google's algorithms amplify these so-called reliable sources of news, so is it any surprise that it becomes difficult to tell them apart from the likes of the *official* fake news industry?

This symbiosis certainly helped to pave the way for the election of Donald Trump. After all, it wasn't so much his provocative and offensive tweets that enabled him to capture the headlines and helped him ascend to the highest political office in the land, but the way in which mainstream news networks were, from the outset, fascinated by his personality and aware of his commercial potential. 'The more offensive, provocative, outlandish the comment – the bigger the lie – the more newsworthy it became. Twitter gave him a platform, but mainstream news provided the microphone, and it is amplification – the ability to be heard – that is the major currency of agenda power.'[31]

So just as elite media were horrified by his politics, they were gripped by his star potential and well aware of the potential financial benefits. According to Victor Pickard:

> Even as Trump attacked the press – mocking and feuding with journalists, threatening to change libel laws, holding campaign events where reporters were corralled and roughed up – he still served major media outlets well. That's because the news organizations covering Trump, particularly television stations, reaped incredible amounts of money from their election coverage. Cable news organizations' expected haul this election season? A record-breaking $2.5 billion.[32]

Pickard quotes research that shows that Trump received 327 minutes of nightly broadcast network news coverage, compared with Hillary Clinton's 121 minutes and Bernie Sanders' 20 minutes and benefited to the tune of $2 billion from free media coverage during his primary campaign. Given that profit-seeking is, as Pickard puts it, 'in commercial media's DNA', it was no surprise to hear the CEO of broadcast media giant CBS declare that '[Trump's candidacy] may not be good for America, but it's damn good for CBS … The money's rolling in and this is fun … this is going to be a very good year for us … bring it on, Donald. Keep going.[33]

This commitment to accumulation and monopolization, whatever the immediate political costs, seems like a pretty obvious and far from unexpected consequence of a neoliberalized for-profit media market. But what of public service media organizations like the BBC that aren't accountable to shareholders, aren't dependent solely on advertisers, and whose underlying logic is not reducible to the need to chase high ratings and to secure customer data? To what extent are they immune from the calling cards of the ambassadors of neoliberalism and able to exploit their limited autonomy for genuinely democratic purposes?

The answer is that public media are just as embedded as private media in a neoliberal discipline that is present in all the restructurings and cultural shifts that have affected the BBC: the emergence of an internal market, the deployment of new public management techniques, the emphasis on value for money, the introduction of public value tests and service licences and, above all, the determination to tie public service media to the needs of their commercial rivals. In all these ways, the BBC has long been structured by and subject to market discipline and, in this sense, the BBC is just as tethered to neoliberalism as BP or Google or Apple.

Leys and Player, writing about the BBC's coverage of the National Health Service (NHS) in the UK in the wake of the 2012 Health and Social Care Act that outsourced a significant portion of health services to the private sector, reveal how the BBC, by defining its commitment to political impartiality in terms of standing mid-way between the views of the major political parties, placed itself near the middle of a neoliberal consensus.[34] This is further inscribed in a regulatory framework that provides for '*due* impartiality', a conception of impartiality that takes account of the mood of the times and bends to the prevailing logic. Thus, views that run counter to a market sensibility and that would have been part of a mainstream *critical* standpoint 20 years ago gradually come to be seen as eccentric, marginal, and unrealistic. We are left, therefore, with a frighteningly singular and apparently depoliticized version of a neoliberal culture that is increasingly normalized, inflexible, and seemingly inevitable. According to this narrative, the NHS is a huge, inefficient beast that requires the market discipline of a privatized industry to function effectively – as opposed to being an incredibly popular universal service that requires additional funding to meet the challenges of an aging population.

Recent policy developments in relation to the BBC exemplify this inability to act independently or to step outside market logic. First, the UK state continues not only to coordinate the overall framework within which the BBC sits but micro-manages its broader orientation, instructing it not to privilege popular formats or provide too much online content lest it tread on the toes of commercial providers, not to pay its talent too much money, and forcing it to outsource more and more content from the independent sector in order to ensure the latter's growth. In turn, the BBC has responded with a news agenda that is demonstrably closer to the Conservative hymn-book than those of other broadcasters: unwilling to challenge the consensus on austerity, morbidly fascinated by what it sees as the cheeky nationalism of the former UKIP leader Nigel Farage, and overtly hostile to the left-wing challenge posed by Labour leader Jeremy Corbyn.

Its affiliation with establishment figures and parties remains remarkably consistent: the outgoing chair of the BBC Trust, Rona Fairhead, was a non-executive chairman of HSBC holdings for many years and chairman and CEO of the *Financial Times*; the chair of the new BBC unitary board, Sir David Clementi, is a former chairman of Prudential and got the job after the government invited him to design a new governance framework. Senior figures in the newsroom, like chief political correspondent Laura Kuenssberg, and the head of news, James Harding, are both robust in their defence of small 'c' conservatism, while James Purnell, a key New Labour figure, was promoted to head of radio without having any experience of actually making radio programmes. Meanwhile, the government has forced the BBC to absorb the enormous cost of providing free licences for the over-75s, thus implicating the corporation in the Conservatives' broader welfare agenda and further cementing the links between state and broadcaster. As with its commercial rivals, a neoliberal logic has been forcibly implanted into the water coolers of the BBC and its management has, in turn, internalized this in its operational manoeuvres.

THE CENTRE FIGHTS BACK

Given the collapse in confidence in many of the institutions of liberal democracy and the fissures exploited by populists on both the right and the left, there is a political (and media) vacuum that is waiting to be filled. In this situation, the outbreak of 'fake news' — choreographed by the Russian security establishment and allegedly responsible for the election of Donald Trump – has presented more established media outlets with the opportunity to reassert their democratic role in winning back trust and re-establishing the importance of 'truth'. The *New York Times*, for example, spent millions of dollars on a television commercial during Superbowl 2017 entitled 'The Truth is Hard' while its commentators argue that independent, fact-based journalism 'has never been more important. Truth has not yet perished, but to deny that it is under siege would be to invite disaster.'[35] This may be true but it overlooks two facts.

First, 'fake news' is not an exception to but the logical result of a market economy that privileges short-term rewards and commercial impact. The rise of programmatic advertising and the domination of advertising by Google and Facebook are hardly peripheral developments, but part of a structural readjustment of the media. In this situation, 'fake news', according to researchers at Columbia University, 'is a distraction from the larger issue: that the structure and economics of social platforms incentivize the spread of low-quality content over high-quality material. Journalism with a civic value – journalism that investigates power, or reaches underserved and local communities – is discriminated against by a system that favors scale and shareability.'[36]

Second, 'fake news' is itself a disputed category that refers to hugely different practices, from falsehoods deliberately concocted to undermine democratic processes (such as elections and referenda), through traditional journalism with its long history of misrepresentations, exaggerations, and distortions (including 'yellow journalism' and sensationalist claims such as Saddam Hussein's Iraq being able to launch weapons of mass destruction within 45 minutes), through to what Tambini describes as '[n]ews that challenges orthodox authority' and that departs from an elite shared consensus.[37] Each of these instances of 'fake news' requires quite different policy and professional responses but, at the moment, it is only the first kind – of deliberate lies designed to disrupt 'democracy' – that seems to absorb the attention of the mainstream media.

In this situation, claims made about the dangers of 'fake news' are hardly innocent but part of a coordinated attempt by the centre ground – the people who used to be known as the establishment until Trump nullified the meaning of the phrase by placing himself outside of it – to construct a narrative that contrasts 'professional journalism' (based on ethical responsibility and objectivity) with 'fake news (anything that departs from established protocols). This is likely to involve the resurrection of the same newsroom agendas and the same authorities of 'truth-telling' and expertise that failed to make sense of the world for so many people and that, at least in part, paved the way for the rapid rise of the 'fake news' mainstream media so deplore. 'The net result of the defense of democracy against populism', writes Thea Riofrancos, 'is, inevitably, a defense of political centrism. Democracy is reduced to the separation of powers and the search for bipartisan consensus.'[38] The fact that the *Daily Telegraph,* a mid-market UK newspaper, recently appointed Andy Coulson, a former editor of the *News of the World* who was jailed following the phone-hacking scandal, to promote the paper as truthful and authoritative, is the final irony in the scramble to protect their commercial product and declare what is 'fake news' and what is not.

Indeed, the centrist response is related to a backlash against voices – admittedly, many of them deeply unpleasant – that epitomizes the breakdown of a neoliberal consensus that has been taken for granted for many years. The revival of political participation that we are now seeing – epitomized by the movements that have emerged around Bernie Sanders in the US and Jeremy Corbyn in the UK – has come with a rejection of the post-war party system and the appetite for those at the bottom to call foul on those at the top. It brings with it different possibilities: both the rise of a populist right as well as the potential for a reimagining of the notion of democracy. Vested interests, however, will always respond to any attack on their own position and privilege by condemning the ignorance of the 'masses' and celebrating the benevolence and rationality of their own motives. Marx identified this nearly 150 years ago when reflecting on bourgeois attacks on the Paris Commune:

> … no sooner do the working men [and women] anywhere take the subject into their own hand with a will, than up rises at once all the apologetic phraseology of the mouthpieces of present society … as if capitalist society was still in its purest state of virgin innocence, with its antagonism still undeveloped, with its delusions still unexploded, with its prostitute realities not yet laid bare.[39]

Without wanting directly to compare a nineteenth century socialist experiment with a twenty-first century populist revolt, the point is that powerful media interests – as with any dominant group whose backs are against the wall – are conducting a propaganda campaign designed to suggest that only they can be trusted with safeguarding freedom of expression and a commitment to truth, and that only they can be guaranteed to preserve democratic rights. Yet while we desperately need a journalism that is both fearless and rigorous, we have no reason to believe that the existing professional model is capable of delivering it.

MEDIA POWER IS NOT ABSOLUTE!

One of the puzzles concerning the media's promulgation of fake democracy is that, while its supporters in the commentariat may imagine that its institutions are robust and its foundational ideas deep-rooted, millions of people think otherwise. This is especially the case when neoliberal administrations make promises that they are unable to keep and then lack the ideological mechanisms to convince electorates that someone else is to blame. As we have already noted, we have seen a backlash against establishment politics in recent elections and referenda – a backlash that has also been aimed at media elites who have themselves been identified as 'part of the problem' and whose power, therefore, has been increasingly brought into question.

Nowhere is this more clear than in the UK general election of 2017, where Corbyn confounded the vast majority of a media class that had sought to undermine him since his very first day as leader of the Labour Party by sensationally depriving Theresa May of a Conservative majority in Parliament. Despite regular headlines about 'annihilation' and 'meltdown', Labour earned its biggest share of the vote since Tony Blair in 2001 and its biggest increase in vote share since 1945. This was an election in which the hostility promoted by the vast majority of the media towards a progressive leader was intense but ultimately ineffectual; a campaign in which the tabloids in particular turned up the heat against the Labour leader but also in which many (although not all) ordinary voters refused to acquiesce to these voices. Yet predictions that the right-wing press have had their day or that, as the *Observer*'s media correspondent put it, media bias is no longer an issue are just as misconceived as *Sun* editor Tony Gallagher's claim that the Brexit vote demonstrated the continuing power of the press only twelve months previously.[40] We need, instead, a far more complex understanding of media power as a phenomenon that distorts democratic processes – and that is, therefore, a central feature of our fake democracy – but that has its own limitations when applied to stubborn publics; a phenomenon that is pervasive but also contingent, fragile, and unstable.[41]

The 2017 election bears this out. Whole swathes of press reporting were hugely biased towards the Conservatives. Despite what was widely acknowledged to have been a disastrous campaign, the Tories attracted coverage that was neutral overall while Labour, running a largely successful and popular campaign, suffered the most negative coverage of all the parties. In terms of endorsements, the Tories received support from 80 per cent of the Sunday press and 57 per cent of the daily press, with Labour receiving 20 per cent and 11 per cent respectively.[42] Titles regularly highlighted Corbyn's alleged links to terrorists and attacked his position on nuclear disarmament, while on the day before polling the *Daily Mail* – with its millions of online and offline readers – devoted 13 pages to attacks on Labour.

It could be argued that these attacks were balanced both by the far more pluralistic agenda of social media as well as by broadcast coverage that was required to respect 'due impartiality' and thus obliged to feature Jeremy Corbyn as much as Prime Minister Theresa May. This certainly benefited Labour, as once Corbyn was given the opportunity to speak, his message was able to resonate with millions of people because of the public's appetite for the party's manifesto policies around redistribution, investment in public services, and anti-austerity. Yet broadcasters also regularly aired memes around Corbyn's 'unelectability', his 'tax-and-spend policies', and his reluctance to condemn people to a horrific death by pressing the nuclear button. The BBC, for example, continued to circulate a report on Corbyn's views on 'shoot to kill' that had previously been censured by the BBC's own regulator because of its misleading editing, which then attracted millions of views during the campaign. It would be foolish to think that this constant repetition of Corbyn as either dangerous or deficient had absolutely *no* impact on what the electorate was discussing.

At the same time, it is also clear that some 40 per cent of the electorate rejected the preferences of media moguls and the cynicism of liberal commentators. When after years of declining wages, disastrous foreign interventions, and cuts in public services, voters were offered the opportunity to strike back against neoliberal policies and support a distinctively progressive, anti-austerity programme, some 13 million people took up this offer to the utter astonishment of the media elite. We can conclude from this that even the most sustained levels of media bias have their limits when faced with an angry and disenfranchised population. Despite voices on the soft left encouraging Corbyn to professionalize his media operation, to be more 'presidential', and to adopt a more conciliatory tone, it was precisely Corbyn's direct engagement with voters through rallies and social media connections, together with his refreshing passion for social justice and his accountability to democratic decision-making, that saw Labour climb so dramatically in the polls.

So while the media play a central role in the legitimation and sustenance of fake democracy, we should be careful not to exaggerate the power of elites in the face of publics who are by no means simply subjects to be brainwashed or herds to be bewildered.[43] Media influence is not predictable or mechanical but connected to the ideas that people hold at any one moment – a consciousness that is not fixed or immutable but profoundly contradictory and volatile. The general election result showed that campaigns, just like media, can change minds if they connect to the actual experiences of publics who, in the UK, were seeking alternatives to a status quo that had let them down. In this case, mainstream media – as epitomized by a memorable *Daily Telegraph* headline less than six weeks before the election: 'Theresa May most popular leader since the late 1970s as Jeremy Corbyn hits all time low' (26 April 2017) – neglected to notice the deep-rooted changes that were going on around them and were outmanoeuvred by a Labour campaign that struck a chord with an electorate increasingly hungry for change.

This also reminds us that to understand power you must first appreciate what powerlessness feels like. Brexit spoke to those who felt cast aside by globalization and forgotten by ruling elites all too willing to stand by and watch communities decimated and social infrastructures weakened. The tag line of the Leave campaign offered the promise of a different future: 'Let's Take Back Control'. It spoke to a disaffection that neoliberal democracy doesn't work for the majority of its members. That the Conservative Party – and their supporters in the press – thought they could win a general election simply by repeating 'Brexit means Brexit' reveals they never fully understood what people had hoped Brexit could give them: the dignity of making their own history. When people feel that they are dispensable and don't need to be listened to, then democracy has failed. The Conservative Party wasn't just *not listening* but it blatantly refused to engage in virtually any debate at all.

Corbyn's Labour campaign, on the other hand, vilified by most of the mainstream press and apparently with nothing left to lose, took to the streets and mobilized thousands of grassroots supporters, often through social media, to knock on doors and discuss the first party political manifesto since the financial crash to attempt to break through the neoliberal force-field, acknowledging that to do this would require a redistribution of wealth via more progressive levels of income tax. They exposed the contradiction between how we are told the world works – that the only way out of an economic crisis is through austerity measures – and our experiences of it – that the more austerity we have, the less economic growth and the higher levels of anxiety we experience. It was a campaign that spoke to people.

Brexit forewarned us of a crisis of the relations of political representation and political parties – what Gramsci referred to as a crisis of authority. But Gramsci also pointed to the 'trenches and fortifications' of civil society as sites where power could be challenged and negotiated.[44] The lessons for us today are stark: first, media power is not an immoveable force; second, activist politics is not a luxury if we are to meaningfully contest mainstream agendas.

LESSONS FOR A DEMOCRATIC MEDIA

In targeting intensified market logic as a major barrier to an independent media, we should be wary of suggesting that neoliberal states inherited fully functioning democratic media systems and set out systematically to roll back their dialogical and 'truthful' qualities. Neoliberalism may have weakened the relationship between mainstream media and democracy but this degeneration has a far longer history. Indeed, we need to ask whether media institutions were ever genuinely accountable to publics apart from those moments when publics themselves hijacked media technologies in the pursuit of democratic aims, from the Chartist press of the nineteenth century to social media platforms during the Arab Spring.[45]

For example, the lack of diversity and accountability of the press has been recognized for many years and, at least in the UK, there is a long history of failed attempts to reform the press that started with the first Royal Commission on the Press in 1947 and continued through to the Leveson Inquiry that followed the phone hacking crisis of July 2011. At each stage, recommendations made were largely rejected by a press that consistently promised to behave and then consistently failed to do so. Governments, always keen to maintain good relations with the press, have time and again bowed down to industry pressure.

Opposition to the mainstream media's amplification of neoliberal 'common-sense' ought not to be based, therefore, on the idea that there once existed – perhaps before Reagan and Thatcher – a meaningfully independent and representative democratic media determined to maintain a check on official power. Tom Mills' excellent history of the BBC demonstrates how even an organization with a reputation for independence has compromised with the state from its very inception: from its involvement in the general strike through its relationship with the security services and its coverage of foreign interventions and its' framing of economic issues.[46] A reading that ties the degeneration of an institution like the BBC – and the media more generally – as exclusively linked to the rise of neoliberalism misses out on a far more complicated picture: one in which, for all the BBC's moments of questioning and creativity, is marked by a history of deference to the state, a lack of geographical and cultural diversity that it is only starting to acknowledge and perhaps address, and a paternalistic political agenda that is intertwined with a legacy of imperial, corporatist, and then neoliberal affiliations. This is a broadcaster that has, throughout its history, served the state more effectively than it has served the public.

These clientilist and paternalistic relationships are resonant of traditional forms of social democracy – precisely the 'democracy' invoked by Crouch as that which existed before 'post-democracy'. This was a political settlement that reached its highpoint after the Second World War and that Crouch describes as 'the democratic moment of most of the western world' when the rulers of Western Europe at least were forced 'to admit the voices of ordinary people into affairs of state'.[47]

Is this the best we can hope for? The limited representation of working people into a state dominated by other forces? Streeck argues that this period was hardly a highpoint of popular participation but was instead characterized by *compromise*, by a contract between capital and labour that entailed accepting 'capitalist markets and property rights in exchange for political democracy'.[48] That involved some huge steps forward in terms of collective provision and the mobilization of working-class pressure to demand basic rights in the sphere of housing, health, and employment – a long way from the rather shriveled democracy on offer in the modern age. But it is still nothing like the expansive definition of democracy proposed by Raymond Williams: that democracy must refer to 'popular power' and an arrangement in which 'the interests of the majority of the people [are] paramount and in which these interests [are] practically exercised and controlled by the majority.'[49]

We ought, therefore, to be sceptical of any simplistic understanding of 'post-democracy' that somehow suggests that we have now superseded an actually existing democracy that was based on popular sovereignty and the equitable control and distribution of all resources, including those of the media. Instead what has happened is that banks, financial agencies, and global conglomerates now compete with states in the management of economies, thus making real democracy ever more distant. In these circumstances, a democratic media will not descend from the heavens nor will it emerge from the compromised models of the past. It has to be fought for and invented out of the struggles that we face in the coming years.

The task for the radical left today, therefore, is not to return the media to an imaginary pre-neoliberal bliss that may well turn out to be even less democratic than the forms of media we have now. Instead we need, first, to challenge some of the most obvious abuses of media power – to oppose further media concentration and to resist the stereotypes and distortions that seek to normalize, for example, racism and war. Second, we need to figure out how best to build a radical political project in which truth-telling and communicative capacity emerge from the bottom up and not through paternalistic diktat or pure market exchange.

This will require not a clever media strategy but the imagination to conceive of a democratic communications system genuinely in the hands of its users as opposed to controlled by billionaires and bureaucrats. 'The principle', as Williams wrote some 50 years ago, 'should be that the active contributors have control of their own means of expression.'[50] The interactive and decentralized affordances of digital media ought to make this easier to achieve – but only if they are freed from the same structures of controlling state and profit-maximizing market that have distorted and undermined previous communication 'revolutions'.

It will also require a commitment to the building of radical political movements given that all major campaigns for social change have had their own channels of communication. The Chartists had the *Northern Star*, the Suffragettes had their own self-titled newspaper, the Bolsheviks had *Pravda*, Gandhi founded *Harijan* to help build his anti-colonial struggle, while Solidarity in Poland had *Robotnik*. Algerians had the unofficial *Voice of Fighting Algeria* during their anti-colonial struggle in the 1950s, a radio station so transgressive that, according to Frantz Fanon, '[h]aving a radio seriously meant *going to war*.'[51] These were all tools of struggle, instruments with which activists communicated with each other, and publicized their activities to others. They were the organizing frameworks of emergent mass movements designed not simply to provide 'alternative' narratives to those of their enemies but to strengthen their own activities and challenge the 'common sense' of elite opinion. These are vigorous examples of democratic media that are utterly distinct from a contemporary 'liberal media' rooted either in a meek and defensive public service or an aggressive market entrepreneurialism, and they are ones that will surely emerge again in the shadow of new struggles for social justice.

NOTES

1   See James Curran, *Media and Power*, London: Routledge, 2002, pp. 217-47 for a comprehensive summary of classic liberal conceptions of the free press.

2   European figures are from European Broadcasting Union, *Trust in Media 2016*, Geneva: EBU, 2016; US figures are from Art Swift, 'Americans' Trust in Mass Media Sinks to New Low', Gallup, 14 September 2016.

3   2017 Edelman Trust Barometer, available at: www.edelman.com/global-results/.

4   Mark Blyth, *Austerity: The History of a Dangerous Idea,* New York: Oxford University Press, 2013, p. 15.

5   UK Department for Work and Pensions, *Simplifying the Welfare System and Making Sure Work Pays*, 2013. available at: www.gov.uk/government/policies/simplifying-the-welfare-system-and-making-sure-work-pays.

6   John Hills, et al., *Falling Behind, Getting Ahead: The Changing Structure of Inequality in the UK, 2007-2013*, London: Centre for Analysis of Social Exclusion, LSE, 2015.

7   Hansard Society, *Audit of Political Engagement 13*, London: Hansard Society, 2016, p. 7.

8   Raymond Williams, 'Democracy and Parliament', *Marxism Today*, June 1982, p. 19.

9   Colin Crouch, *Post-Democracy*, Cambridge: Polity, 2004, p. 6.

10   Crouch, *Post-Democracy*, p. 47.

11   See Natalie Fenton, *Digital, Political, Radical,* London: Polity, 2016, chapter 3.

12   See Andrew Calabrese and Natalie Fenton, eds, 'Media Communication and the Limits of Liberalism', *European Journal of Communication* 30(5), 2015 for a full discussion of these debates.

13   Mike Berry, 'No Alternative to Austerity: How BBC Broadcast News Reported the Deficit Debate', *Media, Culture & Society* 38(6), 2016, pp. 844-63. See also Julian Mercille, *The Political Economy and Media Coverage of the European Economic Crisis*, London: Routledge, 2015; Steve Schifferes and Richard Roberts, eds., *The Media and Financial Crises: Comparative and Historical Perspectives*, London: Routledge, 2014.

14   Des Freedman, 'The Terror News Cycle', *LRB Blog*, 24 May 2017, available at: www. lrb.co.uk/blog/2017/05/24/des-freedman/the-terror-news-cycle/.

15   Tom Mills, 'Is the BBC Biased Against Jeremy Corbyn? Look at the Evidence', *New Statesman*, 1 August 2016.

16   Imogen Tyler, *Revolting Subjects: Social Abjection and Resistance in Neoliberal Britain*, London: Zed Books, 2013.

17   Karl Marx, Letter to Engels, 7 September 1864, in *Marx and Engels Collected Works: Letters 1860-1864*, Volume 41, London: Lawrence & Wishart, 2010, p. 562.

18   Hal Draper, 'Marx on Democratic Forms of Government', in Ralph Miliband and John Saville, eds, *The Socialist Register 1974*, London: Merlin Press, 1973, p. 118.

19   Noam Chomsky, *The Common Good*, London: Pluto Press, 2003, p. 43. The notion of 'legitimate controversy' was also discussed by Daniel Hallin in his critical account of the media's role in Vietnam, *The Uncensored War: The Media and Vietnam*, London: University of California Press, 1989.

20   Jodi Dean, 'Communicative Capitalism: Circulation and the Foreclosure of Politics', *Cultural Politics* 1(1), 2005, pp. 51-74.

21   Read Nick Davies' work for a powerful critique of UK journalism, *Flat Earth News*, London: Chatto & Windus, 2008; and *Hack Attack: How the Truth Caught Up With Rupert Murdoch*, London: Chatto & Windus, 2014.

22   William Davies, 'The Age of Post-Truth Politics', *New York Times*, 24 August 2016.

23   Brian Cathcart, 'Where Press Regulation is Concerned, We're Already Being Fed "Post-Truth" Journalism', *The Conversation*, 3 January 2017.

24   Quoted in Des Freedman, *The Contradictions of Media Power*, London: Bloomsbury, 2014, p. 89.

25   Stephen Cushion, et al., 'Newspapers, Impartiality and Television News', *Journalism Studies*, 2016.

26   Centre for Research in Communication and Culture, '82% Circulation Advantage in Favour of Brexit as The Sun Declares', Loughborough University, 14 June 2016. Available at: https://blog.lboro.ac.uk/crcc/eu-referendum/sun-no-longer-hedging-bets-brexit/.

27   Matthew Garrahan, 'Advertising: Facebook and Google Build a Duopoly', *Financial Times*, 23 June 2016.

28   Justin Schlosberg, 'The Media-Technology-Military Industrial Complex', *openDemocracy*, 27 January 2017.

29   Justin Schlosberg, 'The Media-Technology-Military Industrial Complex'.

30   Jasper Jackson, 'Wikipedia Bans Daily Mal as "Unreliable" Source', *Guardian*, 8 February 2017.

31   Des Freedman and Justin Schlosberg, 'Murdoch's Access to British Prime Minister Shows Media Power Still in Hands of the Few', *The Conversation*, 7 February 2017.

32   Victor Pickard, 'Yellow Journalism, Orange President', *Jacobin*, 25 November 2016.

33   Pickard, 'Yellow Journalism'.

34   Leys and Player, 2011.

35   Roger Cohen, 'Am I Imagining This?' *New York Times*, 10 February 2017.

36   Emily Bell and Taylor Owen, *The Platform Press: How Silicon Valley Rengineered Journalism*, New York: Tow Center for Digital Journalism, 2017, p. 10.

37   Damian Tambini, *Fake News: Public Policy Responses*, Media Policy Brief 20, London: Media Policy Project, LSE, 2016, p. 5.

38   Thea Riofrancos, 'Democracy Without the People', *n+1*, 6 February 2017.

39   Karl Marx, *The Civil War in France*, in Karl Marx and Frederick Engels, *Selected Works*, Volume 2, Moscow: Progress Publishers, p. 223.

40   See Peter Preston, 'This Election Proves that Media Bias No Longer Matters', *Observer*, 11 June 2017; Jane Martinson, 'Did the Mail and Sun Help Swing the UK Towards Brexit?', *Guardian*, 24 June 2016.

41   Des Freedman, *The Contradictions of Media Power*, London: Bloomsbury, 2014.

42   See David Deacon, et al., *National News Media Coverage of the 2017 General Election*, Loughborough University, 2017, available at: blog.lboro.ac.uk/crcc/wp-content/uploads/sites/23/2017/06/media-coverage-of-the-2017-general-election-campaign-report-4.pdf; Freddie Mayhew, 'General Election 2017 Press Endorsements: Tories Backed by 80 per cent of UK National Sunday Newspaper Market, *Press Gazette,* 5 June 2017; Dominic Ponsford, 'Daily Mail and Sun Launch Front-Page Attacks on Corbyn as Fleet Street lines up beind Theresa May', *Press Gazette*, 7 June 2017.

43   Walter Lippmann, *The Phantom Public*, London: Transaction, 2011 [1927], p. 145.

44   Antonio Gramsci, *Selections from the Prison Notebooks*, Quintin Hoare and Geoffrey Nowell-Smith, eds, New York: International Publishers, 1971, p. 243.

45   See for example, Natalie Fenton, *Digital, Political, Radical*, Cambridge: Polity, 2016, pp. 24-51; Stanley Harrison, *Poor Men's Guardians: Surveys of the Democratic and Working-class Press*, London: Lawrence & Wishart, 1974; Linda Herrera, *Revolution in the Age of Social Media: The Egyptian Insurrection and the Internet*, London: Verso, 2014.

46   Tom Mills, *The BBC: Myth of a Public Service*, London: Verso, 2016.

47   Crouch, *Post-Democracy*, pp. 4, 82.

48   Wolfgang Streeck, 'The Crises of Democratic Capitalism', *New Left Review* 71, 2011, p. 10.

49   Raymond Williams, *Keywords: A Vocabulary of Culture and Society*, London: Fontana, p. 96.

50   Raymond Williams, *Communications*, Harmondsworth: Penguin, 1968, p. 121.

51   Frantz Fanon, *A Dying Colonialism*, New York: Grove Press, 1994, p. 93.

DEMOCRACY AND PUBLIC BROADCASTING

TOM MILLS

Even the most limited notions of modern democracy depend upon a functional system of media and communications. Liberal democratic theory is predicated on a politically informed electorate, while more ambitious and inclusive visions of democratic life point to the need for an authentic public sphere to facilitate free and reasoned deliberation between citizens. Twenty-first century capitalist democracies have neither, the actually existing public sphere being dominated by corporate interests. This is most extreme in the United States, where politics is little more than a stage-managed facade, and as Martin Gilens and others have shown, policymaking serves almost exclusively the preferences of a tiny economic elite – a state of affairs which has become increasingly unstable.[1] The news media, which in the imaginations of liberal commentators acts as a check on the powerful, is in reality an aspect of, and accomplice to, this wider state of affairs. The majority of the world's news media is owned by large corporations, and its reporting, even when professionally executed, overwhelmingly reflects these class interests. Many have seen the British Broadcasting Corporation (BBC), a national broadcaster outside of direct commercial or political control, as representing a substantive democratic alternative to capitalist media systems. This essay's account of the BBC's origins and development in the context of capitalist democracy in Britain, however, shows that this has not been the case, even in the heyday of public service broadcasting in the mid-twentieth century.

Raymond Williams once described public service broadcasting as 'an authoritarian system with a conscience', distinguishing the BBC's paternalism from more overtly 'authoritarian' systems on the basis of the former's 'values and purposes beyond the maintenance of its own power' and its mission 'to protect and guide'.[2] But what distinguishes the two systems is not the appeals of the former to the interests of the population, which are common to both, but the relative autonomy afforded to broadcasting professionals in a capitalist democracy like Britain. An important feature of the British system of public broadcasting, which also sets it apart from other European models, is its ostensibly non-political character. Central to the BBC's operations have been the notions of independence and impartiality. These concepts are treated with an almost religious reverence by the BBC and its supporters, but if analyzed sociologically are plainly comparable with the institutional arrangements and ideologies of key sections of the British state that developed in the mid-nineteenth century, such as the permanent civil service and the police. As Williams noted, the relative independence of the BBC from the political system was predicated on Britain's early development as an industrial society, its well-developed 'national culture', and its 'unusually compact ruling-class' which meant that the British state 'in many matters [proceeded] by appointment and delegation'.[3] For Williams, as a result, the BBC's 'independence was at once real, especially in relation to political parties and temporary administrations, and qualified, by its definition in terms of a pre-existing cultural hegemony'.[4] This statement, while understandable in the context of the early 1960s, exaggerates the extent of the BBC's independence and conversely underplays the extent to which ruling-class interests have had to continually work to maintain their hegemony within British broadcasting.

Public service broadcasting and its commercial alternatives – most notably the corporate media system that developed in the United States – each represented distinct elite responses to the emergence of new communicative technologies in the context of industrialization, working-class political mobilization, and universal suffrage. Both sought to unify classes around a shared 'common culture', and thereby to manage conflicting interests in capitalist societies. In the case of commercial broadcasting systems, this was mediated by capitalist enterprises drawing on expertise in marketing, advertising, and public relations,[5] and appealed to the population as consumers. In the case of the BBC, it was mediated by sections of the Oxbridge educated cultural elite with appeals to middle-class culture and the symbols and rituals of the British imperial state.

It is the extent to which the interests of the broadcasting professionals and bureaucrats have been aligned with or subordinated to other institutions, groups, and classes that reveals the democratic potential and limitations of public service broadcasting. Throughout its long history, the BBC has been thoroughly entangled with the British state and embedded within wider networks of social power. An adequate analysis of the politics of the BBC means getting to grips with a complex set of institutional arrangements in a way that social histories of intellectuals and artists rarely do, and paying close attention not only to the BBC itself, but also to wider shifts in society that have impacted on its institutional culture. It is especially important to avoid the all-too-common liberal error of fetishizing public service broadcasting and assuming it has an inherently democratic character. Public service broadcasting is not a coherent blueprint for democratic broadcasting, but a rather a loose set of ideas associated with a historically contingent set of institutional arrangements which have in fact never been particularly democratic. What it has offered is an institutional space outside of capitalist control, which in the absence of much in the way of formal mechanisms of accountability can be regarded as more or less democratic depending on how closely the interests of the broadcasting professionals and bureaucrats, and the institutional structures within which they operate, align with those of the public; or from a more pluralistic perspective, how and to what extent their creative and editorial judgments reflect particular interests in society. This more sociological perspective is particularly important when it comes to analyzing the changes the BBC went through with the gathering crisis of social democracy in the late 1960s and 1970s. As this essay will show, the pressure for democratic reform of the broadcasting establishment, which came from social movements and the left at that time, was eclipsed by the subsequent neoliberal reform agenda that has been the dominant policy paradigm ever since. The essay will conclude with an assessment of current proposals and prospects for radical democratic reform of public service media.

CORPORATE POWER AND THE BIRTH OF BROADCASTING

As the BBC's first official historian, Asa Briggs, noted, British and American broadcasting have served as contrasting ideal types, one publicly owned and the other 'fully integrated into the business system'.[6] What led the same technology to develop along such different lines in relatively similar societies? The development of broadcasting in the US is detailed in Robert McChesney's celebrated account, in which he describes the array of groups that sought to influence the process: 'educators, labor, religious groups, political parties, amateur radio enthusiasts, listeners' groups, and journalists to radio manufacturers, telephone and telegraph companies, naval and military interests, advertisers, electric utilities, and the commercial entertainment industry.'[7] It was the relative power of these different groups and interests, and the outcome of the struggles waged, and coalitions made, between them that determined the distinct structures of broadcasting systems in different polities in Europe and North America in the 1920s and 1930s.

In Britain, the key players were the radio manufacturers, the state administrators, the politicians and the capitalist media. In the formative, innovative stage, the former were the key movers. Capitalizing on their patented technology required the establishment of a broadcasting service, and it was this that gave rise to the BBC, a single state licenced broadcaster formed by the 'Big Six' radio manufacturers in 1922 – what Michael Mann calls an 'electro-technical industry consortium'.[8] The initial members of the British Broadcasting Company Ltd included the industry leader Marconi, General Electric, and the American corporation Western Electric. The major electrical and telecommunications companies were a fraction of capital naturally orientated towards the state, which held the promise of highly profitable military and infrastructural applications. In Britain, they were also seeking state protection from foreign capital.[9] It was through these companies' collective negotiations with state administrators in the Post Office – which also consulted closely with the capitalist media – that British broadcasting as a mass medium was born.

Key to the subsequent emergence of what became known as public service broadcasting as an ideology and a practice was the fact that at this stage broadcasting per se was not recognised as a profitable activity, and so the corporations were not interested in shaping broadcasts according to commercial imperatives. Even at the time of the BBC's reconstitution as a public corporation in 1927, radio was still not turning a profit in the US, in part because advertisers were not sufficiently organized at the national level. This changed only with the effective takeover of the US system by the corporate giants CBS and NBC (and their advertisers) from 1928.[10] It was the chaos prior to this time, combined with the scarcity of available wavelengths, which had persuaded British elites of the need for what was termed 'unified control'.[11] For the convenience of both the state and the corporations, as much as anything else, a single broadcaster was temporally licenced in 1923 with the possibility of others being licenced remaining open for a time. Funding was provided by a levy on the sales of radios, with direct advertising prohibited.[12]

The advertising ban was a crucial development for the trajectory of the UK broadcasting system, and one that would later be interpreted as a reflection of the British upper classes' distaste for commercial culture. But the prohibition in fact reflected the economic interests of the most politically powerful sections of British capital. While the idea of a state monopoly was something of an anathema for liberals and conservatives, and was met with some criticism,[13] the advertising ban was strongly lobbied for by the newspapers and the news agencies (from which the Post Office received considerable revenue) and was opposed by none of the business interests consulted by the British government.[14] The relative underdevelopment of consumer culture compared to the United States was certainly a factor in the trajectory radio took in Britain, but it was decisive because the newspapers for this reason saw advertising revenue as limited and therefore saw radio as a commercial threat.[15] The early BBC was constitutionally obliged not to 'prejudice the interests of newspapers' and prevented from broadcasting any news not already reported by the press. [16]

Once this initial regulatory framework was put in place, the electrical and telecommunications companies, which had been the prime movers in the initial development of British broadcasting, quickly receded. It was the space vacated by these corporate interests that was key to the development of public service broadcasting. It allowed the broadcasting bureaucrats and professionals to exercise a degree of autonomy, while carving out a place for themselves amongst the British establishment. During the 1920s, as 'the concept of public service came to be grafted onto what were originally a set of *ad hoc*, practical arrangements',[17] they developed a distinct philosophical rationale for the shape that the British broadcasting system had already assumed.

A MEDIUM FOR DEMOCRACY?

It was the Sykes Committee of 1923, the first of a number of official inquiries that developed the concept of public service broadcasting over the decades, that initially recommended that the 'wavebands' be regarded as 'public property' and be subject to 'public safeguards'.[18] The reasoning was that since the 'wavebands' were limited, they needed to be regulated, and there should therefore be some stipulation on quality. [19] The association between public service broadcasting and cultural standards is closely associated with the BBC's first Director General, John Reith, who injected into the technocratic arguments about spectrum scarcity, natural monopoly, and public administration a sense of high moral purpose, even a romanticism. His blueprint for public service broadcasting laid out in his hastily written book *Broadcast Over Britain* stipulated that it should be non-commercial, nationally available, under 'unified control' and, most famously, should maintain high cultural standards.[20]

Discussions of 'Reithianism' have usually focused on the latter stipulation, contrasting this patrician ethos with the populism of the capitalist market. The most sophisticated account from this perspective is LeMahieu's *A Culture for Democracy*, which analyzes the response of Britain's artistic and intellectual elite to the emergence of popular culture in the early twentieth century. LeMahieu regards public service broadcasting as an attempt by what he calls the 'cultivated elite' to reassert 'cultural hierarchy' through the imposition of high culture.[21] In LeMahieu's account, the Reithian BBC offered not an egalitarian 'culture for democracy', but 'an idealised version of a fragile, never fully realised, middle-class cultural tradition'.[22] Like others arguing from the 'cultural democracy' perspective, LeMahieu regards mass markets as 'democratic' in that they appeal to the everyday lives, tastes, and preferences of ordinary people as opposed to the politics and culture of society's elite. The problem here, though, is that while consumer markets can create incentives for more popular cultural forms, such a dynamic in itself is neither inherently democratic, nor necessarily even especially egalitarian. As James Curran notes in his discussion of LeMahieu and other 'populist' media histories, it is not irrelevant that the *Daily Mail*, in LeMahieu's account a democratizing force in society, is in fact a middle-class rather than a working-class publication, that it was a supporter of British fascism, and initially welcomed the rise of Hitler.[23] It is also notable from a broader historical perspective that the same commercial press LeMahieu associates with a more democratic culture in Britain during the 1930s would subsequently play a key role in turning the tide against the UK's more egalitarian post-war political economy from the 1970s onwards.

But can the tradition of public service broadcasting pioneered by the BBC be regarded as more egalitarian and democratic by comparison? One of the most forceful and historically informed advocates of this position is Paddy Scannell, co-author with David Cardiff of *A Social History of Broadcasting*, who argues that public service broadcasting 'unobtrusively contributed to the democratisation of everyday life'.[24] As he and Cardiff put it: 'The fundamentally democratic thrust of broadcasting – of which Reith was well aware – lay in the new access to virtually the whole spectrum of public life that radio opened up for everyone. Broadcasting equalized public life through the principle of common access for all.'[25]

Yet the notion that 'universal access' is inherently democratic does not seem a sufficient basis for an authentically democratic arrangement. Indeed, it is surely more suggestive of broadcasting as an instrument of nationalism than a facilitator of democratic public life. Neither is the broader notion of universal culture or education necessarily democratic. To be sure, Reith could at times sound like a committed democrat. The BBC, he argued, could help foster 'a new and mighty weight of public opinion' so people would no longer have to accept 'the dictated and partial versions of others'.[26] Such statements, however, have to be squared with his overt authoritarianism and nationalism, and the extent to which the BBC reflected both. Like many other British elites in the interwar period, Reith was quite open about his admiration for Mussolini and Hitler.[27] In May 1933, he told an audience at Manchester University that in his view: 'A man may be as good a democrat as any other and yet reject, in the light of philosophy, history or experience, democratic process to accomplish democratic ends'.[28] Both fascism and the liberal nationalism of Reith's BBC can be seen as (very different) elite responses to the political enfranchisement of the working classes.

THE POST-WAR BBC

The decidedly conservative BBC of the 1930s underwent some significant cultural shifts in subsequent decades. During the Second World War the BBC strengthened its place in British society through its role as an instrument of public information and propaganda, deepening its relationship with the state. Under the tutelage of the Ministry of Information, it also adopted a more egalitarian nationalism with appeals to 'ordinary' culture, a trend exemplified by the recruitment of left-wing intellectuals like J.B. Priestley and George Orwell. As a public institution modelled on the civil service, the BBC was well suited to the statist politics of the post-war period, and though it lost 'the brute force of monopoly' in 1955, it adapted relatively quickly to the challenge of commercial competition. Over the course of the 1960s, there was a further move away from the elitist and austere culture of the interwar period. As Stuart Hood, who was Controller of Programmes, Television, in that decade, recalled, BBC programmes for the first time attacked 'some of the sacred cows of the establishment – the monarchy, the church, leading politicians and other previously taboo targets'.[29] Hugh Greene, Director-General from 1959 to 1969, considered that the BBC under his leadership was no longer a 'pillar of the Establishment': a 'new and younger generation was in control'.[30] Greene was certainly no radical. A liberal anti-communist, he not only had family connections in intelligence and a background in military propaganda (he had been seconded by the BBC to the Colonial Office during the 'Malayan Emergency'), but as Director-General urged MI5 to extend its secret political vetting of BBC staff.[31] Greene's BBC, though, certainly reflected some of the creative and egalitarian spirit of the sixties, producing celebrated comedies, irreverent satire, and dramas and documentaries more reflective of working-class life. For this Greene was attacked by conservatives, including in the right-wing press and the Conservative Party, and most notably by Mary Whitehouse's National Viewers and Listeners Association (NVLA), a populist conservative movement that blamed the BBC in particular for the shifts in social mores.

After Greene's departure, the BBC took a more conservative turn. The watershed moment was the appointment of Lord Hill, a former Conservative Minister, as BBC chair in July 1967 by Labour Prime Minister Harold Wilson. Hill's appointment was a shock to the BBC management and brought about a definite shift in the BBC's corporate identity – even a 'redefinition of the overall purpose of the BBC'.[32] During his tenure as BBC chair, Hill strengthened the powers of the politically appointed Board of Governors vis-à-vis the Board of Management. He also placed greater emphasis on financial and managerial control, commissioning a series of reports from the influential consultancy firm McKinsey before imposing a top down reorganisation with little consultation.[33] His successor, Michael Swann, though less belligerent was a decidedly conservative figure who actively sought to curtail the influence of sixties liberalism at the BBC. Swann lunched at the neoliberal think-tank the Institute of Economic Affairs and corresponded with its leading figures, Arthur Seldon and Ralph Harris,[34] as well as with Mary Whitehouse.[35] In March 1976, he gave a speech in which he described the BBC's move away from the progressive ethos of the 1960s: 'a change in mood in society, and a change of emphasis in Management,' he said, 'has indeed brought about a change in the Corporation.'[36]

By that point the BBC had found itself in a quite different political situation. While income from television licences had given it considerable financial independence, inflationary pressures meant that during the 1970s it needed to repeatedly negotiate with the government over its licence fee. This drew the BBC into the Labour government's austerity agenda and politicized its operations. The broader social and cultural climate, meanwhile, had also proved challenging. As the Committee on the Future of Broadcasting later noted, the late 1960s saw a growth of hostility 'to authority as such; not merely authority as expressed in the traditional organs of State but towards those in any institution who were charged with governance.'[37] In this context, the BBC, the paternalist institution par excellence, came increasingly to be seen as part of a bureaucratic and unaccountable establishment, and found its hegemony over public life increasingly contested. 'There is increasing awareness of the power that control over channels of communication carries,' the Parliamentary Select Committee on Nationalised Industries noted in 1972, and the 'case is made with increasing cogency that broadcasting is in the hands of a small body not representative of the wider community.'[38] By then a radical movement for media reform had taken shape, incorporating trade unionists, left-wing activists and intellectuals, academics, and left-wing politicians, with the late Tony Benn MP emerging as something of a figurehead as he had for much of the left.

A RADICAL REFORM AGENDA

Tony Benn chaired the Labour Party advisory committee on broadcasting (1957-1964) and then served as Postmaster-General (1964-66). Briggs notes that he was the first Postmaster-General who 'while believing strongly in public service broadcasting, did not identify public service broadcasting with the BBC'.[39] In 1968, he made what became a notorious speech at a Labour Party meeting in which he attacked 'the benevolent paternalism of the constitutional monarchs who reside in the palatial Broadcasting House'.[40] One phrase he used, 'broadcasting is really too important to be left to the broadcasters,' was to be widely quoted by both proponents and opponents of media reform. Three days later, Benn noted in his diary that 'a major row [is] raging over my BBC speech'.[41] The former Labour Minister Ray Gunter was quoted in the press describing it as a 'frightening statement', whilst the Shadow Postmaster General, Paul Bryan, said it was evidence that Harold Wilson, who he compared to Hitler, was planning to take over the BBC.[42] Privately Wilson responded angrily to the speech, and it was soon publicly repudiated by one of Wilson's leading left-wing Cabinet ministers, Richard Crossman.[43]

Benn was at that time going through something of a political transition from technocratic modernizer to a radical democratic socialist. Influenced by the New Left, he became an articulate and charismatic proponent of the democratization of the state and civil society as a route out of the political and economic crisis of the 1970s. He worked closely with groups campaigning on media reform, as well as with academics and trade unions, promoting a critical view of the broadcasting establishment that he said 'the whole left shared',[44] and which was informed by the strongly held belief that there existed a 'bias of the media against working people'.[45] A typical expression of Benn's position on the media was given in a speech in February 1972:

> Nobody wants governmental political control, but the present combination of corporate or commercial control theoretically answerable to politically appointed boards of governors is not in any sense a democratic enough procedure to control the power the broadcasters have.
>
> What is required therefore is some way of developing a new framework to democratise this power without falling into the trap of State control or confusing commercial competition and free enterprise with the free expression of different views on the air.[46]

It is important to note that the critique developed by the left during this period was not directed at journalists or programme makers, but rather at the institutions in which they worked. Indeed, some of the most active and influential campaigners for radical media reform were organized workers within the industry. The Association of Cinematograph Television and Allied Technicians (ACTT), a broadcasting union from 1969 headed by the left-wing Labour Party member Alan Sapper, not only undertook a number of important industrial actions in the television and film industry during the 1970s and 1980s, but was also explicitly 'political' in combining a class-based critique of the media with pressure for structural reforms. It commissioned research on the reporting of industrial disputes and helped to promote the issue of media bias in the wider labour movement. Another radical group of media workers was the Free Communications Group, 'a grouping of journalists and broadcasters campaigning, within a broadly syndicalist perspective against media concentration and what was seen as anti-working-class bias.'[47] The FCG published a periodical called *The Open Secret* and organized discussion groups. Benn was the guest speaker at its first such group, held in July 1969.[48] Later that month, one of the FCG's steering committee members was quoted by *The Times* as describing the BBC as 'ripe for democratic control',[49] and the group subsequently began organising workers in the BBC. [50]

In 1974, the radical critique of broadcasting that had been popularized by this network of journalists, academics, and activists was endorsed by the Labour Party's National Executive Committee, at the time very much under Benn's influence. A report of a Study Group entitled 'The People and the Media', which dealt not only with broadcasting but also with cinema and the press, proposed the break-up and democratisation of the BBC-ITV duopoly. The radical proposals were the result of a number of meetings held between 1972 and 1974, the majority of which were chaired by Benn. The Study Group acknowledged the achievements of the existing British broadcasting system, but was candid about its shortcomings. The 'plain fact,' the report stated, 'is that our broadcasting, for all its reputation and achievements, is now characterized by closed and autocratic institutions and marked resistance to wider public involvement in its decision making processes'.[51] The challenge, according to the Study Group, was 'to devise a framework for the media that avoids the twin dangers of government and commercial control'.[52]

The proposed solution outlined in the report was a system of arm's length non-market and non-governmental regulation and funding allocation, combined with a mix of direct democracy, corporatist arrangements, and workers' self-management all ensuring more representative programme making, editorial decision-making, and regulatory oversight. Government control over broadcasting was to be curtailed, with accountability instead being via 'the introduction of real internal democracy' as well as 'elected representatives on broadcasting management bodies' and the 'democratic determination and control of broad strategies of national broadcasting policy'. The report advocated the phasing out of the BBC licence fee, which was described as a 'clumsy and regressive tax', while commercial advertising was to be strictly separated from programme making. The BBC and ITV would be replaced with decentralized and democratically managed programme units that would afford 'greater diversity of management, [and] programming freedom' and 'the widest practicable access to the media by community groups and by individuals'. These 'dispersed programme units' would produce content for one national and one regional television corporation, and one or two non-commercial radio corporations. [53]

The whole broadcasting system was to be overseen by two quasi-governmental bodies. A Communications Council would act as a research and advisory body for the regulation of all mass media in the UK, as well as an Ombudsman for complaints. The Council would offer policy expertise and recommendations, and would 'include elected representatives from trade unions, local or regional government and national organisations, as well as some MPs.' A Public Broadcasting Commission, meanwhile, would more directly oversee the funding and regulation of broadcasting. 'The People and the Media' emphasised that its proposals would not entail a strengthening of governmental control over the media, arguing on the contrary that if anything the proposals would afford greater independence for broadcasting organisations through 'internal democracy within the framework of public accountability'.[54] The Press Council, however, dismissed this as 'demagogic claptrap',[55] while the industry magazine *Broadcast* wrote that the proposals were 'so strongly based on doctrinaire views about "internal democracy" and concepts of accountability that nobody has bothered to question those beliefs objectively.'[56]

While the left's calls for the democratisation of the media in the 1970s tended to be met with condescension and hysteria from liberals and conservatives, their expression through the Labour Party meant that they could not be dismissed entirely. British officialdom responded with the Annan Committee on the Future of Broadcasting, which became the focal point for broadcasting debates in the 1970s. The committee's final report, published in 1977, stated:

> It has been put to us that broadcasting should be 'opened up'. At present, so it is argued, the broadcasters have become an overmighty subject, an unelected elite, more interested in preserving their own organisation

intact than in enriching the nation's culture. Dedicated to the outworn concepts of balance and impartiality, how can the broadcasters reflect the multitude of opinions in our pluralist society?[57]

This assessment had been strongly denied by the BBC in its submission to the committee, which confidently declared that 'there is no barrier' between the BBC and the public. 'We and the people we serve,' the BBC declared, 'are in a relationship so close that it is difficult to draw a clear boundary between us.'[58] The committee was not convinced. Annan considered the broadcasters to be 'insufficiently accountable to the public',[59] and the BBC in particular came under considerable criticism. An 'organisational malaise' was said to have taken hold[60] and its news and current affairs journalism was found to be too narrow and too timid.[61] It was recommended that the BBC produce more engaging and committed political programming, that it maintain a broader network of contacts, increase the specialisation of journalists, and introduce 'clearer lines of decision-making' and 'better communication'.[62] In all this, the onus was placed on the BBC to implement the changes itself. As Des Freedman has noted, the committee 'embraced the need for change without undermining the basic authority of the existing broadcasting organizations and structures.'[63]

Annan was certainly willing to make concessions to non-elite groups and to encourage their better representation by broadcasters, but he was plainly not willing to endorse measures that might undermine the power and authority of institutions 'charged with governance'. For Annan, as for the BBC leadership, the broadcasters were trusted professionals, while the BBC as an institution was by definition democratic since it was sanctioned by Parliament. In delivering the Granada lecture in July 1977, the committee's chair gave a belated riposte to Benn: 'Do not let anyone tell you that broadcasting is too important to be left to the broadcasters.'[64] By this time the egalitarian movements that had driven the broadcasting agenda since the late 1960s were receding under the pressure of fiscal austerity and a growing conservative backlash. The broadcasting bureaucrats, meanwhile, strongly resisted proposals for democratic reforms being pushed by the left, preferring to defend the quasi-autonomy they had been granted by the political establishment that was legitimated with appeals to Parliament and their own professional expertise. The structures of broadcasting therefore remained largely unchanged during this period. Though the establishment of the pluralistic and occasionally radical Channel 4 was a considerable victory, as was the earlier establishment of the BBC's Community Programme Unit in 1972 – supported 'only in an uncomprehending, lukewarm manner' by the

BBC hierarchy[65] – the momentum for a broader democratic restructuring would not be recovered, and several years later a very different agenda for media reform would be taken up by a potent alliance of neoliberal intellectuals and corporate interests.

A NEW HEGEMONY

With the advent of the neoliberal Conservative government in 1979, a new coalition of forces – comprised of private media interests, advertising firms, neoliberal politicians, journalists, and think-tank intellectuals – was to seize the agenda on media reform. The changes that the BBC then went through have been very poorly understood. The conventional story is that the Thatcher government hoped to privatize the BBC, or at least to abolish the licence fee and force it to take advertising, but that a combination of good luck, pragmatism, and politicking following by an ambitious programme of internal reform at the BBC helped secure the broadcaster's long term future, bringing public service broadcasting into the twenty-first century.[66] This is a misreading based in far too narrow a focus on the immediate political aspirations of Margaret Thatcher, or alternatively on a rather crude caricature of neoliberalism that assumes it to be merely a project for 'rolling back' the state or transferring public assets to the private sector. What in fact happened was that the BBC was radically reformed in line with the new neoliberal, pro-business political consensus.

The beginnings of this long process are fairly well known. In the midst of a series of public attacks on the BBC over its political programming and its financial management, Thatcher set up a committee on the future of the BBC that was dominated by neoliberal experts and chaired by the neoliberal economist Alan Peacock. The committee disappointed the prime minister by not recommending the abolition of the licence fee, instead proposing a number of policy changes intended to institute a more gradual shift towards a market-based model of broadcasting, most notably the stipulation that the BBC should commission content from the private sector, much like Channel 4. The vision essentially was that public funding would be diverted into the private sector so as to foster a plurality of private media companies that could eventually form the basis of a competitive consumer-based media system, displacing the patrician public service model. Whilst the Peacock Committee worked out this medium term plan for shifting the media policy agenda, the Thatcherites gradually filled the BBC's Board of Governors with their supporters, while in partnership with the reactionary press relentlessly attacking the BBC for its supposed left-wing bias and profligate expenditure. This political pressure eventually resulted in the forced departure of BBC Director General Alasdair Milne in 1987. Milne had symbolized the more independent spirit of BBC programming that had taken hold since the 1960s, and his departure was a clear watershed for a protracted but profound process of institutional change at the BBC, which was part and parcel of the broader neoliberal restructuring of British society.

Key to the radical neoliberal reform of the BBC was the person of John Birt, who was brought in from the private media company LWT to head the BBC's journalism after Milne's departure, and who then served as Director General during much of the 1990s. Birt first focused on centralizing editorial authority and implementing script approval for politically sensitive programming. Then, as Director General, he oversaw a radical and hugely unpopular set of reforms that would transform the organisational structure and culture of the BBC, further integrating it into the capitalist market. Producer Choice, as Birt's flagship managerial project was known, was a classic neoliberal initiative similar to the internal market introduced in the NHS in the same period. On the advice of management consultants, it divided the BBC into separate units that each would need to 'break even' in the course of buying and selling services from other sections of the BBC in competition with the private sector, from which programme makers were now encouraged to buy services and the BBC was obliged to commission programming. Naturally the project was justified as an efficiency and cost cutting exercise, but it in fact led to a proliferation of wasteful and demoralising bureaucracy intended to govern the conduct of workers through coercive incentives, targets, monitoring and audits.[67] Another dramatic shift that took place at the BBC over this period was to turn economics reporting away from employment, wages, and trade union politics and towards financial markets, technocratic questions of economic management, and explicitly pro-business perspectives, with even popular and politically moderate policy options absent or completely marginalized.[68] The outcome of this long process of change that the BBC underwent through the 1980s and 1990s was not only that BBC programme makers became more constrained by its highly politicized managerial and editorial hierarchy, but that the BBC became much more fully integrated into the capitalist market, the values of which have shaped its organisational culture.[69]

This was part and parcel of a broader project to construct a political settlement that would bring political institutions much closer to the interests of capital. In the case of the BBC, the result is a broadcaster that remains publicly owned, but in its present form and current trajectory is not able to offer anything like a substantive alternative to the corporate media, nor to perform the sort of role allotted to it in democratic theory. On the contrary, the BBC appears an institution at ease with the neoliberal political settlement and apparently unable to comprehend the seriousness of the crisis in which capitalist democracies find themselves. This was powerfully illustrated during the most recent Charter renewal process, which saw the BBC into its ninetieth year. Trailering its public pitch and negotiating stance in March 2015, Director General Tony Hall referred to the BBC as 'profoundly democratic', but failed to make even a limited case on this basis. He focused instead on the BBC as a global brand for the promotion of British culture that strengthens 'the UK's creative industries' and 'Britain's competitive position'.[70] Hall proposed a 'competition revolution' at the BBC, involving a new wave of radical marketization whereby television programmes, with a few limited exceptions (notably some news journalism), would be fully opened up to private sector competition, as would 60 per cent of radio. BBC programme makers would meanwhile be permitted to sell their programmes to the private sector so as to offset any losses. With some of the limited protections removed, the Conservative government adopted the proposals. This plan, 'Compete and Compare', now being rolled out under the new Charter with familiar rhetoric about cutting overheads, bringing an end to 'working in silos', and calls for staff to be 'more entrepreneurial', and is plainly a revival of the neoliberal managerialism of the Birt era.[71]

THE FUTURE OF PUBLIC AND DEMOCRATIC MEDIA

The twenty-first century BBC, then, not only seems incapable of offering a convincing defence of public service broadcasting, it remains thoroughly committed to a bankrupt political paradigm. This is perhaps unsurprising given the BBC's organisational structure, and the political context within which it was operating during the last Charter renewal. But part of the problem has been the lack of political pressure and alternative vision offered by the left. With the onslaughts of the 1980s, the left tacitly lined up with liberals, moderate conservatives, and right-wing social democrats in defence of the BBC – which was rightly seen to be under existential threat from the New Right and private media interests – and even the most radical of media scholars have been slow to articulate a vision of twenty-first century public and democratic media.

The cutting edge of contemporary debates on public service broadcasting in the UK in recent years is represented by an unofficial inquiry held in 2015-16, chaired by the Labour peer and former television producer David Puttnam. Based at Goldsmiths College, London, a leading centre of critical media scholarship, the Puttnam inquiry brought together industry figures and media academics to develop a defence of public service broadcasting in 'the digital age'. The inquiry drew heavily on the work of academic contributors, especially that of Georgina Born who had conducted a critical ethnography of the BBC in the Birt era.[72] It also explicitly took inspiration from the 1962 Pilkington Committee, which had given a strong endorsement for public service broadcasting and provided a bedrock for the BBC's confident expansion under Hugh Greene. The Puttnam report, published in June 2016, described itself as a reflection on 'the nature of good broadcasting in a democracy'. It offered a considered defence of the BBC and the public service broadcasting tradition as a bulwark against 'market totalitarianism', and as a guarantor of the 'heterogeneous provision of programming' and 'active participation in democratic processes'.[73] But it was rather unambitious in its proposals. The report placed considerable emphasis on pluralism, arguing that public service media can serve both as a 'means of collective experience' and a source of diversity and intercultural dialogue, in many ways echoing arguments made in the Annan inquiry which had similarly advocated more pluralistic provision – in Puttnam's terms 'democratic communicative pluralism' – within a traditional public service framework.

There has, however, been a slow move towards a more radical reform agenda in some circles, especially as the rise of Corbynism has newly politicized questions of media bias, and BBC impartiality in particular. Some inchoate proposals for democratic reform and decentralized governance have emanated from the Media Reform Coalition (MRC), an organisation established by activists and academics in the wake of the phone hacking scandal which has mainly campaigned on regulation of the British press. Its submission to the BBC Charter renewal consultation proposed 'democratising the BBC so that more diverse voices are heard in decision-making at all levels', although details were somewhat scarce.[74] The cultural theorist and Labour left intellectual, Jeremy Gilbert, has called for the democratisation of the BBC.[75] So has the Campaign for Press and Broadcasting Freedoms (CPBF), the legacy body of the media reform movement of the 1970s, which has advocated the replacement of the government appointees on the BBC's new 'unitary board' with staff representatives from trade unions and directly elected board members representing viewers, listeners, and online service users. The CPBF has also called for 'the establishment of a democratically constituted body to set the level of the licence fee'.[76]

Non-market organisational reforms have also been proposed. These were central to the MRC's submission on the Charter renewal, which called for the establishment of an arms-length independent commissioning body, funded by a levy on the profits of the largest media companies in the UK (such as Google, BT, and Facebook), which would support online video channels able to find audiences via BBC cross-promotion.[77] More radical proposals have been put forward by the MRC's chair, Justin Schlosberg, who has advocated a decentralisation of the BBC's structure and governance and a shift towards a 'networked BBC' modelled on the Nederlandse Publieke Omroep (NPO) that would administer a number of audience cooperatives and more specialist news and current affairs organisations.[78]

Dan Hind has made one of the most significant contributions to the contemporary reform agenda with his proposal for a system of democratic commissioning.[79] Drawing on neo-republican democratic ideas, Hind's proposal is for a form of non-market, democratic funding allocation, similar to Robert McChesney and John Nichols's 2010 proposal for a 'Citizen's News Voucher' that would afford all citizens the right to allocate an equal amount of funding ($200 each in their proposal) to support a not-for-profit media outlet of their choice.[80] Hind's proposal for 'public commissioning', however, is distinctive in that it would entail not only the democratisation of resource allocations to media organisations, but also the democratisation of editorial decision-making. Hind proposes that trusts would democratically distribute funding from the licence fee or from general taxation to journalists, academics, and citizen researchers based on specific project proposals that would be publicized, discussed in public forums, and then voted on by the citizenry. The outputs of such projects would then be publicized via the BBC and commercial broadcasters and publishers, but with the form and extent of the outputs also determined by democratic vote.[81]

Such proposals have yet to make their way onto the mainstream policy agenda. The Labour Party's 2017 election manifesto signalled a radical break with the neoliberal policy consensus, but was rather unambitious on the question of media reform. It pledged to support and uphold the independence of the BBC and to 'ensure the BBC and public service broadcasting has a healthy future'.[82] Technological developments and political conditions, however, have quite quickly made radical democratic reform of the media look much more feasible, and there are already enough existing ideas and expertise to sketch out a radical reform agenda. On funding, it seems fairly clear that the licence fee needs to be abolished. This will mean the establishment of an alternative source of funding; perhaps a mix of funds from general taxation and a levy on the new media oligopolies, with both insulated from political influence. In institutional terms, those organisations which currently dominate the media landscape will, at the very minimum, need to be subject to much more public oversight. In the case of the BBC, there seems no good reason why its governance structures shouldn't be democratized via its digital services framework, and at the same time governmental influence be removed altogether. The same technological infrastructure, together with the existing commercial commissioning processes, would also allow for much more radical reform initiatives.

Under the present neoliberal system, all BBC TV programming will be subject to commercial competition. This could be immediately reversed with some programming protected and kept 'in-house', and some subject to public and democratic, rather than market-based, commissioning. If the elite are left to their own devices, the planned future for the BBC is one where it continues to serve as a quasi-state news service, and as a brand and source of revenue for privately owned media corporations. But processes that are currently set to increase profits and precarity could be repurposed so as to foster more diverse, creative and innovative programming, better working conditions, and a more democratic and egalitarian organization and political culture more generally. Given the centrality of the media to public life, this should be a central component of new plans currently being advanced within the Labour Party for developing more democratic, decentralized and regionalized forms of public ownership and governance.[83]

NOTES

My thanks to Dan Hind for some fruitful discussions on media reform while working on this essay.

1   Martin Gilens, *Affluence and Influence: Economic Inequality and Political Power in America*, Princeton: Princeton University Press, 2012; Martin Gilens and Benjamin Page, 'Testing Theories of American Politics: Elites, Interest Groups, and Average Citizens', *Perspectives on Politics* 12(03), 2014, pp. 564-81.

2   Raymond Williams, *Communications*, Harmondsworth: Penguin, 1976, p. 131.

3   Raymond Williams, *Television: Technology and Cultural Form*, edited by Ederyn Williams, New York: Routledge, 2003, pp. 27-8.

4   Williams, *Television*, pp. 27-8.

5   See Alex Carey and Andrew Lohrey, *Taking the Risk Out of Democracy: Corporate Propaganda Versus Freedom and Liberty*, Champaign: University of Illinois Press, 1997; and David Miller and William Dinan, *A Century of Spin: How Public Relations Became the Cutting Edge of Corporate Power*, London: Pluto Press, 2008.

6   Asa Briggs, *History of Broadcasting in the United Kingdom: Volume I: The Birth of Broadcasting*, London: Oxford University Press, 1961, p. 59.

7   Robert W. McChesney, *Rich Media, Poor Democracy*, New York: New Press, 2015, p. 228.

8   Michael Mann, *The Sources of Social Power: Volume 3, Global Empires and Revolution, 1890-1945*, Cambridge: Cambridge University Press, 2012, p. 296.

9   Valeria Camporesi, '"We Talk a Different Language": The Impact of US Broadcasting in Britain, 1922–1927', *Historical Journal of Film, Radio and Television* 10(3), 1990, p. 263.

10   McChesney, *Rich Media, Poor Democracy*, pp. 230-231.

11   Briggs, *The History of Broadcasting Volume I*, pp. 63-4.

12   Briggs, *The History of Broadcasting Volume I*, pp. 188-9.

13   Paddy Scannell, 'Public Service Broadcasting: The History of a Concept', in A. Goodwin and G. Whannel, eds., *Understanding Television*, London: Routledge, 1990, pp. 14-15.

14   Briggs, *The History of Broadcasting Volume I*, pp. 130-31.

15   Camporesi, 'The impact of US Broadcasting in Britain, 1922–1927', p. 261.

16   Briggs, *The History of Broadcasting Volume I*, pp. 106, 164. During the 1930s the BBC remained aligned to newspaper and publishing interests in seeking to prevent the emergence of rival broadcasting and pressure for the BBC to take advertising. See Donald R. Browne, 'Radio Normandie and the IBC Challenge to the BBC Monopoly', *Historical Journal of Film, Radio and Television* 5(1), 1985, p. 7.

17   Scannell, 'Public Service Broadcasting', p. 12.

18   Scannell and Cardiff, *A Social History of Broadcasting*, p. 6.

19   This was affirmed decades later by the Pilkington Committee, which in the heyday of public service broadcasting stated that since 'the frequency space available to broadcasting is limited, it is essential that what is available should be used to the best advantage'. Pilkington Report, 12, para. 33, quoted in Michael Tracey, *The Decline and Fall of Public Service Broadcasting*, Oxford: Oxford University Press, 1998, p. 23.

20   Briggs, *The History of Broadcasting Volume I*, pp. 234-9.

21   D.L. LeMahieu, *A Culture for Democracy: Mass Communication and the Cultivated Mind in Britain Between the Wars*, Oxford: Clarendon Press, 1988, p. 138. LeMahieu situates Reith's paternalism alongside that of the British documentary pioneer, John Gierson, who like Reith combined an interest in propaganda with an emphasis on public education and cultural uplift.

22   LeMahieu, *A Culture for Democracy*, pp. 188-9.

23   James Curran, *Media and Power*, New York: Routledge, 2002, p. 43.

24   Paddy Scannell, 'Public Service Broadcasting and Modern Public Life,' in P. Scannell, P. Schlesinger and C. Sparks, eds, *Culture and Power: A Media, Culture & Society Reader*, London: Sage, 1992, p. 318.

25   Scannell and Cardiff, *A Social History of Broadcasting*, p. 14. Scannell subsequently extends this argument to television also, echoing these very same claims in Scannell, 'Public Service Broadcasting and Modern Public Life,' p. 322.

26   Quoted in Scannell, 'Public Service Broadcasting', p. 14.

27   Marista Leishman, *My Father: Reith of the BBC*, Edinburgh: Saint Andrew Press, 2006, pp. 150, 2. Matthew Arnold, who strongly influenced Reith and saw 'culture' as a basis for transgressing class antagonism, exhibited a quite brutal authoritarianism. He regarded the state as 'sacred' and considered that 'monster processions in the streets and forcible irruptions into the parks, even in professed support of this good design ought to be unflinchingly forbidden and repressed'. Such violence was, for Arnold, an acceptable price to pay for the realisation of cultural perfection in an ordered society. Rioters should be flogged and their leaders executed. See Matthew Arnold, *Culture and Anarchy: An Essay in Political and Social Criticism*, London: Smith, Elder and Co., 1869, pp. 158-9.

28   Quoted LeMahieu, *A Culture For Democracy*, p. 147. See also, Ian McIntyre, *The Expense of Glory: Life of John Reith*, London: HarperCollins, 1995, p. 218.

29   Stuart Hood, *On Television*, London: Pluto Press, 1987, p. 49.

30   Hugh Greene, *The Third Floor Front: A View of Broadcasting in the Sixties*, London: Bodley Head, 1969, p. 133.

31   Christopher Andrew, *The Defence of the Realm*, London: Penguin, 2010, p. 396.

32 Michael Tracey, *The Production of Political Television*, London: Routledge, 1977, p. 162.

33 Victoria Wegg-Prosser, 'Thirty Years of Managerial Change at the BBC', *Public Money & Management* 21(1), 2001, pp. 9-14.

34 Ben Jackson, 'The Think-Tank Archipelago: Thatcherism and Neo-Liberalism', in B. Jackson and R. Saunders, eds, *Making Thatcher's Britain*, Oxford: Oxford University Press, 2012, p. 56.

35 Ben Thompson, *Ban This Filth!: Letters From the Mary Whitehouse*, London: Faber and Faber, 2012.

36 Michael Swann, 'Education, the Media and the Quality of Life', Speech to the Headmasters' Association Annual Conference at St Catherine's College Cambridge, 26 March 1976.

37 *Report of the Committee on the Future of Broadcasting*, HM Stationery Office, 1977, p. 14.

38 Second Report from the Select Committee on Nationalised Industries, Session 1971-72, Independent Broadcasting Authority (formerly Independent Television Authority), London: HM Stationery Office, 1973, p. ixi, para.142.

39 Des Freedman, 'Modernising the BBC: Wilson's Government and Television 1964-1966', *Contemporary British History* 15(1), 2001, pp. 21-40.

40 Quoted in Philip Rawstorne, 'Political Role of BBC Must be Reformed', *Guardian*, 19 October 1968.

41 Tony Benn, *The Benn Diaries: 1940-1990*, London: Random House, 2013, p. 196.

42 George Clark, 'Gunter Broadside at Benn's "Frightening" Attack on BBC,' *The Times*, 21 October 1968, p. 1. John Desborough, 'MPs Join Row Over Benn', *Daily Mirror*, 21 October 1968, p. 32.

43 Hugh Greene praised Crossman's remarks while dismissing Benn's as 'silly and trivial'. Kenelm Jemour, '"Silly" Benn Speech Rapped by BBC Chief', *Daily Mirror*, 22 October 1968.

44 Interview with Tony Benn, 3 February 2011.

45 Leo Panitch and Colin Leys, *The End of Parliamentary Socialism: From New Left to New Labour*, London: Verso, 2001, pp. 59-60.

46 'Voice For the People,' *Guardian*, 9 February 1972.

47 Nicholas Garnham, 'A Personal Intellectual Memoir', *Media, Culture & Society* 27(4), 2005, pp. 472-3.

48 Michael Hatfield, 'New Magazine Hits Out', *The Times*, 5 July 1969, p. 8.

49 Leonard Beaton, 'Who Should Control Press and Television?', *The Times*, 17 July 1969.

50 Des Freedman, *Television Policies of the Labour Party, 1951-2001*, London: Frank Cass, 2003, p. 74.

51 *The People and the Media: The Report of a Labour Party Study Group on the Relationships Between the People, the Press and Broadcasting, Labour Party, 1974*, pp. 11-12.

52 *The People and the Media*, p. 7.

53 *The People and the Media*, pp. 8-14.

54 *The People and the Media*, p. 12.

55 'Shawcross Challenge on Editorial "Democracy"', *The Times*, 4 October 1974.

56 Cited in Freedman, *Television Policies of the Labour Party*, p. 87.

57 *Report of the Committee on the Future of Broadcasting*, HM Stationery Office, 1977, p. 16.

58 National Archives, HO 245/87 Committee on The Future of Broadcasting (1974-1977), Minutes, Evidence and Papers, Copies of Evidence, British Broadcasting Corporation.

BBC Memorandum: The BBC and the Public, British Broadcasting Corporation, April 1975.

59   *Report of the Committee on the Future of Broadcasting*, HM Stationery Office, 1977, p. 32.

60   *Report of the Committee on the Future of Broadcasting*, p. 124.

61   *Report of the Committee on the Future of Broadcasting*, p. 288.

62   *Report of the Committee on the Future of Broadcasting*, p. 124.

63   Freedman, *Television Policies of the Labour Party*, p. 101.

64   Quoted in Kenneth Gosling, 'Annan Plea For Highest Broadcasting Standards,' *The Times*, 5 July 1977, p. 3.

65   Giles Oakley and Peter Lee-Wright, 'Opening Doors: the BBC's Community Programme Unit 1973–2002', *History Workshop Journal* 82 (1), 2016, pp. 213-34.

66   See in particular the account provided by Asa Brigg's successor as the BBC's official historian, Jean Seaton. James Curran and Jean Seaton, *Power Without Responsibility: Press, Broadcasting and the Internet in Britain*, Seventh Edition, New York: Routledge, 2010; and Jean Seaton, *Pinkoes and Traitors: The BBC and the Nation, 1974–1987*, Kindle edition, London: Profile, 2015.

67   Tom Mills, *The BBC: Myth of a Public Service*, London: Verso, pp. 140-66.

68   Mike Berry, 'The "Today" Programme and the Banking Crisis', *Journalism* 14(2), 2013, pp. 253-70; Mike Berry, 'No Alternative to Austerity: How BBC Broadcast News Reported the Deficit Debate', *Media, Culture & Society* 38(6), 2016, pp. 844-63.

69   *Mills, The BBC.*

70   'Hall to Make Case for "Democratic" BBC', *Broadcast*, 2 March 2015.

71   'Director-General Tony Hall's New Year Message to BBC Staff', BBC Media Centre, 11 January 2017.

72   Born, *Uncertain Vision*; Georgina Born and Tony Prosser, 'Culture and Consumerism: Citizenship, Public Service Broadcasting and the BBC's Fair Trading Obligations', *Modern Law Review* 64(5), 2001, p. 676.

73   *A Future for Public Service Television: Content and Platforms in a Digital World: A Report on the Future of Public Service Television in the UK in the 21st Century*, London: Department of Media and Communications, Goldsmiths, University of London, p. 4.

74   Media Reform Coalition, Submission to BBC Charter Review Public Consultation, 7 October 2015, p. 8.

75   Jeremy Gilbert, 'Introduce Democracy and an Elected Director-General', Open Democracy, 30 September 2015.

76   *Save Public Broadcasting: The BBC's Charter Review 2016*, London: Campaign for Press and Broadcasting Freedom, p. 4.

77   Media Reform Coalition, Submission to BBC Charter Review Public Consultation, 7 October 2015, pp. 1, 12.

78   Justin Schlosberg, 'What Would an Autonomous BBC Look Like?', in N. Seth-Smith, J. Mackay, and D. Hind, eds, *Rethinking the BBC Public Media in the 21st Century*, Margate: Commonwealth, 2016, pp. 8-11.

79   Dan Hind, *The Return of the Public: Democracy, Power and the Case for Media Reform*, London: Verso Books, 2012.

80   Robert McChesney and John Nichols, *The Death and Life of American Journalism: The Media Revolution That Will Begin the World Again*, Philadelphia: Nation Books, 2010, pp. 202-212.

81   Hind, *The Return of the Public* pp. 153-74.

82   *For the Many Not the Few: The Labour Party Manifesto 2017*, London: Labour Party, 2017, p. 97.

83   *Alternative Models of Ownership: Report to the Shadow Chancellor of the Exchequer and Shadow Secretary of State for Business, Energy and Industrial Strategy*, London: Labour Party, 2017.

DIGITAL DEMOCRACY?

NINA POWER

We stand on the cusp of enormous change, both politically and technologically, and the two can hardly be separated at this point. To speak from the situation in the United Kingdom at the moment is to recognize a series of sea changes and tendencies that will, and have already, changed much about contemporary life for millions. We need to be wary of both political and technological determinism here – the recent surprising hung parliament in Britain which saw the Conservative government drop more than twenty points in the polls on the back of a terrible election campaign and massive Labour activism shows that politics remains unpredictable, even when austerity and despair have become internalized. Technology's future too remains uncertain, even as it is integrated more and more into the everyday lives of millions to greater or lesser degrees. We cannot begin to discuss the relationship between technology and politics, however, without acknowledging from the outset the fundamental asymmetries in its distribution in the modern world, or without a series of major caveats. As many feminist writers have pointed out, technology cannot be considered as neutrally or inevitably 'progressive'. Cynthia Cockburn put it like this more than thirty years ago:

> It is common sense to suppose that technology, as a medium of power, will be developed and used in any system of dominance to further the interest of those who are on top. As women, then, we have to consider technology from, at the very least, the perspectives of both class and sex.[1]

Similarly, we can also take our cue from the deep concern and suspicion expressed by Marcuse and other twentieth century critical theorists about the ambivalent nature of modern technology:

Technology, as a mode of production, as the totality of instruments, devices and contrivances which characterize the machine age is thus at the same time a mode of organizing and perpetuating (or changing) social relationships, a manifestation of prevalent thought and behavior patterns, an instrument for control and domination.[2]

To think politics and technology together, then, is to rethink what we mean by organization, as well as to understand what it is that is being organized (knowledge, resources, people). The uneven distribution of technology, globally and locally, has put questions of automation, production and consumption firmly on the left's policy agenda, and such questions go to the heart of Marxism's status as a live political and theoretical perspective on the world. Expanding our historical and critical relationship to technology via feminist and ecological perspectives, particularly thinking about the continued dependence on fossil fuels, and how automation might avoid that (or if it can avoid it), there are huge questions at stake: the future of work, the future of politics, the future of global relations of production and consumption, and even the relationship between men and women. Politics and technology must also be understood as intimately intertwined in the everyday lives of millions.

One factor in the success of Corbyn's Labour Party in the 2017 UK election was the massive mobilization of young voters, attracted not only by socially just policies and promises of free university tuition fees, but also influenced, not so much by old media (the right-wing Murdoch-owned press which spent months smearing Corbyn), as by social media which tended irreverently leftward. If older media forms have lost their capacity to influence political decision making, these newer forms of 'digital democratising' need to be understood both at the level of form and at the level of content. Again, we should be wary of overly hasty causal stories (such as the reductionist analyses of the Arab Spring that attributed to Facebook and Twitter some sort of revolutionary determinism), but at the same time it is clear that major shifts in the media landscape and the speed and manner of the dissemination of words and images (or both at the same time in the form of memes and viral videos) are having an enormous impact on the way politics proceeds, for better or worse.

I'll begin here, in the light of the massive Labour resurgence, with an analysis of a brief policy document launched by Labour in August 2016. 'The Digital Democracy Manifesto' indicates some of the core techno-political concerns that interest us here, under the following headings: 'Universal Service Network', 'Open Knowledge Library', 'Community

Media Freedom', 'Platform Cooperatives', 'Digital Citizen Passport', 'Programming for Everyone', 'The People's Charter of Digital Liberties', and 'Massive Mutli-Person On-line Deliberation'. From the slightly clunky titles alone it is clear that politics and technology are here being thought together: albeit a rather narrow image of technology that concentrates on the internet, end-users, and 'networked individuals'. Nevertheless, the Manifesto's call for 'high speed broadband and mobile connectivity for every household, company and organisation in Britain', for 'cooperative ownership of digital platforms for distributing labour and selling services', and for 'publicly funded software and hardware' demonstrate an attempt to make egalitarian services and technologies that are so far unevenly distributed.[3] It is an image of publicness in the form of networks and platforms that nevertheless has security and privacy at its heart – elsewhere the Manifesto talks about the 'Digital Citizen Passport', which will gather information and provide a way of interacting with public services like 'health, welfare, education and housing'. Users will be encouraged to share anonymized data 'for medical, government and academic research', but at the same time individuals will be protected against unauthorized hacking on the basis of 'the human right to individual privacy'. Elsewhere, the 'Open Knowledge Library' will gather 'the digital repository of lessons, lectures, curricula and student work from Britain's nurseries, schools, colleges and universities'.

While caution might be urged here, as technophiles imagine a bright new future of pre-recorded lectures, virtual classrooms, and the elimination of existing lecturers, there is nevertheless a series of oppositions and tensions at the heart of the Manifesto that are worth excavating for any deeper investigation of the current hopes and fears relating to technology and politics. The first is the relationship between the public and the private, and how this relates to various images we have on the left of the 'commons', and especially of the limitations that are often exhibited in thinking the internet and the commons together. The second is the relationship between democracy and technology. The language of 'rights' and 'charters' in the Manifesto harkens back to older civil and revolutionary relations to the commons and public ownership. The Manifesto also tries to integrate unions with the new digital age, summed up in its desire to protect 'the inalienable right of trade union membership to everyone who earns most or some of their livelihood from digital platforms'. The question arises of whether this is adequate. The third question involves the construction and image of a new collective digital subject. The Manifesto states: '[b]y enhancing the on-line rights of every individual, we will facilitate the virtual collectivity of all citizens.' But is this 'new collective' the natural heir of the proletariat, and a potentially revolutionary force, or a more passive beast? Here I will suggest that the crucial question for the left in relation to the ever-pressing question of automation concerns the relationship between jobs that can be automated and those that cannot. Those forms of paid and unpaid employment that fall under the heading of 'care work' or social reproduction in its broadest possible sense will here be posited as the major battleground for future debates regarding how work should be valued, and how we might think about the future of work more broadly.

THE PUBLIC, THE PRIVATE, AND THE COMMONS

An overt focus on technology, particularly the internet, can give the impression that the relationship between the public and private is primarily carried out online, or in virtual forms (albeit with material consequences). There is no doubt that security concerns about individual information, as well as the possibility of elections being 'hacked' by third parties, are real and widespread. Many lives and careers have been wrecked by information and images shared maliciously online (in response to which a 'revenge porn' law was passed in the UK in 2015, making it illegal to share a 'private sexual photograph or film' without the consent of the person depicted in the content, and with the intent to cause them distress). There is no doubt that there are good reasons to be suspicious of a state-managed 'digital citizenship' that claims to be impervious to hacking, or to be willing and able to prevent the misuse of data for political or commercial ends. Yet if we see virtual life in isolation from broader state powers, and material institutions such as the police, the courts, and prisons, we misunderstand the way in which the public and the private are intertwined online and off. While there are calls for some minor offences to be 'tried' online (or at least fines paid online), this is a frightening proposition, given that for serious offences, the jury is the only 'public' element that would be the difference between a conviction and a not guilty verdict.

Furthermore, the massive rise in online use has not eroded the apparent need on the part of the state for its repressive aspects, which still have the monopoly on violence, and can still imprison, torture, and kill with impunity – as we see again and again in the US, UK, and elsewhere where the police routinely kill black men, women, and children without trial or imprisonment. #BlackLivesMatter can be seen as the most important recent political movement that recognizes this violence is in the streets just as much as it ever was. Similarly, issues of housing cannot be solved by getting everyone internet access. The social murder of hundreds of tenants in Grenfell Tower in London because of flammable cladding and economic and technological neglect cannot be separated from our idea of which technologies are available to which people, and which technologies kill those who are poor and dispossessed.

As the policy of austerity in the UK has deliberately destroyed many aspects of the 'public', from libraries to forests, from national resources to the health service and education, we should be extremely wary of images of a new online 'public' that might somehow replace real material provision, whether it be in the form of financial support or free access to resources that belong to everyone. Similarly, while there are clear links between online activism (an important development for those physically unable to attend protests) and public demonstrations against injustice, the idea that the former might one day replace the latter seems ultimately highly attractive to the powers that be, and may not be of much benefit to 'the people'. Outside of the question of direct democracy, some on the left have discerned the potential for liberation at the heart of digital networks of online interactions, from the 'knowledge economy' to models connecting 'leisure' time to work.

Sylvia Federici, amongst others, has addressed this idea directly, placing it firmly in the long history of thinking about the commons. Looking in particular at the work of Hardt and Negri over the past decade or so, she summarises their argument in the following way: 'that a society built on the principle of "the common" is already evolving from the informatization and "cognitivization" of production.'[4] In this model, the internet as an organising structure creates a 'common space' and even a 'common wealth'. Federici points out, however, that despite the appeal of this idea, in that it sees the common as immanent to the organization of work and production, and that the 'multitude' immersed in such networks already have political knowledges suitable for future communist organising (if we flip the capture of knowledge from capitalist profit to the communist general intellect), there are nevertheless serious limitations to this image of the world:

> Its limit is that its picture of the common absolutizes the work of a minority possessing skills not available to most of the world population. It also ignores that this work produces commodities for the market, and it overlooks the fact that online communication/production depends on economic activities – mining, microchip and rare earth production – that, as presently organized, are extremely destructive, socially and ecologically. Moreover, with its emphasis on knowledge and information, this theory skirts the question of the reproduction of everyday life. This, however, is true of the discourse on the commons as a whole, which is mostly concerned with the formal preconditions for the existence of

commons and less with the material requirements for the construction of a commons-based economy enabling us to resist dependence on wage labor and subordination to capitalist relations.[5]

By placing technology in the wider context of production, consumption and reproduction, we can see how an optimistic and utopian image of the internet and internet workers as integrated participants in the commons misses so much. From the dangerous and violent mining of materials necessary to the production of new technologies, overwhelmingly hidden from the everyday sight of the end-users of such machines, to the way in which 'the reproduction of everyday life' is simply neglected by such an account, and the relationship between state violence and the 'private' lives of individuals, we cannot simply and with good conscience talk about the construction of 'new online publics' without serious caveats. When Federici and others bring the commons to the discussion – not merely in terms of the 'formal conditions', but as a verb that encompasses the social reproduction of everyday life – we should be clear what definition of the commons we are working with.

We should note that debates in the literature (and various political struggles) over the years around the enclosure of the commons – originally understood as the 'subdivision and fencing of common land into individual plots'[6] – has moved from primarily being concerned with land and land-ownership to a broader debate concerning multiple types of 'global commons'. This involves everything from social, cultural and intellectual commons (cultures, knowledge, ideas, shared online resources) to DNA, natural features (rivers, forests), and the atmosphere we share. The contemporary resistance to various types of enclosure, whether real or virtual, point to the idea that enclosures (or privatization or 'land-grabs') are not yet 'complete' because access to resources is still a matter of real contestation in many places. The difficulty of pinning down exactly what 'the commons' refers to complicates matters considerably. Are shared internet resources really new commons? What does the verb form – 'commoning' – mean? Can we engage in forms of commoning without having access to the commons, as classically understood? Might focusing too much on digital life mean we forget about common rights to the land?

DEMOCRACY AND TECHNOLOGY

In Labour's Digital Democracy Manifesto, explicit reference is made to the idea of a 'People's Charter of Digital Liberties' which involves a 'digital bill of rights'. Here various forms of communal and civil language are invoked in order to tie the Manifesto to older, but historically disparate, forms of demand and constitution. In this sense, the Manifesto should be seen in the context of other recent attempts to put the commons back on the constitutional agenda, to reconnect the links between civil liberties and the commons (most notably in Peter Linebaugh's 2004 *the Magna Carta Manifesto*), and to demand that the commons – 'the theory that vests all property in the community and organises labour for the common benefit of all' – must exist in both juridical forms and day-to-day material reality.[7] Although enclosure and private property are dominant regimes, reflected in the legal forms that protect them, the commons *understood in a broad sense* remain a site of contestation across the planet, including in legal forms. Thus to resurrect the seemingly archaic term is to acknowledge an ongoing struggle over everything from land to ideas. As Federici puts it: 'Ironically, the new enclosures have demonstrated that not only the common has not vanished, but also new forms of social cooperation are constantly being produced, including in areas of life where none previously existed like, for example, the internet.'[8]

The idea of private ownership as *exclusive* ownership, which dominates both the legal and everyday understanding of property today, is a relatively modern idea, only a few hundred years old.[9] It is also a history that was primarily violent before it was 'legal'. Marx's account of the 'expropriation of the agricultural population from the land' describes the transition from the open field system to the conversion of arable land, to sheep farming at the behest of wealthy landowners, to the complete dispossession of commoners from land previously held in common:

> The 'Glorious Revolution' brought into power … the landlord and capitalist appropriators of surplus-value. They inaugurated the new era by practising on a colossal scale thefts of state lands, thefts that had been hitherto managed more modestly. These estates were given away, sold at a ridiculous figure, or even annexed to private estates by direct seizure. All this happened without the slightest observation of legal etiquette.[10]

Marx argues that the legal formalities for the robbery of land actually came into force long after the seizure and annexation of the land itself (it is only in the eighteenth century that 'the law itself becomes now the instrument of the theft of the people's land'). What Marx's analysis points to, apart from the sheer violence of creating landless populations and depriving commoners of access to the means of sustenance, is a perhaps surprising disconnect between law and common rights. While there were specific 'protections' for practices of commoning in the Magna Carta and the Charter of the Forest, the 'rights' afforded to commoners were rarely, if ever, bestowed from the top down, and were always undermined via the at least implicit consent of the state, which turned a blind eye when landlords kicked people off their land, or permitted the seizure of land and resources from indigenous populations while providing military protection to the companies involved – practices which continue even to this day. The restoration of common rights cannot simply be a matter of petitioning for legal reform, but must involve an active resistance to having these rights taken away in the first place. Common rights do not therefore have the same structure or meaning as human rights or other rights enshrined universally by the state. Linebaugh differentiates common rights from human rights because, amongst other things, 'being independent of the state, commoning is independent also of the temporality of the law and state' and further, they 'inhere in a particular praxis of field, upland, marsh, coast'.[11]

If we link this discussion to Labour's Digital Democracy Manifesto, we can immediately see serious tensions between the language of 'Charter' and the language of 'rights', which points again to the tensions identified in the first part of this essay between the public and the private and how, in the last instance, the state cannot in any straightforward way be invoked in order to protect the public or the private. English and Welsh law put in place so many restrictions on the commons and commoning (between 1750 and 1850 there were approximately 4,000 Enclosure Acts of Parliament) that it cannot in any sense be said to be an obvious first port of call to seek recourse for the protection of the commons, virtual or otherwise. Where can we today find resources to think otherwise about the commons? Not, for Federici, in 'the statist model of revolution that for decades ha[s] sapped the efforts of radical movements to build an alternative to capitalism'.[12] We live in a world where people directly confront rapacious private property-owners, and where the law is rarely able (or willing) to prevent yet further expropriation. The enclosures that began with hedgerows and landowners have expanded to encompass everything that can be owned and sold. As Federici puts it: 'The "new enclosures" have also made visible a world of communal properties and relations that many had believed to be extinct or had not valued until threatened with privatization'.[13] Any move towards a 'digital democracy' necessarily involves global questions regarding enclosures and the commons, and cannot simply restrict itself to consideration regarding participation and representation online, or online voting schemes, for example.

A NEW COLLECTIVE DIGITAL SUBJECT?

Also raised, albeit in the briefest terms, in the Labour Digital Democracy Manifesto is the notion of the 'virtual collectivity of all citizens' as the collective subject of contemporary technology. This resonates with how various writers have attempted recently to link thinking about the commons with the possibility of a new collective subject. In his recent *Omnia Sunt Communia: On the Commons and the Transformation to Postcapitalism*, Massimo De Angelis argues that commoning needs to be rethought in the age of capitalism and what comes after, stressing that:

> commoning must depend on an open attitude that embraces traditions and projection into the future, history and contemporaneity, memory and immanence. We are not just discovering the commons – we are (re)inventing them as well. As we rediscover how to interact and take responsibility in ways that are both old and new, and as we discover more elemental ways of interacting and organising social and economic life, even with high-tech communication tools, when we common we engage in the oldest ways of doing things and relating, the most convivial and democratic.[14]

Nick Dyer-Witheford's *Cyber-Proletariat: Global Labour in the Digital Vortex* directly addresses the relationship between politics and technology today in terms of whether a collective political subject has already been generated by such technology or is perhaps just in the process of emerging. To invoke the idea of the 'cyber-proletariat' is to attempt to capture at once the power and the powerlessness of such a class. On the one hand, Dyer-Witheford argues that:

> the conjunction of automation and globalization enabled by information technology raises to a new intensity a fundamental dynamic of capitalism – its drive to simultaneously draw people into waged labour and expel them as superfluous un- or underemployed. This 'moving contradiction' now manifests as, on the one hand, the encompassing of the global population by networked supply chains and agile production systems, making labour available to capital on a planetary scale, and, on the other, as a drive towards the development of adept automata and algorithmic software that render such labour redundant … digital capital's making of a planetary working class [that is] tasked with working itself out of a job, toiling relentlessly to develop a system of robots and networks, networked robots and robot networks, for which the human is ultimately surplus to

requirements, [is] on a fatal trajectory at once dramatized and protested in the self-immolation of Bouazizi, the death leaps of Foxconn workers and other political suicides in the revolts of 2008 to 2014. It is about a global proletariat caught up in a cybernetic vortex.[15]

The 'vortex' of networks, automation and robots that has at its aim, consciously or otherwise, the elimination of the human as worker, as well as the destruction of the human during the process of production in the literal sense of inducing suicide, is the central point here. But what happens to vast numbers of workers when machines can do their job, whether the task is simple or complex? Here is where the question of what *cannot* be automated becomes central to thinking about the left's position on technology. In this respect, Dyer-Witheford's *Cyber-Proletariat* asks such vital questions as the following:

What then is the relation between cybernetic capitalism and its increasingly disposable working class? What are the interactions between segments of that class with different, yet also sometimes shared, relations to information technologies, such as miners and students, extremes of manual and mental labour? And what is the significance of the networked circulation of the revolts which, beyond Turkey, have so widely disturbed today's algorithmic capital?[16]

Dyer-Witheford argues, among other things, that a new model of 'syndicates' is necessary:

[C]ross-segmentary struggle organizations are urgently needed: without invoking too much left-historical baggage, let us call these 'syndicates'. Some principles that should inform such organizations are: a) alliances of the working, workless, and precariously employed; b) taking responsibility for the social reproduction of the destitute and crisis-struck, without becoming a voluntarist substitute for a destroyed social safety net, but instead maintaining a fighting front; c) adopting a stance of 'raising from the bottom up', prioritizing the needs the most precarious and pauperized workers in a racialized and feminized workforce.[17]

Here let us stay with the question of the 'most precarious and pauperized' workers in the context of ever-dominant automation. Firstly, it should be noted that environmental crises may involve massive restrictions on the possibility of automation in the sense that it continues to be based largely on a fossil fuel economy. Secondly, and more positively, we might imagine a reversal in value, as those jobs that are currently unpaid, under-and poorly paid, particularly in the care sector, become the most vital and important (after all, what is there to compare in the protection and maintenance of life and someone manipulating an algorithm?). Popular discussion is turning more and more to the realization that the future of work must centre care and social reproduction. As Livia Gershon puts it:

> There's an enormous opportunity before us, as robots and algorithms push humans out of cognitive work. As a society, we could choose to put more resources into providing better staffing, higher pay and more time off for care workers who perform the most emotionally demanding work for the smallest wages ... This isn't something our economic system, which judges the quality of jobs by their contribution to GDP, is set up to do. In fact, some economists worry that we haven't done enough to improve the 'productivity' of service jobs such as caring for the elderly the way that we have in sectors such as car manufacturing. Emotional work will probably never be a good way to make money more efficiently. The real question is whether our society is willing to direct more resources toward it regardless.[18]

What is clear is that care work, despite the best efforts of corporations, states and individuals to privatize it, cannot primarily generate profit. Nor can we conceive of 'care strikes' in the same way we might envisage strikes in a more classical industrial sense: turning away from life has much higher stakes than laying down tools or sabotaging machines. In addition to simply paying attention to shifts in the economy, the left has an opportunity here to draw upon (often intertwined) feminist and ecological thought to conceive of a collective political subject that is not first and foremost digital. The role of an exclusively digital subject is granted to very few and only at the cost of massive exploitation and dependency on the labour of others, as well as increasingly finite raw materials. Discussions about forming new collective subjects through struggles for alternative sources of livelihood that do not depend upon labour (such as Universal Basic Income schemes) are one aspect of the discussion – though it should be noted that UBI is not straightforwardly progressive in and of itself, and could easily be used by right-wing governments to close borders to 'reward' only their own citizens and to push flexibilization, wage subsidization, and administrative rationalization.

We would be better off shifting the debate around digital democracy and a new collective subject towards larger and more fundamental questions concerning the commons (virtual and actual), the role of care in our societies, and how we value all the paid and unpaid work that goes into reproducing life at all levels. Corbyn's Labour Party has pledged £8 billion to solve the 'care crisis', which includes paying a living wage to all care workers. Centring care alongside education generated a lot of support for the party in the recent election, which surely points to the potential for shifting popular perceptions of how these aspects of social, personal, and political life should be regarded. We can, however, ask even more radical questions of the relation between 'digital democracy' and all the work and relations that fall outside of the virtual and online worlds. A collective communism of care that would reclaim the commons such that there were enough resources for the global community seems utopian in the extreme. Yet in the face of new enclosures, private property, and asymmetrical global violence, we have little choice but to address the future of technology, work, and politics in the broadest and most direct of ways.

CARE, TECHNOLOGY, AND DEMOCRATIC PLANNING

Care presents some difficult planning issues. Because of its often private and multiply-located nature, it is harder, on the face of it, to see how centralization could be used to 'redistribute' care, to ensure fair provision of skilled labour, and to facilitate use of expensive facilities. Care involves a collective condition – as is evident from the fact that we all need care at various points, and far more often than the liberal and neoliberal image of the self-standing, self-generating subject ideologically presupposed. But it also involves diverse geographical workplaces and an immense amount of self-management and individual decision-making. Moving from a classical image of work as centralized, geographically concentrated, and with an obvious 'product' means rethinking completely what we value and even what image of being human lies behind our policies. Care is ignored, assumed to always be there, undervalued both socially and economically, gendered and racialized. Yet if we were to centralize it, and to acknowledge that automation may not be able to replace care (even if it might be able to help in its planning), then we might begin to recognize its foundational political and social importance. Care work is often extremely gruelling as well as poorly, under- or unpaid; making it a public issue and something to be valued and collectively discussed and democratically planned would be a revolution.

How might the new digital technologies help us to think about democratic economic planning, taking the care sector as our central example? As part of this process, we might also want to reverse the question and ask what technology can learn from care work. Hilary Wainwright, in her discussion of the 'Lucas Plan', where in the face of redundancy workers at Lucas Aerospace came up with their own plan to keep jobs via proposing 'socially-useful applications of the company's technology and their own skills',[19] points out that the democratic egalitarianism central to the plan made it possible to imagine what 'socially useful production' might mean. We might build on such examples to imagine what 'socially useful reproduction' might look like, particularly as we move into service, knowledge, and care economies. As Wainwright puts it:

> We are in new times for trade union organisation but interest in democratic economics is increasing with the spread of green and solidarity economies, commons-based peer-to-peer production, and grassroots fabrication in 'hackerspaces' and 'fab labs'. All of which has deepened ideas about connecting tacit knowledge and participatory prototyping to the political economy of technology development, as was the case with Lucas.[20]

We need to think beyond the separation of the virtual and the real, although it is hard to avoid the thought that one is ineffable and the other is all-too-material. How can technology not replace or subsume care work, but assist in its redistribution? How can technology help people organize without simply removing social responsibility from the state? The latter we have seen in all too cynical detail: playing upon people's genuine willingness to help in their communities, the Conservative government's 'Big Society' slogan provided the cover for removing state responsibility for libraries, or even welfare safety nets. It handed over responsibility to unpaid volunteers, who were left to manage formerly planned and paid for infrastructure in unbalanced and difficult circumstances. The massive rise in foodbanks in the UK, not to mention teachers buying food for undernourished pupils, is also indicative of this handing over of central planning to well-meaning citizens. Technology will need to be put in the service of people's needs, and not fetishized for its own sake, nor used to relieve responsibility for the vulnerability of populations.

Possibilities for rethinking the role of technology in dealing with the distribution of care will be enhanced if, as Ursula Huws argues, we can avoid the trap of thinking of 'digital labour' as somehow isolated from the rest of the economy:

it is worth noting that digital labor cannot be regarded as a discrete form of labor, separated hermetically from the rest of the economy … the existence of a separately visible sphere of non-manual labor is not evidence of a new 'knowledge-based,' 'immaterial,' or 'weightless' realm of economic activity. It is simply an expression of the growing complexity of the division of labor, with a fragmentation of activities into separate tasks, both 'mental' and 'manual', increasingly capable of being dispersed geographically and contractually to different workers who may be barely aware of one another's existence. This is a continuing process, with each task subject to further divisions between more creative and/or controlling functions on the one hand, and more routine, repetitive ones on the other.[21]

The possibilities afforded by geographical dispersal should alert us to possible positive uses of digital technologies (think of the way, for example, epidemiologists can already track potential illness outbreaks by tracking people's web-searches). Of course, fragmentation and atomization suit particular aspects of the capitalist economy, but there are potentials here, particularly if we imagine what it might mean to use the same technologies to overcome the lack of awareness of each other's existences.

THE FUTURE OF DIGITAL DEMOCRACY

Jeremy Corbyn's recent challenge to neoliberal austerity under Conservative rule was in good part predicated on a mobilization of the youth, addressing education and care with a progressive image of the future. To a lesser extent, it addressed questions of technology, drawing on various historical and contemporary rhetorics in 'The Digital Democracy Manifesto' to present a sketch of how technology might expand rather than restrict democracy. Social media was integral to the recent mobilization of young people in registering to vote and pushing a left-wing agenda which was often old-fashioned in its social democratic impulses, but highly contemporary in the dissemination of its message. How could it go further? How can social media increase social agency? In connecting online activism and activity to grassroots, on-the-streets mobilising, Corbyn's Labour Party has been extremely successful, indicating not a divide between technology and everyday life, but rather an optimistic kind of continuity.

It is clear that old media is over: it cannot poison the young in the same way. There are of course newer forms of right-wing influence that use the internet at their base (the rise of the 'alt-right' and a particular kind of online violent irony that too spills over onto the streets and into the ballot box needs careful understanding and attention). It would be foolish to trust too much in technology in and of itself without being permanently critical of malign uses, whether they be in terms of surveillance, commercial data gathering, or even personal upset caused by the often cruel mediation afforded by the internet, but it is imperative that the left take seriously the challenges and opportunities provided by technology, not only at the level of social and political participation, and feminist and environmental concerns, but also at the level of economic infrastructure. The central question of care can help us to orient our thinking and practice to the core questions that will dominate the next few decades. Let us hope that a future Labour victory will allow this discussion to proceed in such a way that human needs and the redistribution of the commons are treated as paramount.

NOTES

1   Cynthia Cockburn, *Machinery of Dominance: Women, Men and Technical Know-How*, London: Pluto Press, 1985, p. 8.
2   Herbert Marcuse, 'Some Social Implications of Modern Technology', *Technology, War and Fascism*, London: Routledge, 1998, p. 41.
3   'The Digital Democracy Manifesto', released in August 2016 and available here: http://www.jeremyforlabour.com/digital_democracy_manifesto.
4   Silvia Federici, 'Feminism and the Politics of the Commons', 2011, available here: http://www.commoner.org.uk/wp-content/uploads/2011/01/federici-feminism-and-the-politics-of-commons.pdf
5   Federici, 'Feminism and the Politics of the Commons'.
6   Simon Fairlie, 'A Short History of Enclosure in Britain', *Land Magazine*, Issue 7, Summer 2009.
7   Peter Linebaugh, *The Magna Carta Manifesto: Liberties and Commons for All*, Berkeley: University of California Press, 2008, p. 6.
8   Federici, 'Feminism and the Politics of the Commons'.
9   Fairlie, 'A Short History of Enclosure in Britain', p. 3.
10   Karl Marx, *Capital*, Volume 1, Chapter 27, (1867), available here: http://www.marxists.org/archive/marx/works/1867-c1/ch27.htm
11   Linebaugh, *The Magna Carta Manifesto*, p. 45.
12   Federici, 'Feminism and the Politics of the Commons', p. 1.
13   Federici, 'Feminism and the Politics of the Commons', p. 1.
14   Massimo De Angelis, *Omnia Sunt Communia: On the Commons and the Transformation to Postcapitalism*, London: Zed, 2017, p. 208.
15   De Angelis, *Omnia Sunt Communia*, p. 15.
16   Nick Dyer-Witheford, *Cyber-Proletariat: Global Labour in the Digital Vortex*, London: Pluto, 2015, p. 3.
17   Dyer-Witheford, *Cyber-Proletariat*, pp. 201-2.
18   Livia Gershon, 'The Future is Emotional', *Aeon*, June 2017, available here: https://aeon.co/essays/the-key-to-jobs-in-the-future-is-not-college-but-compassion.

19   Hilary Wainwright, 'When the Workers Nearly Took Control: Five Lessons from the Lucas Plan', *OpenDemocracy*, November 2016, available here: https://www.opendemocracy.net/neweconomics/when-the-workers-nearly-took-control-five-lessons-from-the-lucas-plan/.

20   Wainwright, 'When the Workers Nearly Took Control'.

21   Ursula Huws, *Labor in the Global Digital Economy: The Cybertariat Comes of Age*, New York: Monthly Review Press, 2014, p. 157.

BARCELONA EN COMÚ: URBAN DEMOCRACY AND 'THE COMMON GOOD'

GREIG CHARNOCK
AND RAMON RIBERA-FUMAZ

In June 2017, the city of Barcelona hosted the 'Fearless Cities' summit: a three-day programme of public events organized by the city council to celebrate 'international municipalism'. The event included the participation of mayors, city officials, and activists from cities across Europe, Latin America, and the United States.[1] Themes discussed included 'Austerity, Globalization and Democracy', as well as 'Social Syndicalism' and the question: 'how are community, housing rights and labour organizations building power across different movements?' The event's organizers, the citizens' municipal platform Barcelona en Comú (Barcelona in Common, or BeC), branded the event a significant opportunity to build 'global networks of solidarity and hope among city halls and citizens in the face of hate, walls and borders' – networks built on the principle that 'democracy was born at the local level, and that's where we can win it back'.

At the summit's opening event, Ada Colau and Manuela Carmena – the mayors of Barcelona and Madrid – together took to a stage in Barcelona's Plaça dels Àngels to discuss topics ranging from 'resisting state authoritarianism and combatting the far right' to 'fighting speculation and guaranteeing the right to the city'. These two women appeared to epitomize the new municipalism, at least insofar as they were both well-known within and outside Spain for being activists and campaigners for human and social rights long before they each entered politics to lead the newly formed citizens' platforms BeC and Ahora Madrid in the 2015 local elections. The Fearless Cities event offered the opportunity to present an image of solidarity between two cities' fledgling governments, and to reassert once again that this new citizen-focused municipalism stands for new forms of democratic government, and against the entrenched and corrupt political classes that have fomented a 'climate of fear' made worse by the jobs, housing, and refugee crises.[2] As Colau underlined from the stage: 'we are anti-system mayors, revolutionaries, and we believe in love'.

Alongside the rise of Podemos as a national political movement in Spain, there are several significant examples in which a remarkable revitalization of grassroots participation in local political organizing has led to taking control of municipal governments, in cities such as Cádiz, Pamplona, Oviedo, Santiago de Compostela, Vitoria and Zaragoza. It is important to note that most have not assumed outright majority control of their councils, but depend upon coalitional agreements with more established parties of the left. Though most share common characteristics, the Barcelona case nonetheless stands out, not least because Colau herself has been celebrated as 'the world's most radical mayor'.[3] For many, BeC's victory evoked the historical memory of the arrival of the Second Spanish Republic in Barcelona on 14 April 1931. The crowds waving the Republican flag that greeted Colau's inauguration evidently saw in BeC some affinity with the egalitarian spirit of the pre-civil-war city. BeC was also born in a digital age, and none of the other 'new municipalist' governments in Spain have been quite so oriented as BeC towards what John Postill terms a 'rare admixture of techno-political savvy and neo-leftist social justice ideals'.[4] In standing out as a beacon of new municipalism, BeC has been vaunted by international supporters who see its victory as a wake-up call for a global network of 'rebel cities' with the means and wherewithal to resist the 'worst excesses of authoritarian central government' bent on imposing right-populist agendas.[5]

BeC's sudden rise to power in the city is quite remarkable. In the fall of 2014, BeC formed the 'citizen platform' Guanyem Barcelona (Let's Win Barcelona) as its electoral vehicle, and 'crowd-sourced' its code of ethics and allowed online citizen input into the design of its manifesto. Just ten months later, BeC won a quarter of the vote in local elections in the capital city of the Catalonia region (Spain's second largest city, with a population of around 1.6 million people), and took control of the city council (albeit, in 2016, in coalition with the Catalan Socialist Party). In 2016, BeC maintained its commitment to participatory democracy by using a new open source online platform alongside regular public assemblies, allowing for citizens' input into strategic city planning, citizen initiatives, and budgeting. This process, involving over 10,000 initial proposals, was coined Decidim Barcelona, 'we decide Barcelona'.[6]

Guanyem Barcelona's bold aim in competing for office was therefore to bring about a 'democratic rebellion in Barcelona' that would 'be the trigger for a citizen revolution in Catalonia, Spain, Southern Europe and beyond'.[7]

This, they understood, would require a new form of democratic organization – like BeC – whose task would be to realize the political potential of the popular movement that had arisen in the midst of crisis, to seize control of local government, and to dis- and reassemble the city's institutions from within on a more transparent and participatory basis. As their 2014 manifesto put it:

> Taking advantage of the economic crisis, economic powers have launched an offensive against the rights and social achievements of the majority of the population … We can't afford another institutional blockade from above that leaves us without a future. We need to strengthen, more than ever, the social fabric and spaces for citizens to self-organize. But the time has also come to take back the institutions and put them at the service of the majority and of the common good.[8]

At first glance, then, BeC would appear to represent what Leo Panitch sand Sam Gindin in the *Socialist Register 2017* posit as a constructive first step toward taking power at the sub-national scale in order to effect meaningful political and social change. This requires the strategic development of new party forms 'oriented to developing capacities for complex democratic representation and administration'.[9] Once a sufficient degree of institutional control has been attained, early steps towards delivering on a radical agenda might include 'developing alternative means of producing and distributing food, health care and other necessities' – steps that would have to be supported by appropriate 'coordinating agencies of democratic planning'.[10] These first steps, in other words, address pressing fundamental subsistence needs and the endemic crisis of the social reproduction of the working class through recalibrated democratic institutions. The question of how to move beyond immediate issues and formulate a longer-term radical, interoperable, and up-scalable programme of radical social transformation could then, presumably, be addressed through building political momentum and popular legitimacy.

It is this kind of strategic approach that inspires many within Guanyem Barcelona. Their principles of openness and participation combined with their deployment of new digital-technological means of developing democratic capacity to foster new democratic experiments at the local or regional scale. The hope is that that particular movements will thereby be able to learn and demonstrate to others like them what might and might not be achievable. This essay attempts to gauge the potential of BeC to realize transformative change in Barcelona on such a basis. We focus first on the capacities for complex representation and administration being developed within the movement, as well as the 'first steps' BeC has made to recalibrate municipal institutions and effect policy change at the city level 'in the service of the majority and the common good'. In order to do this, we first elaborate on the broader political-economic circumstances within which Guanyem Barcelona was conceived as an essential means to comprehend why certain issues have been prioritized under BeC's initial tenure in office. We then go on to ask whether there is the political will and capacity within the movement[12] to push beyond addressing immediate issues of institutional democratization, particular grievances around housing, and the amelioration of the worst manifestations of a crisis of social reproduction within the city to push for a transformative agenda beyond formal 'citizenist' democracy.

THE HOUSING CRISIS

The significance of Barcelona's housing crisis for understanding BeC's popular mandate cannot be overstated. The housing question has come to frame and dominate sentiment within the broader movement behind BeC, and therefore to determine the formulation of policy across several key strategic areas after May 2015. Of course, the housing issue is not particular to Barcelona, but must be seen as an outcome of the unfolding international, national, and urban dynamics of Spain's decade-long property boom and the state's management of the crisis that erupted in 2009. These dynamics have been covered in detail elsewhere, so can be summarized in brief here.[11] From the early 2000s the Spanish real estate market became a highly attractive destination for the speculative recycling of overaccumulated capital from the European 'core', especially of German origin. Much of this was switched through the highly securitized Spanish savings bank system (the *cajas*). Several interrelated factors worked together to created a fertile context for a housing bubble in Spain: increased competition among the *cajas* to lend as a result of deregulation and the introduction of the euro, rising land and housing prices as a result of the 1998 Land Act reform, rising levels of immigration and tourism, and a general tendency in international markets that saw huge volumes of capital investment diverted to housing and real estate ventures (especially after the 2001 'dot.com' crash). By 2007, the *cajas* share of the European covered mortgage bond market stood at around 30 per cent (worth a total 248.8 billion euros).

Overproduction in the construction sector was endemic: between 2001 and 2011, Spain's housing stock increased by 24 per cent to over 26 million units, in a country of 47 million people (up just 5.8 per cent in the same timeframe).[12] Meanwhile, estimated net household debt as a percentage of disposable income grew from 79.7 per cent in 1999 to 150.1 per cent in

2008, as an increasing number of families and individuals across Spain either took out mortgage debt for the first time or cashed in on the equity available from rising house prices.[13] All this meant that when German and French banks in particular began redirecting funds to cover their own national liabilities in 2009, the Socialist government had to act quickly to shore up the Spanish banking system through a series of emergency measures that amounted to the highest proportion of GDP committed to the financial system by any OECD government during the crisis.

The restructuring of the banking system under the right-wing Partido Popular (PP), elected in 2011, saw significant fresh public investment in bank recapitalizations, a concentration of banking capital through mergers, and the partial nationalization of Spain's fourth largest bank, Bankia, in a 4.5 billion euro bailout. In 2012, the Rajoy government secured a 100 billion euro rescue package from the European Union in return for the implementation of an especially austere program of public spending cuts and broad based tax increases (including VAT). In return, the government also established Sareb, a new 'bad bank' (*el banco malo*), to which 'toxic' real estate assets were transferred from the *cajas* with the aim of divesting a portfolio of 200,000 units worth an estimated 50.45 billion euros by the year 2027.[14]

In the fall of 2014, around the time Guanyem Barcelona was formed, the IMF announced that the Spanish economy had finally resumed growth. President Mariano Rajoy of the conservative Popular Party greeted the news with characteristic hubris, publicly lauding the 'recovery' and the 'stupendous' resilience of the Spanish banks. But the crisis had already exacted an enormous toll on the Spanish population. By 2013, according to government figures, 12.6 million people were at risk of poverty or social exclusion. The unemployment rate peaked that same year at 27 per cent, with youth unemployment then at 57 per cent,[15] while real wages were in the midst of a decline of 6.1 per cent between 2010 and 2014.[16] But the politics of the crisis were ever more intensely focused on housing issues after 2009. While the banking system was rescued by the state, homeowners in Spain were put under extreme duress – a problem exacerbated by the idiosyncrasies of Spanish law. No less than 600,000 foreclosures were recorded across Spain between 2008 and 2014, while the number of court-ordered evictions during the same period was a staggering 378,693. By 2014, campaigners estimated that there were 40,000 homeless people in Spain, with 1.5 million families living in shelters.[17]

'LET'S WIN BARCELONA'

The housing crisis was acutely felt in Barcelona, where there were 20,117 evictions between 2008 and 2011 (second only to Madrid).[18] It was in this context, on 22 February 2009, that housing activists based in the city – including Ada Colau – formed the Plataforma de Afectados por la Hipoteca (PAH): 'a horizontal, assembly-based, non-party-affiliated movement denouncing the mortgage-scam and political-economic machine that drove it.'[19] The PAH's immediate aims were to raise awareness of the growing number of evictions taking place, to campaign against Spanish laws that ensured that most foreclosing and evicted households retained their mortgage debt even after their homes had been surrendered or seized, and to demand that empty housing stock owned by the banks be given over to rent-controlled social housing. The PAH's activities escalated in 2010, when activists turned up to an eviction in the Catalan province of Tarragona to successfully prevent a court order from being presented to a homeowner by forming a human barrier to the property. (By June 2017, the PAH had prevented 2,045 evictions across Spain, and had managed to rehouse 2,500 people in empty bank-owned units.)

The PAH gained further prominence in 2011 as a significant component of the 15-M movement (the *indignados*), which encouraged hundreds of thousands of people across Spain to flood the streets and squares of major city centres in opposition to austerity and the indifference of the established political parties to the plight of the general population. In 2012, the PAH collected over 1.4 million signatures in support of a Popular Legislative Initiative (permissible under the Spanish Constitution) to reform Spanish law pertaining to foreclosures and mortgage debt. Colau presented the Initiative to the Spanish Congress on 5 February 2013. Several minutes into her televised hearing, she broke from the script, her voice breaking with visceral rage, to openly denounce the 'expert' testimony of the Deputy General Secretary of the Spanish Banking Association: 'this man is a criminal.'[20] Her outburst quickly went viral, cementing her own status as an icon not simply of the right to housing movement but popular indignation in general. Emboldened by an upswell of popular support over subsequent months, the PAH together with other social and leftist political movements formed the platform Guanyem Barcelona, and in June 2014 secured the support of 30,000 city residents to begin the process of constituting BeC and its electoral programme through a series of thematic and territorially organized commissions (*comisiones*) involving a high degree of citizen participation and input through what became the Decidim Barcelona platform.[21]

Any evaluation of BeC therefore has to be mindful of the movement's antipathy towards the political establishment, its harnessing of online and open source (i.e. replicable) methods of maintaining a commitment to popular participation, and the fact that its mandate is centred around the housing crisis. All three of these factors have clearly shaped the initial direction and sequencing of reform since the movement took control of the municipal government in May 2015.

'WIPE THE SLATE CLEAN'

One of BeC's first steps in office was to publish its 'Emergency Plan for the first months in office'. The plan denounced the outgoing city council led by the nationalist right-wing CiU (Convergencia i Unió, now the main opposition party) for its privileging of elite private interests and lobbies in the city since 2011. Framing the plan as one founded on popular consultation and 'for the common good', it recognized the imperative to prioritize the needs of those most adversely affected by the crisis. It called for addressing pervasive inequalities by cutting funding and subsidies to unnecessary, partial, and unsustainable projects, and by investing 160 million euros over an initial 18 month period to improve the growth, security, and quality of employment in the city (in liaison with public sector unions). As an unambiguous expression of political will, the plan announced:

Barcelona has enough resources to tackle inequalities and to become a model of a city where people live well, in common, with respect for others and for the environment. To harness these resources, we need a credible and courageous council that is able to stand up to powerful groups that put their own interests above those of the majority, and a council that taps into the collective intelligence of the people and neighbourhoods of Barcelona.[22]

The Plan affirmed the BeC government's commitment to guaranteeing social rights by means of 'long-term pre-distributive and redistributive policies that allow us to build a set strong of universal, adequately financed socials rights for citizens'. Foremost among these rights is, unsurprisingly, housing. The Plan pledged to force banks to enter into negotiations with the council over evictions and the allocation of vacant housing, to reform emergency housing protocol in partnership with social service professionals, to push for vacant housing to be ceded to the council, and to investigate new measures to allow the city council first refusal in the purchase and sale of housing at below market rates.[23] This clearly represented a continuing commitment to addressing issues central to concerns of the right to housing movement and the PAH. And it did so in terms that made it very clear that any struggle to guarantee housing as a fundamental right will need to take on entrenched interests – especially the banks.

In addition to the right to housing, BeC's Emergency Plan committed to guaranteeing food security to the city's children and teenagers in recognition that one in five children are at risk of poverty and over 2,800 are malnourished; it guaranteed the right to healthcare (while recognizing that broadening public healthcare provision requires reforms at the level of the Catalan regional government); it pledged to boost the city-wide use of affordable public transport; and it promised universal municipal income support to poorer families, guaranteeing an income of 600 euros per month (60 per cent of the average wage in Barcelona). The red thread that permeates all of these guarantees is the need to address the underlying causes of the housing crisis, whether in terms of foreclosures or the lack of availability and affordability.

Significantly, the plan also committed to guaranteeing energy security through bold measures to take on the private utility companies. Despite the fact that Catalan regional law obliges private utility companies to allow low-income families to suspend energy payments, and to notify social services in the event of vulnerable customers being cut off, non-compliance has been rife. Across Spain, several deaths in separate house fires attributable to using candles and cheaper but unsafe alternative sources of heating have been reported in recent years, with the death of an 81 year-old woman in Reus, a city south of Barcelona, provoking widespread public outrage. In recognition of the inefficacy of regional law, BeC announced in March 2016 that it would look into the establishment of a public energy supplier, issuing a new tender for interim energy provision in the city for the next two years and stipulating that interim providers would not be able to cut off households suffering energy poverty. The largest Spanish energy providers refused to participate in the tender and the contract was awarded to Som Energia, a Catalan renewable energy cooperative. Spain's two energy giants, Endesa and Iberdrola, successfully pursued legal action to annul the tender through the Spanish courts. BeC responded by announcing that it would be immediately instating a publicly managed electricity supplier, Barcelona Energia, with a view to supplying low-cost, 100 per cent renewable energy to public facilities and 20,000 households by summer 2018.

The energy case reveals the degree to which BeC is prepared to tear up the old institutional rulebook. City council officials affiliated to BeC are often at pains to point out that many of the people now running council departments on a daily basis are 'citizens', not professional politicians. This obviously places upon them certain demands to learn how institutions function and processes work. But, as they also point out, this means they are more than willing to 'undo' the way things have traditionally operated if and when they need to. In public procurement, for example, BeC were quick to overhaul the pre-existing, cozy relationship between the CiU and the major consultancy firms involved in the tender process ('the usual suspects', as one council official put it to us), and to make the 'everyday business' of procurement compliant with their commitment to sustainability, gender equality, and transparency. In formulating new protocols (*guies*) in public procurement and applying these with full accountability, BeC is acting on its promise to execute 'a real audit and analysis of our public institutions and inherited city accounting books, so that we can put an end to bad practices and create less bureaucratic, more efficient institutions with more citizen involvement ... to wipe the slate clean, end perks and privileges, and practice what we preach'.[24]

BEYOND 'CITIZENISM'

While many admirers abroad see BeC as a significant prefigurative experiment in substantive participatory democracy at the municipal scale, the movement it represents has not been without its critics. Manuel Delgado, a prominent Barcelona-based leftist intellectual, has launched a scathing attack on 'citizenism' (*ciudadanismo*), which he defines as 'nothing more than a programme of renewal of old bourgeois republicanism and its goal of a tranquil democratization of society that does not alter nor threaten the plans of capitalist accumulation, that does not question the real mechanisms of control over society, [and that is] inoffensive to official political agendas'.[25] For Delgado, the 'citizenists' of the 15-M movement, Podemos, and the various En Comú platforms have accomplished what fascism sought to achieve but could never could: 'the end of the class struggle', so that that individuals 'may be invited to "participate", that is, to be partners in their own domination'.[26]

While Delgado's critique might well be dismissed as an attempt to rehabilitate antiquated 'reform or revolution' debates, it is nonetheless the case that any recognizable socialist content has been conspicuously absent from public discourse within BeC. The 'common good', for instance, is usually defined in terms of guaranteeing immediate subsistence needs and opposing an entrenched and self-serving political class in the name of 'the citizen'. At the very least, Delgado's critique raises the question of who the privileged political subject at the heart of this new municipalist project really is. Is he right to warn that this 'citizen' is really nothing other than the abstractly free and independent subject of radical bourgeois liberalism in a new guise? And, if he's right, does this mean that, beyond guaranteeing basic rights in the city in the context of an immediate crisis of social reproduction, municipalism need not necessarily deliver on anything other than safeguarding the means of participation through novel, complex, transparent, but nonetheless formal technologies of democratic administration?

An area in which there is evidence that BeC is willing to challenge the 'citizen' as the privileged subject of democratic and substantive reform, as well as to think through challenges facing the city in broader political economy terms, is tourism. BeC's 'Strategic Plan for Tourism', published in September 2016, evinces how the movement is developing a more holistic and systemic approach to fundamental questions of social reproduction, questions that have become even more pressing since the PAH first mobilized around issues of evictions and the anomalies of Spanish law in 2009. The still alarming rate of mortgage foreclosures in Barcelona due to rising mortgage repayments, precarity, and joblessness is today only one dimension of a complex crisis scenario that has been compounded in recent years by an absolute lack of available social housing (only 2 per cent of the total stock).

Private landlords opting en masse to enter a different rental market, made possible by digital 'sharing economy' platforms, have exacerbated the relative scarcity and high cost of private rental housing in comparison with other European cities.[27] A May 2014 survey revealed that there were then already over 12,000 Airbnb listings in the city (and over 57 per cent of these were entire apartments). This number has certainly increased since, bringing with it not only an ever more intense squeeze on housing availability and affordability within the city, but also contributing to problems of *massificació* (dense overcrowding in areas of touristic interest), transport and mobility issues, and pervasive forms of inappropriate or downright anti-social behaviour.[28]

BeC's Strategic Plan acknowledges the intractability of the problem, and in proposing a wholesale reconceptualization of tourism in the city as being more than simply an industry or sector, it offers a more realistic assessment of the scale and impact of the tourism economy (for example by taking into account that though 6 million tourists stayed in Barcelona's hotels in 2015 – the previous method of accounting for tourist numbers – the actual number of visitors that year was found to be closer to 25 million).[29] It also goes some way toward challenging the powerful hoteliers' lobby, which has set the agenda concerning tourism reform for decades. Moreover, re-conceptualizing 'the tourist' as a temporary 'city user' undermines the populist 'citizenist' discourse of '*they* are destroying *our* city', and instead focuses critical diagnostic attention on *the urban process* – that is, on a comprehension of the city as a node within a broader, systemic political economy that implicates the European Union, central government (as, for example, the manager of the main airport), the hoteliers' lobby, 'disruptive innovators' like Airbnb, and indeed the city council itself for its erstwhile aggressive international marketing campaigns. It establishes grounds, therefore, for a more collective dialogue on tourism, such as by incorporating the neighbourhood assemblies and trade unions. This is aimed at fostering fresh solutions to intensifying problems of housing availability and high rents, along with insufficient jobs and wages (not only within the hotel industry). The goal is to raise the quality of life in the city for all, whether they are residents, *sans papier* migrants, refugees, or even tourists.

A broader, systemic and critical diagnosis of the challenges facing the city also underpins BeC's aspiration to achieve 'technological sovereignty'. Disruptive intermediaries like Airbnb are deemed to be but one small component of a global 'digital capitalism'.[30] The BeC-appointed Chief Technology Officer, Francesca Bria, frames the problem at stake thus:

> The reason why Uber and Airbnb and all these corporations can be platforms is because they are building on top of the large-scale infrastructure that's already been built by the security state and run by the US. It's very clear that for instance here in Europe, we are not doing that in a democratic way. We are not rolling out this civic, democratic infrastructure for the future, to run hospitals [and] preserve some kind of welfare state and education.[31]

For critics, like Bria, the lifeblood of the information economy – dominated by a global cartel comprising the likes of Amazon, Cisco, Google, Microsoft, and Facebook – is data extracted, often without users' knowledge, and monetized to generate huge profits. Under BeC, moves are already underway to re-appropriate a public-private programme of urban management instigated under the former CiU municipal government, which aimed to make the city a world-leading 'smart city',[32] and instead to work towards a 'commons-based sharing economy … where the data that is generated and gathered by citizens, the Internet of Things, sensor networks, and open city level data is available for broader communal use with appropriate privacy protection'.[33] In September 2016, CiU-instigated contractual negotiations with Cisco and Schneider Electric to invest 37 million euros in a 'smart city campus' were suspended pending review by the BeC government, with Deputy Mayor Gerard Pisarello openly stating that the 'logic behind' the project was one the new city government 'could not allow to continue'.[34] Since then, BeC has announced it will invest in its own open source digital economy projects such as La Comunificadora (an incubator for collaborative economy start-ups), and it has launched a new public digital technologies procurement process that discriminates in favour of cooperatives and collaborative economy-based SMEs. In February 2017, it announced that it would be investing 300,000 euros in social innovation programmes and digital fabrication spaces with the generative potential to boost the local digital manufacturing economy on participatory and ecologically sustainable bases.

These initiatives demonstrate that elements within the BeC government are indeed willing to think beyond ameliorative solutions to immediate problems of social reproduction at the urban scale, and to critically frame more generative policy interventions within a broader systemic diagnosis. While it is true that the term 'class' does not feature in any of BeC's various strategic plans or press releases, it is also the case that city officials are willing to think in political economy terms and to posit democratic and 'commons-based' models of public administration and social innovation. However, the city is still divided in political, socio-economic, and therefore electoral terms. The same business lobbies exert a powerful influence in the city, not least in the heavily financialized hotel sector.[35] And the ever-looming question of Catalan secession from Spain further blurs any attempt to envision a longer-term prognosis. It thus remains to be seen whether Barcelona en Comú will be able to develop the capacity to 'trigger a citizen revolution'. But if it does it will have reverberations across Spain, and well beyond.

NOTES

This work was supported by the Spanish Ministry of Innovation and Science.

1   'Fearless Cities' website: www.fearlesscities.com.

2   Toni Sust, 'Colau y Carmena: "Somos antisistema y revolucionarias que creen en el amor"', *El Periódico*, 9 June 2017.

3   Dan Hancock, 'Is This the World's Most Radical Mayor?', *The Guardian*, 26 May 2016.

4   John Postill, 'Freedom Technologists and the Future of Global Justice', in Nick Buxton and Deborah Eade, eds, *State of Power 2016: Democracy, Sovereignty and Resistance*, Amsterdam: Transnational Institute, 2016, p. 159.

5   Kate Shea Baird, 'America Needs a Network of Rebel Cities to Stand Up to Trump', International Committee of BeC, 25 November 2016.

6   At the time of writing, the online platform has been adopted by six other cities in the wider Barcelona metropolitan area.

7   BeC, *How to Win Back the City en Comú: Guide to Building a Citizen Municipal Platform*, Barcelona: Barcelona en Comú, 2016, p. 4.

8   Guanyem Barcelona, 'Manifesto: Let's Win Back Barcelona', 2014.

9   Leo Panitch, 'On Revolutionary Optimism of the Intellect', in Leo Panitch and Greg
      Albo, eds, *Socialist Register 2017: Rethinking Revolution*, London: Merlin Press, 2016.

10   Leo Panitch and Sam Gindin, 'Class, Party and the Challenge of State Transformation',
      in Leo Panitch and Greg Albo, eds, *Socialist Register 2017: Rethinking Revolution*, London:
      Merlin Press, 2016.

11   Greig Charnock, Thomas Purcell and Ramon Ribera-Fumaz, *The Limits to Capital in
      Spain: Crisis and Revolt in the European South*, Basingstoke: Palgrave Macmillan, 2014,
      Chapter 4.

12   Mark Stücklin, 'Spanish Housing Stock Increases 24pc in a Decade', *Spanish Property
      Insight*, 12 April 2013.

13   Melissa García-Lamarca and Maria Kaika, '"Mortgaged lives": the Biopolitics of Debt
      and Housing Financialisation', *Transactions of the Royal Institute of British Geographers*
      41(3), 2016.

14   Fondo de Reestructuración Ordenada Bancaria, 'The Transfer Prices to the Asset
      Management Company (Sareb) Will be Sharply Adjusted to Ensure its Profitability',
      Press Release, 29 October 2012.

15   At the time of writing (June 2017), the official national unemployment rate is 18.75 per
      cent, and 41.6 per cent for under-25s.

16   Thorsten Schulten and Torsten Müller, 'European Economic Governance and its
      Intervention in National Wage Development and Collective Bargaining', in Steffen
      Lehndorf, ed., *Divisive Integration: The Triumph of Failed Ideas in Europe – Revisited*,
      Brussels: ETUI, 2015, p. 350.

17   Data from the RAIS Fundación, cited at https://www.homelessworldcup.org/
      homelessness-statistics.

18   Ada Colau and Adrià Alemany, *Mortgaged Lives: From the Housing Bubble to the Right to
      Housing*, Journal of Aesthetics and Protest Press, Leipzig/London, 2014, p. 209.

19   Melissa García-Lamarca, 'From Occupying Plazas to Recuperating Housing: Insurgent
      Practices in Spain', *International Journal of Urban and Regional Research*, online first
      version, p. 9.

20   Available at https://www.youtube.com/watch?v=LtNBnc6khHg. Colau's denunciation
      begins at around the 10:35 mark.

21   BeC, *How to Win Back the City en Comú*.

22   BeC, 'Emergency Plan for the first months in government', Ajuntament de Barcelona,
      18 February 2016, p. 3.

23   This was followed up in September 2016 by BeC's 'Plan for the Right to Housing
      2016-2025'.

24   BeC, *Emergency Plan*, p. 8.

25   Manuel Delgado, *Ciudadanismo*, Madrid: Catarata, 2016, p. 15.

26   Manuel Delgado, 'Los ciudadanistas seran el sustituto del PSOE', *El Nacional*, 24
      October 2016; Delgado, *Ciudadanismo*, p. 16.

27   Observatori DESC and PAH BCN, *Exclusión residencial en el mundo local: Informe de la
      crisis hipotecaria en Barcelona (2013-2016)*, Barcelona, 2016, p. 74.

28   Albert Arias Sans and Alan Quaglieri Domínguez, 'Unravelling Airbnb: Urban
      Perspectives from Barcelona', in Antonio Paolo Russo and Greg Richards, eds.,
      Reinventing the Local in Tourism, Bristol: Channel View Publications, p. 213.

29 Dirección de Turismo, 'Plan Estratégico de Turismo de Barcelona 2020: Diagnosis estratégica', Ajuntament de Barcelona, September 2016.

30 Dan Schiller, *Digital Depression: Information Technology and Economic Crisis*, Urbana: University of Illinois Press, 2014.

31 Evgeny Morozov, Francesca Bria and Richard Barbrook, 'Digital Democracy and Technological Sovereignty', Rosa Luxemburg Foundation, Berlin, 3 December 2016.

32 Hug March and Ramon Ribera-Fumaz, 'Smart Contradictions: the Politics of Making Barcelona a Self-Sufficient City', *European Urban and Regional Studies* 23(4), 2016.

33 Francesca Bria in Esteve Almirall, et al., 'Smart Cities at the Crossroads: New Tensions in City Transformation', *California Management Review* 59(1), 2016, p. 151.

34 'Colau frena una inversión de 37 millones de euros en Barcelona, *Bolsamanía*, 13 September 2016.

35 Ismail Yrigoy, 'Financialization of hotel corporations in Spain', *Tourism Geographies* 18(4), 2016.

COOPERATIVE DEMOCRACY OR COOPERATIVE COMPETITIVENESS: RETHINKING MONDRAGON

SHARRYN KASMIR

Cooperatives play an important role in the imagination of the left for their purported potential to democratize the workplace, nurture non-capitalist social relations in the interstices of capitalism, and anchor social or solidarity economies. They are seen, as well, as levers for a soft transition to socialism, 'quiet democratization everywhere',[1] and as preferred alternatives to top-down labour unions and the bureaucratic enterprises of state socialism. Worker occupations and cooperatives inaugurated the twenty-first century in Argentina, Venezuela, Greece, Spain, and the US, testifying to people's persistent impulse to find novel ways to secure their livelihoods and organize their workplaces. We therefore need sharp analysis of the on-the-ground realities of actual cooperatives, as they exist in, navigate, and make alliances in a political world.

Mondragon is widely recognized as the most successful worker-owned enterprise in the world, and its influence extends far. A vast scholarly and popular literature recounts Mondragon's history and details its cooperative principles and structures, but it largely avoids tough political questions. In this essay, I draw on my earlier ethnographic fieldwork and my decades-long acquaintance with Mondragon to revisit how we think about worker-owned cooperatives and workplace democracy.[2] After outlining Mondragon's organizational model, I turn to the social and political terrain, where problems of a segmented global workforce and working-class agency and capacity come to the fore. While the literature on Mondragon often has a narrow frame, focusing on the cooperative institutions themselves, I broaden the picture to situate Mondragon within both the political field of the Basque region of Spain and processes of working-class formation. Specifically, I trace connections between coop workers' apathy and lack of agency in their own workplaces, their insularity, and the resulting fragmentation of the local working class. The long erosion of working-class alliance and solidarity in the local context, in turn, laid the groundwork for Mondragon worker-owners to later accede to a global labor hierarchy, whereby the privileges of coop ownership are underwritten by an exploited, international wage-labour force. This uneven class dynamic should, by rights, challenge how we think about cooperatives as places of equality and democracy in socialist imaginaries.

MONDRAGON AS MODEL

The Mondragon cooperative group began as a Catholic Action project to further technical education and spur local employment in its home city of Mondragón (Arrasate in the Basque language Euskera) and in the Alto Deba industrial belt.[3] The first cooperative factory opened in the 1950s to produce paraffin stoves for a domestic market stimulated by the development policies of the Franco state. The cooperative federation today includes 261 financial, industrial, retail, and research and development concerns, and it employs more than 74,000 people worldwide. Industrial coops manufacture a wide range of goods, from automotive parts to machine tools and commercial kitchen equipment. The retail giant Eroski boasts 2,000 outlets throughout Spain, including 90 super-centres that sell everything from groceries to furniture and house cafes, travel agencies and cell phone outlets. The Caja Laboral bank and the social security coop Lagun Aro provide financial services, insurance, and pensions to individual members and affiliated businesses. Students pursue degrees in engineering, management, education, and culinary arts at Mondragon University and its partner institutions internationally.

Mondragon limits managers' salaries to about nine times the pay of the lowest-level coop members, an admirably flat scale compared to Spain's overall ratio of about 127:1. Annual distributions are deposited in members' capital accounts in the Caja Laboral, where they are held as private savings but made available for investment in the coop group. This shared access to capital manifests the principle of solidarity between affiliated coops, and it secures members' jobs. Mondragon guarantees employment to members, and during downturns, cooperators preserve their jobs by voting to invest additional capital funds or cut their salaries, while access to inter-cooperative loans and the system of transferring members between coops further secures their employment. These practices express labour's sovereignty, or 'the instrumental and subordinate nature of capital', a signal principle of Mondragon. Mondragon's business success – without standard capitalist ownership – makes it a model for worker-self-directed enterprises worldwide.

Mondragon's democratic structures also attract thousands of international visitors who travel to the Basque region for study tours and to take lessons back to their home countries. Democratic organization and participatory management are among Mondragon's guiding principles, and distinct and intersecting organs give nominal (though not necessarily substantive) form to workplace democracy. Each coop is fully owned by its members, workers and managers alike, and there are no outside stockholders. When a member joins a cooperative, he or she contributes the equivalent of one year's salary (this can be borrowed from the Caja Laboral) and opens a capital account in the Caja, into which a share of yearly surplus is credited or losses debited. The distribution of surplus versus salaries or other expenditures is decided by the general assembly, in accordance with the minimum established by Spanish law. Each member has one vote in the general assembly, the highest governing body, which meets annually to approve business plans, allocate earnings, vote on mergers and acquisitions, decide on the admission of new members or the punitive expulsion of existing members, and elect the governing council. Beyond the annual meeting, members can collect signatures to convene an extraordinary general assembly. Although workers, like managers, can exercise this right, in practice it is management that does so. The general assembly elects the cooperative governing council – president, vice president, secretary and several other coop members. This body prepares annual plans, proposes the distribution of surplus, and presents annual reports and accounts. The governing council appoints and oversees the general manager, and the management council is composed of department heads and supervisors who are nominated jointly by the general manager and governing council, and who advise the manager.

Mondragon cooperatives are not unionized; instead, a social council, an elected committee that brings grievances to management, represents worker-members in their workplaces. In this regard, it functions like a union committee in a standard capitalist firm; however, the social council not only exerts pressure upwards from the shop floor but communicates decisions and conveys information downward as well. There is a good deal of criticism of social councils for not adequately representing workers and advocating in their interest, but rather persuading them to acquiesce to management. Predictably, there is a difference between rights and the power to exercise rights in the coop governing structure. Local, firm-level power is circumscribed by sectoral groups (industrial, retail, financial, educational) that centralize business functions and decision making, and Mondragon has a system-wide general council that further concentrates control. The Cooperative Congress is made up of 650 delegates from all the general assemblies, but given the high-level nature of this body, representatives tend to come from management rather than the ranks of manual workers.

While the coops are centered in the Basque region, Mondragon began global expansion in 1990. Mondragon now has investments in 60 countries, employing 12,000 workers, many in developing or post-socialist countries. The majority of Mondragon's firms are *not* worker-owned – 101 are coops, while 160 are not – and coop members constitute only one-third of its workforce. The rest are wage laborers in subsidiaries and joint ventures, many poorly paid and insecure. In the Basque country too, cooperatives rely on temporary workers on short-term contracts. Faced with a majority of workers who do not have the rights or privileges of membership, Mondragon's Cooperative Congress established a policy of 'social expansion' to help extend participation and democracy. There is continued talk of converting subsidiaries into coops, and there is a plan to boost worker-ownership, particularly in Eroski stores, where there are very high rates of workers on temporary contracts, most of them women. Mondragon's Mundukide NGO encourages social economy initiatives, and its educational mission includes spreading cooperative expertise beyond the Basque country, especially in the southern hemisphere, and Mondragon recently joined with the United Steel Workers to develop a union-coop business model for the United States.[4] Despite these initiatives, Mondragon relies on wage labourers at home and abroad. Mondragon has a three-tier workforce – members in the Basque country, temporary workers in the Basque region and in Spain, and wage labourers in international subsidiaries. Spatially segmented labour is not simply an unfortunate and recent consequence of globalization, but a core feature of the Mondragon model. Mondragon is thus fertile ground for assessing what cooperatives may mean for working-class formation, agency and political capacity.

WORKING-CLASS AGENCY AND POLITICS IN MONDRAGON

An internal study of Mondragon's Fagor coops in 1981 identified a growing problem: worker members were not actively involved in governance and the formal right to participate did not translate into meaningful workplace democracy. In one telling case, social council members regularly missed meetings, and when they did attend, they were largely uninterested in the proceedings. The causes of their apathy were not personal but structural, the report concluded. Since cooperative ideology intended to convince members that their workplaces were free from labour-management conflict, workers ceded power to engineers and managers. The report further found that although strategic plans were supposed to be discussed in the general assembly, in reality workers rubber-stamped management proposals without generating critical dialogue. The document recommended restructuring social councils to increase participation, but the changes were never carried out.[5]

More, there was mounting evidence that the coops fragmented the local working class and created a privileged stratum in Mondragón/Arrasate. By the 1960s, left factions of the Basque socialist independence organization Euskadi ta Askatasuna (ETA) criticized coop workers' apathy and lack of involvement in factory decision making. They referred to a survey that documented complaints about the increasing pace of manufacturing work; in the market-driven business environment, they argued, the possibility of real self-management was denied to workers and surrendered to a 'new technocratic class'. This bred cynicism, which, turned inward, became passivity, and turned outward, manifested as class division. The growing reliance on short-term contracts was turning worker-owners into an 'artistocracy in the factory', who acted like self-appointed, petty supervisors of temporary workers and who were increasingly disconnected from area workers and their struggles. Cooperators did not support a series of important local labour strikes in the early 1970s, and there was a growing rift between them and the rest of the local working class. Critics, including the Diocesian social secretary, believed that cooperators had become isolated and had grown 'egotistical' at a time when collective action and resistance to the Franco regime shaped working-class experience in the Alto Deba. The left labour union Langile Abertzaleen Batzordeak (LAB), affiliated with the radical Basque movement, challenged the coops in 1985 for their 'fake internal democracy, a division of labour, economism, technocracy, education subordinated to production, [...] consumerism, [...] production of socially unnecessary goods.' Cooperatives do not transform the capitalist mode of production, LAB maintained; to the contrary, they 'reproduce the defects of the capitalist system'.[6]

My own ethnographic research on the Fagor Clima washing machine coop in the late 1980s to the early 1990s found important connections between thwarted internal workplace democracy and working-class division. (Clima later merged with other Fagor domestics appliance coops into Fagor Electrodomésticos.) Shop-floor conditions, rank-and-file participation in decision making, and workers' involvement in Clima were not meaningfully better than they were in Mayc S.A., a nearby capitalist-owned factory with a union workforce that I studied in comparison. During my fieldwork, Fagor hired consultants to lay the groundwork for just-in-time production. Assembly jobs were redesigned for greater efficiency, flexible work schedules replaced regular shifts, and there was a speed up. Coop workers were physically exhausted and emotionally stressed by the changes. One young woman on a six-month contract described the strain of being observed by the time-management consultant: 'I was very nervous. It was stressful. I didn't know what to do. He stood behind me while I was working, watching me. I was afraid that I wasn't working right. He just watched.' She was a temporary employee, and as much as she disliked her job preassembling washing machine parts, she hoped to become a coop member because her family needed the income and the financial security. A few months later her application was approved, and she was made a member of another appliance cooperative; she was grateful for the steady work, but the consultants' recommendations led to a speed up throughout Fagor. I met her one day after work and saw that her hand was shaking; she told me she was now nervous all the time. Worker-ownership and formal structures of democracy did not shield cooperators from a factory regime that was devised for profit maximization and workplace discipline in the capitalist market.[7]

Neither did they translate into active participation or the real exercise of power on the shop floor. Managers and engineers were notably engaged in cooperative governance, while Clima workers were mostly inactive and uninvolved. In Mayc, to the contrary, an activist union committee used contract provisions to exert meaningful control over their workplace. This was due, in part, to the fact that the collective bargaining agreement provided substantial release time for union activities. Members of Clima's social council, on the other hand, got only a few hours a month to prepare position papers or economic studies. Those who were especially conscientious spent hours outside of work dealing with problems and evaluating plans, but others assented to management proposals without fighting back. Whereas members of Mayc's union committee had access to union lawyers, economists and engineers who helped them examine business plans and present a considered response, the social council had no recourse to outside experts. The premise that workers and managers shared the same interests in the business meant that management proposals supposedly stood for the whole. In fact, it was against regulations for social council members to consult anyone but coop staff; thus, they had little ability to develop an independent voice on technical, business, or social matters. Consequently, and despite the formal right to a wealth of information about their firm, the social council was less effective than the union committee in controlling the shop floor. This, in turn, dampened coop workers' activism.

Perhaps most significantly, coop workers were disempowered by their lack of collective struggle. Union workers in Mayc had a shared identity and purpose from years of job actions, at their own workplace and in larger mobilizations during negotiations of the metal contract or general strikes, and their activity developed leadership in the factory that strengthened area unions. Cooperators did not have similar experiences. Internal strikes over workplace grievances are forbidden by cooperative regulation, and cooperators were less involved in sector-wide, external actions; they therefore did not have the resources of a collective history or cadre of leaders. As a result, they showed less solidarity with the Basque labour movement, which at the time was part of a dynamic left coalition for socialism and independence for the Basque country. They were more often absent from metal-sector strikes, which were external and therefore permissible by coop rules, less likely to be union members (individual membership without shop floor representation is permitted by Spanish law), and less involved in other activities and affiliations that would have linked them to the organizations of the regional working class.

One telling example was the 1990 strike over the provincial metal contract. The event was an annual ritual in Mondragón/Arrasate, as it was throughout the Alto Deba zone, dating to 1962 when the Franco government first permitted state-sanctioned vertical unions to bargain with employers. In a city where the metal contract affected the daily lives of so many people, the strike was a significant event in which hundreds of workers and supporters took part. Even in years when talks were going well, workers stopped production for several hours in a show of collective strength and a performance of solidarity. In 1990, a walk-out was called for the morning, but in some factories workers did not assemble before their shifts to vote to join the action, while in others they held general assemblies but voted to remain on the job. The afternoon demonstration was also discouraging, and union leaders were worried about the poor showing. Notably, not a single cooperator was in attendance. Although coop salaries were not determined by the contract, payouts were usually pegged to area wage levels, therefore coop workers had some interest in the strike. Unionists did not blame cooperators for the disappointing turnout since they never counted on their meaningful participation, but they were nevertheless disheartened that not a single cooperator showed up in solidarity.[8]

The tepid nature of substantive workplace democracy, coop workers' apathy and acquiescence to managerial expertise, and the fracturing of Mondragón/Arrasate's working class were intertwined processes. Coop workers lacked internal organizations and external alliances that could have built a strong rank and file to confront the automation, speed up, and reliance on contract labourers that came to characterize their work lives as I observed them in the late 1980s–early 1990s. Their ineffectiveness in their firms and their isolation set the stage for worker-members to support the acquisition of foreign subsidiaries and to leverage the unevenness of global capital accumulation for their own benefit.

CONTRADICTIONS OF GLOBALIZATION: COOPERATIVE COMPETITIVENESS

Mondragon responded to Spain's entry into the European Union in 1986 by centralizing governance and business operations and by internationalizing. The first foreign acquisition in 1989 was a factory in Mexico operated by the cooperative Copreci to manufacture fittings for copper tubing and components for gas appliances. Copreci recorded losses in the previous year, and simultaneous with the purchase of the Mexican facility it introduced a new time management system in its Mondragón/Arrasate plant. Copreci hired a consulting firm to conduct time motion studies and to reorganize production through an even more exacting process (known by the acronym MMT) than in Fagor. With the new standard, output increased by 25 per cent, and Copreci determined it had excess workers, who were transferred to other coops. There were serious complaints about the system, and the Basque left newspaper *Egin* carried an article that criticized the 'anti-democratic' way it was imposed over the objections of Copreci's social council. A group of cooperative workers joined the local union offices of LAB and the Spanish Communist affiliate union Comisiones Obreras (CCOO) to host a forum on the impact of MMT in a General Motors facility in Zaragoza, Spain. Workers from Zaragoza came to Mondragón/Arrasate to warn of the stress-related illness they suffered when the system was put in place. Cooperators in the audience voiced their protest: 'The cooperatives have created a culture in Mondragón of working more and more hours, of living more for yourself [...] They know they are not going to encounter any struggle against MMT. We have to coordinate forces.'[9] The forum was valuable for animating cooperators to act in their own interest, for linking them with union workers in common cause, and for fostering ties to area unions. It was a rare moment when conflict within a cooperative workplace energized broader solidarity, but the activism did not last and the MMT system was instituted in Copreci and other coops. Unfortunately, the forum did not draw connections between the speed up/downsizing and erosion of shop floor democracy in the Basque country and Copreci's move to internationalize manufacturing, nor did it pay attention to the wage-labour workforce that the acquisition of a private firm supposed.

In the following years, as Fagor cooperatives merged into the home appliance group Electrodomésticos, sectoral divisions and system-wide governance were established to consolidate business strategy and investment.

Most significantly, the 1993 Cooperative Congress approved the Strategic Corporate Plan for Internationalization for 1994-96, which set targets for international sales, countries for expansion, and production plants abroad. Mondragon and its member coops and groups invested in numerous joint ventures and wholly owned subsidiaries in the 1990s in Europe, Latin America, North Africa, and Asia. In 2003, the Cooperative Congress planned for 24 new international industrial facilities, and a second strategic plan projected 60 production centres, employing 23 per cent of Mondragon's workforce by the end of 2004.[10]

The acquisition of Brandt Electomenager by Fagor Electrodomésticos in 2005 offers a window into the tensions and contradictions caused by globalization. Brandt was Fagor's long-time competitor in the European home appliance market. At the time of the purchase, Brandt had a sizeable unionized workforce of 5,500 in six plants, five in France and one in Italy. The purchase price was high, costing over €165 million, and Fagor held an extraordinary general assembly to consider the deal; 83 per cent of members favoured the acquisition, betting it would increase Fagor's market share and strengthen its position in the highly competitive sector. Fagor Electrodomésticos had already bought nine other businesses at the time of the vote. Most were in nearby Basque towns, but three were international: Extra-Electomenager, S.A. in Morocco in 1995; Mastercook Poland, S.A. in 1999; and Shanghai Minidomésticos Cookware, Ltd. in 2001. Only Edesa in the Basque city of Basauri was legally constituted as cooperative. Workers in all the others were wage labourers.[11] Although Fagor Electrodomésticos was not the only coop to turn to joint ventures and subsidiaries, the Brandt deal was especially significant. This was, first, for its symbolic weight as Fagor was heir to Ulgor, where Mondragon's founders began manufacturing gas stoves in 1956 and where the cooperative experience began. Second, Fagor was a leading employer in Mondragón/Arrasate and the livelihoods of thousands of households depended on its fortunes. Third, since Brandt had a large workforce, the merger brought a lot of non-members into the Mondragon system and thus exacerbated frictions already in evidence. Finally, Brandt was the most expensive acquisition in Mondragon's history, and the considerable debt burden had serious consequences for Fagor. For these reasons, Brandt had a decisive impact on workers' attitudes and visions.

The home appliance sector was characterized from the 1980s on by the concentration of capital. Some thirty mergers and takeovers resulted in the market dominance of three European corporations, Bosch-Siemens, Electrolux, and Merloni, while Whirlpool controlled the US market. Unlike its capitalist competitors, Fagor was constrained by the cooperative framework. The principle of the subordinate nature of capital, in particular, prioritized employment security for coop members, and business plans had to meet the approval of members who were unlikely to vote themselves out of jobs. Fagor therefore did not systematically downsize in high-labor-cost coops in the Basque country in order to relocate to cheaper labor environments. Instead it outsourced small-scale, low value-added products to Poland and China, while pursuing acquisitions, like Brandt, with valuable brand recognition, trademarks, and sales networks, but (counterintuitively) expensive workforces. As a result, Fagor had more plants in high-cost countries than did other European manufacturers.[12]

Fagor's plan was to cut jobs at Brandt. Shortly after the purchase, production at the Italian plant was outsourced to Morocco, and Confédération générale du travail (CGT) union leaders in France feared their members would be the next victims. They tried for months to get information, review plans, and negotiate with Mondragon directors, but corporate reorganization and layoffs proceeded without their consultation. One CGT leader observed that dialogue and democracy stopped at the Spanish border; he charged that the coops were engaging in an exercise amounting to 'protectionism', since Fagor members safeguarded their own employment at Brandt workers' expense. Fagor worker-members were troubled by the growing conflict with the CGT and Brandt workers. 'We are not an NGO. We are a business', one member insisted, 'We are doing this so we have work, and our children, and our children's children.'[13] His assertive tone did not so much convey his conviction that Fagor was justified in its dealings with Brandt as it betrayed his attempt to reassure himself that if the decision to lay off workers did not demonstrate solidarity, it was nonetheless necessary and unavoidable.

After decades of global neoliberal reign, his words may not surprise. In the US, for example, the continual threat of plant closures and whipsawing regularly pits workers in one locale against those in another in a zero-sum game. Powerful unions, including the United Auto Workers (UAW), have been sorely weakened by competition among locals for corporate investment and jobs, and workers' alliances and political visions are narrowed in the process. But before joining Fagor, this cooperator worked in a standard capitalist factory where he was a union delegate for LAB. In the Basque left context in which LAB elaborated its positions, international solidarity was a valued attribute of working-class consciousness and action. The comments of the LAB member-turned-cooperator – 'We are a business. We are doing this so we have work' – thus resonate deeply in that social environment, and raise questions about the ideological and political consequences for Basque workers of Mondragon's global expansion.

Coop members voted to buy Brandt in order to preserve their own jobs, but the dismissals at Brandt did not shore up Fagor. Competitive pressure continued to squeeze the coop until the global financial crisis of 2007/8 dealt the decisive blow. The Spanish real estate market was hard hit, and the drastic fall off in housing starts halted orders for home appliances. Fagor's sales dropped 40 per cent in 2007, and over the next six years, losses mounted to €200,000 million. Fagor reduced its workforce from 11,000 to just over 5,600, with 3,000 jobs eliminated in the Basque country. The shock was cushioned for cooperators, who voted to cut their wages and surplus distributions and make additional contributions to their capital accounts. Where these steps were not sufficient, cooperators were relocated to affiliated coops or took early retirement. In these ways, members were protected but inter-firm cooperation and solidarity did not extend to temporary workers at home or to wage labourers abroad.[14]

Trying to stay afloat, Fagor restructured its debt and sold its plants to Mondragon Corporation, leasing them back for operation. Affiliated coops contributed a portion of their surplus to buttress Fagor and a solidarity fund was established. In a last-ditch effort, Fagor proposed a strategic plan that would close eight plants and finally shift all production to Poland. Fagor's General Assembly approved the plan, but it was never implemented. After a cash injection of €120 million from Mondragon and the Basque government, Fagor recorded additional losses of €90 million. Mondragon's general council refused a second bailout, and Fagor was forced to declare bankruptcy in 2013. It was over €1 billion in debt, including €240 million to the Mondragon group, €75 million to the Basque government, and €79 million to members' capital accounts and voluntary additional investments. Fagor factories closed or were sold to competitors (Bosch/Siemens and CAN-Cata) to reopen in the future with dramatically reduced, wage-labour workforces.[15]

A forensic account of Fagor's demise finds ample evidence of inter-firm cooperation and intra-firm solidarity, principles for which Mondragon is acclaimed. Cooperatives notoriously have difficulty accessing capital and Mondragon is rightly credited with pioneering practices to secure financing for affiliated businesses. Also manifest is the commitment to preserve members' jobs – the instrumental and subordinate nature of capital to labour – even at great cost. At the same time, however, the events laid bare social and political processes often hidden from view, particularly Mondragon's three-tiered and spatially segmented labour force. The 5,634 workers who remained at the time of bankruptcy faced different fates: most of the 1,600 members in the Basque country transferred to other, more financially sound coops, and many now commute to neighboring cities to permanent or temporary placements. Others opted for retirement through Lagun Aro, Mondragon's pension management institution or went on unemployment until they qualified for early retirement (the Spanish government allowed self-employed workers affected by the crisis to collect unemployment). Some took buyouts or were retrained. Two hundred remaining temporary workers in the Basque country and 3,500 wage labourers in international subsidiaries were not afforded these protections. As the CGT leader observed at the outset of the Brandt acquisition, democracy and solidarity did not cross national borders, nor did it apply to Fagor's full workforce.

MONDRAGON'S SEGMENTED WORKFORCE

Fagor's bankruptcy spotlighted underlying contradictions of cooperative-owned subsidiaries. Mastercook in Wroclaw, Poland contributes further insight. Fagor acquired majority stake in Mastercook in a 1999 auction that privatized the state-owned enterprise. Although Fagor's was not the highest bid, both the Solidarity union and Polish government favored it since the offer included social improvements, maintained jobs, and appointed worker representatives to the board of directors. Mastercook was located in a special economic zone, where along with Opel, Volkswagen, and other multinationals, it accessed state subsidies and tax breaks. Solidarity had a long history and a lot of members in the plant, and upon the union's recommendation, Fagor-Mastercook was recognized by the Polish president as an exemplary employer. In 2008, however, an adjustment plan sparked unrest. The wages of the majority female workforce were cut to barely higher than the state-mandated minimum and to below the average Polish wage. Leaders of a left-wing dissident minority union known as WZZ Sierpen 80 accused Solidarity of being a company union that collaborated with management and was conciliatory in face of the cuts, and they called a short strike over wages and conditions. When union leaders were fired, activists organized an indefinite strike and launched an international solidarity campaign. In an interview with the Basque newspaper *Gara*, WZZ Sierpen 80's president charged that Fagor reacted to the strike with repressive methods, including vigilance and surveillance that had not been seen before in the special economic zone. CGT in Fagor-Brandt sent a message of solidarity, reviewing the chain of threats that linked workers across the subsidiaries: French workers were warned that their jobs could go to Poland at any time, while in Wroclaw, management threatened capital flight to Ukraine or Russia. The secretary general of the centrist Basque union ELA-Metal likewise regretted that a cooperative would act like an 'aggressive capitalist business' and 'trample on the rights of workers'. Meanwhile, governing councils and directors in

Mondragón/Arrasate ignored WZZ Sierpen 80's request that they intervene to help resolve the dispute.[16]

The Fagor-Mastercook labor conflict (including the presence of the dissident union) may have been more acute and the inter-union politics more complex than in other subsidiaries but the circumstances in Wroclaw were not singular. Brandt's strong union culture and French labour legislation gave the union committee leverage, and there were work stoppages and strikes across Brandt facilities whenever jobs were at stake. Fagor was therefore pressed to preserve employment where it might have otherwise proceeded with dismissals. Nevertheless, there was little evidence of cooperative practices or of worker participation. As the economist Angel Errasti found, 'in the opinion of practically everyone, including workers, management and trade union representatives, and even members of Fagor itself, there were no noteworthy differences' between cooperative and capitalist management styles.[17] Moreover, none of the subsidiaries had a European Works Council. (In firms with 1,000 or more employees, and a minimum of 150 workers in two or more member states, an EWC has the right to access business information and to be consulted on company decisions.) Fagor directors were uninterested in promoting EWCs in their subsidiaries, and no Mondragon multinational had a social or works council of any kind.

Workers in coop-owned subsidiaries in Kunshan Industrial Park in China, near Shanghai fared worse than their European counterparts. (Mondragon has eight other plants in China.) A comparison of eleven Mondragon-owned factories with conventional corporate multinationals in Kunshan found little to distinguish them. Most of the firms produced auto parts and were small-to-medium-sized, labor-intensive concerns in which the majority of assembly workers were women and machine operators were men. Pay was equally low in both the Mondragon and the conventional subsidiaries; Kunshan workers earned €1.5 per hour compared with €21 in Basque coops. So too were the hours similarly long and conditions harsh. To get overtime pay, workers put in eleven hours, six days a week and regularly forewent vacations and holidays.[18] That said, when the Chinese state set new limits on overtime, Mondragon complied with the restrictions, even while other firms in the industrial park did not. But many workers relied on the extra pay, and when they struck over the loss of hours, 300 workers were fired for the job action. The dismissed strikers quickly found new jobs, but to a Mondragón/Arrasate-area resident who told me about the event, that was not the point. He believed that Mondragon acted correctly in observing the overtime restrictions but was distressed that cooperators in the Basque country would fire the Chinese workers. Echoing complaints from France and Poland, he remarked at the high-handed treatment of subsidiary workers compared to the solidarity coop members expected for themselves, and he noted the lack of solidarity across both the cooperator-wage labour divide and national borders.

Errasti considers that Mondragon has a Basque, cooperative 'core', with stable jobs and benefits accruing to owners, including 'making profit for themselves by the employment at wages outside their association.' Outside is a 'capitalist periphery' of European, North African, and Asian subsidiaries. Errasti uses the term 'coopitalist multinationals' to characterize Mondragon's transformed labor arrangements since the 1990s.[19] Yet there is a longer trajectory of working-class fragmentation to account for, since the global hierarchy and spatial division of labor were built upon conditions created by the coops in Mondragón/Arrasate decades before. Problems of solidarity surfaced early on, when cooperators were absent from collective actions that were important for the fledgling local labour movement as it fought the Franco Regime. These contradictions are etched into Mondragon's history, and they matter for how we assess cooperatives.

MONDRAGON IN SOCIALIST PERSPECTIVE

Coop advocates contend that worker-ownership nurtures workers' capabilities to manage and plan production, thereby transferring technical know-how from the capitalist class and its allies to workers, and they predict that worker-owners will either be actively involved in business decisions and day-to-day operations or will exercise control over directors and managers. The evidence from Mondragon does not bear this out. The cooperative project motivated directors, managers and engineers but not rank-and-file workers; there was a gap between formal rights to participate and worker-members' ability to command their workplaces; and coop workers were uninvolved and disempowered, in part because the ideology of a conflict-free firm made workers compliant.[20] This state of affairs facilitated the practical dominance of a technocratic stratum of managers and engineers over everyday matters and long-term strategies, including decisions that consolidated a cooperative core in the Basque country and a subsidiary periphery elsewhere. The fact that from 2007 domestic employment was double in coops with overseas plants compared to those without suggests the extent of privilege the hierarchical arrangement afforded.[21]

When Fagor announced its closure in 2013, coop workers took to the streets to defend their jobs. The eruption of protest was unusual since coops prohibit internal strikes, but the situation was dire. Mondragón/Arrasate's population of approximately 22,000 depended in good measure on Fagor factories, and the bankruptcy dealt a further blow to a city already suffering from state-imposed austerity, salary cuts, and job loss. Workers from non-coop factories came out to support coop members, since their union affiliations habituated them to solidarity, and they knew that despite measures that would save members' jobs, the suspension of temporary contracts and net loss of employment were setbacks for the city's working class. A long-time labour movement activist joined the demonstrations in defence of jobs, but not the subsequent actions to fight for members' capital investments that were lost in the bankruptcy.[22] To him, that money was a symbol of how cooperators separated themselves from regional labour struggles. Drawn-out legal battles to reclaim their investments represented personal financial interests over collective aims, and their capital accounts were a measure of their social and political distance from their wage-earning counterparts.

Apathy and fatalism about the degeneration of cooperative principles persist. A recent study of member-workers found little participation in decision-making and little debate or internal reflection regarding governance and business decisions. Democracy is not exercised in daily work life, yet Mondragon workers do not aspire to greater involvement. Rather they 'comply' with management. They value their job security but little else of cooperative philosophy, and they use a managerial discourse that reprises the pressures of global competition to express their 'sense of neglect or of giving up' and to give reason that democratic principles must necessarily be sacrificed for the coops to remain viable. Since Mondragon is an influential corporate actor in the Basque country with pull in the Basque autonomous government, this discourse has an important impact on economic policy, and it spreads 'dominant regimes of managerialism and productivity' throughout the region.[23]

The mantra of globalization has a depoliticizing effect on cooperators, just as it does on workers in many other parts of the world, and in distinct workplace regimes – from unionized assembly plants in France, to privatized factories or small sub-contractors in special economic zones in Poland or China. Anxiety about job security is acute among Mondragon members who reached adulthood from 1980-95 and who lived through economic crises and persistent unemployment, when joblessness was regularly reported in the mass media. The social climate of economic insecurity 'influenced the mentality of that generation' and intensified their apathy.[24] Their experience in the cooperatives did not counter this tendency, nor spur their activism. When Basque labour unions called a one-day general strike in May 2009 to protest the austerity measures, job losses, and economic hardship that followed the financial crisis, the majority of cooperatives voted not to participate. There was no debate about the significance of the action; social councils did not foment discussion about the positions that businesses engaged in the social economy could take in the face of a crisis of the magnitude they confronted; and only 500 members signed a statement supporting the strike, even as the cooperatives were hit hard by the crisis and general assemblies cut salaries by 7-10 per cent. Wall graffiti asked directly: 'Fagor, Mondragon where is the solidarity?'[25] The graffiti might also have referred to the history that foreclosed solidarity, and it might have asked cooperators: Where is your shop floor power and how will you organize to defend your self-interest?

Socialists have disagreed about worker cooperatives for more than 150 years. The terms of the debate were set out early in the socialist movement and reflected in Marx's 1864 Inaugural Address of the International Working Men's Association. In an often-quoted passage from that speech, Marx praised cooperative factories as a practical expression of the spirit of 1848: 'The value of these great social experiments cannot be overrated. By deed instead of by argument, they have shown that production on a large scale, and in accord with the behests of modern science, may be carried on without the existence of a class of masters employing a class of hands.' Marx, however, immediately tempered his optimistic appraisal with caution. Cooperative experiments were confined to 'the narrow circle of the casual efforts of private workmen', and they remained subordinate to the pressures of market competition. They would never fundamentally challenge capitalist social relations unless they were organized at a national level, but at that scale, they would face opposition from 'the lords of the land and the lords of capital'.[26] That struggle would inevitably come up against capital and the state. Marx expressed his ambivalence about cooperatives in later writings as well. In *Capital*, and again after the Paris Commune decreed that abandoned factories be turned over to the cooperative association of workers, he recognized their promise and he lamented their limitations.[27] Some of Marx's concerns have been well rehearsed in recent years, while others have been sidelined. We know a good deal, for instance, about the kinds of structures and practices that help promote democracy in coops – including restricting ownership to workers, safeguarding the principle of one worker-one vote, and locating decision making in bodies like a general assembly – and we have many accounts of new coops and worker-self-directed enterprises. Yet the more difficult political discussion is neglected. As Sam Gindin observes, 'short shrift is given to political agency and the kinds of political capacities' required for cooperatives to 'contribute to building a working class with the vision, confidence, class sensibility, smarts, and institutional strength to democratize the economy.'[28]

The observation that global neoliberal capitalism engendered insularity and self-interest in Mondragon lends weight to Marx's prediction that economically successful cooperatives ultimately succumb to market pressures. Mondragon depends upon the flexible, cheap labour of temporary workers at home and wage labourers abroad, and it cannot extend beyond its (now wide) 'circle of the casual efforts of private workmen' without challenging the pressures of global capitalism that segment the labour force. Yet the deterioration of working-class capacity and political agency make that hard confrontation more unlikely. The measure of cooperatives' ability to democratize the workplace or transform social relations cannot be taken in individual firms, or even in large cooperative systems. It must be assessed in the political arena, by the impact on workers' alliances and on their capacity to imagine and undertake meaningful campaigns for general social betterment.

This is where the current celebration of cooperatives and worker self-directed enterprises disappoints as left analysis. Writings by post-structuralists or anarchist/horizontalists and by social democratic pragmatists exhibit this shortcoming. Some consider cooperatives to be on capitalism's 'outside', finding 'ontological difference' from capitalist social relations in these and other forms of 'everyday communism'. Others focus on achievable goals, foremost that workers purchase their own firms, whether those enterprises are foundering under capitalist ownership, threatened by capital flight, or face closure when owners retire without heirs ready to run family businesses. The feminist geographers who write under the shared pen name J.K. Gibson-Graham well represent a post-structuralist version of the first position, while the Marxist economist Richard Wolff advances the latter pragmatic stance. Both are highly influential authors on the left, promoting cooperatives as alternatives to capitalism, and both cite Mondragon as an inspiration or model.[29]

Gibson-Graham recognize problems with Mondragon – including, the use of cheap, insecure wage labour and dependence on the market – but they insist that these are remediable because Mondragon's more commendable achievement is *difference*: 'It is in this pluralist spirit that we have taken Mondragón as our inspiration (rather than model) for the intentional community economy and the political and ethical project of its institution.' They chastise writers who connect Mondragon to global capitalism or see its development in that explanatory frame. 'Its failures and shortcomings are often read as inherent weaknesses of the cooperative form rather than reversible errors, and are frequently taken as evidence of the impossibility of establishing a truly noncapitalist intentional economy in a system dominated by global capitalism.'[30] There is no way out of this formulation, since no empirical data can intervene in the argument. Evidence that Mondragon is entwined with the historical processes of working-class formation, by virtue of the ways it is inserted in the world capitalist system is irrelevant. The argument is circular: If Mondragon looks to be determined by capitalist competition, this is a failure of inspiration, stemming from the inability of 'strong theory' to perceive capitalism's 'outside'. The expression of difference, in and of itself, puts Mondragon on the road to non-capitalism. To connect Mondragon to world capitalism is, by their definition, to be 'capitalocentric' and to use 'strong theory' to defeat hope; no socialist wants this charge on their record.

Richard Wolff takes a different approach, favouring a pragmatic solution to capitalism's many failings, but one that also avoids the socialist traps of statism, central planning, and the failure to change the micro-level organization of the workplace. Worker coops such as Mondragon can tackle key problems: the democratization of enterprises, the distribution of surplus, and capital flight (since workers will not opt to outsource their own jobs.) Notably, rather than assessing coops by the measure of (strong or weak) Marxist theory, Wolff takes it to be an agreeable fact that coops share a political environment which bends against left ideology. The notion that workers can be their own bosses is an easier sell and a more realistic starting point, he believes, for mobilizing a new left. Moreover, workers *should* form cooperatives because they *can*; some capitalist owners want to sell their firms to workers, and coops are permissible under law. They have broad, cross-party and NGO support, and can be strengthened by enabling legislation at different political scales.[31]

Wolff's enthusiasm for cooperatives, however, falls short of aspiring to social and democratic transformation. He largely concedes to the terms of the capitalist market, preferring to look for niches where worker cooperatives might compete. Worker-self-directed enterprises get their start in the market and do little to mitigate the pressures of competition. If they go down easily in capitalist-dominated societies for their resemblance to business as usual – workers can become their own bosses – there is good reason to be sceptical that they could mobilize a new left of any sort. Conceptualizing social change in the form of a business model, as Panitch and Gindin argue in an earlier critique of such an approach to workers' control in *Socialist Register*, limits 'the meaning of change to fit what capital and the state will accommodate' and re-inscribes capitalist ideology by positing 'the premature harmonization of social contradictions' within the confines of existing social relations.[32]

CONCLUSION

Though Gibson-Graham and Wolff articulate distinct proposals, they both champion cooperatives as democratic alternatives to capitalism. Yet they steer clear of all the thorny problems of working-class agency and political capacity that coops present, and in this respect their assessment of Mondragon is apolitical. Significantly, they also avoid a systematic investigation of actual cooperatives enterprises over time, allowing a model (even when taken as inspiration and not blueprint) to stand in for on-the-ground realities. When they point to Mondragon, they rehearse the standard narrative of its achievements, reproducing the discourse of executives and managers, while marginalizing the experiences of worker-members, contract workers, and wage labourers in foreign subsidiaries. As we have seen in this essay, when these workers' perspectives are included, our view of Mondragon changes. By squarely facing working class formation – tracing the historical connections between cooperators and workers in standard firms, in the context of a Basque left movement, and in relation to Mondragon's segmented global workforce – we can see that the abstract model of coops as transformative will not hold. Mondragon does not conform to a socialist imaginary of a diverse collective of workers in action, building organizations, creating alliances with other politically engaged groups. Indeed, we only glanced this when Copreci workers made common cause with GM workers and unions in their shared protests against a punishing manufacturing regime.

Lauding practices because they are diverse and purportedly outside of capitalism without closely examining their history and impact in actual communities is to succumb to a post-structuralist incarnation of neoliberal market ideology, where plurality stands against a coherent theory of social transformation.[33] Promoting worker-owned enterprises because capitalist ideology and social relations can accommodate them similarly capitulates to the hegemony of the market. Lessons from Mondragon are not about the triumph of workplace democracy in worker-owned coops, but they are nonetheless indispensable for socialists. They advise scepticism regarding calls to socialism that set aside politics in favour of quiet, easily sold, or already-existing, everyday forms. This is not to argue that socialist seeds cannot be sown within capitalism, but it does mean that such planting requires struggle if it is to yield much in the way of radical transformation, either in specific workplaces or in society more broadly.

NOTES

1   Gar Alperowitz, *What Then Must We Do? Straight Talk About the Next American Revolution*, Vermont: Chelsea Green Publishing, 2013, p. 35.

2   Sharryn Kasmir, *The Myth of Mondragon, Cooperatives, Politics and Working class Life in a Basque Town*, New York: SUNY Press, 1996; 'The Mondragón Cooperatives and Global Capitalism: A Critical Analysis', *New Labor Forum* 25(1), 2016, pp. 52-9.

3   The cooperative system underwent name changes with expansion and transformation of its corporate identity. In the 1990s, it became Mondragón Cooperative Corporation and later simply Mondragón.

4   Saioa Arando, et al., 'Assessing Mondragon: Stability and Managed Change in the Face of Globalization', William Davidson Institute Working Paper #1003, November 2010. Ramon Flecha and Pun Ngai, 'The Challenge for Mondragon: Searching for Cooperative Values in Times of Internationalization', *Organization* 21(5), 2014, pp. 668-82. Robert Witherwell, Chris Cooper, Michael Peck, 'The Union Co-op Model', 26 March 2012, available at: http://www.usw.org/union/allies/The-Union-Co-op-Model-March-26-2012.pdf.

5   Kasmir, *Mondragon*, pp. 138-9.

6   Langile Abertzalean Batzordeak (LAB). Kooperatibismoari buruz txostena eta LAB-en jarrera S.A.L-aren aurrean (Ponencia sobre cooperativismo y posición de LAB ante la S.A.L.) September, 1985. Kasmir, *Mondragon*, pp. 86-7, 114-20, 174-6.

7   Kasmir, *Mondragón*, p. 183.

8   Kasmir, *Mondragón*, pp. 169-71.

9   Kasmir, *Mondragón*, pp. 186-9.

10 Flecha and Ngai, 'The Challenge for Mondragon', p. 669; Anjel Mari Errasti, Inaki Heras, Baleren Bakaikoa, and Pilar Elgoibar, 'The Internationalisation of Cooperatives: The Case of Mondragon Cooperative Corporation' *Annals of Public and Cooperative Economics* 74(4), 2003, pp. 557-8.

11 Jon Balda Odriozola, 'El Impacto del Cooperativismo el la Economía Vasca. El Caso Fagor y la Apuesta Por Empleo', Masters Thesis, Univesidad del País Vasco, 2015; Anjel Errasti and Antxon Mendizabal, 'The Impact of Globalisation and Relocation Strategies in Large Cooperatives: The Case of the Mondragón Cooperative Fagor Electrodomésticos S. Coop'. in Sonja Novkovic and Vania Sena, eds, *Cooperative Firms in Global Markets: Incidence, Viability, and Economic Performance*, 2007, pp. 265-95; Anjel Errasti, Baleren Bakaikoa, Ignacio Bretos and Enekoitz Etxezarreta, 'What do Mondragon Coopitalist Multinationals Look Like? The Rise and Fall of Fagor Electrodomésticos S. Coop and its European Subsidiaries', *Annals of Public and Cooperative Economics* 87, 2016, pp. 433-56; Anjel Errasti, Ignacio Bretos, and Aitziber Nunez, 'The Viability of Cooperatives: The Fall of the Mondragon Cooperative Fagor', *Review of Radical Political Economics* 47, 2017, pp. 1-17.

12 Odriozola, 'El Impacto del Cooperativismo el la Economía Vasca'; Errasti and Mendizabal, 2007, 'The Impact of Globalisation'; Errasti, et al., 'The Viability of Cooperatives'.

13 Anne Argouse and Hugues Peyret, 'Workers Divided: The Fagor-Brandt Merger' documentary film (English version).

14 Errasti, et al., 'The Viability of Cooperatives'.

15 Errasti, et al., 'The Viability of Cooperatives'.

16 Errasti, et al., 'What do Mondragon Coopitalist Multinationals Look Like?'. Juanjo Besterra, 'Fagor Mastercook superexplota a los trabajadores de Polonia', *Gara* 2 August 2008; 'Declaración de los miembros CGT en el Comité Central de Empresa Fagor Brandt', 11 July 2008.

17   Errasti, et al., 'What do Mondragon Coopitalist Multinationals Look Like?', p. 13.

18   Anjel Errasti, 'Mondragón's Chinese Subsidiaries: Coopitalist Multinationals in Practice', *Economic and Industrial Democracy* 36(5), 2015, pp. 479-99.

19   Errasti, et al., 'The Viability of Cooperatives', p. 13; Errasti, et. al., 'What do Mondragon Coopitalist Multinationals Look Like?'.

20   A similar situation pertained in white line factory in Wroclaw (not Fagor.) Through activism and struggle workers self-organized to take control of their state-run factory after the end of the communist regime in Poland. The rise of a technocratic, EU-aspiring class to state power, however, turned the factory into a cooperative that was managed and led by technocrats. Workers felt undermined and deceived and turned away from active self-management. Don Kalb, 'Worthless Poles and Other Dispossessions: Toward and Anthropology of Labor in Post-Communist Central and Eastern Europe', in Sharryn Kasmir and August Carbonella, eds, *Blood and Fire: Toward a Global Anthropology of Labor,* Oxford: Berghahn Press, 2015, pp. 250-89.

21   Arando, 'Assessing Mondragon', p. 12.

22   'El Modelo de Mondragón Tiene Pies de Barro', *El Diario Vasco,* 20 October, 2013, p. 37; 'Los Socios de Fagor Elecotrodomésticos se Juegan 131 Milliones Imvertidos', *El Diario Vasco,* 26 October 2013, p. 36.

23   Iñaki Heras-Saizarbitoria, 'The ties that bind? Exploring the basic principles of worker-owned organizations in Practice', *Organization* 21(5), 2014, pp. 645-65.

24   Arando, 'Assessing Mondragon', p. 27.

25   'La huelga general de 21 de mayo en las cooperatibas', *Ahots Kooperatibista,* 23 June 2009, pp. 2-3.

26   Karl Marx, 'Inaugural Address of the International Working Men's Association', 21-27 October 1864, available at www.marxists.org.

27   Robert Tombs, 'Harbingers of Entrepreneurs? A Workers' Cooperative During the Paris Commune', *The Historical Journal* 27(4), 1984, p. 969. For a discussion of Marx's position on cooperatives, see Bruno Jossa, 'Marx, Marxists and the Cooperative Movement', *Cambridge Journal of Economics* 29, 2005, pp. 3-18.

28   Sam Gindin, 'Chasing Utopia', *Jacobin,* 10 March 2016, https//www.jacobinmag. com/2016/03/workers-control-coops-wright-wolff-alperovitz/

29   See J.K. Gibson-Graham, *A Postcapitalist Politics,* Minneapolis: University of Minnesota Press, 2006; and Richard Wolff, *Democracy at Work: A Cure for Capitalism,* Chicago: Haymarket Books, 2012. For further examples of the former position, see Maria Sitrin and Dario Azzelini, *They Can't Represent Us: Reinventing Democracy From Greece to Occupy,* New York: Verso, 2014; David Graeber, *Toward an Anthropological Theory of Value, The False Coin of Our Own Dreams,* New York: Palgrave, 2001; and 'On the Moral Grounds of Economic Relations: A Maussian Approach', Open Anthropology Cooperative Press, Working Paper Series #6, 2010, available at: www.openanthcoop. net/press. For the latter position, see also Gar Alperowitz, *What Then Must We Do?;* and Eric Olin Wright, *Envisioning Real Utopias,* New York: Verso, 2010.

30   See Gibson-Graham, *A Postcapitalist Politics,* pp. 101-2, 124. In 'Rethinking the Economy with Thick Description and Weak Theory', *Current Anthropology* 55, 2014, Gibson-Graham affirm the existence of a 'landscape of economic difference', involving multiple relations and practices outside of market exchange and circuits of capitalist value. The long list includes both positive and negative relations of care, sharing, reciprocity, cooperation, bondage, coercion, self- exploitation, solidarity, etc. For some, this inventory immediately urges connection or explanation, but Gibson-Graham plainly reject the impulse to 'strong theory' because it is a 'powerful discourse that organizes events into understandable and seemingly predictable trajectories'. Their preferred 'weak theory' instead prizes the complexity of non-capitalist practices and

alternative moralities without tying them to capitalist histories or logics. Their argument ignores how Marxist theory charts unevenness as both the lifeblood and consequence of capital accumulation, and it elides the manifold ways that capital and states produce difference, including uneven proletarianization and non-wage labour relations. See a related critique by Don Kalb, 'Class, Labour and Social Reproduction. Towards a Non-Self Limiting Anthropology', *Soumen Anthopologi, Journal of the Finnish Anthropology Association* 4(2), 2015.

31   Richard Wolff, *Democracy at Work*.

32   Leo Panitch and Sam Gindin, 'Transcending Pessimism: Rekindling Socialist Imagination', in Leo Panitch and Colin Leys, eds, *Socialist Register 2000: Necessary and Unnecessary Utopias*, London: Merlin Press, 1999, pp. 12, 4.

33   Susana Narotzky, 'On Waging the Ideological War: Against the Hegemony of Form', *Anthropological Theory* 16(2-3), 2016, p. 5.

NEW AGRARIAN DEMOCRACIES:
THE PINK TIDE'S LOST OPPORTUNITY

LEANDRO VERGARA-CAMUS
AND CRISTÓBAL KAY

With the electoral defeat of Cristina Fernández de Kirchner in December 2015 in Argentina, the removal from power of President Dilma Rousseff in August 2016 in Brazil, and the debacle that has unfolded since the death of Hugo Chávez in Venezuela, the latest cycle of left-wing politics has come to an end in Latin America. The fall of Brazil's Workers' Party (Partido dos Trabalhadores – PT), after being entangled in several corruption scandals and pushed out of power on the back of a wave of massive street protests over 2013-2016, in particular closes this cycle in a tragic manner. The inability of social movements to take the lead in articulating this discontent against corruption and the rising cost of living, unable even simply to defend 'their government' against right-wing protests, is a testament to the limits of their strategic alliance with the PT. The PT that came to power in 2003 was, however, already no longer the PT that was born out of the wave of mobilization that began in the early 1980s with the rise of a new trade unionism and the Landless Rural Workers' Movement (MST). Its behaviour in government was such that by the time of Dilma's impeachment, visions of maintaining a 'party of movements' – that is, a party form that would be capable of melding successful electoral politics and more participatory government practices with support for social mobilization – had already come to a definitive end.

What crumbles with the cresting of the 'pink tide' is a particular way of bringing together social movements and political parties, which never really shook off the remnants of populist and clientelist forms of mobilizing, organizing, and representing the popular classes. In this essay, we will look back at the new types of rural democracy that rural workers, peasant and indigenous movements were developing in the 1990s while they were struggling against neoliberal policies in order to assess what was achieved under left-wing governments. We use the term 'new agrarian democracies' as an umbrella under which we place their different projects to radically transform the countryside, as well as the actual way in which they began to organize decision-making in the communities under their influence. New agrarian democracies are designed to be built on a more equitable distribution of land and natural resources and their democratic and sustainable management by local communities, allowing labourers to control their means of subsistence and production and engage freely in some degree of cooperation. The political form of organizing would include forms of community self-government linked to other popular classes outside the countryside through larger participatory political and planning bodies. The development of agrarian democracies requires the support of the state, not only in terms of a more equitable distribution of land and natural resources but also in terms of facilitating the processes through which rural labourers would control their means of subsistence and production.[1]

Against this backdrop, we will critically analyze the main agrarian policies of the 'pink tide' governments in Argentina, Bolivia, Ecuador, Nicaragua, Paraguay, Uruguay and Venezuela, as well as Brazil. Through this analysis we seek to contribute to strategic discussions in the *Socialist Register* regarding the relationship between social movements and political parties in projects for radical social change, and the importance of the democratic transformation of the state in this process.[2] An analysis of Latin American rural politics is particularly relevant to these questions, given that peasant and indigenous movements had managed by the 1990s to reach significant levels of mobilization and politicization by territorializing their struggles and organizing self-governing power structures, while maintaining some degree of autonomy from the market, the state, and political parties.

Our main argument is that overall, even if they improved the living and working conditions of subaltern rural classes, these governments did not modify the pro-agribusiness model of rural development. Following the policies of their neoliberal predecessors, they continued to support large-scale export farming and did little, if anything, to roll back the growing control by agribusiness of the different stages of agricultural production. To be sure, they created or expanded policies supporting small-scale producers and introduced measures to improve living and working conditions of rural labourers. But with the partial exceptions of Brazil, Bolivia, and Venezuela, these governments did not carry out redistributive land reforms that would have tackled the historic unequal distribution of land in the region. Moreover, the measures that were directed at supporting peasant and rural workers did not politically empower their social movements so as to further the development of new agrarian democracies. On the contrary, these policies had a demobilising effect, which reinforced clientelist tendencies and increased internal class differentiation, weakening the unity which had previously been created between different fractions of the rural subaltern classes.

At the opposite end of the rural class spectrum, the diversified yet compact and highly organised fractions of the dominant classes – combining landed, industrial, and financial capital to make up what Zeitlin and Radcliff call a *coalesced bourgeoisie*[3] – leveraged positions within the state to secure their continuing economic dominance and block any substantial agrarian reform. While in many regions of Latin America until the 1970s, an important component of the dominant classes were 'traditional landlords' as their wealth accumulation strategies relied mainly on land rent and the different modes of surplus value extraction, the neoliberal restructuring and globalization of agriculture led to the transformation of these strata into an agrarian bourgeoisie. This landed agrarian bourgeoisie has become fully integrated with finance and industrial capital through land markets, infrastructure, and technological investment, as well as through non-agricultural capital investment, essentially abolishing any significant distinction between landowners and non-agrarian capitalists. These coalesced bourgeoisies now combine several strategies of wealth accumulation that correspond with processes of primitive accumulation and the expanded reproduction of capital, as well as a rentier use of the state.[4] As this essay shall show, in failing to alter the unequal distribution of land and create new economic and societal forms in the countryside, pink tide governments not only missed a valuable opportunity to begin the construction of new agrarian democracies in Latin America, but also facilitated the development of the powerful coalesced bourgeoisies that opposed it.

PARAMETERS OF THE STRUGGLE AGAINST NEOLIBERALISM

Except for the Zapatista movement, in practice most peasant and indigenous movements in Latin America viewed state power as a necessary ingredient for scaling-up the struggle against neoliberalism, gaining access to land, and implementing pro-peasant policies, in addition to securing or consolidating control over their territory in the case of certain indigenous movements. The main issue for these movements was to assess what kinds of alliances to strike with left-wing political parties that were often already in a process of 'social democratization' by the time they reached office. Although some peasant and indigenous movements were themselves already in decline when the left reached government, as in Ecuador, there were several experiences of autonomous organizing that could have played an important role in transforming and democratizing state power and society more broadly.[5] Hence peasant and indigenous movements also faced the challenge of how to critically support left-wing political parties while continuing to develop the capacities that gave them a certain degree of autonomy. None of them managed to successfully navigate this tension under the pink tide governments.

The major achievement of the peasants and indigenous movements in the 1990s had been to unite politically rural subaltern classes that were going through a process of de-peasantization and internal social differentiation. From the outset, the struggle of the peasant and indigenous movements against neoliberalism was complicated by two major contradictions. First, most national movements brought together a great diversity of agricultural producers (market-oriented landed peasants, land-poor subsistence peasants, semi-proletarianized rural workers, indigenous colonists of newly opened jungle areas, small-scale capitalist family producers linked to agribusiness-led commodity chains, etc.) around an uneasy and fragile subaltern historical rural bloc. This had been made possible, to a great extent, by the crisis triggered by the neoliberal restructuring of the countryside. Where indigenous peoples were at the forefront of the movement, as in Bolivia and Ecuador, important differences existed between indigenous peoples from the highlands and those from the lowlands and the Amazon, not only as a result of their different forms and levels of market integration.

Hence, the first contradiction underlying this uneasy alliance revolved around the need to maintain politically the subaltern historical rural bloc as various elements were being pushed and pulled toward different policies, ranging from state subsidies for small-scale agricultural production to the protection of territorial rights for indigenous communities facing the expansion of extractive industries. The second contradiction was that while the movements' proposals for new agrarian policies called for an interventionist state, these movements did not have the ability to control the state through their alliance with political parties or politicians. This contradiction derived in fact from the movements' inability to sustain the politically active and cohesive rural communities that they had been developing through their struggles against neoliberalism.

It is impossible in a short essay to be faithful to the great diversity of experiences of peasant and indigenous struggles in Latin America. There are, however, various common elements that afforded these movements an unprecedented ability to mobilise and politicise the grassroots, and develop a high degree of cohesion and autonomy. The central demand of all these movements was access to land, in addition to calls to reverse the expansion of agribusiness and expand state support for small-scale agriculture in terms of market control, credits, and technical assistance. The demand for land was not always associated with parallel plans to create new institutions to resist the expansion of capitalist social relations. More often, in fact, peasants demanded more equitable market integration.

The rise of peasant and indigenous movements coincided with the transition to limited liberal representative democracies, which was itself coupled in certain cases, especially in Ecuador, with a neoliberal multiculturalism oriented to decentralising certain social policies to indigenous communities and organizations so long as they did not challenge the core principles of neoliberalism.[6] This new state configuration opened certain avenues for the mobilization of popular sectors while preserving the effective control of the state by the dominant classes. Movements took advantage of the opening of the regime by occupying the public space with land occupation, marches, rallies, blockades, sit-ins, and the like. Leaders of indigenous movements, especially in Ecuador, also took advantage of the devolution of education programmes to reinforce the territorial presence of their organizations. However, despite the democratic opening, all the movements faced significant levels of state and non-state violence. As the movements needed to constantly display their mobilizing capacity in the face of repression, these frontal confrontations with the state triggered broader participation and increased politicization of the grassroots membership. This saw the adoption by several movements of participatory practices for making decisions through a successive series of nested assemblies, involving constant dialogue between the base and the leadership as well as the rotation of leaders, and the training of new cadres whereby militants learned how to become leaders. Traditional gender roles were also challenged through increased, and sometimes autonomous, participation of women. Of course, these democratic practices coexisted with more traditional top-down forms of leadership in an uneasy balance corresponding to the ebbs and flows of different moments, and requirements of the struggle, as well as the personal ambitions of specific leaders. In Bolivia, old community institutions like the indigenous *ayllus*, or more recent ones like the *sindicato* (rural unions created by the state through its agrarian reform in the 1950s to represent agrarian reform beneficiaries), were reinvented and used to amplify the struggle.

Hence, it was peasant and indigenous movements, more than political parties, that were playing the role of what Gramsci called the 'modern prince'. But most movements also had a pragmatic attitude toward party politics. Peasants and indigenous movements in Bolivia and Ecuador created their own political parties, the *Movimiento al Socialismo-Instrumento Político para la Soberanía de los Pueblos* (MAS-IPSP)[7] in Bolivia and the *Pachakutic* in Ecuador. In Brazil, they participated through the PT, while in other countries they established alliances with populist parties. Many movement leaders directly participated in local municipal elections, and when they were elected used their office to mediate between the movements and the state or even to channel resources to the movements.

While such participation in electoral politics generated all kinds of tensions, including splits and conflicts between leaders, these seemed to be kept under control when the electoral field was at the municipal or regional level. It was when the battle jumped to the national scene that the ruptures and conflicts became much more acute—and sometimes fatal— for political unity, as it was for the *Confederación de Nacionalidades Indígenas de Ecuador* (CONAIE) after it participated in Lucio Gutiérrez's short-lived government in 2003. In Bolivia, the internal dynamic of the MAS was built on the practice of submitting leadership decisions to grassroots scrutiny or discussion in large regional assemblies (*ampliados*) of the *cocalero* movement in the 1990s. In the early phase of its development, the party required other movements to follow this same practice when indicating whom they would put forward as candidates for office. In a move to appeal to the middle class and become a national option, in 2005 the MAS leadership decided to open the party to almost anyone. The party was turned into a mass party where the National Directorate, made up of a few leaders (Evo Morales, Álvaro García Linera, Félix Santos Ramírez, Iván Iporre and Julio Salazar), came to centralise decisions, and later subordinated them more and more to the needs of the government.[8]

Although the peasant and indigenous movements showed an unusually high degree of cohesion in comparison to other popular sectors, nowhere was a single organization able to impose the direction of the struggle. If in Brazil and Ecuador the MST and the CONAIE, respectively, were able to play a central role in leading the mobilisation of the subaltern classes of the peasantry throughout the 1990s, in all cases the successful mobilization depended on fluid coalitions of popular forces. These coalitions rested on the common experience of exploitation, and grievances stemming from the crisis of the peasant economy. The opening up of the state to some of the demands of peasant and indigenous movements under the pink tide governments weakened these coalitions. Each organization attempted to find political space within the new configuration, but none had the strength to radicalise these governments or to lead a struggle against them.

Looking back at the height of the cycle of anti-neoliberal protests at the end of the 1990s and early 2000s, the crises that brought the left to government in Latin America were in most cases 'conjunctural (or occasional) crises' and not 'organic crises', because the governing parties, their leaders, and their policies were the real targets of discontent rather than the whole model of domination.[9] Even in countries like Argentina, Bolivia, and Ecuador where the discrediting of neoliberalism was probably the deepest, this did not extend all the way to a full-blown crisis of hegemony. However, the political conjuncture was perfect for the appearance of a *Bonaparte*, whether in the figure of Rafael Correa in Ecuador and Néstor Kirchner in Argentina, both of whom first established opportunistic alliances with social movements before later fatally weakening them through a subtle combination of repression, cooptation, and *transformismo*.[10]

That these were not crises of hegemony was evidenced by the way in which many left-wing parties that came to power in the mid-2000s allied themselves with conservative forces. The running mates (and later vice presidents) of Lula Da Silva and Dilma Rousseff in Brazil were from the conservative right. Michel Temer, Dilma's Vice-President, would later lead the impeachment process against her and become president himself in August 2016. Néstor Kirchner's vice president Julio Cobos also played a critical role against Kirchner, casting the decisive vote in the Senate to bring down a motion to increase the export tax on soybeans in 2007.[11] The policy choices of left-wing governments were thus constrained from within their own political coalitions. Nor did the right lose access to the state, though it lost the presidency and sometimes even the parliament, as in Ecuador and Bolivia. In many countries, it remained powerful in the parliament, the bureaucracy, and the judiciary, as well as at the regional level of governance. In all cases, right-wing entrepreneurs maintained lines of communication with presidents.

Right-wing forces were not only present inside these governments, but also rapidly reorganized themselves to confront them from the outside. In the early years of left-wing government in Venezuela, Brazil, Bolivia, and Paraguay, the landed classes reacted vehemently to the threat of redistributive agrarian reform. They adopted a diversity of tactics ranging from the use of parliamentary and judiciary activism to criminalize agrarian movements (Brazil), social confrontation and economic boycott (Venezuela), the threat of secession (Bolivia), and finally military or parliamentary coups (failed in Venezuela in 2002, successful in Paraguay in 2012 and Brazil in 2016).

AGRARIAN POLICIES OF THE PINK TIDE

Limited by the correlation of forces that brought them to power as well as by their own ideological inclinations towards neo-developmentalism, left-wing governments did not attempt to transform the existing agrarian structures, but tried instead to make markets more inclusive by encouraging agricultural growth and exports and by linking small family producers to agribusiness-led commodity chains. Everywhere they relinquished control of ministries of agriculture to representatives of agribusiness. They carried over or even expanded support to large capitalist farmers, while also increasing support for landed sectors of the peasantry through a variety of programmes. Only in Brazil, Bolivia, and Venezuela did the state distribute a substantial amount of land to poor peasants and rural workers. But even in these countries, this distribution was not sufficient to modify the historic concentration of land in the hands of a minority.

In Brazil between 2003 and 2016, the four presidential administrations of the PT are said to have 'distributed' over 51.2 million hectares to 721,442 families, an area more than twice the size of Great Britain or equivalent to Spain.[12] No matter how impressive these numbers are, this land distribution did not change the highly concentrated and unequal nature of land ownership in Brazil. Indeed, between 2003 and 2010, the area controlled by large properties (including by the state) increased by 104 million hectares (four times the size of Britain, twice that of Spain). By 2010, large private owners controlled 244 million hectares.[13] Moreover, most of the land was not distributed; instead, the status of small-scale producers already in possession was merely regularized by extending them titles. Critics estimate that only between 120,000 to 250,000 families benefited from agrarian reform.[14] Thirdly, rather than being expropriated from private landowners, land was distributed from public land and mainly in the Amazon.

A similar pattern took place through a different route in Bolivia. By 2014, the Morales government had distributed 28.2 million hectares to 369,507 beneficiaries, a bit more than half the area distributed by the PT but in a country eight times smaller. However, just like its Brazilian counterpart, the Morales government distributed mainly public land. This land distribution was to a great extent actually a large land legalization and titling programme. An important difference in this case, however, is that close to 15 million hectares (53 per cent) were titled as '*Territorio Indígena Originario Campesino*' (Indigenous Aboriginal Peasant Territory, TIOC), which is a collective form of land tenure and is supposed to give more autonomy to indigenous people. Nonetheless, the Bolivian case may be even more problematic in some respects than the Brazilian one, as a significant quantity of land (almost

14 per cent) was distributed to medium and even large property owners – including 56 titles to properties over 5,000 hectares. Moreover, the Morales government's land law effectively protects large properties by establishing a ceiling of 5,000 hectares that can be owned by an individual, but allowing that limit to be multiplied by the number of associates participating in an agribusiness and exempting large properties existing before the enactment of the law.[15] Within this overall pattern of land concentration, more land was titled to women, either individually or as co-owner, in both Bolivia and Brazil, to a great extent due to pressure from autonomous rural women's organizations.[16]

Venezuela is probably the most surprising, but also the most tragic, case of failed agrarian reform under a left-wing government. Until 2013, the government had redistributed 6.3 million hectares and regularized 10.2 million hectares, benefiting over a million people. However, the policies deployed to support this transfer of land to small-scale family producers and their organization into collectives to generate economies of scale did not translate into a significant increase in land area under cultivation or increased production. It slipped instead, as in other moments of Venezuelan history, into an extreme distortion of agriculture that resulted from the appropriation of oil rents.[17]

THE UNDISPUTED ADVANCE OF AGRIBUSINESS

The first two decades of the twentieth century will be remembered for the dramatic geographic expansion of agribusiness in Argentina, Brazil, Bolivia, Uruguay, and Paraguay, now referred to by some as the 'Soybean Republics of South America'. While grown by numerous small and medium-scale farmers, large-scale industrial farming and agribusiness dominate almost all stages of production of this cash crop. In Argentina the areas planted with soybeans jumped from 6.7 million hectares in 1997 to more than 20 million hectares in 2013 – close to half of the country's arable land. In Paraguay, this area increased from 1.2 million hectares in 2000 to 3.2 million hectares in 2015. In Uruguay, soybean fields covered only 30,000 hectares in 2001 but jumped to 1.3 million hectares in 2014, covering 72 per cent of the cultivated area. In Bolivia in 2013, soybeans were planted on 1.1 million hectares, representing 35.5 per cent of the cultivated area, ten times more than at the end of the 1980s. In Brazil, this expansion has been more phenomenal. In 2003, the year that Lula took office, 18.4 million hectares were planted with soybeans. By the time Rousseff was impeached in 2016, this area had grown to 33.3 million hectares.[18] Similar expansionary trends occurred across Latin America in sectors like cattle ranching, forestry, sugarcane and palm oil.

These last two are flex-crops,[19] which have benefited from the creation of protected markets established through mandates adopted by several countries to blend agrofuels with gasoline as a strategy to mitigate climate change. In Brazil alone between 2004 and 2014, the state infused $23 billion into the sector, while the area planted with sugarcane almost doubled between 2005 and 2013, reaching close to 10 million hectares.

This expansion of agribusiness has been accompanied by a substantial increase in the price of land and its transfer into foreign hands, notably Brazilian and to a lesser extent Argentinian.[20] Particularly because of its extensive use of agro-chemicals, agribusiness expansion has also increased deforestation and the loss of biodiversity, decreased soil fertility, contaminated surface and ground water, and has been linked with health problems of the local population. Regardless of the green rhetoric of some of the pink tide governments and the mobilization of rural communities, they did not put in place stricter environmental regulations or devote sufficient funding to properly monitor agribusiness.

The left-wing Latin American governments have presided over an intense phase of market concentration that was particularly acute in downstream activities such as processing, commercialization, and export. In country after country five to seven companies, often including transnational giants like Archer Daniels Midland, Cargill, Louis Dreyfus, Bunge, and Syngenta, control anywhere between 70 to 90 per cent of the agro-export. Only in the largest countries like Argentina and Brazil have a few national companies been able to tag along with this select group. For instance, two of the world's largest meat processing companies, Marfrig and JBS, are Brazilian, with JBS accounting for 10 per cent of world meat production. In smaller countries where markets are less interesting and profitable for transnational capital, like Ecuador and Nicaragua, market concentration tends to happen through the increasing dominance of national conglomerates, without precluding the presence of transnational capital often of the *translatino*[21] or subimperialist kind.

This general trend toward concentration is a bit more complex for upstream activities, such as companies providing seeds and other inputs and in the machine and equipment industries, which vary according to commodity chains and countries. For soybeans and cereals, agribusinesses of different sizes are involved in all stages of the commodity chain. Some investors rent land from medium or large landowners, or even from family farmers, while some companies simply provide farmers with the technological package. Thus there is still substantial room for different smaller national entrepreneurial groups within the agricultural market. However, large-scale producers are gaining ground in all the commodity chains, and Brazilian agrarian capital is playing an important sub-imperialist role in soybean expansion in Paraguay and Bolivia. Similarly, Argentinian capital has been participating in Uruguay's agribusiness expansion. As far as the labour market is concerned, this sector hires fewer and fewer rural wage-workers due to increasing mechanization.

In fresh fruits and vegetables, as well as cut flowers, agribusiness also has a commanding position. These crops are very capital intensive, require a substantial amount of energy and water, and are oriented toward both the domestic and the global market depending on the quality of the produce. In comparison to soybeans and cereals, however, they still require a substantial amount of seasonal wage-labour, very often women and sometimes children. Though they have been squeezed out of the export market by the standards imposed by supermarket chains, peasant and family farmers still produce a substantial amount of the fruits and vegetables for the domestic market. Finally, in typically peasant crops such as coffee and cacao, production is still in the hands of peasant and family producers although agribusiness, both domestic and foreign, focuses on controlling processing, commercialization, and export.

As a consequence of this expansion and economic dynamism, agro-exports accounted for a very significant portion of the overall exports of these countries. In Brazil, from 1999 to 2010 agricultural exports accounted for around 42 per cent of total exports – and only around 7 per cent of imports. Gross agricultural exports in 2014 of $96.75 billion (and a corresponding net surplus of $80.13 billion) broke all records. In Uruguay in 2014, total exports were just over $10 billion, 76 per cent of which were agricultural and agro-industrial exports. In Paraguay in 2016, more than 83 per cent of the total exports were agricultural, with soybeans and its derivatives representing 53 per cent and meat representing 18 per cent.[22]

The agricultural policies of the pink tide governments have clearly been pro-agribusiness. In Brazil and Argentina, the state mobilized its full range of policy instruments: institutional reforms to protect land, strengthening intellectual property rights, and facilitating the purchase of land; investment in infrastructure, fiscal incentives, soft credits, and direct subsidies; labour conflict mediation and favourable environmental regulations; and others. To illustrate, in 2015 alone the Brazilian government is said to have distributed $46.6 billion to agribusiness, mainly through credit to finance production, but also in the form of subsidies, debt equalization, purchase and price guarantees, stock exchange shares, etc. The Argentinian state also supported agribusiness, but in contrast to Brazil's lack of taxation on agribusiness, the government of Néstor Kirchner imposed a 35 per cent export tax on soybeans. However, in a typically Argentinian populist fashion, the state took money from agrarian capital with its left hand and gave it back with its right: agribusiness received more than 80 per cent of the $7,359 million pesos distributed between 2007 and 2010 as subsidies to the agricultural sector as a whole.[23]

States with less capacity and no significant peasant movements, like Nicaragua and Uruguay, tended to adopt measures supportive of agribusiness institutionally, such as protection of property rights, allocation of land titles, and fiscal incentives. But this was also the case in Bolivia and Ecuador, where peasant and indigenous movements had been crucial to creating the conjunctural crisis that allowed left-wing politicians to reach office with commitments to curb the power of agribusiness in favour of peasant and family producers. Rhetorically, both governments adopted food sovereignty and *buen vivir* as guidelines for their agricultural policies, enshrining it in their constitutions. In Ecuador, Correa never followed through on his promises.[24] As for Morales, after an intense three year confrontation with the large landowners of the Eastern Lowlands (which he managed to diffuse by 2009), he ended up allying himself with them anyway through the promotion of soybean production, which now is also produced by an important fraction of indigenous producers. This accentuated already-existing divisions between indigenous colonists in the agricultural frontier and long-term indigenous occupiers less connected to agribusiness. In late 2011, the *Consejo Nacional de Ayllus y Markas del Qullasuyu* (CONAMAQ) of the highlands and *Confederación de Pueblos Indígenas de Bolivia* (CIDOB) of the lowlands (both of which organize along ethnic lines), withdrew their support for the Morales government over its law of autonomy and the weak protection of indigenous territories against extractive industries. In contrast, the *Conferación Sindical Única de Trabajadores Campesinos de Bolivia* (CSUTCB), where the *cocaleros* play a critical role, has continued to support Morales.[25]

POLICIES FOR SUBALTERN RURAL CLASSES

Regardless of the differences, with the commodity export boom in many Latin American countries levels of employment rose, poverty significantly decreased, and income inequality declined, albeit marginally.[26] Rural poverty tended to decline fastest in those countries that rolled out different types of cash transfer programmes for the poor. With the commodity boom and increased resource royalties, Bolivia, Ecuador, and Venezuela managed to significantly reduce extreme poverty and boost the incomes of the rural poor. The incidence of rural poverty between 2000 and 2012 declined most in Ecuador (by 49 per cent), followed by Brazil (44 per cent), Bolivia (34 per cent), Paraguay (31 per cent) and Nicaragua (15 per cent). While in 2012 rural poverty ranged from 65 per cent in Nicaragua to 31 per cent in Brazil, it was only two per cent in Uruguay.[27]

The pink tide governments clearly distinguish themselves from right-wing ones by increasing the minimum wage, regulating and formalizing rural labour markets, and providing wider access to pensions – policies that also contributed greatly to reducing poverty. The *Frente Amplio* in Uruguay was very active in bringing rural labour markets on a par with urban ones by extending most social and labour rights such as collective bargaining, the eight-hour working day, and regulated breaks. It doubled the minimum wage and created a special unit for rural labour within the Ministry of Labour. In Brazil between 2003 and 2010, the minimum wage increased by 81 per cent even after inflation, and levels of labour formalization in agriculture rose from 33 per cent of the labour force in 2004 to 50 per cent in 2013.[28] In Ecuador under the Correa government the minimum wage doubled, and the subcontracting of labour, which allowed employers to avoid their legal obligations to workers, was made illegal, although this measure has been difficult to enforce.

Regardless of the past links of some of their officials with the food sovereignty movement, most of the pink tide governments seem to have improvised the policies oriented to small-scale producers instead of following a clear programme. They expanded policies that already existed, and in some cases also created new institutions or policies to support peasant and family producers. First, they distributed small credits ranging from a few hundred to a few thousand dollars to family farmers to help develop their farm infrastructure, raise productivity, improve the quality of their crops, or generate new sources of income. Such policies already existed in countries like Argentina, Brazil, and Uruguay. During its time in power in Brazil, the PT also substantially increased the size and scope of these programmes, reaching $7.2 billion in 2015. Critics pointed to the fact that this only represented 15.5 per cent of what was distributed to agribusiness that same year. Furthermore, 80 per cent of the loans went to the richer strata of family farmers, and promoted their insertion into the soybean or sugarcane complexes.[29] Following a similar logic in Bolivia, EMAPA, the state-owned enterprise in charge of supporting food production, used most of its $148 million budget to provide credit and support for family farmers to plant soybean in the region of Santa Cruz.

The second type of support policies attempted to link small-scale producers to agribusiness-controlled commodity chains, along the lines promoted by the World Bank. These policies involved fiscal incentives to encourage agribusiness to buy the production of peasant or small-scale producers. The PT government in Brazil offered tax exemptions to biodiesel plants if a certain proportion of their raw materials were bought from family producers. The Correa government in Ecuador did the same by mandating sugarcane ethanol plants purchase a certain percentage of the artisanal alcohol production of peasant producers. However, no left-wing government attempted to implement policies that could have led to the growth or improvement of markets that are in principle favourable to peasants or small-scale farmers, not to mention markets organized under non-capitalist principles.

The third type of support policy for small-scale producers involved market regulation, but also the creation by the state of various markets strictly limited to family producers. Ecuador and Venezuela, the largest oil producers of the region, were the only countries to establish guaranteed minimum prices for commercial crops. These were justified as a way to help the poorest producers, but as they applied to a crop regardless of the type of agricultural producer, medium and large-scale producers were most likely to be the beneficiaries. In Venezuela, the floor prices combined with a deep economic crisis, over-valued currency, and a generalized practice of profiting from trading commodities between the parallel and the official market (called *bachaqueo*), were part of a disastrous socioeconomic cocktail that derailed the government's attempts to transform agriculture.[30] In Brazil, the PT government's experimentation with public procurement programmes through which the federal government requires municipalities to buy food from family producers stands out from the rest. The largest of these programmes was the National School Feeding Programme (PNAE) with a budget of $1.15 billion in 2014, of which $340 million was reserved for the direct purchase of family farming products.

THE LONG COMMODITY BOOM

The relative economic and social success and sustained popularity of pink tide governments stood on the shoulders of the recent 'long commodity boom', to a large extent fuelled by the Chinese demand and investment.[31] This favourable conjuncture led leftist governments to fall into the easy temptation of 'progressive neo-extractivism', or what can be termed state 'social rentierism': continuing to promote extractive industries while using the income these generated to fund social programmes. The flip-side of this strategy was that social mobilization waned during the commodity boom, even though there were numerous conflicts between peasant and indigenous communities and extractive industries and agro-exports. The national 'celebration' of the export boom, be it based on oil, gas, mining, or agriculture, made it more difficult for groups suffering the negative social and environmental effects of extractivism to make their voices heard. The consolidation of agribusiness and the way it was able to interlock with the interests of other sectors, placed a wedge between the richer landed peasantry – which sold their product to agribusiness or leased land to them – and the poorer peasantry and landless rural workers. Several sectors of the peasantry, including unionised rural workers, began to see the benefits of a thriving agribusiness sector. For these sectors of the peasantry in Brazil, Bolivia, and Ecuador, land struggle or agrarian reform – not to mention a radical transformation of the agricultural model – was no longer a priority. Policies designed to shore up peasants and family farmers also supported the richer strata of the peasantry. This prompted some of the peasantry to plant export crops themselves, while others decided to rent their land to large capitalist farmers and extract ground rent from them.

The pink tide policies that supported small-scale farming reinforced the ongoing process of internal class differentiation of the countryside. This was epitomized by Brazil, as anti-poverty policies directed at increasing the incomes of the poorest sectors of the peasantry discouraged them from embarking on more uncertain struggles, such as land occupations. From the 1990s until the first years of the Lula government, the internal strength and vitality of the MST relied on maintaining an alliance between the 'land-poor' peasants, the landless rural workers, and the fragile small-scale capitalist family producers. The MST's ability to constantly produce highly politicized militants trained in the heat of the land occupations sustained an organizational inner vitality which could be projected throughout the countryside to other rural movements. As the agrarian reform stalled while the PT government deployed cash transfer payments and support policies for landed family producers, the political terrain shifted under the feet of the MST. As its ability to influence other rural movements and pressure the PT government declined, its capacity to lead the previous alliances among subaltern agrarian classes was weakened.[32]

Similarly in Bolivia, a sector of the poor indigenous peasantry transformed itself through internal class differentiation into a petty-capitalist fraction linked to the soybean complex. Poor indigenous peasants also saw their living conditions improved with the cash transfer payments and land distribution. These traditional supporters of the MAS became less vocal in calling for radical agrarian reform. This was not possible in Ecuador, where agribusiness is not as large nor soybeans the crop of choice for its expansion. But Correa has nevertheless been successful in dividing the national peasant movement by striking deals with local leaders and providing micro-development projects for grassroots members.[33] The reincarnation of neoliberal multiculturalism in the state discourse of *buen vivir*, and the granting of limited rights of self-determination to indigenous peoples in certain areas of the Amazon, in particular pre-figuring access to financial compensations in exchange for consenting to oil exploitation, has led a section of the Amazonian indigenous movement to change its strategy away from radical mobilisation.[34] Working out how to deal with the new institutional framework around indigenous self-determination in countries like Bolivia and Ecuador also further weakened the peasant and indigenous movements.

CONCLUSION

As the pink tide recedes, a historic opportunity for moving toward new agrarian democracies has been lost. Regardless of their rhetoric in favour of participatory democracy, pink tide governments – with the exception of Venezuela, where there was a genuine attempt to create 'popular power' – remained firmly within the limits of Latin American-style liberal representative democracy. The pink tide governments surfed the wave of a long commodity boom and took the easy route of state social rentierism. None of them democratized access to land or challenged private property and all facilitated the growth and power of agribusiness. The agrarian policies of these regimes ranged from an almost classical populism (Argentina) and a reconstituted landlordism (Paraguay), to all the shades of neo-populism in between: neo-developmentalism (Ecuador), sub-imperialist developmentalism (Brazil), patrimonial rentierism (Nicaragua), and neo-nationalist modernization (Bolivia). The term neo-populism is probably the most appropriate for describing the pink tide regimes, as they remained firmly within the realm of Latin American style 'national-populist' politics, signalling the overarching tension within labouring classes between clientelism and autonomy.

In no country were peasant movements able to successfully pressure the government into taking more assertive measures in favour of the subaltern rural classes, or to develop their collective control and governance over land and agricultural production. Correa, Lula, Chávez, and Morales can all, to different degrees, be said to have fostered populist and clientelist linkages with the grassroots memberships of the great majority of the rural social organizations, while actively attempting to co-opt their leaders. For their part, beyond their general demand for regional autonomy in governance, peasant and indigenous movements reverted to more state-centric strategies. As governments offered positions within the national state to their leaders, many movements gave up their ability to mobilise their social base in exchange for marginal influence on the policy process. They ended up at the mercy of state programmes over which they had very little input and without their own self-sustained autonomous model of development.,

The pink tide governments lacked a long-term democratization and transformation strategy to rebuild a viable democratic peasant-centred economy in the shadows of an agribusiness-dominated agriculture. They had neither a clear idea of the types of reforms that were required to empower rural workers, peasant producers and family farmers, nor of the sequence of these reforms. No plan was drawn up to begin to reorganise the peasant sector so that it could acquire a collective dynamism through the creation of cooperatives, rural production networks, and locally-controlled agro-industries and distribution capacities. Instead, the pink tide agrarian policy regime seldom departed from the implementation of isolated policies oriented to income support or tenure stabilization of the individual producer.

The most tragic example of this is to be found in the long march of the PT in Brazil. In the 30 years from its creation to its electoral victory in 2003, the PT abandoned its original thinking with respect to internal party democracy, participatory processes, and workers' control in the workplace. It moved from one electoral campaign to another, ever closer to a typical clientelist populist party. When the time came to call in 'the masses' to defend it from the parliamentary coup in 2016, this social base was no longer there. Instead of using its executive command over the state when in power to build an active, politicised, and committed citizenry, the PT built its own clientelist network. Most left-wing parties in Latin America have followed similar trajectories.

Finally, any class hegemony or agenda of social transformation needs to also build new social relations of production, such as new ways of organising production, new ways of exchanging, and new property relations. This is probably where the pink tide of the 2000s suffered its most resounding defeat. Absolutely nothing of this kind was even attempted. The struggle to rebuild a political project that builds on the strength of grassroots mobilization and self-organization to challenge the limits of capitalist liberal representative democracy, clientelism, and populism will be a long one.

NOTES

This essay builds on the analysis in 'Peasants, Agribusiness, Left-wing Governments and Neo- Developmentalism in Latin America: Exploring the Contradictions', *Journal of Agrarian Change* 17(2), 2017.

1   We use the term 'new agrarian democracy' to build on the Marxist critique of capitalist democracy. Although it is close to the demands of the most radical peasant

and indigenous movements, this is not the term they have used. The concept that has come out of their struggle has been 'food sovereignty', which they use to indicate the collective and national control of agriculture. The term however is neither unanimously adopted nor understood in the same way by the different movements. For an overview and critical discussion of the term and its usages see the forum on 'Food Sovereignty: A Critical Dialogue,' *The Journal of Peasant Studies* 42(1), 2014.

2   Leo Panitch and Sam Gindin, 'Class, party and the challenge of state transformation', in Leo Panitch and Greg Albo, eds., *The Socialist Register 2017: Rethinking Revolution,* London: Merlin Press, 2016; Michael Lebowitz, 'The State and the Future of Socialism', in Leo Panitch, Greg Albo, and Vivek Chibber, eds., *Socialist Register 2013: The Question of Strategy,* London: Merlin Press, 2012; Atilio Borón, 'Strategy and Tactics in Popular Struggles in Latin America', *Socialist Register 2013*; and Greg Albo, 'The Limits of Ecolocalism: Scale, Strategy, Socialism', in Leo Panitch and Colin Leys, eds, *Socialist Register 2007: Coming to Terms with Nature,* London: Merlin Press, 2006.

3   Maurice Zeitlin and Richard E. Ratcliff, *Landlords and Capitalists: The Dominant Class of Chile,* Princeton: Princeton University Press, 1988.

4   For our theorization of these strategies of wealth accumulation and the place of the state in them see: 'Agribusiness, Peasants, Left-Wing Governments, and the State in Latin America: An Overview and Theoretical Reflections', *Journal of Agrarian Change* 17(2), 2017.

5   See: Leandro Vergara-Camus, *Land and Freedom: The MST, the Zapatistas and Peasant Alternatives to Neoliberalism,* London: Zed Books, 2014; Raúl Zibechi, *Dispersing Power: Social Movements as Anti-State Forces,* Chico, CA: AK Press, 2010; Jeffery Webber, *From Rebellion to Reform in Bolivia: Class Struggle, Indigenous Liberation, and the Politics of Evo Morales,* Chicago: Haymarket Books, 2011; Marc Becker, *Pachakutic: Indigenous Movements and Electoral Politics in Ecuador,* Lanham: Rowman and Littlefield, 2011.

6   See generally, Charles Hale, 'Neoliberal Multiculturalism: The Remaking of Cultural Rights and Racial Dominance in Central America', *Polar (Political and Legal Anthropology Review)* 28(1), 2005, pp. 10-28.

7   The complete and official name of the MAS is 'Movement Toward Socialism – Political Instrument for the Sovereignty of Peoples'. It signalled the idea that initially the political party was thought to be at the service of the popular and indigenous movements and not the other way around.

8   See Sven Harten, 'Toward a "Traditional Party"? Internal Organisation and Change in the MAS in Bolivia', in Adrian K. Pearce, ed., *Evo Morales and the Movimiento al Socialismo in Bolivia: The First Term in Context, 2006-2010,* London: Institute of the Americas, 2011, pp. 63-92.

9   Antonio Gramsci, *Selections from the Prison Notebooks of Antonio Gramsci,* edited by Quentin Hoare and Geoffrey Nowell Smith, London: Lawrence and Wishart, 1971.

10   *Transformismo* is a term that Gramsci uses to refer to the incorporation of left opposition leaders and parties within right-wing governments or forces, or when leaders switch from one party to the other without any ideological coherence. See: *Prison Notebooks,* pp. 58-9.

11   Pablo Lapegna, 'The Political Economy of the Agro-export Boom Under the Kirchners: Hegemony and Passive Revolution in Argentina', *Journal of Agrarian Change* 17(2), 2017.

12   Fernando Gaiger Silveira, et al., *Public Policies for Rural Development and Combating Poverty in Rural Areas,* Brasilia: UNDP, 2016, pp. 11-12.

13   Tatiana Farah, 'Concentração de Terra Cresce no País', *O Globo*, 9 January 2015.

14   Sérgio Sauer and George Mészáros, 'The Political Economy of Land Struggle in Brazil Under Workers' Party Governments', *Journal of Agrarian Change* 17(2), 2017.

15   Jeffery Webber, 'Evo Morales, Transformismo and the Consolidation of Agrarian Capitalism in Bolivia', *Journal of Agrarian Change* 17(2), 2017.

16   Carmen Diana Deere, 'Women's Land Rights, Rural Social Movements and the State in the 21st-Century Latin American Agrarian Reforms', *Journal of Agrarian Change* 17(2), 2017.

17   Thomas F. Purcell, 'The Political Economy of Rentier Capitalism and the Limits to Agrarian Transformation in Venezuela', *Journal of Agrarian Change* 17(2), 2017; Laura J. Enríquez and Simeon J. Newman, 'The Conflicted State and Agrarian Transformation in Pink Tide Venezuela', *Journal of Agrarian Change* 16(4), 2016.

18   Lapegna, 'The Political Economy'; Arturo Ezquerro Cañete and Ramón Fogel, 'A Coup Foretold: Fernando Lugo and the Lost Promise of Agrarian Reform in Paraguay', *Journal of Agrarian Change* 17(2), 2017; Diego F. Piñeiro and Joaquín Cardeillac, 'The *Frente Amplio* and Agrarian Policy in Uruguay', *Journal of Agrarian Change* 17(2), 2017; Webber, 'Evo Morales'; CONAB, *Séries Históricas de Área Plantada, Produtividade e Produção, Relativas às Safras 1976/77 a 2015/16 de Grãos*, 2016. Available at http://www.conab.gov.br/conteudos.php?a=1252&t=2.

19   Flex crops are crops that have multiple uses, such as for food, animal feed and fuel. See Saturnino M. Borras Jr., et al., 'The Rise of Flex Crops and Commodities: Implications for Research', *Journal of Peasant Studies* 43(1), 2016.

20   Sérgio Sauer and Sergio Pereira Leite, 'Agrarian Structure, Foreign Investment in Land and Land Prices in Brazil', *Journal of Peasant Studies* 39(3-4), 2012, pp. 890-91; Piñeiro and Cardeillac, 'The *Frente Amplio*'.

21   *Translatino* capital refers to capital originating from a Latin American country being invested in another Latin American country. See Saturnino M. Borras Jr, et al., 'Land Grabbing and Global Capitalist Accumulation: Key Features in Latin America', *Canadian Journal of Development Studies* 33(4), 2012.

22   Sauer and Mészáros, 'The Political Economy'; Piñeiro and Cardeillac, 'The *Frente Amplio*'; J Vázquez, 'Evolución de Subsectores Agroexportadores', in Marielle Palau, ed., *Con la Soja al Cuello 2016: Informe Sobre Agronegocios en Paraguay*, Asunción: BASE Investigaciones Sociales, 2016, pp. 32–7.

23   Sauer and Mészáros, 'The Political Economy of Land', p. 406; Lapegna, 'The Political Economy of the Agro-Export Boom', pp. 320, 325.

24   Patrick Clark, 'Neo-Developmentalism and a "*Vía Campesina*" for Rural Development: Unreconciled Projects in Ecuador's Citizen's Revolution', *Journal of Agrarian Change* 17(2), 2017.

25   See Webber, 'Evo Morales'; and John Crabtree and Ann Chaplin, *Bolivia: Processes of Change*, London: Zed Books, 2013, especially chapters 2 and 5.

26   Claudio Katz, 'The Singularities of Latin America', in Leo Panitch and Greg Albo, eds, *Socialist Register 2012: The Crisis and the Left*, New York: Monthly Review Press, 2011.

27   CEPAL, FAO, IICA, *Perspectivas de la Agricultura y del Desarrollo Rural en las Américas: Una Mirada Hacia América Latina y el Caribe 2015-2016*, San José: IICA, 2015, p. 208. There are no data for rural poverty in Venezuela, but poverty dropped nationally by 27 per cent between 2000 and 2012.

28   See Sauer and Mészáros, 'The Political Economy'; Silveira et al. *Public Policies*, p. 4.

29   Silveira et al. *Public Policies*, p. 4.

30   Purcell, 'The Political Economy of Rentier Capitalism'.

31   Katz, 'The Singularities'.

32   Vergara-Camus, *Land and Freedom*, pp. 232-41.

33   Thomas Paul Henderson, 'The Class Dynamics of Food Sovereignty in Mexico and Ecuador', *Journal of Agrarian Change*, 2016.

34   For an overview of the effects of neoliberal multiculturalism on the peasant indigenous movement in Ecuador from its emergence in the 1990s to its transformation in the state discourse of Buen Vivir under the Correa government, see Víctor Bretón Solo de Zaldívar, 'Etnicidad, desarrollo y "Buen Vivir": Reflexiones críticas en perspective histórica', *European Review of Latin American and Caribbean Studies* 95, 2013, pp. 71-95. Javier Martínez Sastre, *El Paraíso en Venta. Desarrollo, Etnicidad y Ambientalismo en la Frontera Sur del Yasuní (Amazonía Ecuatoriana)*, Quito: Ediciones Abya-Yala, 2015 provides a fascinating analysis of the strategy of two Amazonean indigenous families, the Viteri-Gualinga and the Villamil, and their relationships within the indigenous movement on the one hand, and international development agencies, including the World Bank, on the other, as well as within the Correa regime.

PRACTISING DEMOCRATIC COMMUNISM: THE KERALA EXPERIENCE

MICHELLE WILLIAMS

The twentieth century was marked by the emergence and growth of mass political parties that sought to control their respective states through either democratic or authoritarian means. For parties operating in democratic contexts, their relations to civil society tended to be more autonomous and revolved around support for electoral contests. For many communist parties, by contrast, the relation to civil society was top-down, with the mobilization of a mass base by a vanguard party vital to the communist project.[1] Kerala's Communist Party of India (Marxist) was trying to break with this tradition of heteronomous[2] relations to its base through pioneering a new road to socialist democracy in which the party prioritized democratic institutions, practices, and processes as both means and end. In this process, the party was refashioning relations between the state and civil society, as well as between the party and state-civil society.

In this essay I argue that in the 1990s the CPI(M)'s *People's Plan Campaign for Democratic Decentralization* represented a fundamental shift in the way politics and civil society interface: civil society mobilization went from redistributive claims-making protest politics to a generative politics[3] that deepened and extended democratic practices. Indeed, it has been suggested that 'the campaign' (as it is popularly called) 'in both its scope and design … represents the most ambitious and concerted state-led effort to build local institutions of participatory democratic governance ever taken in the subcontinent'.[4] For the CPI(M) the campaign had twin goals: (1) institutional transformation making local governments more accountable and responsive to local needs; and (2) mass mobilization to build the capacity and culture for democratic participation among ordinary citizens. The CPI(M) was trying to extend civil society's influence in the political and economic spheres through institutional changes and mobilizational efforts. It envisioned empowering ordinary citizens through democratizing local government in order to effect economic development and social justice. The party recognized, at least implicitly, that popular sovereignty requires the autonomy of popular movements.

This shift required a fundamental reorientation in the way both the state and the communist party related to civil society. The CPI(M)'s transformative politics entailed combining responsibilities for holding state power with the need to redistribute wealth while generating new arenas of economic, political, and social development. This involved innovating in terms of democratic planning: essentially democratizing democracy. As I observed directly through interviews with officials, community residents, women's groups, and party activists, and participant observation in communities between 2002 and 2014, the campaign unleashed new organizational capacities in civil society that were autonomous from political party control. Even though it did not transform the structural underpinnings of the economy, there is much to learn from Kerala for attempts at socialist democracy in the twenty-first century.

CIVIL SOCIETY AND PARTY POLITICS

Kerala's vibrant civil society has a long history. Since its formation in the 1930s, the Communist Party in Kerala has busied itself with subaltern class interests in both the state and in its engagement with civil society. The successful claims-making protest politics won it redistributive gains rarely achieved in the developing world, and which far outstripped the rest of the subcontinent. By the mid-1980s, however, Kerala was at a crossroads with its lagging economy threatening to undermine its redistributive gains and with its failure to attract the younger generation to political activism. Some within the party started looking for ways in which a generative politics enlisting new practices and strategies could be cultivated in order to stimulate productive investments, expand the economy and engender democratic self-government.[5] In keeping with its commitment to promote growth without jeopardizing hard-won social gains, the CPI(M) began developing ways in which the social and institutional advancements (for example, vibrant civic associations, a dynamic political climate, legitimate state institutions, capable bureaucracies, and human capacities) could be harnessed for economic and political development. This debate occurred in the context of increasing focus by scholars of development[6] on the importance of participation for enhancing the capabilities of citizens, 'strengthening fragile democracies, improving the quality of governance, and countering the influence of organized and powerful dominant groups'.[7]

Since the early 1980s the two main parties – the CPI(M) governing in the alliance of the Left Democratic Front (LDF), and the Congress Party, through the United Democratic Front (UDF) – have alternated forming the government with neither party ever winning two consecutive elections.[8] This alternation has led to a contradictory dynamic for the CPI(M), concentrating when in government on programmes, policy and legislation to advance subaltern class interests, but then shifting its emphasis towards organizing and mobilizing when it is out of government. This alternation made it appear less hegemonic in comparison to West Bengal's 34 consecutive years of rule until 2011; yet the Kerala Party has had to fight much harder to gain access to state power and thus remain in touch with its base of support. The hegemony the CPI(M) built over four decades in Kerala has been more deeply rooted in society, with the effect of shifting the entire political spectrum to the left. In the process, it has shifted politics in the state to the left. As a result, even the Congress-led UDF has adopted left policies championed by the LDF, to the point of actually running its 2001 campaign on the promise that it would improve on the CPI(M)'s democratic decentralization. The Kerala CPI(M)'s deep presence in civil society had been reflected in its continued strong electoral performance over the past decade, the same period in which the West Bengal party has lost support. The pendulum of occupying state power in Kerala reinforces a noisy but effective politics in which the CPI(M) acts as a vehicle for shaping and articulating subaltern class interests in both political society and civil society. In this process the party is a dominant force that has a great deal of influence over the nature of civil society and has consolidated its hegemonic presence in society.

The CPI(M) began investigating the possibilities for democratic decentralization in which people's involvement would drive social, economic, and political development in the wake of its 1987 election victory. The LDF government it led until 1991 launched a series of novel initiatives, undertaking a literacy campaign, mapping popular resources, promoting group farming initiatives, and starting a limited democratic decentralization process.[9] These were all part of the larger project of preparing citizens to participate in both local government institutions and grassroots economic initiatives, such as democratically controlled micro-enterprises producing for local consumption.[10] All this reflected a common commitment to activate and educate the subaltern base, as well as galvanize the middle strata of society into volunteering their time and labour in these efforts. The Total Literacy Campaign was a mass movement involving popular committees in every ward, mobilizing 350,000 volunteer teachers to conduct thousands of hours of literacy classes.[11]

In 1993 the national government passed the 73rd and 74th constitutional amendments allowing for power, authority, and resources to be devolved to local governments, leaving it up to states to work out the details of implementation. Until this time, there were few opportunities for ordinary people to participate in decision making in local development and allocation of state funds. E.M.S. Namboodiripad, the Party leader and first Chief Minister of Kerala, captured this when he explained that 'if at the level of centre-state relations the constitution gave us democracy, at the level of state-panchayat relations the constitution gave us bureaucracy'.[12] The CPI(M)'s response was *democratic decentralization*, which essentially redefined subaltern class interests beyond economistic working-class demands to a societal project that harnesses a broad sector of society along non-party political lines. In other words, the CPI(M) was attempting to make subaltern class interests hegemonic by redefining the relation between the state, party, and civil society. To do this required moving from primarily protest politics to generative politics.

In the late 1970s, the CPI(M)'s membership exploded with the all-India membership increasing from 161,000 in 1978 to 579,000 in 1991, to 796,073 in 2001[13] and still further to 1,065,406 in 2013, with a total membership in mass organizations of over 40 million. But the growth was uneven in the country, with West Bengal and Kerala accounting for the majority of new members.[14] The Kerala CPI(M) is a cadre party with strict membership requirements (such as an extended probation period), and it claimed a membership of approximately 320,000 throughout the 2000s— which translates into one party member for every 106 people in the state.[15] Its affiliated mass organizations[16] have a combined membership of over 10 million. To be a member of the party requires levels of commitment in one's personal life (e.g. code of conduct, no alcohol), and also in one's public life (e.g. participate in activities, read and popularize party publications, and place the interests of the people and the party above personal interests). In order for members to remain involved in civil society, the party requires members to be active in at least one mass organization. In addition, the CPI(M) has a vast network of 4,700 full-time activists and almost all of its leadership are full-time party members.[17] It has numerous print media (vernacular and English newspapers, theoretical journals, and popular magazines), television stations, and social media outlets, which gives it a direct channel for disseminating its views in society.

In various indicators of electoral participation, Kerala's electorate registers among the highest in India. Its voter turnout is well above the rest of India and averages above 70 per cent for both local and national elections. Even among the four southern states – Kerala, Tamil Nadu, Andrah Pradash, and Karnataka – which all share the same history as part of the Madras Presidency,

Kerala registers the highest voter turnout and Malayali[18] households are more likely to participate in political activities than households in the other states.[19] In the 2016 Legislative Assembly elections voter turnout was 77 per cent, and the CPI(M)-led Front got the majority with 43 per cent. While West Bengal voter turnout has consistently registered in the 80th percentile, the West Bengal CPI(M)'s share of the votes has gone down over the last decade whereas the Kerala CPI(M) has managed to maintain its share of votes. One indication of the degree to which class-based organizations and the Communist Party have shaped political affinities is the fact that Malayalis are least likely to vote based on caste or religion.[20] Kerala also registers the highest turnout at *Gram Sabhas*[21] (three times more likely than the other southern states), and those who attend are more likely to speak than other states, indicating a highly engaged populace.[22]

Beyond electoral measures, Malayalis also register high levels of political consciousness and engagement with local developments, with repeated surveys showing them as reporting 'significantly higher political interests than the average Indian'.[23] Political and civic associations have a long history of making claims on officials in government for social services, especially in health and education, and publicize the issues in vernacular presses. Failure to meet demands is often met with mass protests and 'gheroes', where protestors surround an official and refuse to allow him/her to leave until the demands are met. There is also vibrant community engagement with local development initiatives. On my visits to communities in Mararikulum between 2002 and 2014, community members actively engaged and attended local initiatives such as *Gram Sabhas*, cooperatives, festivals, and development projects. An aubergine festival celebrating the local organic varieties (and indirectly challenging the threat to local food cultures brought by neoliberal globalization) attracted thousands of local participants (from community residents, state officials, elected representatives to party activists) every day of the multi-day festival. Singh tells a similar story of her field experience where whole communities – government officials, elected representatives, party officials, local leaders, teachers, parents, medical professionals, ordinary community members – were involved in the opening of government schools or medical clinics.[24]

Clearly the party represents a highly organized force that exacts firm commitment from its members and overlaps extensively with civil society organizations. While I have focused on the CPI(M)'s linkages with civil society, all the major political parties have dense relations with mass organizations. Malayalis are active in the associational life of their affiliated party organizations and the influence of party politics permeates nearly all aspects of associational life. On every level, politics infuses civil society to the extent that the fabric of Kerala's civil society is fundamentally fashioned by political parties.

Kerala's robust civil society is not characteristic of India in general.[25] Despite India's relatively stable democracy, voluntary associational life remains weak. Chibber describes this as 'democracy without associations'.[26] In Kerala, however, where civil society is strong, dense, vibrant, noisy and heteronomous generative politics did not require building civil society from scratch, but rather taking the densely developed and routinized relations in civil society and remaking them into democracy-promoting civic spaces of participation. The campaign was such an innovative and transformative initiative precisely because it not only built on the organizational strength of civil society, but also involved deploying generative politics to remake state-civil society.

THE 1996 DEMOCRATIC DECENTRALIZATION CAMPAIGN

The earlier initiatives laid the foundation for the 1996 *People's Plan Campaign for Democratic Decentralization* in which the CPI(M) articulated a comprehensive participatory democratic vision. The 1,214 local government institutions in Kerala – the three rural tiers of district, block, and gram panchayats and urban municipalities – were given new powers of decision making and control of planning, budgeting, and implementation. Local governments were given discretion over 35 to 40 per cent of state expenditure. With local funds increasing as they did from Rs. 1,000 million in 1996-97 (the year before the campaign started) to over Rs. 5,000 million by 2000-2001, Kerala attained 'the greatest degree of local expenditure' in India and second in the developing world after Colombia.[27]

In addition to decentralizing power and discretionary control over budgets, the campaign also established participatory democratic institutional structures and processes, creating new arenas within local government for public participation. The institutional design made line department officials – who previously enjoyed patronage and high status – accountable to local elected representatives, which ultimately placed democratic control over local government bureaucracies. Heller, Harilal, and Chaudhuri note that as 'planning and development in India have long been dominated by politicians and officials, the challenge has been to incorporate civil society actors. The campaign appears to have done just that. Over 56 per cent of those who attended Task Force general body meetings in 1999-2000 were either civilian experts or civil society activists, and 19 per cent were party activists.'[28] Moreover, it was widely observed that 'felt needs' were reflected in the Task Force proposals and panchayat plans, suggesting civil society was expanding its role.

The party recognized that widespread citizen participation requires the creation of new institutions as well as immense organizational support in the actual process of participatory governance. To meet these demands, the CPI(M) established clear phases for the annual planning cycle in its institutional design. The first phase is the *Gram Sabhas* (village assemblies), held at ward level (each panchayat has about 10 to 12 wards),[29] which bring together approximately 1,500 to 2,000 participants to identify local problems and priorities and create sub-sector Development Seminars, each of which creates a list of 'felt needs'. Typically four *Gram Sabhas* are held per year, with delegates to the sub-sector Development Seminars selected at the first of these while subsequent assemblies select beneficiaries for targeted programmes. The *Gram Sabhas*, which are supposed to be held on public holidays in public spaces, are inclusive of anyone who wants to participate and are publicized through popular avenues such as media, festivals, jathas (marches), newspaper advertisements and articles, leaflets, radio talk shows, and television slots.

The second phase is the creation of sub-sector Development Seminars that use participatory studies to develop solutions for the 'felt needs' into comprehensive 'Development Reports'. The Development Seminars include representatives from the *Gram Sabhas*, members of the panchayat, government officials, political leaders, and key experts. The third phase is the constitution of Task Forces (later renamed Working Groups) responsible for turning the development reports into project schemes that are then integrated into the panchayat development plans. The Task Forces include elected representatives, officials, experts, ordinary citizens elected at the *Gram Sabhas*, and activists. The fourth phase of the planning cycle integrates the various Task Force planning schemes into a panchayat budget plan that aligns the local proposals with the state's development plans.[30] At certain stages of development planning high-level technical knowledge is necessary, hence experts and officials can exercise inordinate amount of power. To try to counter this problem, and help the planning process remain community driven, the campaign launched a 'voluntary technical corps' made up of retired technical experts.

The campaign succeeded in attracting widespread participation with 1.8 million people attending *Gram Sabhas* in the first years of the campaign. Women constituted 41 per cent of these participants, and those from India's subordinate scheduled and tribal casts were overrepresented in relation to their proportion of the overall population, in sharp contrast with the usual patterns of socio-economic, caste, and gender participation in India.[31] To ensure inclusionary participation, neighbourhood groups were designed to provide women a less intimidating avenue for engagement, allowing for discussion of issues among themselves before they bring them to the village assemblies. The neighbourhood groups essentially became the lowest tier of participatory governance and were a crucial institutional innovation that increased women's participation.

The CPI(M) was clearly trying thereby to promote participation through intentional design, and in so doing shape political agency. Creating participatory institutions is only the first step in engendering a civil society-led politics. Recognizing the need to train everyone, from ordinary citizens to government officials, elected representatives, and political party leaders, the State Planning Board provided one of the largest training programmes ever launched in Kerala. One hundred thousand volunteers were trained for every phase of the planning process in order to educate and mobilize people to actively participate in the people's assemblies and the overall development process. In the first year of the campaign, three hundred thousand participants attended development seminars, with one hundred thousand volunteers learning to formulate village projects, subsequently condensed into village plans with the assistance of twenty-five thousand volunteers.[32] Seven rounds of training were held at various levels of government to fifteen thousand elected representatives, twenty-five thousand officials, and seventy-five thousand volunteers.[33] In addition to this sort of formal training, informal learning also flourished. In my field visits to villages, ordinary citizens and elected representatives often mentioned the increased opportunities for learning since the campaign. In one community I visited in central Kerala activists held informal meetings at the village library every morning. These began with a public reading of local newspapers, and usually led to very informal discussions of community issues, which those who attended saw as not only helping them to understand the issues, but also to prepare them to participate in *Gram Sabhas*.[34]

Moreover, alongside the unions and party-affiliated mass organizations which already had a long history of vibrant activity in civil society, the campaign inspired participation from a wider spectrum, including women's groups, secular associations and religious organizations. Some organizations such as the Kerala Sastra Sahitya Parishad (KSSP, the People's Science Movement) were directly involved in designing and implementing the campaign.[35] The KSSP supplied training officers and officials in the State Planning Board as well as mobilizational support for the campaign.

One of the most successful institutional innovations of the campaign involved women's neighbourhood groups, called Kudumbashree, which became the *de facto* lowest tier of participatory governance. These were initiated under local leadership in 1998 to empower poor women through micro-credit and micro-production units, and to turn women from passive recipients of social services and government programmes to active participants in local development through collective involvement in the provision of public goods as well as individual economic advancement. By 2007 there were over 177,000 Kudumbashree groups across the state, involving over 3.8 million households – representing half of all households in Kerala.[36] This has proved vital for forging a direct link between civil society and local government around women's empowerment and gender issues. While Kudumbashree receive state support and directly participate in state-designed participatory institutions, they are intended to be autonomous organizations engaged in economic activities. It is this dual characteristic of autonomy combined with direct linkage to local government that marked Kudumbashree apart. But this very linkage also posed a potential threat to their autonomy. The degree to which the groups are autonomous depends in part on the local dynamics, and in some instances they fall under the influence of the party.

The campaign combined the CPI(M)'s vision of participatory politics with novel attempts at fostering economic and social development, and nurtured a civic culture that promotes grassroots democratic institutions. The organizational efforts it put into educating and training subaltern classes initiated new ways in which the party related to civil society, as communities were mobilized based on wards and panchayats, not along political party lines. Training focused on processes and procedures, not on providing a predetermined blueprint for communities to follow. Government officials, elected representatives, and community activists – regardless of political affiliation – all received training. As a result, successful decentralized planning developed in wards across the political divide, and all political parties embraced the campaign and indicated that it had positive concrete impact.[37] Given the highly partisan nature of Kerala's political scene and Malayalis' tendency to vote along party lines,[38] support from across political party affiliations is noteworthy and suggests that space was created for a more non-partisan and autonomous civil society. The fact that subaltern classes (especially dalits, women, and people below the poverty line) have been the primary beneficiaries of decentralization further supports the non-partisan character of the campaign.[39]

In order to understand the way in which civil society's relation to the state changed, I regularly asked villagers in my various field visits over a twelve-year period whether people had become more active in local development initiatives as a result of democratic decentralization. While not everyone participated in the campaign, villagers across the state consistently told me that people had become more involved. For example, villagers from Karakulam Grama Panchayat, near the capital city Thiruvanthapuram, explained that because of the campaign they started holding regular neighbourhood meetings that grew into micro-production units in which 2,500 women in 96 women's self-help groups and 174 neighborhood groups participated.[40] In field visits in Mararikulam in 2010, I met similar groups that started as a result of the campaign and cascaded their activities from women's neighbourhood groups into Kudumbashree groups. One group of 24 women in Thaneermukkom Grama Panchayat in Mararikulam cultivated vegetables with each member earning 1000 rupees per month from their activities. In their weekly meetings, many of which I attended, they also discussed local development issues, which they presented to the *Gram Sabha*. For these women, they were directly engaging local government in development planning, registering their community's needs, and engaging in economic activities.

The importance of these initiatives lies both in the new accumulation patterns that were being forged in cooperative production and the increased participation of ordinary citizens, especially women, through their voluntary associations in development planning. Civil society was more involved in local government institutions, and the party's influence over these processes was tentative as groups were organizing independently from political parties.

There were also tangible outcomes in pro-poor areas such as housing, child services, small-scale production units, and roads. The majority of the targeted scheme beneficiaries were from poor households. In the years since the campaign, democratic decentralized planning and fiscal devolution has been successfully institutionalized, and is continuing.[41] In 2001, the Congress-led UDF government institutionalized decentralized planning and changed the name from the People's Campaign to 'Kerala's Development Programme', but continued the devolution of funds with per capita funds released rising from Rs.201 in 1996-1997 to Rs.909 in 2007-2008.[42]

DECENTRALIZATION IN NEOLIBERAL TIMES

The campaign had positive outcomes in both enhancing civic participation and achieving concrete developmental projects, but did it change power relations among civil society, parties, and the state? Did it initiate a new phase of development, one marked by civil society-led politics, in which the CPI(M) used the state to empower civil society, which in turn further transformed local government? Did the expansion of alternative political and civil society institutions create spaces for building an alternative hegemony and societal transformation from below? Did the devolution of financial and administrative powers and decision-making authority to lower tiers of government combine with organizational efforts to educate ordinary citizens and engender active civil society participation? Were popular capacities for class struggle developed? Did the campaign represent a transformative politics of socialist democracy?

The campaign did achieve dramatic change in many of these dimensions. Approximately 200 of the nearly 1,000 local government bodies registered real and meaningful processes of deliberative development planning. The emergence of Kudumbushree groups, the expansion of micro-production units, the involvement of women and dalits in participatory processes, and the tangible deliverables in housing, infrastructure, and social services are concrete and impressive achievements. There were also meaningful changes in a number of local governments where officials embraced the campaign and sought participatory development planning. However, over time it has become clear that the campaign has not ushered in a new phase of transformative politics in which democratic institutions drive social and economic development. While power relations were reconstituted during the campaign, this redistribution of power has gradually eroded and in some areas local elites have captured the planning process. The campaign experience has demonstrated the difficulties in maintaining transformative politics once a project becomes institutionalized within class-divided societies.

In 2007, the Government of Kerala set up a commission to review ten years of decentralized planning and found that institutionalization was largely successful. However, it also highlighted a number of challenges such as skills shortages among government officials and elected representatives, lack of organizational support, shortage of staff given the increased workload of democratic planning, the routinization of participatory structures, and inconsistent participation in people's assemblies – a serious concern as participation was the linchpin of the democratic decentralization process.[43] Indeed, it is the last two challenges that are especially worrying. While attendance remains relatively stable, *Gram Sabhas* have lost their vibrancy in the planning process and in some areas are manipulated by local elites.[44] Moreover, the campaign required levels of commitment from local officials, volunteers, and ordinary citizens that were difficult to maintain in the post-campaign period.

In this context, what were once participatory forums have often become the 'crowd politics' of consultation rather than deliberative assemblies. Without people's active and continual participation, the process is vulnerable to capture by local officials and party bosses, especially in areas with long histories of charismatic local 'strongmen'. In addition, over time stringent and onerous rules, procedures, and regulations have come to dominate every aspect of the planning process, starving it of its participatory drive. Rather than participatory bodies disciplining the bureaucracy, the bureaucracy disciplines participation.[45] With bureaucratic capture, participatory planning has become routinized and hollow in many locations.

In terms of gender, the campaign also threw up contradictory processes. On the one hand, there were more women elected in reserved seats, and women widely participated in the various local planning phases. On the other, the elected women representatives were dependent on their parties, the masculinist cultures of which reinforced traditional norms of femininity and hyper-moralized views of women.[46] While their gendered roles are reinforced on the one side, women's participation in deliberative forums of development seminars and Task Forces was 39 per cent and 30 per cent respectively, suggesting that women were involved in the actual decision-making processes.[47]

For the party itself, the campaign period was followed by one of the most debilitating and vicious periods of factional politics that the Kerala party has ever experienced. Exactly how far this was a result of the contradictions the campaign raised in the party as opposed to other factors is difficult to say, but it appears that the shift in the party's relation to civil society unleashed a backlash from the old guard within the party. The campaign took the party out of its traditional working class organizing around redistributive and economistic demands and into a multi-class arena of common interests, democratization, redistribution and socio-economic development while attempting to maintain its working-class orientation. It was extending redistribution from a narrow connection to the wage by decentralizing resources to local communities. While the party was very conscious of ensuring subaltern classes were the major beneficiaries and key participants, the campaign inaugurated a new form of politics for the party. Notably, in the years after the campaign, the party has not maintained the drive to refashion its relation to autonomous civil society, and has often reverted back to heteronomous control and patronage politics.

Without strong organized forces in civil society and renewed political mobilization, transformative, democratic local-level development has proved extremely difficult to maintain. While autonomous civil society continues to exist, its power is relatively weak and delinked from political forces. It was the combination of decentralized authority and finances to local government, political support from the party, and civil society autonomy that gave the campaign its widespread appeal and created a virtuous cycle of democratization. While the party and civil society set a process in motion, the party was not able to maintain its support for autonomous civil society. While these local challenges limited the long-term goals of social development and inclusive growth, there were also serious impediments stemming from the national and global scale.

One of the goals of the campaign was to inaugurate dynamic local economic activity that would arrest the stagnant growth of the previous period and engender inclusive economic growth and development. Despite the campaign's attempt to initiate productive investment in local economies, there were challenges here too. For example, while the campaign earmarked 40 per cent of funds for productive investment, funds were chronically underspent in this area or diverted to unproductive investment and in some cases misused altogether.[48] The impressive growth that Kerala experienced since the 1990s has not been inclusive growth and inequality has increased in income and land ownership.

Harriss and Törnquist suggest that Kerala's history of 'social justice by democratic means' has been in retreat due to the onslaught of neoliberal globalization.[49] In fact, the structural transformation of Kerala's economy has brought a new class dynamic to the fore that challenges many of the gains of the campaign. Despite its efforts, democratic decentralization has not overcome the pernicious effects of neoliberal globalization. Democratic decentralization came at the same time as national-level market-oriented reforms were setting roots on the subcontinent and a paradigm of exclusive growth emerged. While poverty declined and human development indicators remain impressive in Kerala, other worrying trends have emerged especially in income inequality and skewed land distribution. The liberal economic reforms imposed by the national government registered impressive growth in the service sector in Kerala, but were characterized by a dual structure of earnings that ultimately increased inequality. After decades of stagnation, per capita income growth began registering upward trends in the late 1980s, and shot up spectacularly in the 2000s.[50] Over a period of fifty years Kerala's economy underwent a structural transformation with agriculture and its allied sectors plunging from almost 60 per cent of net state domestic product (NSDP) in 1960/61 to 8.5 per cent in 2009/10. Most of this decline occurred over the twenty years since 1990, when agriculture accounted for 36.5 per cent of NSDP.[51] As agriculture declined, the service sector registered massive increases, jumping from 26.6 per cent of NSDP in 1960/61 to 63.8 per cent of NSDP by 2009/10. Service sector growth (over 10 per cent between 2000 and 2010 alone) has generated high income inequality, with two distinct streams emerging: low-wage traditional services such as tourism, retail, trade, transport and construction comprising half of the sector, and a high-wage technology-driven service sector such as computer technology, renting, real estate, telecommunications, and finance the other half. Many of those pushed out of agriculture went into the low-wage service sector, while the high-wage side consists largely of the educated middle classes. Exacerbating the inequality within the service sector is the fact that the high-wage stream grew over 30 per cent per annum, much more than the low-wage stream.[52] Together with the significant number of relatively wealthy migrants to the Gulf States, the basis of Kerala's economy has shifted from agriculture to services with a significant injection from middle class emigrant remittances.

As a result of the neoliberal tide, overlapping as it did with the period of democratic decentralization, the economy underwent a dramatic transformation that brought increases in inequality, a decline in state expenditure in social services, privatization of education and healthcare, significant remittances to middle income families, and growing inequality in consumption. Decentralization has not been able to ameliorate the impact of these changes in the economy and many of the micro-production units inaugurated through decentralization remain survivalist. Exacerbating the situation is increasing inequality in land distribution, as Oommen explains: 'The widely known land reforms virtually bypassed the poor and the state now has a highly skewed land distribution.'[53] With middle-class migrant remittances flowing into the state, land became 'a lucrative means of accumulation of capital and wealth' and by the mid-2000s the wealthiest were acquiring land. With the growing market in land, a new land-owning class emerged who are largely dependent on farm workers for cultivation.

These inequalities are reflected in the growing inequality in per capita consumer expenditure, which grew 'from 0.341 to 0.417 [...] for rural areas and from 0.400 to 0.498 for urban areas' between 2004/5 and 2009/10. Kerala now has the ignominious place among the highest inequality in per capita consumption in India. The state government has also overseen inequality through its administration of state pensions and social security. Social security accounts for only 2.79 per cent of state revenue expenditure compared to 18.87 per cent for state employee pensions.[54] Even within state employee pensions a widening gap has emerged between the highest and lowest paid. The impact has also registered through the reduction in the once-universal (98 per cent of households) subsidized public distribution system that distributed essential commodities such as food grains, sugar, and kerosene. Together with the increasing privatization of healthcare and education, the wellbeing of the poorer sectors of society has been hard hit.

Neoliberalization of the economy placed important limits on the transformative potential of participatory planning as it undermined a number of the egalitarian developmental goals underpinning decentralization. Nevertheless, decentralized planning continues to be a locus of popular participation, and one of the few arenas where attempts to assert alternatives to neoliberalism are being nurtured.

CONCLUSION

In the campaign, the CPI(M) essentially created avenues for transformative politics. New state-civil society relations were constituted as a more autonomous civil society emerged and local government became more attuned to democratically generated demands. For a period, social development was being co-produced through the intentional design of democratic spaces in local government. In effect, the campaign created a public arena for a vibrant civil society to practice democratic decision making in local development planning, creating an enabling environment for local government to co-deliver developmental goals and in the process diminishing the role of party politics. The institutional goal was to create new local self-government bodies, the organizational goal was to mobilize autonomous civil society into the planning process, and the political goal was to create new forms of agency. The new forms of agency created through the campaign challenged the way in which the CPI(M) as a vanguard party related to its base of support, and thus indirectly and unintentionally challenged Leninist vanguardism in favour of a more Gramscian synergistic relation to the base. The CPI(M) was introducing a new era of party politics into the highly contested political field of Kerala. In the process it was redefining the party's own relation to civil society as well as state-civil society relations.

In terms of democratizing local government, decentralized planning faced two challenges. First, over time decentralization succumbed to bureaucratic capture and participatory processes and institutions ossified. Second, structural changes in the economy brought a fundamental change to the class structure of Kerala, introducing levels of inequality never seen in the state before. The experience demonstrates the importance and the limits of the local. The local is where people's 'felt needs' are experienced and where new agencies, cultures, and capacities for democratic socialist experiments are built. Yet structural transformations in the economy undermine initiatives of local development. Too often, debates about socialism, democracy, and development focus on national levels, forgetting that *the* fundamental constituent part of democratic society lies in local communities. But maintaining vibrant deliberative spaces of development planning have proven extremely elusive in the face of neoliberal national developments. For the renewal and realization of the potentialities in decentralization, a new initiative that seeks to overcome these local and national challenges is necessary.

While these two challenges to the egalitarian aspirations embedded in the campaign undermine the long-term impacts of democratic decentralization, there is no gainsaying that the campaign was a novel and creative attempt to initiate a radical democratizing project in the interests of subaltern classes. The party was trying to create a new subaltern class hegemonic politics of people-led development. For the first time in Kerala's history, ordinary people participated – even if in imperfect conditions and with less efficacy than once hoped – in local government and helped shape the development of their local communities. Kerala's decentralization campaign still represents one of the few major attempts on the left to challenge the neoliberal hollowing out of democracy.

NOTES

I would like to thank Vishwas Satgar, Devan Pillay, and Eddie Webster for their comments on an earlier draft. Thanks also to Thomas Fraser for research assistance.

1   For a fuller discussion of civil society see Dylan Riley and Juan Fernández, 'Beyond Strong and Weak: Rethinking Postdictatorship Civil Societies', *American Journal of Sociology* 120(2), 2014, p. 432-503. Also see Antonio Gramsci, *Selections from the Prison Notebooks*, Q Hoare & G. N. Smith, eds, New York: International Publishers, 1992.

2   Heteronomous is the opposite of autonomous, and refers to dependence on an external actor and being subject to the rules or laws of another organization. I am using it to refer to the party's influence and control over organizations in civil society.

3   Generative politics refers to a constructive politics of building something new. For a fuller discussion of generative politics see Michelle Williams, *The Roots of Participatory Democracy: Democratic Communists in South Africa and Kerala,* London: Palgrave, 2008.

4   Patrick Heller, K. N. Harilal, and Shubham Chaudhuri, 'Building Local Democracy: Evaluating the Impact of Decentralization in Kerala, India', *World Development* 35(4), 2007, p. 627.

5   Most prominent in this respect were I.S. Gulati, E.M. Sreedharan, M.P. Parameswaran, and Thomas Isaac, among others. As seen below, the party's leader, E.M.S. Namboodiripad, supported the shift to democratic decentralization.

6   Jean Dre'ze and Amartya K. Sen, *India: Economic Development and Social Opportunity,* New York: Oxford University Press, 1995. Peter Evans, *Embedded Autonomy: States and Industrial Transformation*, Princeton: Princeton University Press, 1995. Joel Migdal, Atul Kohli, and Vivienne Shue, *State Power and Social Forces: Domination and Transformation in the Third World*, New York: Cambridge University Press, 1994.

7   Heller, et al., 'Building Local Democracy', p. 627. Leonardo Avritzer, *Democracy and the Public Space in Latin America*, Princeton: Princeton University Press, 2002.

8   The two fronts have alternated power as follows: 1982-87 UDF, 1987-91 LDF, 1991-96

UDF, 1996-2001 LDF, 2001-06 UDF, 2006-11 LDF, 2011-2016 UDF, 2016 to present LDF.

9   At this time, there were limits on the devolution of funds, power and authority. In 1993 new national legislation was adopted, which allowed for the decentralization of finances, power, and authority.

10 The People's Science Movement (KSSP) was instrumental in most of these campaigns, but especially the literacy campaign. It is a 45,000 strong volunteer-based organization that has pioneered a politics that integrates ecologically sensitive, sustainable development with egalitarian and redistributive politics. Through membership overlap, the KSSP and CPI(M) have worked closely on a number of projects since the 1970s, but it remains autonomous from any political party.

11 Olle Tornquist, 'The New Popular Politics of Development: Kerala's Experience', in G. Parayil, ed., Kerala the Development Experience: Reflections on Sustainability and Replicability, London: Zed Books, 2000.

12 VK Ramachandran cited this at the International Conference on Democratic Decentralization, Thiruvananthapuram, 27 May 2000.

13 CPI(M), 'Report on Organization', Congress Report, 17th Congress, Hyderabad, March 19-24, 2002.

14 For example, the growth from 717,645 in 1998 to 796,073 in 2001 West Bengal and Kerala accounted for 68.91 per cent of the growth. CPI(M), Political-Organizational Report, Congress Report, 17th Congress, Hyderabad, March 19-24, 2002, p. 32.

15 This ratio was derived by dividing the population in 2012 (34 million) by membership number of 320,000.

16 The affiliated mass organizations include the Democratic Youth Federation of India (4,403,081), Students Federation of India (815,896), Centre of Indian Trade Unions (973,102), All India Kisan Sabha (peasant organization) (1,796,520), All India Agricultural Workers Union (1,549,233), and All India Democratic Women's Association (1,737,240), and the smaller organizations Kerala non-Gazetted Officers Union, Bank Employees Federation of India, All India Lawyers Union, and Adivasi Kshema Samithi (tribal organization). CPI(M) 'Political-Organizational Report', pp. 54-61. These numbers have remained relatively stable through 2016.

17 CPI(M), 'Political-Organizational Report'.

18 Malayali is the name for people from Kerala and stems from the Malayalam language.

19 Prema Singh, How Solidarity Works for Welfare Subnationalism and Social Development in India, Cambridge: Cambridge University Press, 2016, pp. 144-145. Timothy Beasely, Rohini Pande, and Vijayendra Rao, Panchayats and Resource Allocation in South India, World Bank, 2004.

20 The BJP has been slowly making inroads into Kerala and in 2016 it won a seat in the National Assembly.

21 Gram Sabhas are open village assemblies officiated by local elected representatives.

22 Beasely, et al., Panchayats and Resource Allocation.

23 Singh, How Solidarity Works, p. 143.

24 Singh, How Solidarity Works, p. 144.

25 Partha Chatterjee, 'Democracy and the Violence of the State: A Political Negotiation of Death', Inter-Asian Cultural Studies, 2(1), 2001, p. 8.

26 Pradeep K. Chibber, Democracy Without Associations: Transformation of the Party System and Social Cleavages in India, Ann Arbor: University of Michigan Press, 1999.

27 GOK, *Economic Review 2001*, State Planning Board, 2002; Heller et al., 'Building Local Democracy', p. 631.

28 Heller, et al., 'Building Local Democracy', p. 637.

29 I attended two Grama Sabhas and numerous community meetings, neighborhood group meetings, and women's group meetings during 2002.

30 Thomas Isaac & Richard Franke, *Local Democracy and Development: The Kerala People's Campaign for Decentralized Planning*, Lanham, Md: Rowman and Littlefield, 2002, p. 100.

31 In the second year, 10.6 per cent of the electorate participated and by the fourth year the participation rate had declined to 7.8 per cent but the percentage of women and SC/STs stabilized. Shubham Chaudhuri and Patrick Heller, 'The Plasticity of Participation: Evidence from a Participatory Governance Experiment', Columbia University ISERP Working Paper, New York, 2003. Bina Agarwal, 'Participatory Exclusions, Community Forestry, and Gender: An Analysis for South Asia and a Conceptual Framework', *World Development* 29(10), 2001, pp. 1623-48; Pradeep K. Chibber, 'Why Some Women are Politically Active: The Household, Public Space, and Political Participation in India', *International Journal of Comparative Sociology* 43, 2003, pp. 409-29; T. N. Seema and Vanita Mukherjee, 'Gender Governance and Citizenship in Decentralized Planning', Paper Presented at the International Conference on Democratic Decentralization, Thiruvananthapuram, 23-27 May 2000.

32 Archon Fung and Erik O. Wright, *Deepening Democracy: Institutional Innovations in Empowered Participatory Governance*, London: Verso, 2003, p. 14.

33 Thomas Isaac and Patrick Heller, 'Democracy and Development: Decentralized Planning in Kerala', in A. Fung & E. O. Wright, eds., *Deepening Democracy: Institutional Innovations in Empowered Participatory Governance*, London: Verso Press, 2003, p. 83.

34 Visit to village in Kanjikuzhi Panchayat, 17 April 2002. I visited the Panchayat again in 2010 and heard similar stories.

35 K. P. Kannan, 'People's Planning, Kerala's Dilemma', *Seminar*, 458, 2000, pp. 92-7. M. P. Parameswaran, 'Role of the Kerala Sastra Sahitya Parishad in the Movement for Democratic Decentralization', Paper Presented at the International Conference on Democratic Decentralization, Thiruvananthapuram, 23-27 May 2000; M. P. Parameswaran, *From Voters to Actors: People's Planning Campaign and Participatory Democracy in Kerala*, Kerala Sastra Sahitya Parishad, Trichur, 2001.

36 M. A. Oommen, 'Microfinance and Poverty Alleviation: The Case of Kerala's Kudumbashree', Working Paper 17, Kochi, Kerala, Centre for Socio-Economic and Environmental Studies, 2008; Glyn Williams, Binitha V. Thampi, D. Narayana, Sailaja Nandigama, and Dwaipayan Bhattacharya, 'Performing Participatory Citizenship – Politics and Power in Kerala's Kudumbashree Programme', *Journal of Development Studies*, 2011, pp. 1-23.

37 Heller, et al., 'Building Local Democracy', p. 633.

38 Beasely, et al., *Panchayats and Resource Allocation*, World Bank, 2004.

39 Heller, et al., 'Building Local Democracy', pp. 626-48.

40 Field Trip, 6-7 June 2002.

41 The last review of decentralized planning by the State Planning Board was in 2007-2009.

42 GOK, *Report of the Committee*, p. 30.

43   GOK, *Report of the Committee for the Evaluation of Decentralized Planning and Development*, State Planning Board, 2009.

44   GOK, *Report of the Committee*, pp. 307-36.

45   K.N. Harilal, 'Confronting Bureaucratic Capture: Rethinking Participatory Planning Methodology in Kerala', in *Economic and Political Weekly*, XLVIII/36, 2013, pp. 52-60.

46   S. Anitha, Reshma Bharadwaj, J. Devika, Ranjini Krishnan, P.R. Nisha, K.P. Praveena, Reshma Radhakrishnan, S. Irudaya Rajan, Rekha Raj, A.K. Rajasree, S. Santhy, Binitha V Thampi, and Usha Zacharias, 'Gendering Governance or Governing Women? Politics, Patriarchy, and Democratic Decentralisation in Kerala State, India' Final Report, Centre for Development Studies (CDS), 2008.

47   Heller, et al., 'Building Local Democracy', p. 637.

48   B.A. Prakash, 'Decentralised Planning in Kerala', in D. Rajasenan D and G. de Groot, eds., *Kerala Economy: Trajectories, Challenges, and Implications*, Kochi: Cochin University Press, 2005, p. 323.

49   John Harriss and Olle Törnquist, 'Comparative Notes on Indian Experiences of Social Democracy: Kerala and West Bengal', Simons Papers in Security and Development 39, 2015, pp. 5-47.

50   M.A. Oommen, 'Growth, Inequality and Well-Being: Revisiting Fifty Years of Kerala's Development Trajectory', *Journal of South Asian Development* 9(2), 2014, pp. 177-9.

51   M.A. Oommen, 'Growth, Inequality and Well-Being', pp. 173-205.

52   Oommen, 'Growth, Inequality and Well-Being', p. 183.

53   Oommen, 'Growth, Inequality and Well-Being', p. 173.

54   Oommen, 'Growth, Inequality, and Well-Being', pp. 190-1.

FROM DEMOCRACY TO SOCIALISM: THEN AND NOW

PAUL RAEKSTAD

In recent years, we've seen more and more calls for 'democracy' – not only among familiar reformist and liberal groups, but from far more radical ones as well. Radical calls for democracy are seen in movements and organizations from the Arab Spring, Occupy, and the Movement of the Squares[1] to the efforts at constructing Democratic Confederalism in Rojava. This poses a number of important questions. What does and can democracy mean today? Is it inherently tied up with states and statehood, whether liberal and capitalist or not? How, if at all, can it be used to critique capitalism and guide its replacement? This essay seeks to contribute to thinking about democracy from a socialist perspective, in significant part through a reading of Marx's development into a socialist thinker through the period during which he is a radical democrat – albeit one opposed to both capitalism and the modern state.[2] Marx's commitment to democratization remains at the core of his commitment to socialism (communism),[3] which is based on subjecting all aspects of our social life to the collective self-governance or self-rule of its participants. As we will see, this vision is universalistic, admits of no divisions between sex, race, ethnicity, religion, etc., and presupposes full freedoms of speech, press, association, and conviction. It also replaces both capitalism and the state, and overcomes alienation to realise human freedom and thereby greatly enhance human development and flourishing.

We can reconstruct and use this concept of democracy without privileging an earlier Marx to a later Marx in any significant sense. Taking this concept of democracy up again does not commit us to rejecting any of the views of the later Marx – his commitment to socialism, his views on social revolution, his economics, and so on. However, it does mean that we need to be careful not to read *this* concept of 'democracy' back into later Marxist thought, which may use the term differently. We must also be careful to distinguish it from the later Marxist critiques of 'democracy' in a very different sense. As we know, democracy has gradually come to be associated with modern representative states, in particular as a result of the popularity of social democratic and populist politicians who described themselves as 'democrats'. It is because of this that many in the later Marxist tradition critique notions of 'democracy' or 'bourgeois democracy', which refer essentially to representative state structures with expanded (not necessarily universal) suffrage. According to the radical Marxian concept of democracy defended here, these are arguably not instances of democracy at all.

DEMOCRACY AGAINST ALIENATION IN THE EARLY MARX

We're often given the impression that the early, pre-socialist Marx was essentially a progressive liberal focused only on questions of law, polity, and/ or the state. Against this, there's a great deal of evidence from Marx's early letters, his doctoral dissertation, early journalism, and more that support a more radical reading. In fact, before becoming a socialist the early Marx seems generally to subscribe to the doctrines of what Jonathan Israel calls the 'Radical Enlightenment'.[4] This tradition includes thinkers like the Marquis de Condorcet, Denis Diderot (one of Marx's favourite writers), Mary Wollstonecraft, and others, originating in the work of van den Enden and Spinoza.[5] Its core doctrines include substance monism and atheism, a commitment to democracy or democratic republicanism, a commitment to freedom and equality, commitments to full freedoms of speech, press, conviction, and association, secularism, anti-sexism, and anti-racism. We see virtually all these elements in the early Marx, and will discuss some of them in the next section. Of course, Marx was no uncritical adopter of these ideas. His vision of democracy, though drawing heavily on his reading of Spinoza, goes beyond the democratic republicanism of the radical enlightenment to also consider the democratization of the economy – and note that this is before he becomes a socialist. Nevertheless, the influence of radical enlightenment thought on the early Marx provides us with a better framework for understanding his political thought and activity than more traditional readings, which place greater or even exclusive emphasis on the influence of liberal ideas.

This is not to argue that other strands of thought, such as Hegel's work, Young Hegelianism, and some of the ideas that are associated with liberalism don't have considerable influence on the early Marx. No doubt they do. It is only to stress that we also need to be aware of the influence of specifically radical enlightenment tenets in order to understand his political ideas properly. One of the most important examples of this is how Marx, throughout his early writings, presents alienation as a critique of emerging capitalist society for thwarting human freedom, and how he presents democracy as a solution to this unfreedom. In so doing, he works out a radical concept of democracy that contemporary radical politics should find useful.

We find the early Marx's most extensive discussion of democracy in his notebooks on the *Critique of Hegel's Doctrine of the State*, where it's presented as the cure for his critical diagnosis of the ills of modern society: alienation. Although earlier societies have also been alienated,[6] the advent of modern society marks a split of society into distinct political and economic spheres – the separation of state and civil society. This process of separation began under absolute monarchies and was perfected by the French Revolution, which 'accomplished the separation of political life and civil society'.[7] This process transformed the system of (legally recognised and politically enforced) feudal estates into social classes (lacking juridical recognition or political enforcement). Recalling that, for Marx, economic activity is one of the most important components of human social life, we see why the characteristic capitalist 'atomism into which civil society is plunged by its *political* actions' results from the fact that the 'community' within 'which the individual exists, civil society, is separated from the state'.[8] In the political state of capitalism, one is the imaginary member of a fictitious sovereignty, where one 'is divested of his real individual life and filled with an unreal universality'.[9] This universality is an illusion, since the modern (overwhelmingly monarchical) states that Marx was discussing exclude the vast majority of their subjects from any real political power. People are therefore alienated under modern political states because they don't participate in any meaningful way in its deliberation and decision-making on public affairs.

But Marx doesn't stop here. For the early Marx, the modern capitalist economy (or civil society) is also alienated. This analysis of economic alienation sets the early Marx apart from liberalism, and marks an important further development upon the radical enlightenment and Young Hegelian thought he inherited. The early Marx writes that modern capitalist society 'isolates the *objective* essence of man, treating it as something purely *external* and material'; as such, it 'does not treat the content of man as his true reality'.[10] By the 'content' of man, Marx means the everyday social processes of production and reproduction of human life as something external to human society – perhaps as necessary prerequisites, but little more insofar as real politics is concerned. In terms of what overwhelmingly constitutes human life, processes of production and reproduction, especially economic processes of production, are what constitutes the real 'content' or 'objective essence' of human beings, which these capitalist forms of consciousness tend to misconstrue. Importantly, Marx further writes:

The perfected political state is by its nature the *species-life* of man in *opposition* to his material life. All the presuppositions of this egoistic life continue to exist *outside* the sphere of the state in *civil* society ... Where the political state has attained its full degree of development man leads a double life, a life in heaven and a life on earth, not only in his mind, in his consciousness, but in *reality*. He lives in the *political community*, where he regards himself as a *communal being*, and in *civil society*, where he is active as a *private individual*, regards other men as means, debases himself to a means and becomes a plaything of alien powers.[11]

Here we see why the early Marx thinks people are alienated not just under capitalism's political state, but in the capitalist economy as well. There are two reasons for this. First, by removing an economic sphere from political – or any other conscious and collective – control, its participants are excluded from any meaningful deliberation or decision-making on economic public affairs. Secondly, the capitalist economy not only separates people from one another – destroying forms of collective empowerment, and reducing one's relations of others to merely using them as means for one's individual ends – it also means that one becomes 'a plaything of alien powers'.[12] Since the economy is not subject to the control of any conscious and collective organization, and since it subjects people to socially constructed powers and imperatives beyond their control, those subject to it are alienated. This is one reason why the early Marx's conception of democracy goes beyond any mere democratic republicanism. A democratic republic implies a continued separation between economic and political spheres, thus retaining an alienated economic system.

The cure for the alienation of capitalism and the state is, according to the early Marx, democracy. While Marx speaks of democratizing *der Staat* in his early writings, he is using it as a translation of the Latin term *res publica*, meaning the public thing or public affairs. This is how he defined it in his *Critique of Hegel's Doctrine of the State*, where he writes that 'the *state* is the "matter of general concern", and by "matters of general concern" we mean the state'.[13] As such, he distinguishes between this broader concept and a narrow concept of the 'political state'.[14] This is further supported by Marx's earlier 1842 complaint to Ruge about not finding an adequate German translation for *res publica* for his planned critique of Hegel,[15] as well as his use of the term in that way throughout his early journalism.[16] This is important, because it means that just as alienation supplies a critique of both capitalism and the modern state, democracy proposes a solution to the alienation of both.

How, then, do we subject public affairs, or matters of general interest, to democratic rule? First, Marx writes that '[d]eliberation and decision are the means by which the state becomes *effective* as a real concern'. Thus, for people to be real members of the state in the sense of public affairs implies that 'their very *social existence* already constitutes their *real participation* in it', and that to 'be a conscious part of a thing means to take part of it and to take part in it consciously.[17]

Marx adds that in 'a democracy the constitution, law, i.e. the political state, is itself only a self-determination of the people and the determinate content of the people'.[18] Democracy is thus unique in that it 'proceeds from man and conceives of the state as objectified man', rendering human beings the 'one and only' subject of the social process.[19]

The conception of democracy laid out in the *Critique of Hegel's Doctrine of the State* owes much to his earlier reading of Spinoza's *Tractatus Theologico-Politicus*,[20] and focuses above all on the real participation of all in society's deliberation and decision-making. This in turn requires subjecting all major aspects of human social life – including both economic and political decision-making – to the control of the totality of their participants. Marx writes that:

> Only when real, individual man resumes the abstract citizen into himself and as an individual man has become a *species-being* in his empirical life, his individual work and his individual relationships, only when man has recognised and organized his *forces propres* as *social forces* so that social force is no longer separated from him in the form of *political* force, only then will human emancipation be completed.[21]

There are a number of points that set the early Marx's vision of democracy apart from less radical views. First, democracy goes beyond any merely democratic republicanism to also include the economy, thereby overcoming the opposition between economic and political spheres that characterises capitalism and doing away with the contradictory interests arising from both.[22] This democratic society further excludes no adult human beings, e.g. based on race, gender, sexuality, ethnicity, religion, or anything else. Finally, by overcoming human alienation, democracy will make human beings the true sovereigns of their own social existence, removing the need for compensatory religious illusions and thereby leading to the end of religion as we know it. In this sense, democracy remains central to the later Marx's vision of a future society. Democracy is at the core of socialism, and we must never forget this fact.

THE DEMOCRATIC CORE OF MARX'S SOCIALISM

Much changes when Marx goes from radical democrat to socialist, but one thing does not: his commitment to a future society that is consciously and collectively self-governed by its participants. In the *German Ideology*, Marx and Engels write that '[m]odern universal intercourse cannot be controlled by individuals, unless it is controlled by all'.[23] In the *Communist Manifesto*, they write of a future socialist society where 'class distinctions have disappeared, and all production is concentrated in the hands of associated individuals',[24] and in the *Grundrisse* Marx speaks of socialism based on the 'free exchange among individuals who are associated on the basis of common appropriation and control of the means of production'.[25] There is of course more to Marx's conception of socialism than this, and that commitment goes far beyond his earlier commitment to democracy. Among other things, Marx insists that a future socialist society must be planned from the bottom up; it must eliminate the hierarchical capitalist division of labour, and must include people contributing to their abilities and receiving according to their needs.[26] More than anything, Marx's transition from democracy to socialism reflects his deepening analysis of the capitalist mode of production from 1844 onwards. The importance of democracy to both Marx's vision of socialism and his views on the kinds of organisation required to reach it are well known.[27] As Hal Draper put it, for Marx 'popular control meant unlimited popular control, the elimination of all juridical, structural and socio-economic restraints on or distortions of popular control from below'.[28] This in turn 'pointed to socialism'[29] because popular control from the bottom up can be realised only if the inherently undemocratic aspects of capitalism are removed, and this can only be done by replacing capitalism with socialism.

Marx's conception of socialism not only retains the commitments of his earlier vision of democracy, it also retains their rationale in terms of realising human freedom and through that human development. Socialism is 'the true *appropriation* of the *human* essence through and for man; it is the complete restoration of man to himself as a *social*, i.e. human, being'.[30] It is able to do this by producing and reproducing '[u]niversally developed individuals, whose social relations, as their own communal [*gemeinschaftlich*] relations, are hence also subordinated to their own communal control'.[31] Marx was not alone among socialists in his continued commitment to democracy. It is no coincidence that the early socialist parties called themselves 'social democratic', or that Bakunin's Alliance was called the 'Alliance for Socialist Democracy'. They were self-consciously appealing to the idea of democracy as collective self-governance or self-rule, which they wanted to replace the oligarchies and monarchies governing social – economic and political – life.

It is this commitment to democracy as central to the vision of socialism that makes it so relevant for us today, and to the recent growth of radical movements calling for 'democracy' and 'democratization', frequently in opposition to both capitalism and the state. The early Marx's concept of democracy offers a useful interpretation of 'democracy' as a coherent, radical, and anti-capitalist political value. When the young Marx stops talking about 'democracy' in his original sense, it's because for him it referred to the kind of society he wanted to replace capitalism and the state. When he becomes a socialist, he no longer needs this less specific term for his vision of the future, and he therefore drops it – at least in that sense. He still talks and writes about democracy of course, but it never plays the same kind of role that it did in his earliest writings, and for understandable reasons.

Resurrecting this concept of democracy can be very useful today. Democracy is an existing political concept with a great deal of power and appeal, and has played a significant role in recent radical political movements critical of capitalism and the state.[32] The Marxian concept of democracy as the full participation in social deliberation and decision-making, i.e. collective self-governance or self-rule, is still an important part of what democracy means, and is taken to mean, by people today. Lastly, this concept of democracy is not problematically tied either to ancient institutional forms that are arguably unsuited to large-scale, complex societies (such as the Athenian Assembly) or to abstracted state structures which most people have little or no real control over (such as modern representative states).[33]

This concept of democracy can also form the basis for a powerful critique of both capitalism and the capitalist state. In the case of capitalism, this is blindingly obvious. Capitalism does not allow the vast majority of the population to control either their working lives or the economy as a whole. Decisions about who gets hired and fired, what a workplace makes, how it makes it, in whose interests it does so, and to whose benefit are made by managers and directors, subject to the vagaries of the capitalist marketplace. The same is true for broader questions of the economy as a whole, as well as for modern states. Here too most people don't participate in decision-making in any meaningful way. A recent study of the United States concluded that a minimum of two thirds of the population exerted no detectable influence whatsoever over the decisions of their so-called representatives.[34] This is clearly inconsistent with a commitment to democracy in the sense sketched above. The radical concept of democracy drawn from the early Marx can thus provide a good basis on which to critique capitalism and the capitalist state.

Michael Lebowitz, in particular, has made a powerful case that Marx's concept of democracy has a valuable role to play in contemporary radical politics. As a Marxian socialist perspective on democracy and why it's important and valuable, this has much to recommend it. Yet, I disagree with his argument for a 'definition of democracy as a process of production, a process of producing "the all-round development of the individual"', as embodied in the vision of socialism for the twenty-first century,[35] i.e. democracy 'defined as the process of developing capacities'.[36] For one, if democracy is defined as human development, or even human development of a certain kind or degree, then a commitment to democracy might not be meaningfully different from e.g. all-round human development – which is something I would argue we don't need another term for. As a definition of democracy, it is also too far removed from what people think about under that term. Like all political concepts with a long and contested history, and which have been used in a multitude of different struggles and movements, 'democracy' has no single and coherent definition that can capture all its past and present uses and associations. Instead, such a concept is necessarily a confused composite of several different layers of historical deposits, and is associated with a range of different things that there's no reason to assume will always occur, or be able to occur, together. This includes the ancient idea of the collective self-rule of a group of citizens in a *polis*, connections to freedom and equality, the idea of voting for some or many of one's rulers, and much more. A practical concept of democracy cannot capture all of this in a coherent way, and thus it shouldn't try to either. However, it is important that a definition of democracy doesn't deviate too much from at least some of the most important things that democracy is taken to mean. In that case, we wouldn't have a definition of 'democracy', but a different concept disguised under the same word. To my mind, this is what Lebowitz's definition risks.

Notions of human development, all-round human development, and the like are simply not a part of, or sufficiently close to, what 'democracy' is generally taken to mean. Like the realisation of any political value or kind of political institution, democracy naturally requires and implies certain modes of human development, and it may certainly be expected to promote human development in numerous ways. But requiring and resulting in something is different from consisting in it, and being defined as it. Monarchy also implies certain forms of human development, and arguably implies thwarting human development to a great extent. But this does not mean that we can and should define monarchy as insufficient human development or as thwarting human development. So too with democracy. Although democracy implies certain forms of human development, and can rightly be expected to promote it, this does not mean that we should define democracy in terms of human development. Instead, we need a definition of democracy that makes determinate demands on institutions; that we can use to criticize institutions like capitalism and the state and use to guide their process of replacement. This is what the early Marx's definition of democracy gives us, and that is why we should resurrect it today.

While it is true that the invocation of the term democracy today, as Jodi Dean observes, is often presented as 'a defence of the status quo, a call for more of the same' – i.e. more of the same capitalist state[37] – this doesn't invalidate our use of the term in the early Marx's sense. If this objection were accepted, it poses a serious problem for the usefulness of the early Marx's conception of democracy for those who want to do away with the capitalist state as well as capitalism. However, calling for democracy in the sense of collective self-rule does not amount to more of the same representative state precisely because the modern representative state is not democratic in this sense. Rather, this amounts to calling for a different structure of social deliberation and decision-making altogether. Moreover, Marx's concept of democracy entails overcoming the separation between the economic sphere and the capitalist state. Since the existing capitalist state is premised upon this separation, calling for democracy in Marx's sense is logically incompatible with calling for more of the same representative capitalist state.

Dean's argument presupposes the idea that current associations between democracy and representative states are impossible to change. If there's one thing that's apparent from the complicated history of all our important concepts – freedom, equality, democracy, socialism, communism, etc. – it's that they change their meanings and connotations over time, sometimes dramatically, in complex interactions with the needs, desires, goals, and ideas of their users in particular natural, social, cultural, and historical contexts. Postulating a currently dominant meaning of an important and heavily contested political concept and dogmatically declaring that any appeal to such a concept necessarily and irrevocably adverts to this one meaning, denies this contextual and malleable nature of our concepts. This is not a conception of, and approach to, human linguistic praxis that socialists should accept.

A socialist reclamation of democracy is not only still worthwhile, it is increasingly likely to yield positive results – indeed, we see that it's already happening. The early Marx's radical concept of democracy can provide us with a coherent, compelling, and uncompromisingly radical way of spelling this value out both for critiquing capitalism and the capitalist state and for guiding their replacement.

NOTES

1   On Democratic Confederalism, see esp. Abdullah Öcalan, *The Political Thought of Abdullah Öcalan: Kurdistan, Women's Revolution and Democratic Confederalism*, London: Pluto Press, 2017 and Michael Knapp, Anja Flach, and Ercan Ayboga, *Revolution in Rojava: Democratic Autonomy and Women's Liberation in Syrian Kurdistan*, London, Pluto Press, 2016.

2   I do not think that anything socialist needs to or should necessarily be traceable back to some past great thinker. This would deny the importance of growth, development, and creativity within any living body of theory and practice. However, in this case I think a return to Marx's writings serves a purpose, because it can allow us to extract a concept of democracy that is useful for radical socialist politics today.

3   As the reader will no doubt know, it is not uncommon today to talk about 'socialism' where Marx himself chose to speak of 'communism', for essentially pragmatic reasons. I will follow this convention throughout this article.

4   Jonathan I. Israel, *Radical Enlightenment: Philosophy and the Making of Modernity 1650-1750*, Oxford: Oxford University Press, 2001; *Enlightenment Contested: Philosophy, Modernity, and the Emancipation of Man 1670-1752*, Oxford: Oxford University Press, 2006; *A Revolution of the Mind: Radical Enlightenment and the Intellectual Origins of Modern Democracy*, Princeton, NJ: Princeton University Press, 2009; and *Democratic Enlightenment: Philosophy, Revolution, and Human Rights 1750-1790*, Oxford: Oxford University Press, 2011. I should note that Israel's reading of several important enlightenment figures (e.g. Adam Smith and Immanuel Kant) is heavily contested in the literature, and his interpretation of the French Revolution (in Jonathan I. Israel, *Revolutionary Ideas: An Intellectual History of the French Revolution from the Rights of Man to Robespierre*, Oxford: Princeton University Press, 2014) has been very strongly criticized. I don't want to wade into these debates here. For our purposes, it's sufficient to note that the main tenets that Israel attributes to the radical enlightenment seem to accurately reflect the values and beliefs of the early Marx.

5   For some excellent discussion of Marx's relation to Diderot, see David Leopold, *The Young Marx: German Philosophy, Modern Politics, and Human Flourishing*, Cambridge: Cambridge University Press, 2007, pp. 262-71. For Spinoza's influence on Marx, see Albert Igoin, 'De l'ellipse de la théorie politique de Spinoza chez le jeune Marx', *Cahiers Spinoza* 1 1977, pp. 213-28; Alexandre Matheron, 'Le Traité théologico-politique lu par le jeune Marx', Cahiers Spinoza 1 1977, pp. 159-212; Etienne Balibar, *Spinoza and Politics*, London: Verso, 2008; Miguel Abensour, *La Démocratie contre l'État: Marx et le moment machiavélien*, Paris: Éditions du Félin, 2004; Stathis Kouvelakis, *Philosophy and Revolution: From Kant to Marx*, London: Verso, 2003; and Paul Raekstad, 'The Democratic Theory of the Early Marx', *Archiv für Geschichte der Philosophie*, forthcoming.

6   See my argument for this in Raekstad, 'The Democratic Theory of the Early Marx'.

7   Karl Marx, *Karl Marx: Early Writings*, London: Penguin, 1992, p. 146.

8   Marx, *Karl Marx: Early Writings*, pp. 147-8

9   Marx, *Karl Marx: Early Writings*, p. 220. Brackets in the original. English translation modified from 'estrangement' to 'alienation' (for the original German, see Karl Marx and Friedrich Engels, *Marx-Engels Gesamtausgabe*, Berlin: Dietz Verlag, 1975-, I, 2, p. 149).

10   Marx, *Karl Marx: Early Writings*, p. 148.

11   Marx, *Karl Marx: Early Writings*, p. 220.

12   Marx, *Karl Marx: Early Writings*, p. 220.

13   Marx, *Karl Marx: Early Writings*, p. 187.

14   Andrew Chitty, 'The Basis of the State in the Marx of 1842' in D. Moggach ed., *The New Hegelians: Politics and Philosophy in the Hegelian School*, Cambridge: Cambridge University Press, 2006, pp. 220-41; and Hal Draper, *Karl Marx's Theory of Revolution, Volume I: State and Bureaucracy*, New York: Monthly Review Press, 1977.

15   Marx and Engels, *Gesamtausgabe*, I, 3, p. 22.

16   Marx and Engels *Gesamtausgabe*, I, 1, pp. 153, 156, and 276-7.

17   Marx, *Karl Marx: Early Writings*, p. 187.

18   Marx, *Karl Marx: Early Writings*, p. 89.

19   Marx, *Early Writings*, p. 87. See also David McLellan, *Marx Before Marxism*, London: Penguin, 1970, p. 150.

20   Compare his characterisation in Marx and Engels *Gesamtausgabe* IV, 1, pp. 233-76 to his notes on Spinoza in Marx and Engels, *Gesamtausgabe*, IV, 1, pp. 240-1.

21   Marx, *Karl Marx: Early Writings*, p. 234.

22   Marx, *Karl Marx: Early Writings*, pp. 145-7, 220.

23   Karl Marx and Friedrich Engels, *Marx-Engels Collected Works*, Volume 5, London: Lawrence & Wishart, 1975, p. 88.

24   Karl Marx and Friedrich Engels, *Karl Marx: Later Political Writings*, Cambridge: Cambridge University Press, 1996, p. 20.

25   Karl Marx, *Grundrisse: Foundations of a Critique of Political Economy*, London: Penguin, 1973, p. 159.

26   For more, see Bertell Ollman, 'Marx's Vision of Communism: A Reconstruction', *Critique* 8(1), 1977, pp. 4-41.

27   See among others Hal Draper, 'Marx on Democratic Forms of Government', in Ralph Miliband and John Saville, eds, *Socialist Register 1974*, London: Merlin Press, 1973, pp. 101-24; and *Karl Marx's Theory of Revolution, Volume I*; August Nimtz 'Marx and Engels on the Revolutionary Party', in Leo Panitch and Greg Albo, eds, *Socialist Register 2017: Rethinking Revolution*, London: Merlin Press, 2016, pp. 247-64; and *Marx, Tocqueville, and Race in America: The 'Absolute Democracy' or 'Defiled Republic'*, Oxford: Lexington Books, 2003; and especially Richard N. Hunt, *The Political Ideas of Marx & Engels, Marxism & Totalitarian Democracy, 1818-1850*, Volume I, London: Macmillan, 1974.

28   Draper, 'Marx on Democratic Forms of Government', p. 104.

29   Draper, 'Marx on Democratic Forms of Government', p. 104.

30   Marx, *Karl Marx: Early Writings*, p. 348.

31   Marx, *Grundrisse*, p.162.

32   David Graeber, *The Democracy Project*, New York: Spiegel & Grau, 2013; Marina Sitrin and Dario Azzellini, *They Can't Represent Us! Reinventing Democracy From Greece to Occupy*, London: Verso, 2014; Mark Bray, *Translating Anarchy: The Anarchism of Occupy Wall Street*, Washington: Zero Books, 2013; and Gerbaudo, *The Mask and the Flag: Populism, Citizenism, and Global Protest*, Oxford: Oxford University Press, 2017.

33   Confirming this well-known Marxist view, the most extensive study shows that in the United States, at least two thirds – and according to the authors probably more – of the population wield no detectable power whatsoever over the actions of their supposed 'representatives' in local and national government. See Martin Gilens and Benjamin I. Page, 'Testing Theories of American Politics: Elites, Interest Groups, and Average Citizens', *Perspectives on Politics* 12(3), 2014, esp. p. 575.

34   Gilens and Page, 'Testing Theories of American Politics'.
35   Michael Lebowitz, *The Socialist Imperative,* New York: Monthly Review Press, 2015, p. 153.
36   Lebowitz, *The Socialist Imperative*, p. 154.
37   Jodi Dean, *The Communist Horizon*, London: Verso, 2012, pp. 57–8.

CHALLENGING THE COMMON SENSE
OF NEOLIBERALISM:
GRAMSCI, MACPHERSON, AND THE NEXT LEFT

IAN McKAY

The term 'neoliberalism' has become a kind of common sense, and it would be unrealistic to imagine its early departure from the scene. Yet in many ways it misleads us. It allows us to imagine that 'neoliberals' constitute one troglodytic faction within a wider liberal family, pining for the age-old verities of the nineteenth century. But a better term might well be 'authoritarian liberalism'. In essence, such authoritarian liberals, now hegemonic throughout much of the West, though stoutly affirming their loyalty to conventional liberal values and practices, consistently defend an implicit theory of politics that radically departs from them. Aware that a kind of grassroots liberalism – a belief in fairness, honesty, and accountability – has deep roots in the populace, such authoritarians continue to pay lip service to compassion, equality, and democracy while blatantly contravening any such commitments. They can be counted upon to wax eloquent about government openness and operate discreetly to conduct a foreign policy beholden to the interests of the armaments industry. They emote about no children being left behind as they smooth the way for charter schools. Guantámano survives after eight years of a 'liberal' US president. The tears shed over the infringed rights of LGBTQ minorities worldwide somehow do not detract from mouth-watering deals with beheading autocrats. China is simultaneously reprehended as a human rights abuser and courted as a lucrative market. The consistent core of all these moral and logical *and liberal* contradictions is their origin in an order founded on private property and the rights of the individual – even if that 'individual' is an arms-manufacturing multinational in cahoots with queer-executing Saudis.

Wendy Brown has brilliantly explored the novelty of authoritarian liberalism. Rather than confronting age-old liberalism, she argues, leftists are up against something relatively new:

We are not simply in the throes of a right-wing or conservative positioning within liberal democracy but rather at the threshold of a different political formation, one that conducts and legitimates itself on different grounds from liberal democracy even as it does not immediately divest itself of the name.

In this formation, citizens are produced as 'individual entrepreneurial actors across all dimensions of their lives', civil society reduced 'to a domain for exercising this entrepreneurship', and the state comes to be considered as one firm among many, 'whose products are rational individual subjects, an expanding economy, national security, and global power'. They confront, that is, not a particular liberalism readily critiqued by noting its blatantly anti-democratic consequences, but a far more totalizing political order, in which all such consequences can be attributed to individual miscalculations and self-interested manoeuvres: 'This is serious political nihilism, which no mere defence of free speech and privacy, let alone securing the right to gay marriage or an increase in the minimum wage, will reverse'. This 'political nihilism' constitutes not the mere continuation of the old liberalism in a new guise, but something more ambitious: the drive to integrate into one commanding logic principles, institutions, and practices that were once differentiated from each other. As Brown suggests:

> Neoliberal governmentality undermines the relative autonomy of certain institutions – law, elections, the police, the public sphere – from one another and from the market, an independence that formerly sustained an interval and a tension between a capitalist political economy and a liberal democratic political system.

The state legitimates itself, not as the supposed representative of the people, but the facilitator of economic activity: its success is indexed 'according to its ability to sustain and foster the market'. Although undoubtedly this can be read as a direct confirmation of Marx's thesis that capital 'penetrates and transforms every aspect of life – remaking everything in its image and reducing every value and activity to its cold rationale', and of Weber's analysis of the 'evisceration of substantive values by instrumental rationality', neoliberalism might be better seen as the contingent, historically-specific 'organization of both'.

The implications of this transformation are significant. Whereas nineteenth-century Marxists hoped dialectical oppositions within capitalism would ultimately transform the system, and many of their twentieth-century successors reluctantly came to the conclusion that capitalism had proved itself capable of 'delivering the goods', neoliberalism now means that, as Brown puts it, 'democratic principles of governance, civil codes, and even religious morality are submitted to economic calculation …. no value or good stands outside of this calculus'. Thus 'sources of opposition to, and mere modulation of, capitalist rationality disappear'. This means that the traditional left-wing strategy – of dwelling upon the glaring contrast between the promises of liberalism and its lived experiences – has diminishing effectiveness, for 'the space between liberal democratic ideals and lived realities has ceased to be exploitable'. Both freedom and equality have been redefined and reduced, in essence, to the market.[1]

In the eurozone, for instance, the 'will of the people' in a given country has little bearing on the monetary union. The example of Greece's Syriza, elected on an anti-austerity programme, is instructive in this regard, and Andreas Karitzis has drawn the appropriate lesson: 'today's neoliberal configuration is ever harsher towards other political orientations. A large bureaucratic apparatus of processes and mechanisms, a vast network of regulations, norms, and directives, discards without the need for political argumentation any attempt to follow an economic and social path.' This apparatus has taken over 'policies and powers that once belonged to the state', which are now vested in external authorities or financial elites, while 'a vast number of neoliberal regulations and norms increasingly govern the state and social life'. Thus state power refers not to '*the* political power, but just one pole of such a power, shaping a hostile environment in which considerable effort is needed just to open some space for the implementation of a different policy'.[2]

This world – one in which 'There Is No Alternative' has become a mantra for apostles of the market – is an inauspicious place for democrats who, at a minimum, still believe that more than a small number of people should be able to engage in reasoned public deliberation. Or, as Wolfgang Streeck puts it in a more down-to-earth manner:

Who is to demand and force through the democratic reforms that will, for example, end and reverse the growth of precarious employment; stop privatization and restore equitable public services; tax Google and its ilk; increase public social investment, to make for more equal starting positions and opportunities in the marketplace; control working time; make the production and regulation of money more transparent, less oligarchic and less dangerous?

In Streeck's estimation, the 'American Dream' has attained such power that it has perhaps become 'the most powerful impediment to political radicalization and collective action'.[3] Failure to 'achieve the Dream' indicates not the limitations of the ideal of happiness via infinite consumption, but personal failing, and it calls out for our pity and our charity.

And inherent in The Dream is an entire common sense perspective about property. To acquire property is, in a capitalist liberal order, to *belong* and to *be secure*. All sane and sensible persons may agree that the forces of supply and demand determine wages and prices, that capitalist economic growth is beneficial for all, that the world should become ever-flatter (i.e., more accessible to global capital), and that what really matters in life is individual excellence, duly rewarded. One seeks membership in, or to forestall one's ejection from, 'the middle class' – a maddeningly vague category, resistant to sustained efforts to make it more precise and repeated *ad nauseam* by every mainstream politician. But like 'the Dream,' the 'middle class' also connotes a subjective ideal with very real and material consequences, a real-world projection of down-to-earth hopes for pleasant or at least endurable accommodation, good health, economic security, autonomy at work, and a measure of self and social respect.

Rather than sneer at the people who cherish such hopes, we need to realize that many of them are in flux, caught up in a perpetual and worsening property-based crisis over which they have little control, and wide-open in many (often youthful) cases to alternative theorizations of their predicament. This essay proposes that by drawing on such ostensibly different thinkers as Antonio Gramsci and C.B. Macpherson,[4] a radical democratic movement could effectively place the property rights enshrined in liberal theory, and now entrenched around the globe, in question.

GRAMSCI AND THE LIBERAL ORDER

As John Scharzmantel remarks in his introduction to his extremely useful guidebook to Gramsci's *Prison Notebooks*, one colleague recently advised him that Gramsci has 'gone off the boil' in recent years. Scharzmantel's exposition goes on to suggest one underlying reason why: 'Gramsci's totalistic view of Marxism is certainly at odds with contemporary scepticism towards "grand narratives".' As he notes, Gramsci's claim that it would constitute a philosophic event of world-historic significance if the masses could be 'led to think coherently and in the same coherent fashion about the real present world', seemingly places him radically at odds with all for whom the celebration of difference and pluralism is the epitome of progressive politics.[5] For an influential cohort of anarchist thinkers, proclaiming 'Gramsci is Dead' has been a near-obligatory rite of passage – proof that one has understood and overcome the toxic traditions of Marxism.[6] Moreover, the *Prison Notebooks* are notoriously difficult to interpret, especially for Anglophone readers unattuned to the nuances of the western philosophical tradition as it was refracted in Italy through the writings of Benedetto Croce. After a brief vogue, they were swiftly overshadowed (in North America at least) by Michel Foucault, whose work (often construed in an overly functionalist manner) came to enjoy an immense influence across many humanities and social sciences from the 1980s to today.

Yet, thanks to Kate Crehan's *Gramsci's Common Sense: Inequality and its Narratives*,[7] a fresh appreciation of Gramsci as a resource for an emerging left is possible, one that highlights in particular one key theme of the *Notebooks*: the necessity for Marxists to critique, absorb and overcome – in a word, sublate – the liberal inheritance. Appreciative of the malleability but also the political power of the word 'liberty' so central to the liberal imagination, Gramsci counsels us to be sympathetic, critical, and above all rigorous in our attention to liberalism. He insists – and on this point, if only on this one point, he agrees with Hayek & Co. – that liberalism is not a 'natural occurrence' but a class-based and state-mediated project. Liberalism in education, as in many forms of 'progressivism', often involves a dereliction of the duty to truly empower the oppressed by giving them a command of the abstractions that shape the culture around them, and leave them isolated from it. Liberalism in international relations often means a form of abstracted cosmopolitanism inattentive to the transnational economic forces consigning some regions and countries to subordinate status. Liberalism in formal politics often involves – and not only in Gramsci's Italy – the diversion of democratic energies into non-revolutionary ('passive revolutionary') directions, often by prioritizing the interests of 'the individual', that bourgeois category Gramsci also subjected to a searching criticism. Since authoritarian liberalism has become hegemonic – i.e. maintaining its hold not only by coercion but by the diffusion of ideas 'which block off any alternative vision of society'[8] – Gramsci's insights, crafted during an earlier phase of the same phenomenon, are of obvious interest today. Captive of a regime endorsed by countless high-ranking and prestigious liberal intellectuals around the world, he was an understandably keen student of the precursor of today's authoritarian liberalism.

It is important to note that Gramsci was not dismissive of the liberal tradition. Like Marx, who thought one could find anticipations of a more egalitarian social order in the formal principles of equality and freedom,[9] Gramsci dwelt so long and hard upon liberal order because he wanted, not to reject the liberal ideal of freedom from tyranny, but to liberate it from the thralls of bourgeois individualism. He counselled militants to adopt many habits often called 'liberal', such as for instance a respect for human complexity, a due regard for evidence-based science, and not least, a fair-minded entertainment of opposing opinions.[10] He was in search of what he called a 'method of liberty'. The new structure of liberty has to emerge from below to the extent that 'an entire stratum of the nation – that is, the lowest stratum, economically and culturally – would participate in a radical historical event that affects every aspect of the life of the people and makes everyone mercilessly face their own ineluctable responsibilities'.[11] None of this was about the relegation of the individual to the dustbin of history. Rather, Gramsci wanted to rethink liberty in the context of mass production and mass consumption and grossly unequal relations between town and country, north and south. One might even say, to the discomfiture of some of his followers, that he sought not to bury liberalism but to *retrieve* it from the liberals who had so travestied their own tradition.

Central to Gramsci's 'method of liberty' was the strategy of mounting a challenge to 'that comforting set of certainties in which we feel at home, and that we absorb, often unconsciously, from the world we inhabit'. Gramsci calls this matrix the *senso comuno,* a concept only partly captured by the English 'common sense' – because in English, the term has more positive connotations of 'sound popular wisdom' than it does in Italian. A hegemonic common sense plays a crucial role in modern politics. Hegemony is not the epiphenomenal reflection of underlying, and more 'real', socio-economic forces – an interpretation often implied by the expression 'cultural hegemony' and giving rise to numerous mischaracterizations of the Gramscian position as one focused on fleeting and ephemeral fads and fashions. Rather, the ideas and beliefs that are 'embodied in institutions and social practices' exist not just in 'the minds of individuals but need to be seen as an inherent part of the material realities of oppression and exploitation'. Popular beliefs and the *senso comune* to which they contribute 'are themselves material forces'.[12] The American Dream is an intangible if commonsense entity – but the sub-prime mortgages were its real-world, all-too-material manifestation, which when progressively commodified and abstracted through a world financial order, had drastic all-too-material consequences.

Challenging such beliefs, when they are part of a liberal *senso comune* as is the case in much of the West, is far more difficult than merely assenting to them, because their almost endless repetition makes them seem aspects of reality with which any functional adult must agree. Yet mounting such a critique is not necessarily a Quixotic exercise in 'demanding the impossible,' because the ruling order generates contradiction after contradiction that routinely disrupts its claim to stability and coherence. Besides, there is the 'chaotic aggregate of disparate conceptions' making up the *senso comune* that might yield oppositional meanings.[13] In these early days of resistance to authoritarian liberalism, moments of such 'counter common sense' – Gramsci would call it 'good sense' – proliferate: it is the task of an emergent cadre of activists and thinkers both to preserve such moments and to reshape them into more far-ranging counter-narratives.

Such people are, one might say, subaltern organic intellectuals – meaning that they are organically, i.e., enduringly, concretely and dialogically, linked to subalterns, i.e., groups of people living in a 'commonsense world rooted in the narratives of those who dominate them'.[14] If members of such groups are accustomed to being objectified, treated as things and not historical actors, they nonetheless grasp their situation in flashes of insight – in visual images, jokes, slogans, songs, even bodily gestures. But in order for these flashes to generate a lasting challenge to the ruling order, they must be given more permanent form by subaltern intellectuals, activists and thinkers with the ability to connect such flashes with more lasting forms of thought and practice – to transform them into compelling counter-narratives.[15] Such oppositional narratives must have their origin and sustain themselves in the implicit philosophy of subalterns, systematizing flashes of insight into a coherent and lasting philosophy. There is no shortcut to fundamental social change that can skip this path, and it is steep: for the narratives it develops run against the grain of the 'very fabric of the institutions and practices of everyday life'.[16]

And this cannot be merely a process of imposing upon people coldly rationalistic schema that have no resonance in their daily lives: 'Only a political narrative that explains inequality and oppression in a way that connects with subalterns emotionally as well as intellectually can hope to mobilize the kind of movement that might actually bring about significant change.'[17] We may support the democratic rights of everyday Arabs as an abstract ideal; the self-immolation of street vendor Tarek el-Tayeb Mohamed Bouazizi in Tunis, protesting against the confiscation of his wares by a petty bureaucrat, concretized the struggle for democracy in a way that connected with millions of people. Details of the 2007–9 financial crisis may be forgettable (even if they entail billions of dollars and have immense practical consequences), but the occupation of the allegedly public property of Zuccotti Park in Manhattan in 2011 brought the inequities they embodied down to earth. And it is no accident that both of these transformative incidents concerned property – which names a crucial zone of interaction between the average person and an otherwise difficult-to-grasp economic order.

It was because he took the formation of a cadre of organic intellectuals – a contingent of people who, grasping abstract issues, could also connect them to everyday people – so seriously that Gramsci was impatient with the many people who treated *senso comune* sentimentally. It called out for a much more rigorous and critical treatment. At their most reactionary, common sense narratives could often be 'crudely neophobe and conservative'.[18] It was never Gramsci's aim to salvage quaint aspects of popular culture for the edification and amusement of his readers. Rather, he sought an all-encompassing social revolution to which common sense might contribute, but only if it was subjected to critical analysis and intellectual transformation. There could be no democratic revolution without a widely-diffused critique, in a language accessible to most people, diffused by organic intellectuals linked directly to them. And at the core of that critique was a critical evaluation of property.

RETRIEVING C.B. MACPHERSON

If Gramsci unsettles many liberals, because of his undeniably revolutionary socialist outlook, he also unsettles many Marxists, suspicious of someone who, just as undeniably, had incorporated so many aspects of liberal thinking into that outlook. In that sense, he was a liminal figure – working within the Marxist tradition, yet often operating at several degrees removed from the received opinions (one might even say, the deterministic *senso comune*) that many Marxists relied upon. Liberal or Marxist? Materialist or Idealist? Some asked these questions in a stand-and-deliver manner, and found incriminating answers in Gramsci's complex reflections.

The same accusatory questions have been put to C.B. Macpherson (1911-1987), once renowned as the author of the concept of 'possessive individualism', a phrase that has endured in critical thought. *Possessive Individualism* (1962) was seen in its day as a major revision of received understandings of John Locke, Thomas Hobbes, and other seventeenth-century thinkers; *The Real World of Democracy* (1965) was widely debated as an accessible introduction to contemporary debates about democracy that challenged polarized Cold War assumptions about the global south and the Communist bloc. Three decades after his death, Macpherson has re-emerged as one of liberal capitalism's most powerful critics, whose wonderfully accessible but fiercely rigorous writings shed light on some of its most deep-seated contradictions.[19]

The major, yet often overlooked, writings of Macpherson's last decade – *The Life and Times of Liberal Democracy* (1977), *Property: Mainstream and Critical Positions* (1978), and *The Rise and Fall of Economic Justice* (1987) are much more than afterthoughts to his more famous writings of the 1960s. Rather, although developing ideas broached by Macpherson for decades, these works take them in new, more radical directions. It was in his late works – especially in the generally overlooked edited collection *Property* (the Cinderella of the Macpherson corpus) and *The Rise and Fall of Economic Justice*, which appeared after many had pronounced their verdicts on his life's work – that Macpherson engaged in a sustained way with the Marxist tradition. He did so with such intensity that, contrary to his own explicit injunction (he kept saying he was borrowing ideas from the Marxists, not himself becoming one), many of his readers thought he had fully converted.

One can see why they thought so. There was a Marxist atmosphere in his post-1975 corpus. *The Life and Times* warned liberals they faced a potentially fatal crisis, as once-successful Keynesian remedies 'failed to cope with the underlying contradiction' – one of the few times Macpherson used 'contradiction' to mean something other than a logical error.[20] As the economic order experienced 'economic difficulties of near-crisis proportions', liberals inclined to defend traditional property rights would find themselves entering a period in which the class realities they habitually discounted would be uncontainable by the party system. They were led by their political tradition to pay minimal attention to the 'capitalist relations of production', and instead followed J.S. Mill in focusing on the more distant past when it came to explaining 'the existing inequitable distributions of wealth, income, and power'.[21] For its part, Macpherson's *Property* pronounced Marx's critique of capitalist political economy 'incisive', and proclaimed that 'his outraged ethical rejection of its reduction of human beings to commodities, and his argument that that reduction was required by the property relations of capitalism, gave his work a strength which is more formidable in the twentieth century than it was when he wrote'.[22]

Small wonder, then, that many readers of the late Macpherson considered him a Marxist. They were missing something. Macpherson's borrowings from Marx (but, with rare exceptions, not Marxists) were about his quest to retrieve the possibility of an authentic, autonomous, 'developmental' individualism.[23] Macpherson had recourse to Marx as a way of uncovering what was authentically radical about liberalism as he construed it – which was the doctrine that a test of a good society was how well it allowed individuals freely to flourish, to develop their capacities, to enjoy life without overbearing oppressors procuring many of their human powers and so limiting their possibilities. His heretical break with his fellow liberals came with his critical realist realization that, in a liberal capitalist order, foremost among such overbearing oppressors were those who used their privileged access to the means of life to benefit from the powers and capacities of others.

Many liberals smelled a Marxist rat, a deceptively subtle one, but their preternaturally sensitive nostrils were deceiving them. Macpherson was clear about who he was and what he was about, i.e., a humanist radical liberal democrat, keen to retrieve what was best in his tradition from the dehumanizing context of capitalism. Macpherson was pointing out that, in a world divided between extremely wealthy people and the rest, the latter transferring powers over their lives to the former, liberal talk of equal rights for all did not correspond to social or political realities.

Macpherson's many foes discerned in this line of thinking little more than a rehash of Marx's labour theory of value, class analysis, and critique of surplus extraction – but they were wrong. They missed, inter alia, what was most truly path-breaking about Macpherson's writings on property. In them, Macpherson uncovered a hidden radical liberal tradition critical of present-day liberal conventions. He repeatedly turned to liberal theorists for inspiration: Adam Smith on the class inequities of accumulation, for example, or John Stuart Mill on liberals' true vocation, which was to create the conditions for the optimal development of human capacities.

Macpherson's critics also missed what might be unsettling for orthodox Marxists in his position on property, since it signalled the insufficiency of the ubiquitous 'public/private' and 'state/capitalist' distinctions many had made the foundation of their 'revolutionary' politics. A state-owned coal mine in China or a Taylorized auto factory in the Soviet Union (which, unusually for leftists of his generation, Macpherson never glamourized), were not necessarily steps towards a fuller democracy if they merely relabelled age-old institutions of property and disempowered the average working person. And this was especially so in a globalized world in which such self-described socialist states, having implicitly accepted a narrow definition of human flourishing, merely played catch-up with their capitalist competitors. As they did so, they came inevitably to resemble their competitors more and more. The politics of property remained fundamental to any project of human emancipation[24] – but this politics required a searching and rigorous examination of the social ends that property relations were meant to accomplish.

Macpherson's rare capacity to unsettle liberals emanated from his being himself a liberal,[25] with a peerless command of the tradition's core texts, not to speak of an equally formidable grasp of the tools of logical analysis. He did not deploy an easily-othered 'Marxist' vocabulary, but for the most part used the well-established tools of empirical historical research to challenge the reputations of many of liberalism's most venerated figures (John Locke in particular never quite recovered from his dissection by Macpherson).

Macpherson made liberals look again, more critically than they really wanted to, at their own tradition. Since liberals often resent being reminded that they are partisans of one historically specific and contingent and class-specific ideology, rather than spokespeople for the interests of humanity in general, their orchestration of the elimination of Macpherson often had an 'écraser l'infame' intensity about it.

Perhaps the clearest insight into this can be obtained from the work of William Leiss, whose book-length indictment of Macpherson in 1988 (reprinted in 2009)[26] set out to expose his 'artful deficiencies' as part of an army of new scholars 'striving to ferret out and overcome them' (p. 25). In Leiss's polemic, Macpherson was a prisoner of the 1930s, pining for his lost Depression-era ideological certainties. Allegedly blithely confident in his own capacity to distinguish false from true consciousness (p. 101), Macpherson imagined a 'socialist utopia' (p. x) entailing the omission of '*any* form of market exchange among citizens' (p. xiv). He allowed for no 'half-measures' in his 'vision of the future' (p. xvii).

Perhaps the only reason to re-visit Macpherson in the twenty-first century, in Leiss's feverishly hostile reading, is to re-experience the drabness and clunkiness of a bygone age: like visitors to Berlin's DDR Museum beholding the melancholy and pathetic relics of a now-vanished era of socialist certainty, we may visit Macpherson if we wish to bask in our own liberal superiority. Go to Macpherson, suggests Leiss, if you want a 'commonplace', 'conventional' analysis of 'the dependence of political on economic power' (p. 51). The page has turned on this aged, sad, Trabant-like relic, obstinately (and, most of Leiss's readers might well conclude, stupidly) repeating the insipid bromides of his Fabian mentors Harold Laski and R.H. Tawney. Here was a man who did not appreciate, perhaps did not have the intelligence to appreciate, the wonders of a globalized capitalist world – in which 'quasi-market' societies generally offered their happy citizens 'genuine gratification of quite genuine and deeply-felt needs' (p. 140). For all twenty-four of these quasi-market societies – with Ireland and Iceland sharing honours with North America and Japan – enjoyed secure welfare programmes, rising levels of prosperity, and consumers enraptured by 'a rich mixture composed of both real and vicarious experiences of buying and selling' (p. 134).

A point-by-point refutation of Leiss would perhaps pay his hatchet job of an interpretation too much credit.[27] It was Leiss's misfortune to bring out the reprinted version of his paean to property and his celebration of the wonders of quasi-market societies in 2009, just as the global impact of the property-induced financial crash was becoming apparent – not least for those lucky citizens of such 'quasi-market societies' as Ireland and Iceland.

In fact, everywhere in a post-2008 world we find disconfirmation of Leiss's core theses. Income inequalities have reached unprecedented and devastating levels. Even in the affluent United States, life expectancies for industrial workers are declining. Students of socio-economic inequality scramble to find a period that can best serve as a model for contemporary patterns. The Great Depression? The Gilded Age of the Robber Barons, 1890-1920? The dire 1820s in Britain? Or perhaps even the Roman Empire?[28] As capital has globalized, with supply-chains linking sweat-shops in China, Indonesia, and the Philippines with retailers in Europe and North America, it has liberated itself from the political and social forces that once mitigated its inequality-inducing effects. As one Javanese woman quipped in 2017, her minimum-wage job making clothes for Ivanka Trump's brand makes it difficult for her to live up to her boss's ideal of a 'work/life balance', beyond her dream of seeing 'her children more than once a month'.[29] The environmental devastation accelerated by unbridled capitalism is poisoning the atmosphere and warming the entire planet – a consequence of possessive individualism against which Macpherson persistently warned.[30] And, under conditions of global authoritarian liberalism, Leiss's conviction that democratically-elected governments can regulate the global economy now seems as tragically dated as any of the exhibits in the DDR Museum.

Marxists were also vexed by Macpherson. Often thinking in black-and-white terms – one must be *either* a liberal or Marxist: stand and deliver! – they tended to miss the extent to which Macpherson had been influenced by Tawney, whose *Acquisitive Society* provided him with a direct inspiration for his *Possessive Individualism*. From Tawney one could draw the general precept that it was legitimate and indeed necessary to commit oneself to an ethical strategy of redeeming the social order. Such a commitment did not necessarily require an emphasis on one class achieving domination over another. Rather, at its core was a vision of releasing the invaluable freedoms achieved since the seventeenth century from the fetters of capitalist social relations. Such a moral opposition to capitalism per se could lead one to conclusions more radical, because more uncompromising, than many a unilinear Marxist narrative in which capitalist accumulation was a necessary if painful step towards the dawn of a socialist order.[31]

In a 1978 article in the *Socialist Register* focused on *The Life and Times of Liberal Democracy*, Ellen Meiksins Wood roundly declared that 'Macpherson's theory and method are not... Marxist'. He seemed indifferent to any *analysis* of capitalist social relations. Was he writing in a kind of Aesopian language, so as not to alarm liberals but sweet-talk them into socialism? Or, more likely, had he (and the British socialist tradition from which he drew) been 'seduced' by liberalism, a fate that might now befall Marxists unwise to listen to his siren Fabian song? How could he at one and the same time tell his readers that liberalism 'had always meant freeing the individual from outdated restraints of old established institutions' and show them how intimately liberalism and capitalism had mutually constituted each other? It was important to pay due acknowledgment to the legitimate claims of liberalism, but never at the cost of avoiding any confrontation with liberalism's 'mystifications ... on their own ground'.[32]

Following up on Wood's article, Leo Panitch suggested that Macpherson was like other non-Marxist writers – C. Wright Mills or Barrington Moore, for example – who used the insights of Marxism to enrich their analyses. In Panitch's view, Macpherson used Marx as an 'ethical benchmark to measure how far change has to go to realize human potential'. Yet, in doing so, Macpherson tended to gloss over the gross deficiencies of Marxism itself, particularly with respect to democratic theory, and by emphasizing the deleterious circumstances under which they had been born, gave Marxist dictatorships an easy ride. Macpherson had failed to take responsibility for the tradition upon which many of his central concepts – such as the net transfer of powers – supposedly depended.[33] Overall, Panitch thought Wood had underplayed the extent to which Macpherson had relied on Marx for his conceptions of the state and class, indeed over-relied upon him in adopting his economic determinism – which made it all the more 'puzzling' why he so stubbornly located himself within the liberal tradition. Confronting Macpherson's blithe remark, 'Where there's a will, there's a way' – the context was a consideration of past obstacles to the real-world application of socialist theory – Panitch exclaimed: 'So we move from the extreme of economic determinism to the extreme of sheer voluntarism ... Only an intellectual who does not see Marxism and its revolutionary project as his personal business can afford such theoretical luxury'.[34] Wood concluded the debate with a third instalment by rejoicing that, at the very least, she and Panitch had agreed that Macpherson was woefully deficient in the class struggle department, and insisted that he was, at bottom, an individualist and a Fabian, oblivious to the crying need to re-think – and 'de-alienate' – power. His intricately formal analyses of liberal ideology were 'devoid of social content'.[35]

Although Macpherson to my knowledge never replied to these critics, one might venture to do so on his behalf. First, he would offer an appreciation for the subtlety, intensity and political passion with which his work had been read by his fellow leftists. But where they saw evasion, inconsistency, or naiveté, Macpherson saw logical deductions – the logical deductions of socialist conclusions from liberal premises. To be a consistent modern liberal democrat meant freeing the individual from the dead hand of outmoded institutions, capitalism foremost among them. It meant, in fact, resisting received versions of liberal order itself. The 'individualism' they had quite correctly noted in him did not in fact refer to 'a monolithic concept'.[36] Were not they as socialists also in favour of the freeing of individual creativity from the thralls of the capitalist marketplace?

He discerned a sharp dichotomy among individualism's defenders. In contrast to celebrators of possessive individualism – Bentham and James Mill in their day, F.A. Hayek and Milton Friedman in Macpherson's, their innumerable neoliberal progeny in our own – stood thinkers like J.S. Mill, T.H. Green and John Dewey, and above all Tawney, committed to a free society in which each person was empowered to exert, develop, and enjoy his or her powers.

And, in the good company of Gramsci, this Macpherson would have enjoined his Marxist critics to spend more time with the concept of property – 'all roads lead to property'[37] – not just as an economic reality but as a complex politico-cultural ideal. As early as 1941, Macpherson had argued that 'not only the genesis of democracy but also its present and future are bound up with the problem of property relations'. An 'inclusive historical method' of political theory necessarily made it a central topic.[38] But – what was property and why was it so fundamental? 'Property' in everyday speech often denoted a physical object or tract to which someone claimed exclusive ownership – yet behind each such thing was a complex set of relationships necessary for that thing to be so categorized. As liberal democracy cohered as an influential theory and practice in the early nineteenth century, property came to mean 'the individual right to exclude others from the use or benefit of something', which had grown into the dominant 'paradigm of property for historical rather than logical reasons'.[39]

Macpherson had learned from his savvier critics in the 1960s that, for social commentators before Locke and Hobbes, and often including them, 'property' had once had far wider connotations than it does today. An early modern person might claim 'property' in his or her honour, matrimonial happiness, good health, offspring, indeed in pretty much anything.[40] Yet the upshot of Lockean liberalism had been progressively to narrow the concept, on the seemingly egalitarian argument that a justifiable claim to property derived from the labour invested in it – a thesis that, once applied in a market society to employees, slaves, colonial plantations or, ultimately corporations, created a plausible justification for the glaring inequalities inherent in capital accumulation. Macpherson thought that by accepting this 'labour derivation of the property right' liberals had been forced into two profound errors: they had come to argue for a severely constricted, pacifying, and reductionist notion of human nature and they had become complicit in socio-economic relations that blatantly undermined the democratic equality they supposedly championed. They had gone astray in accepting as a permanent facet of human existence what was 'only a special case', i.e., property as it had come to be defined since the late eighteenth and early nineteenth centuries.[41]

Property was so fundamental because society had come to be divided into classes (i.e., groups of people standing 'in the same relations of ownership or non-ownership of productive land and/or capital').[42] And once generalized to the entire planet, the tensions between owners and non-owners could entail entire countries entering extractive relationships with other countries.[43] Property was 'always a political phenomenon'. It had assumed its seemingly natural and self-evident character through a political process depending on ideas and perceptions. 'How people see the thing – that is, what concept they have of it – is both effect and cause of what it is at any time', Macpherson argued in 1978. If what such people saw necessarily bore *some* relation to what was actually there, this correspondence was not exact – and 'changes in what is there are due partly to changes in the ideas people have of it'. Property was both an institution and a concept, and 'over time the institution and the concept influence each other'.[44] Remember 'The Dream': and remember the great capitalist institutional crisis of 2007-9! And remember, too, Gramsci explaining that commonsense beliefs could themselves become 'material forces'.

It was thus possible for property's egalitarian critics to contemplate influencing the institution by changing its 'justificatory theory', i.e. all the authoritative arguments conventionally brought forward (often in courts of law) to legitimize it. Macpherson, who was such a critic, recommended the definition of property be changed, so that it became 'an individual right not to be excluded by others from the use or benefit of something'.[45] As someone who esteemed classical logic, Macpherson thought this provided a tidy resolution of the contradictions afflicting liberals and 'most of their critics' (at least those who wanted to retain 'the most important values of liberal-democratic society').[46] Rather than marching under banners proclaiming 'Human Rights Not Property Rights' – a slogan that inadvertently and ironically paid homage to the widespread conflation of property with private property – egalitarians could march under banners demanding 'Equal Property Rights For All'. He saw concrete indications of this new thinking in widespread notions of property as a right to a revenue, i.e., 'a right to an income from the whole produce of the society, an income related not to work but to what is needed for a fully human life', and in the notion of 'an equal right to access to the accumulated means of labour, i.e., the accumulated capital of society and its natural resources'. [47] The guaranteed annual income might be one modest step towards the realization of such rights.

Macpherson envisaged a time when the looming crisis of capitalism would prompt 'a new, or an increasing, popular awareness of the structural incompetence of the present system, and will lead increasing numbers of people to a more articulate view of their own best interests or long-run real wants'.[48] He was, in short, a liberal who wanted his tradition to respond realistically to contemporary Marxist challengers. And to do that, liberals had to achieve 'a more realistic concept of what it is to be human': with an intensity partly derived from listening closely to his Marx-leaning critics in the late 1970s, Macpherson insisted that the 'individual' at the heart of liberal theory, whose free and full development was at the core of his own political imagination, needed to be grasped as being 'fully human only as a member of a community'.[49]

MARX FOR THE MIDDLE CLASS?

A 'Marx for the Middle Class' – the title of a book Macpherson was planning a few years before his death[50] – would have to convince people who thought themselves as 'middle class' that socialists were offering them something more practical than a lovers' leap into a revolutionary void. Guarantees of the right to a stable and healthy environment, for example, would require not the tweaking but the transformation of the global social order. It would be difficult for liberals to resist this case, especially if it was cast in terms of fundamental rights, but it would also be impossible for them to concede such demands and leave capitalist social relations as they were. And once the human right to a quality of life came to be considered a property right, it would not be so easily discounted, for property's 'whole prestige' – a very Gramscian turn of phrase and insight - 'will work against it rather than for it'.[51]

This 'Marx for the Middle Class' might, for example, point out to middle-aged middle-class people that their own debt-encumbered economic insecurity, the pervasive precariousness of their children's jobs, and the seeming inability of their governments to supply even a modicum of affordable housing, day care and universal public health, is the outcome of a global system of property that rewards the wealthiest with immense fortunes and leaves most everyone else high and dry. This 'Marx' would also build upon massive *middle-class* discontent with meaningless and repetitive jobs and argue that the majority of professionals themselves stand on the brink of a massive process of global deskilling and deprofessionalization.[52] And this 'Middle-Class Marx' would insist, in the midst of the serious political nihilism diagnosed by Brown, that a valid distinction can be drawn between true and artificial needs, with the former defined as those which 'could be met by a rational, non-class-dominated, organization of production (work and leisure), given the presently available technology'.[53] The 'human essence' could be realized 'only in free, conscious, creative activity', an 'essential humanity' capitalism denied 'to most of its inhabitants'.[54]

Or – to translate this insight into a more familiar Marxist language – if you truly want to defend individualism, commit yourself to overcoming capitalism. If you really want to build a post-capitalist alternative, it is not enough to concentrate your energies on Marxist theory. Rather, you need to question – and persuade fellow citizens to question – the *senso comune* that surrounds 'property', that pith and substance of so much of our political and legal tradition, the dynamic interface wherein the tectonic plates of economic structure are integrated with the hopes and (now often disappointed) dreams of a vast public. Accepting conventional acquisitive notions of property – often based, certainly in North America, on Locke's 'labour derivation of the property right' – meant, in the end, buying into a distorted and partial doctrine of human nature, one that treated the essential human being as a 'consumer, desirer, maximizer of utilities,' not a 'doer, exerter, and developer of uniquely human attributes'.[55] This, in short, is what I imagine Macpherson might have said to his Marxist critics in the *Socialist Register* – but, I imagine he would have also added: 'Our struggles, our sense of history, our belief in a radical democratic future, are so very, very close to each other.'

In fact, if the crisis of twenty-first-century capitalism can be conceived of as one of property – the 'centre of gravity and the core of our entire juridical system' (Gramsci)[56] and 'always a political phenomenon' (Macpherson) [57] – then both thinkers could play key roles in a radical democratic movement that, in the face of global oligarchy, must necessarily place the property rights enshrined in liberal theory, and now entrenched around the globe, in question. The property right not to be excluded from adequate housing could, under twenty-first-century conditions of authoritarian liberalism, come to be considered a revolutionary property demand – as might the right not to be excluded from gainful employment, medical care, and affordable advanced education. If the liberal buzzword 'inclusivity' is given this more down-to-earth, materialist connotation, new theoretical and analytical space would suddenly be opened up. Not only might Marxists and radical liberals start to have useful conversations with each other, but they also might be able to forge dramatically new forms of praxis.

Might the working-class occupiers of the factories deserted by capital find new intellectual inspiration, and new bases of support, if they argued their claims with reference to a 'Macphersonian' concept of property, i.e., their human property right not to be excluded from the means of labour? Might this not provide an interesting linking concept between two modes of discourse that often seem mutually exclusive? And possibly a way of making their case to a broader 'middle class' otherwise susceptible to easily-aroused fears of expropriation? Could we find in such liminal strategies an updated Gramscian 'method of liberty', both materialist and idealist, suitable to our time? Or, if we attend to a point made by Leo Panitch in his commentary on Macpherson – that Marxists need to incorporate 'those elements of the liberal democratic theory of the state that can be found consistent with a non-market, classless society'[58] – might there not be a way of thinking through how such grassroots struggles can find their way into a genuinely democratic party politics? Might there not be, inherent in Macpherson's rethinking of property, an element useful to the long 'war of position' against capitalism that will confront us – if we are lucky — for the remainder of the twenty-first century?

To date, the tectonic shifts of a capitalist order in crisis have not generated a worldwide cultural shift analogous to those of the 1920s and 1930s. Yet, against more fatalistic and apocalyptic analyses, one might from a longer-term perspective find promising indications that this crisis is shaking many loose from their customary ideological positions and political identities. Many people, including many young middle-class people, are rethinking capitalism and its property relations. In a starkly oligarchic world, most of them are likely to be forever numbered among the excluded. Confronting similar issues of precariousness, propertylessness, and stagnant or declining living standards, and likely to find little of substance in the morally and politically bankrupt positions of mainstream liberals, people in such strata are good candidates to become subaltern organic intellectuals of a radical democratic movement. And when and if they do, there is a rich treasury of thought, much of the best of it coming from liminal theorists defying ready-made labels, for such subalterns to learn from. Much – perhaps even human civilization itself – depends on the success of their struggle.

NOTES

My thanks to Peter Graham for his research assistance and to Frank Cunningham for his encouragement and sound advice.

1   Wendy Brown, 'Neoliberalism and the End of Liberal Democracy,' *Edgework: Critical Essays on Knowledge and Politics*, Princeton, New Jersey and Oxford: Princeton University Press, 2005, citations at pp. 41, 45-6, 56-7, 59.

2   Andreas Karitzis, 'The Dilemmas and Potentials of the Left: Learning from Syriza', in Leo Panitch and Greg Albo, eds., *Socialist Register 2016: The Politics of the Right*, London: Merlin Press, pp. 374, 376.

3   Wolfgang Streeck, *How Will Capitalism End? Essays on a Failing System*, New York: Verso, 2016, pp. 93, 42.

4   Here I follow in the steps of Frank Cunningham, who linked these two theorists together in presentations in 1988 and 1992: 'The Gramscianism of C.B. Macpherson', Canadian Political Science Conference, Windsor, 9 June 1988; 'Le Mariage de Macpherson et Gramsci', Instituo Gramsci, Rome, 19 June 1992. Macpherson himself wrote of a 'euphoric vision' of adherents of the two traditions either beneficially coexisting in 'friendly rivalry', or a 'still more euphoric, even utopian, vision' of their merger: 'If that were to happen, the political-theory profession could be said to have entered the late twentieth century', C.B. Macpherson, *Rise and Fall of Economic Justice*, Oxford: Oxford University Press, 1987; reissued with an introduction by Frank Cunningham, Toronto: Oxford University Press, 2013, pp. 74-5.

5   John Schwarzmantel, *The Routledge Guidebook to Gramsci's Prison Notebooks,* London and New York: Routledge, 2015, pp. xii, 225; Antonio Gramsci, *Selections from the Prison Notebooks*, ed. and trans. by Quintin Hoare and Geoffrey Nowell Smith, London: Lawrence & Wishart, 1971, p. 325; Q [Quaderni] 11§ [Note] 12.

6   See Richard J.F. Day, *Gramsci is Dead: Anarchist Currents in the Newest Social Movements*, Ann Arbor: Pluto Press, 2005; for my critique, see '"O Dark Dark Dark. They All Go into the Dark": The Many Deaths of Antonio Gramsci', *Capital and Class* 98 (Summer 2009), pp. 131-40.

7   Kate Crehan, *Gramsci's Common Sense: Inequality and its Narratives*, Durham and London: Duke University Press, 2016.

8   Schwarzmantel, *Guidebook to Gramsci's Prison Notebooks*, p. 93.

9   Karl Marx, 'On *The Jewish Question*', available at: www.marxists.org/archive/marx/works/1844/jewish-question/.

10 Cf. 'The tendency to belittle the enemy. It seems to me that exhibiting this tendency is itself proof of one's inferiority. Belittling one's enemy is in fact an effort to enable oneself to believe that he can be vanquished; such a tendency therefore is also an instinctive judgment on one's own inability and weakness.' Antonio Gramsci, *Prison Notebooks* Volume 3, ed. and trans. Joseph A. Buttigieg, New York: Columbia University Press, 2007, 324; Q8§158. Or, again, 'one must be fair to one's enemies, in the sense that one must make an effort to understand what they really meant to say and not dwell on the superficial or immediate meaning of their expressions' (p. 347; Q8§196).

11 Gramsci, *Prison Notebooks* Volume 3, pp. 121-2; Q6§162.

12 Crehan, *Gramsci's Common Sense*, p.20; Gramsci, *Selections from the Prison Notebooks*, p. 165; Q13§18.

13 Gramsci, *Selections from the Prison Notebooks*, p. 422; Q11§67.

14 Crehan, *Gramsci's Common Sense*, p. 61. One might add that, if Gramsci's concept of subalternity applies mainly to classes, it can be brought to bear on other social groups as well.

15 As both Marcus Green and Crehan have pointed out, it was a fundamental error on the part of 'subaltern studies' to assume that Gramsci's intellectuals were *individuals* possessed of certain skills, when Gramsci referred to the 'social relations that organize the production of authoritative knowledge on which we should focus'. Crehan,

Gramsci's Common Sense, p.189; Marcus Green, 'Gramsci Cannot Speak: Presentations and Reinterpretations of Gramsci's Concept of the Subaltern', in Marcus Green, ed., *Rethinking Gramsci*, New York: Routledge, 2011, pp. 68-89.

16   Crehan, *Gramsci's Common Sense*, p. 181.

17   Crehan, *Gramsci's Common Sense*, p. 186.

18   Gramsci, *Selections from the Prison Notebooks*, p. 423; Q11§67.

19   It could well be that the accessibility of an author who modelled himself on Voltaire has also stood against his posthumous reputation. His clarity was easily mistaken, especially among intellectuals in quest of European sophistication, for simple-mindedness. They often tended to read his writings without attending to their context or nuances – or to the Aristotelian logic structuring many of his logical dissections of his opponents' positions. Much of his declining stock post-1980 may also be attributed to the now-fading vogue of the Cambridge School of Political Thought. The reissuing of most of his major works under the editorship of Frank Cunningham by Oxford University Press can be seen as an indication of his revival.

20   C.B. Macpherson, *The Life and Times of Liberal Democracy*, Oxford: Oxford University Press, 1977; reissued with a new introduction by Frank Cunningham, Oxford University Press, 2006, p. 106.

21   Macpherson, *Life and Times*, pp. 55, 66.

22   C.B. Macpherson, 'Introduction to Karl Marx', in C.B. Macpherson, ed., *Property: Mainstream and Critical Positions*, Toronto: University of Toronto Press, 1978, p. 59.

23   University of Toronto Archives and Records Management Services, C.B. Macpherson Fonds [hereafter MF], B87-0069/004, Folder 'Letters re Festschrift', Macpherson to Steven Lukes, 8 January 1980. Macpherson so staunchly adhered to 'a Millian individualist concept of human essence' that his arch-critic Quentin Skinner once quipped that, when he came to define his 'own positive credo', Macpherson, seemingly sanguine about 'liberal individualism as a proper basis for social life', sometimes called to mind 'a more embattled John Stuart Mill'. Quentin Skinner, 'Liberty and Property', *New Statesman*, 2 March 1973.

24   One of the most striking examples of this centrality of property to meaningful twenty-first-century radicalism can be found in the indigenous people's movements that have arisen throughout the Western Hemisphere. Liberal strategies of 'truth and reconciliation' have predictably entailed much moralizing about the sins of past generations and the generous tolerance of future ones – but without a fundamental conception of long-standing liberal processes that transformed homelands into alienable property, 'reconciliation' here is just a prettier word for 'assimilation'. For a suggestive analysis, see Glen Sean Coulthard, *Red Skin White Masks: Rejecting the Colonial Politics of Reconciliation*, Minneapolis: University of Minnesota Press, 2014. Late in his life, Macpherson came to appreciate (albeit in an unpublished research file) that indigenous land claims provided evidence that notions of property now taken for granted were but '200/300 years old'. MF, B87-0069/009, Folder 'Native Land Claims'.

25   A supposed 'Marxist' forgetful of the class struggle, the expropriation of surplus value, the necessity of some sort of socialist revolution, peaceable or otherwise, and the dialectic, not to speak of almost all writings in the Marxist tradition apart from those of Marx himself – which was the case with Macpherson prior to the mid-1970s – would be an odd bird indeed. He did read more broadly in Marxist scholarship in his last 15 years.

26 William Leiss, *C.B. Macpherson: Dilemmas of Liberalism and Socialism,* Montreal and Kingston: McGill-Queen's University Press, 2009.

27 Although one specific point *does* call out for rebuttal (and reveals some of the polemical fervour that transformed this imaginary Macpherson into political theory's equivalent of Pol Pot). Leiss answers one suggestion that Macpherson might have considered the survival of some form of market relations under socialism – emanating from David Morrice, 'C.B. Macpherson's Critique of Liberal Democracy and Capitalism', *Political Studies* 42(1994), pp. 646-61 — to be out of keeping with the alleged tendency of Macpherson toward rigid either/or thinking, which inclined him to favour '*bureaucratic, non-market socialism*' (p. xi, emphasis in original). Yet Macpherson in fact clarified this point in an important letter of 1980: 'A centrally-planned and administered socialist economy may use markets as a distributive mechanism without permitting market incentives to determine investment or pricing decisions or the whole direction of the economy'. Macpherson imagined such states could use markets without 'letting the market use them'. The recipient of this letter was, interestingly enough, one William Leiss. MF, 887-0069/004, Folder, 'Letters re Festschrift,' C.B. Macpherson to William Leiss, 13 January 1980.

28 For which, see Jeffrey A. Winters, *Oligarchy,* Cambridge: Cambridge University Press, 2011, who works with a 'material power index'. In one version, he compares the income of the top 400 American taxpayers to that of the 134,887,500 souls who find themselves in the bottom 90%; on this calculation the rich have an advantage of 10,327 to 1 (p. 215, table 5.1). Actually, this estimate underestimates levels of inequality, because it excludes home equity and offshore and untaxable accounts. In contrast, Winters estimates that Roman senators enjoyed a 10,000 to 1 material advantage over the slaves who kept their empire going (p. 92, table 3.2). Granting all the difficulties of statistical analysis stretching over many centuries and areas, his attempt at a comprehensive survey is impressive. For more recent data, see the much-discussed Thomas Piketty, *Capital in the Twenty-First Century,* Cambridge, MA: Harvard University Press, 2014; Branko Milanovic, *Worlds Apart: Measuring International and Global Inequality,* Princeton: Princeton University Press, 2005; and, best of all, the highly sophisticated analysis of Göran Therborn, *The Killing Fields of Inequality,* Cambridge: Cambridge University Press, 2013. Therborn also provides an accessible distillation of much recent literature in 'Dynamics of Inequality', *New Left Review* 103, January-February 2017, pp. 67-85.

29 http://portside.org/2017-05-31/activist-probing-factories-making-ivanka-trump-shoes-china-arrested

30 Macpherson, *Economic Justice,* pp. 27, 65-6, 73, 98.

31 R.H. Tawney, *The Sickness of an Acquisitive Society,* London: Fabian Society, 1920; *Religion and the Rise of Capitalism,* New York: New American Library, 1937 [first published 1927]; for an insightful study, see Lawrence Goldman, *The Life of R.H. Tawney: Socialism and History,* London: Bloomsbury, 2014.

32 Ellen Meiksins Wood, 'C.B. Macpherson: Liberalism and the Task of Socialist Political Theory', in Ralph Miliband and John Saville, eds., *The Socialist Register 1978,* London: Merlin Press, 1977, pp. 215-40, citations at pp. 216, 217, 219, 240.

33 The 'net transfer of powers' offers us interesting insight into the strengths and limits of this debate. As Macpherson explained the theme in 1965: 'Human beings are sufficiently unequal in strength and skill that if you put them into an unlimited contest for possessions, some will not only get more than others, but will get control of the

means of labour to which others must have access ... So in choosing to make the essence of man the striving for possessions, we make it impossible for many men to be fully human. By defining man as an infinite appropriator we make it impossible for many men to qualify as men'. C. B. Macpherson, *The Real World of Democracy*, Toronto: Anansi, 2006 [orig. published 1965], p. 79. It was a theme Macpherson thought so important that he regarded it as a key to whether people had really grasped his theory or not. With respect to its theoretical roots, Macpherson references Jeremy Bentham and Charles A. Reich in *Property*. This concept *could* be assimilated to the Marxist theme of the expropriation of surplus value – but it could also be integrated into a wide range of radical democratic theories quite separate from it. It seems to me that in their drive to assimilate this theory to their own, Marxists were overlooking its originality and usefulness – as a theorization of unequal power relations not directly reliant on the labour theory of value.

34   Leo Panitch, 'Liberal Democracy and Socialist Democracy: The Antinomies of C.B. Macpherson', in Ralph Miliband and John Saville, eds., *The Socialist Register 1981*, London: Merlin Press, 1980, pp. 144-68, citations at pp. 145, 152, 159. It was indeed true that Marx's radical humanistic writings did give Macpherson such a benchmark – but one should never underestimate the extent to which he also turned to Tawney, John Stuart Mill, and T.H. Green.

35   Ellen Meiksins Wood, 'Liberal Democracy and Capitalist Hegemony: A Reply to Leo Panitch on the Task of Socialist Political Theory', *The Socialist Register 1981*, pp. 169-89, citation at p. 181.

36   C.B. Macpherson, 'Pluralism, Individualism, and Participation', *Economic and Industrial Democracy* 1(1980), p. 21.

37   C.B. Macpherson, *Democratic Theory: Essays in Retrieval*, Oxford: Oxford University Press, 1973; reissued with an introduction by Frank Cunningham, Toronto: Oxford University Press, 2012, p. 121.

38   C.B. Macpherson, 'The History of Political Ideas', *Canadian Journal of Economics and Political Science* 1(4), 1941, pp. 576-7.

39   C.B. Macpherson, 'Liberal-Democracy and Property', *Property*, p. 205.

40   See, for instance, Jacob Viner, 'Possessive Individualism as Original Sin', *Canadian Journal of Economics and Political Science* 29(4), 1963, p. 554.

41   C.B. Macpherson, 'Liberal-Democracy and Property', in *Property*, p. 201.

42   Macpherson, *The Life and* Times, p. 11.

43   From the 1930s on, Macpherson was almost always sceptical about the transformative potential of class conflicts in the West, but sometimes thought these had been transposed onto the global scale in the form of struggles between the developed and the underdeveloped world.

44   Macpherson, 'Meaning of Property', Introduction to *Property*, pp. 1, 13.

45   Macpherson, 'Liberal-Democracy and Property', p. 201.

46   Paraphrasing Macpherson, *Rise and Fall*, pp. 32-3. They would thus be returning, he adds in a nice twist, to 'the original liberal meaning of property, as when Locke and his contemporaries spoke of a property in one's person, one's life and liberty, as well as one's worldly goods'. This was a point with which Macpherson's critics had belaboured him in the 1960s and 1970s.

47   Macpherson, 'Liberal-Democracy and Property', p. 206.

48   MF, B87-0069/006, Folder, APSA Paper: A Primary Question for Democratic Theory, CBM, 'A Primary Question for Democratic Theory', Contribution to Panel on Democracy, as APSA meeting, Chicago, 1 September 1983.

49   Macpherson, *Rise and Fall*, p. 33.

50   MF, 887-0069/005, Folder, 'Marx for the Middle Class', draft notes. *This* Marx was to reveal to middle-class people the denigration of humanity implicit in Bentham's 'utilitarian vision', which on Macpherson's reading had triumphed over other, more humanistic variants of liberalism. Notions of an unvarying human nature were to be challenged: 'Man has changed & can change again'. And the socialist vision did not merely entail 'distributive change via welfare-state floors & transfers'. The rough notes peter out before we learn what socialist vision might fully appeal to middle-class people, but elsewhere one discerns something of its dimensions — self-management at work, women's liberation, the end to environmental devastation, and a fundamental rethinking of narrowly individualistic concepts of property, which confined everyone living and working in a capitalist society.

51   Macpherson, *Rise and* Fall, p. 84.

52   For an accessible discussion, see Peter Frase, *Four Futures: Visions of the World After Capitalism*, London and New York: Verso, 2016, pp. 1-18.

53   C.B. Macpherson, 'Second and Third Thoughts on Needs and Wants', *Canadian Journal of Political and Social Theory* 3(1), 1979, p. 49.

54   Macpherson, *Rise and Fall*, p. 64.

55   Macpherson, 'Liberal-Democracy and Property', in *Property*, p. 201.

56   Gramsci, *Prison Notebooks* Volume 3, p. 125; Q6§167. Gramsci is citing, by and large approvingly, Alessandro Chiappelli.

57   Macpherson, 'Meaning of Property', p. 1.

58   Panitch, 'Liberal Democracy', p. 163.

RADICAL DEMOCRACY AND SOCIALISM

ALEX DEMIROVIĆ

It appears that the advanced capitalist social formations have arrived at an impasse. None of the problems that have defined capitalism for several hundred years have been solved; that is to say, poverty and unemployment, heteronormative violence between genders and sexual orientations, racism and the colonial domination of many global regions by privileged centres, the exploitation of human labour capacity and the massive increase of social wealth concentrated in the hands of a small rich minority, all alongside the destruction of nature (not just climate change, but soil erosion, desertification, and shortage of clean drinking water too) as a prerequisite for human life.

The dominant bourgeois forces are evidently incapable of tackling these problems, which is not to say that they cannot see the need for action too – annual debates at the World Economic Forum testify to this, as do the national and international commissions, expert committees, conferences, and studies addressing these issues that have been institutionalized for years§. Yet, no relevant decisions are made – nor can they in fact be made. No common interest can be established and no consequent joint actions decided. If attempts are made, they are blocked by powerful heterogeneous interests. Agreements, coalitions, and contracts fail or are maintained only temporarily. The argument revolves around the definition of reality, strategies for action, and ultimately the question of which parties' group interests are put at an advantage or disadvantage. The lowest common denominator model inevitably overrides particularistic interests. Consequently, what tends to take place could be described as negative coordination rather than a positive collective quest for solutions. In past years, then, we have observed a back and forth movement in the bourgeois camp: the rights of wage earners are reduced, only to be marginally reformed again; civil rights are extended, then restricted; environmental legislation improves and then worsens again; renewable energy is championed, as is fossil energy thereafter. Meanwhile, some people get wealthier and enjoy comprehensive services, while many get poorer and experience daily humiliation and violence. Some live longer, while many continue to die early. Climate change proceeds and environmental disasters are more frequent and severe.

In light of this situation, a common social interest – that is to say, humanity's interest – ought to come to the fore and assert itself. Yet the opposite seems to be true. State apparatuses are captured by rich oligarchies and virtually privatized; fraud and corruption proliferate. At the same time, evident facts are denied, the media attacked, and the sciences ridiculed as false teaching. As has been the case during all authoritarian periods in modern capitalist history, not just specific facts are disputed: the very notions of truth and reason are discredited. Liberalism, which has always tended to relativize truths as mere opinions, is thus carried to extremes.

THE EROSION OF DEMOCRACY
AND NEW DEMOCRATIC MOVEMENTS

In such a muddled situation, it would indeed seem reasonable to get back to a central tenet of the self-conception of the modern social formation: democracy, that is, the sovereign people from whom all power supposedly derives. At the same time, no solutions can be expected from the institutions of representative democracy – after all, erosion and crisis of the dominant democratic institutions brought about by the neoliberal reorganization of capitalist society have been diagnosed for some time.[1] Nationalist, nepotist, populist and authoritarian political tendencies are evident in a number of states; even in countries where parliaments and political decision-making authorities have remained intact, technocratic politics of governance are practiced.[2] It will not be possible to find solutions or put them into practice by this means – everything will just continue to revolve around the reproduction of existing power relations on an expanded scale.[3]

Humanity can only solve these problems transnationally, on the basis of commitment, intelligence, and the cooperation of many. The cycle of radical democratic protests that began in 2011 was a positive sign.[4] Along with material demands against finance capital, austerity policies, privatization, forced evictions and tuition fees, demands for democracy were also prominent. That is to say, democracy not based on the model of representative democracy, but real, genuine democracy practiced today by people who join in debate in the here and now.[5] Political parties and managerial elites were accused of not representing the people, being corrupt, only carrying out bureaucratic necessities, and ultimately orientating their policies towards powerful interests. Remarkably, debates were indeed often held in a democratic fashion – yet these assemblies were not enough to generate anything permanent or effective by themselves. Demands for democracy alone, even when raised and discussed democratically, are not enough to capture collective life. For this to happen, they have to coalesce with everyday life and intervene in the machinery of powerful decision-making processes. People need to have the time to come together and debate, and the debates have to involve concrete decisions.

This implies that to a certain degree, they have to be binding. They must be held in a way that addresses relevant problems and makes any involvement meaningful: once a decision has been made, it remains relatively valid; it cannot simply be overturned by a random gathering or different committee at the next opportunity. In instances such as Occupy Wall Street and Nuit debout, the assemblies soon hit their limits and dissolved: many activists involved did not have enough time at hand, and since there were no prospects of putting ideas into practice, democratic debate began to slack. Where that did not occur, new parties such as Syriza and Podemos emerged and produced new managerial staff. Elsewhere, people supported alternative leaders in existing parties hoping they would bring about democratization (such as Sanders, Corbyn, and Mélenchon). Radical democratic movements thus reached a limit that was impossible to overcome solely by making demands for democracy more forceful. They were detached from the processes of everyday life, as well as administrative processes. Crucially, they were detached from the processes by which they reproduced their own material existence. Often taking place on the margins of mainstream society and everyday life, the protests and assemblies typically involved the unemployed, the homeless, students, and passers-by who participated in debates after work. They only obtained any power when they organized concrete cooperation regarding medical and food supplies, struggles against forced evacuation and water privatization in the neighbourhoods, and opposition to corrupt politicians. However, the existing state managers generally stood their ground and state apparatuses remained intact. Where new apparatuses were built or top positions taken over by new managerial staff – as, for example in Greece, which saw a Syriza-led government emerge thanks to the social movements – the divide between self-organized solidarity networks on the one hand, and the political sphere with its parties and state apparatuses on the other, soon became manifest in everyday life. Despite great efforts, it proved difficult – if not impossible – to maintain a connection between the two spheres.

The representatives of bourgeois forces found various ways to exploit this weakness, which characterized radical democratic movements. They persistently ignored criticism and practical proposals, defended their institutions and functions, employed legal and police measures to persecute the movements, and manipulated public opinion. Sections of the bourgeoisie mobilized with a view towards authoritarian-populist ruling coalitions. On a superficial level, the latter efforts had similarities to the social movements' critique of democracy: after all, authoritarian populists also hold the view that the people are not represented by existing political institutions and administrative staff. True to the tradition of authoritarian elite theory, they claim that elected politicians constitute a 'political class' that seizes political institutions in the name of democracy, yet solely to pursue vested interests. Authoritarian populists, who claim to represent the unmediated voice of the people, aspire to bring about an immediate representational relationship between top and bottom. This way, they can neutralize the crisis of representation and help reorganize the power bloc. In a sense, their claim to independence is accurate: the political parties that are geared to their interests rarely subject them to genuine political decision-making processes. Unlike most politicians, to use Gramsci's words, they are not intellectuals 'at the service' of the ruling class. Like Berlusconi, Trump, and Blocher, they directly belong to that class because of their property, or they use their position to join that class (as in Eastern Europe and Turkey).

It is becoming apparent that these forces erode democracy to a significant degree when in charge of top positions within state apparatuses: systems of knowledge are reformed (read: restrictions on scientific freedom, reductions in funding, new tools to control universities and research),[6] scientists intimidated and persecuted, the judiciary reorganized and re-staffed, media and press freedom attacked, administrative processes dismantled through legislative changes and staff cuts, and responsibilities transferred. Crucially, an authoritarian climate is engendered in everyday life to undermine civil rights and liberties, as well as devalue well-substantiated knowledge, standards of rationality and accepted ethics. Facts are denied and the opposite claimed. Those who stand up for democratic rights are discredited as 'politically correct'; those who deconstruct ingrained ideological practices are labelled ideological. A rigid and hypocritical sexual morality, religious sectarianism, ideological abstrusities, and racist discrimination proliferate within, and by means of, democratic institutions. It is sheer mockery when the German Minister of Finance – one of the key advocates of hard austerity policies in the European Union – explains the rise of authoritarian populism by stating that people are disaffected and want more participation in decision-making, yet in the same sentence demands that trade union influence is weakened and the job market deregulated.

The advanced capitalist societies have arrived at an impasse: dramatic problems require social solutions. Democracy itself, which should serve to develop these, is in crisis. Given this disastrous state of affairs, we need to ask particularly what ideas democratic theory has contributed that might help us out of the impasse. I do not mean the kind of democratic theory that practices 'business as usual' in the belief that there is no alternative to representative democracy, and insists that the system is not in a crisis. Rather, I am referring to radical democratic theory. Some of its ideas are closely linked to social movements, inspire them, or seek to draw conclusions based on their experiences. In my understanding, the radicalization of democratic theory since the 1960s, which has been partly informed by a close dialogue with social movements, and partly by a distanced and critical one, essentially evolved in two steps. I will therefore distinguish between Radical Democracy I and Radical Democracy II. Before addressing these concepts, I will briefly reiterate the assumptions of conventional democratic theory.

THE CONVENTIONAL CONCEPTION OF DEMOCRACY

The conventional conception of democracy is based on the assumption that the democratic constitution rests on the will of a sovereign people. The people are represented by the state, and their will assumes the shape of general legislation. The state is synonymous with the public sphere; it guarantees the legal framework that allows all members of society to pursue their interests in safety and equal freedom. To the extent that the general will has to be investigated, this responsibility is held by parliament, where the representatives of the whole people discuss and decide bills. The political agenda is set by the representatives of the people and by the government. Consequently, the understanding of popular participation in representative democracy is narrow: citizens are expected to participate in elections. In addition, they can form an audience that stays informed about political debates and decisions made in political caucuses through the media. Malcontents are expected to express their dissent in elections and public speech within a conventional framework, i.e. in citizens' assemblies, letters to delegates or newspapers, or through participation in a political party. The logic of parties is such that competition for votes pushes them into a certain distance from the diverse interests of the electorate, which renders the representative relationship precarious.

Although complaints about insufficient legitimacy are often heard, this distance between political parties and 'the people' poses no formal problem for representative democracy – after all, elected delegates always represent the people as a whole. Hence, even a minuscule election turnout would legitimize parliaments and governments. A critical situation is only diagnosed when competition to established parties emerges or citizens become politically active in unmediated ways. To be sure, citizens' involvement is regarded as a political virtue and moral resource for the stability of existing political institutions. However, unconventional political activities such as demonstrations and blockades are often perceived as an affront to public order rather than perfectly normal democratic expression. Activists involved are discredited as anti-democratic, extremist, and subversive forces that state bodies must confront with tough measures to protect the democratic constitution.

The concept of a sovereign people is distinguished by further democratic deficits. For one, it suggests that the reach of its decisions is consistent with territorial borders. In reality, the 'democratic' decisions made by most OECD countries' affect territories far beyond their borders. The constitutions of these countries safeguard property rights and lifestyles that seriously interfere with the lives of people who live in different states and have no democratic say in these matters. Moreover, representative democracy is inwardly restrictive with respect to participation rights as well. For in most cases, those who belong to the sovereign people are narrowly defined. After the American and French revolutions, it took a great deal more than a hundred years until universal suffrage was formally adopted in the OECD states. In reality, suffrage is still constrained and conditional. In many states, migrant workers pay taxes, but do not have the right to political participation; and in numerous countries, people who have been integrated with the domestic working class for many years are still illegal, and can thus be super-exploited. Suffrage and elections themselves are subject to a number of formal and informal interventions. For one, constituencies can be customized to deliver the expected election results. In some countries, parties and voters are required to undergo strict registration processes to participate in elections. Elections are held on working days, preventing many from voting. There may only be a few geographically distant polling booths. Poorer sections of the populace and those who have no hope of wielding any influence over political parties do not partake in debates and elections. The weight of political party funding and advertising shows them plainly what aims the rich and powerful pursue, whereas opinions backed by less powerful interests cannot be voiced as publically or are discredited. Finally, voting ballots are misappropriated, illegitimately added, or miscounted. Candidates, delegates and political parties are openly threatened with violence and their campaigns disrupted. Ultimately, the formal concept of a sovereign people belies the material bases of different forms of representative democracy. In each individual case, the material basis embodies a specific balance of forces and compromise between social classes. Thus the welfare state democracies after the Second World War were constituted on the basis of steadily increasing workers' wages brought about by increased productivity and economic growth – which in turn was due to state subsidies and demand. They integrated workers in an extended circulation of consumer goods, which included basics such as food and furniture, but also durable consumer goods. The culture industry facilitated the mass consumption of culture just as automobility and tourism transformed workers' lifestyles. Furthermore, working-class families and large sections of the traditional petty bourgeoisie could now invest in the education and upward mobility of their children, who were in fact integrated by state apparatuses with an expanded scope of duties. Initially, the phase of neoconservative neoliberalism from the early 1980s onward was characterised by attacks on trade unions. In the 1990s, under the auspices of social-democratic neoliberalism, mechanisms of governance proliferated and civil-society actors – especially in the shape of NGOs, business consultants, and think-tanks – gained importance. Today, authoritarian neoliberalism rolls back these forms of participation. Governments continue to cut staff, close advisory channels, withdraw from public life, and manipulate the media in order to create a one-way and one-sided communication between populist leaders and the people.

RADICAL DEMOCRACY I

Radical democratic theory is dissatisfied with the restrictive dominant conception of democracy, which ultimately falls back on existing institutions and processes. This formalist orientation indeed allows for a distanced, institutionalist approach, which favours order and lacks any inner commitment to democratic standards. Radical democratic theory, in contrast, calls for a different conception: democracy should not be defined by a rigid canon of rules that can be followed on a mere formal level, but tied to a political culture, which involves a living process of participation, questioning and change.

In this sense, what we are calling Radical Democracy I, epitomized by Jurgen Habermas (and also so Claus Offe) aims to democratize democracy. It does not question existing constitutional institutions, but wishes to reconstruct the meaning they contain to update them. Thus, it is assumed that democracy is the result of a contract between equals who join a community on the basis of equality and freedom; by partaking in democratic arguments, they fight to prevent anybody's rights from being disadvantaged by the institutions of the community. To ensure this, one must not solely rely on formal institutions, but expand the public sphere to the effect that no issues, actors or practices can be simply fended off as illegitimate. The theoretical assumption is straightforward: it is alleged that in the institutions of representative democracy, collectively binding decisions are made. These decisions are legitimate because they are made by way of constitutional processes rooted in the principles of freedom and equality. As a rule, it is to be expected that legislative decisions prove to be particularistic, incomplete, one-sided or wrong in factual, social, spatial, or temporal terms. That is to say, they interfere with existing lifestyles in such a way as to disadvantage them or give rise to new interests. Illegitimate power emerges when interested parties immunize decisions against arguments and shield them from opposing parties.

To democratize democracy, then, means to voice doubt and assert the need to revise laws. This may pertain to the consequences that decisions have, but also to the ways in which decisions have come about. Despite their claim to universality, laws are never truly universal, and a number of problems arise when they are applied. Governments and administrations may violate laws and legal requirements, as when applying legislation to administrative regulations, due to delayed execution or staff shortage, or when acting arbitrarily for strategic reasons, possibly even accepting the risk of prolonged court trials. Because of the general nature of legislation, which only restricts liberties, but does not determine actions, non-regulated loopholes appear; interested parties take advantage of them. Conversely, in many cases, the rights of individuals and groups are disregarded or violated because formal and universal legislation is applied to individuals of different backgrounds and personal circumstances. What is more, the execution of democratic laws assumes bureaucratic forms, which further reinforces such limitations even when the state bureaucracies act in a proper fashion. To be sure, the abuse of power by authorities is itself a systemic component of executive force.

In all of these cases, citizens feel that their equality and freedom are violated. This gives them reason to question the legitimacy of decisions and push for the process to be reopened. When interest groups guard a decision that might have only been made due to their pressure by blocking any avenues of questioning and revising it, this undermines the normative foundations of the democratic social contract. When this occurs, the radical democratic idea envisions that the affected, instead of disassociating themselves from the democratic institutions, demand compliance with the standards by which they constitute a commonwealth of individuals with equal rights. When active citizens (*Aktivbürger*) initiate a public discussion to put a past decision up for debate, they appeal to these norms of equality and freedom. Because of the doubts they express in debate, the decision must be justified again – and in detail. The debates may take many different forms: citizens' assemblies, talks and presentations by experts, media reports, protests and demonstrations, occupations of public spaces, sit-ins, hunger strikes, and pickets. It is an important aspect of Radical Democracy I to regard many unconventional, non-procedural ways of public communication as valid contributions to public debate.

From the point of view of Radical Democracy I, new forms of public communication do not jeopardize the legitimizing basis of the democratic political system. On the contrary, by claiming democratic rights, new actors help to universalize and democratically refound that basis. The women's movement is cited to illustrate this: it led a struggle demanding that the separation of the private family sphere should be understood as a political decision granting men special powers backed by the state, and it was on the rejection of this particular decision that women campaign for unrestricted access to the bourgeois public sphere was founded. The women's movement is never radically excluded in the sense of a complete communication breakdown: rather, women fighting for emancipation constitute a specific public arena. When arguing different interpretations of needs in debate, they follow the self-conception of the liberal public sphere. Using criticism to transform the bourgeois public sphere from the inside, the women's movement asserts universal norms that are constitutive of bourgeois society.[7] A new interpretation of the norms of freedom and equality results in a deeper and broader understanding of democracy, which lends the system new legitimacy. In this way, a crisis is averted and democratic institutions are effectively re-founded.

If voicing the need for revision is made difficult by democratic decision-making processes, or if decisions tend to privilege specific social groups, then the need to revise these very processes democratically becomes evident. However, in the liberal tradition, constitutions are deemed to provide the required rules for legislation and – consequently – social change. Thus codifying the present for the future, they make change difficult or even impossible. Any effort to broaden the procedures of democratic decision-making is dismissed as an illegitimate attempt to question the constitution itself. Radical democratic theory therefore envisions procedural approaches as very far-reaching. It argues that democratic procedures must be reflexively extended to the democratic procedures themselves: deliberations are to be held in the form of debate; they must be inclusive and public, nobody must be excluded; they must be free of external pressure and tied solely to the procedural rules of debate; everybody must have an opportunity to be heard; conferences may be continued indefinitely, although they should lead up to a decision passed by majority vote; no matters that concern everybody may be barred from conference – this applies especially to the resources on which equal communication and the exercise of participation rights depend; debate extends to the discussion of needs and pre-political attitudes, i.e. it is not guided by values and traditions.[8]

Democratization takes place not outside of constitutional political institutions, but within and through the procedural frameworks; these are supplemented by public communications, which rest on the civic infrastructures of bourgeois society. Social problems are laid out in multiple heterogeneous public arenas. This public sphere consists of an intermediary structure, which mediates between lifeworld relations and the political and administrative system. It forms a channel through which numerous instances of exclusion, suffering, and dysfunctional consequences brought about by systemically integrated processes of the economic, political, and administrative systems can be addressed, generalized, and communicated to political decision-making bodies. In this periphery of civil society that surrounds the political power centre, a communicative influence unfolds, which nonetheless must overcome the barrier of institutionalized processes before it can gain communicative power and pass into legitimate legislation.

It is on this basis that Jurgen Habermas thus deviates from conventional constitutional thought in proposing that we expand the concept of popular sovereignty and make it communicatively fluid: in addition to the checks and balances of the state, the communication flows of civil society should also be regarded as components of democratic popular sovereignty.[9] Even so, Habermas explicitly stresses that radical democratic practice must be restricted to civil society and may not mistakenly become a form of social self-organization for society as a whole. Public discourse may only assume authorized forms when tied to the institutionalized power of political processes.[10] Put differently, as much as the governmentally grounded public sphere is opened up to society through democratic debate, ultimately it is still defined by the decision-making entities of the state. The division of society into separate functional systems - economy and politics on the one hand and the lifeworld on the other - and the intermediary public sphere are not subjected to democratic deliberation.

In this sense, 'how we want to live as members of a specific collective'[11] is already largely predetermined. Habermas rejects socialism, but surprisingly, he argues like a functionalist rather than from the point of view of democratic theory: according to him, society is too complex; socialism cannot work because it rejects functional differentiation and intervenes in the economy by means of politics (a functional system), thus impairing the specialized services of the economy. Incidentally, Habermas thus names exactly one of the problems: the issue is indeed the democratization of the economic sphere.[12] Yet that is not all, for the public sphere and the political system must also be examined according to the criteria of democratic theory. Above all, the form that the complexity of bourgeois society takes must be subjected to democratization: that is to say, the logic of differentiation or put differently, the social division of labour.

RADICAL DEMOCRACY II

In the 1980s, radical democracy began to evolve further. This development was inspired not only by the authoritarian tendencies the New Left observed in the state socialist countries, but also by those it encountered in its own organizations. The new social movements brought new issues, new actors, and new forms of action that eluded both the vocabulary of the traditional left and conventional democratic theory. As neoliberalism attacked Fordism's welfare state class compromise and reorganized capitalist economies and politics, it became clear that this marked the end of a specific period of capitalism. Radical democracy I (not only the particular approach of Jürgen Habermas but also that of John Rawls)[13] was criticized for assuming a rational, universally shared consensus upon which collectively binding decisions were to be based. Radical Democracy II champions dissensus, argument, conflict and antagonism – however, it does not return to the notion of class antagonism. Radical Democracy I conceives of politics as an argument about the general good that is fought out in public; its results are legally fixed in cooperation with existing political institutions. Radical Democracy II, in contrast, is interested in processes that put new issues on the agenda, overcome marginalization, present a new vocabulary and new ways to look at things, and during which previously unknown actors appear. Habermas emphasized the normative public sphere, communicative compatibility, and the merging of different horizons of meaning through communicative rapprochement, reclaiming the concept of politics for this process. The new emphatic conception of politics, on the other hand, wanted to call attention to the irreducible emergence of entirely new horizons of meaning, the appearance of unexpected constellations, and sudden shifts in the balance of forces.

In my view, this critique misunderstands consensus orientation, proceduralism, and ultimately itself. Both forms of radical democratic theory highlight the importance of conflict and base their democratic theory on linguistic assumptions. I will briefly demonstrate this by clarifying a) Habermas's conception of conflict, and b) Jacques Rancière's references to language.

The proceduralism championed by Habermas indeed assumes that there are fundamental conflicts between social interest groups. However, they are considered particularistic and neutralised in the functional subsystems by monetary or administrative means. Universally relevant subjects, on the other hand, become the subject of public debate and argument. When arguing about the interpretation of standards that opponents appeal to, they performatively renew them as shared foundations of social coexistence.[14] Habermas recognized this principle in the ability of humans to speak to each other in a communication-oriented fashion, thus recognizing each other as equals. By speaking, people assert their intention to coordinate their actions through communication. Therefore, they implicitly or explicitly raise a truth claim to the effect that their interpretation of the world is correct. This claim to a universally binding interpretation that coordinates actions normatively assumes that everybody else can raise argumentatively substantiated objections as a free and equal speaker. Discourse is therefore by no means free from conflict, nor will this be the case in the future.

To be sure, Habermas recognizes an evolutionary process whereby humans, as a community of speakers, only gradually assert the universal norms that are intrinsic to their sociality and language faculty. The public sphere, according to him, aims for unrestricted inclusion. However, his conception holds that there will never be an evolutionary stage without conflict: humans not only have divergent interests, the wayward processes of differentiated functional systems will often have negative consequences for lifeworld relations. Hence, arguments brought forward by individuals will still be publicly debated, and there will still be debate as to whether they can be generalized. Nonetheless, it is conceivable that in a universalist setting, individuals will no longer pursue their particular interests in an instrumentalist fashion or accept decisions in a functionalist manner. That is to say, they will no longer make themselves immune to arguments. Rather, they will conduct themselves in a truth-apt manner and put their interests up for debate; they will also seek decisions that minimize the negative effects of systemic processes that colonize lifeworld cultural relations.

As shown above, Habermas rules out the prospect of abolishing capitalist relations of production and bureaucratic rule through the democratic self-determination of society. He argues for a theory of social equilibrium that allows pushing back encroachment from the functional systems and synchronizing them, the lifeworld and the public sphere by the means of democratic participation to obtain a more purposive arrangement.[15] Since the operational mode of the systems frequently allows imbalances to reappear anew, democracy is theoretically downgraded to the point of becoming a structural correction mechanism. It remains subordinated to the social totality and constitutes a channel for individual experiences of suffering in the lifeworld sphere. The notion that it should shape the totality and social development is rejected.

In a broad sense, the advocates of Radical Democracy II also follow the linguistic turn. For Ernesto Laclau and Chantal Mouffe, who primarily refer to Derrida's theory of the sign, democracy is internally produced by the logic of discourse. According to Rancière, humans are speaking beings. When speaking, they aim for communication. By performing the speech act, they claim equality; even an order, although based on inequality, must assume the equality of the addressed to be heard and understood.[16] Yet speaking has a radical meaning. For Habermas, the excluded are barred from putting forward their arguments in public. They can, however, form their own subcultural public arena to assert their identities, problems, and issues. By doing so, they claim the norms of communication-oriented action that define the bourgeois public sphere as a whole and frequently make it susceptible to the coercion-free force of better arguments.

In Rancière's view, when those who have no part in anything begin to speak, an argument takes place on what it means to speak and be heard rather than just issue forth noise.[17] The same word might be used to name a different object, or a previously unseen object is made visible. A fundamental reordering of constituent parts occurs, different classifications emerge, the sensible is partitioned in new ways, and the world is divided according to a different system of coordinates. The difference between proceduralist Radical Democracy I and Radical Democracy II is not that the former ignores conflicting interpretations; conversely, new radical democratic approaches primarily appeal to the standard of equality as a universally binding democratic benchmark that no longer allows for radical exclusion – and they draw similar conclusions.[18] Indeed, Mouffe, who strongly advocates a conflict theory of democracy, even insists that all conflicts must be carried out within the consensual framework of a constitution and be compatible with the acceptance of pluralism that is constitutive of modern democracy.[19] The critique is aimed at the fact that democracy is always tied down to already existing constitutional institutions, and that the institutions of the state, which are in fact particularistic and led by sectional managerial staff, are always considered universal at the outset.

In contrast, newer forms of Radical Democracy II undertake a double displacement, namely from institutionalized communication and decisions to constitutive actions, and from politics to the political. Even if the first variation of radical democratic theory regards political and moral standards as fundamental for human coexistence, it still views democracy as a specific trait of modern society and a feature of a differentiated political system.

Radical Democracy II, in contrast, is concerned with the political as a distinct rationality and conduct. The political is no longer understood as a special sphere of society, nor can it be deduced from it. Politics is not confined to a constitutionally defined sphere where fixed interest groups pluralistically argue what to accept as universal. The political is not that location of power that is structurally void now that the king's head has rolled and, as a result of democratic struggles, always temporarily filled with a concrete universality.[20] If one could say that in this case, modern democracy still cleaves to feudality, Radical Democracy II argues in a more radical fashion: it asserts that the political is constituent action, that is, the very actions that institute society and politics, social institutions, the order of the sensible and its partition to begin with. 'The problem of the political is the problem of the institution of the social.'[21]

Democracy is the emphatic element of the political, for it is participation in the fact of domination without any entitlement. Democracy is the 'beginning without a beginning, the rule of those who do not rule', as Rancière puts it.[22] It is 'the institution of politics – the institution of both its subject and its mode of relating'.[23] Those who partake in what they have no part in, those who speak when they are not to speak assert themselves in a democracy. Therefore, democracy is synonymous not with normal everyday processes of coordinating, preparing, and making decisions, but with sudden acts of open speech and participation. It asserts itself solely in those rare and eruptive cases in which political acts produce new institutions or new arrangements of the political space in such a way that issues, modalities of collective decision-making, and actors change.[24] Out of this instituting political moment, the entire social space is reorganized. Society itself is conceived as the merely temporary result of efforts to fix and totalize a specific political constellation.[25]

Rancière refers to the established distribution of the sensible, the arrangement of people, and the regulated practices of communication as the police. He differentiates politics from this arrangement, and distinguishes politics from Radical Democracy I as advocated by Habermas:

The essence of politics is the manifestation of dissensus. Dissensus is not the confrontation between interests or opinions ... Politics makes visible that which had no reason to be seen, it lodges one world into another (for instance, the world where the factory is a public space within the one where it is considered a private one) ... This is precisely why politics cannot be identified with the model of communicative action since this model presupposes the partners in communicative exchange to be preconstituted, and that the discursive forms of exchange imply a speech community whose constraint is always explicable. In contrast, the particular feature of political dissensus is that the partners are no more constituted than is the object or the very scene of discussion ... The worker who argues for the public nature of a 'domestic' matter (such as a salary dispute) must indicate the world in which his argument counts as an argument. Political argument ... is the construction of a paradoxical world that relates two separate worlds. Politics thus has no 'proper' place nor does it possess any 'natural' subjects.[26]

I would add two critical remarks to this observation. First, regarding the question of whether politics consists of antagonism, argument, and dissensus whereby radical politics disrupts the established order and results in a new one. Both in Laclau's and Rancière's view, antagonism and argument emerge from a constitutive *externality*. They are not reproduced according to *internal* processes and contested as continued contradictions that define everyday social life. This is why they appear without any determination. They embody groundlessness and contingency – a beginning without a reason. Politics is the absence of reason; it exists because every social order is contingent.[27] This is also the basis upon which Laclau distinguishes radical democratic theory from Marxism. The latter, in his view, reduces democratic action causally to social conditions – relations and compromises between capital owners and wage labourers, rulers and ruled – and therefore fails to take it seriously. By invoking the contingency argument, Laclau, like Rancière, claims the element of irreducible free action for democratic theory. However, their logic of freedom is belied by the fact that there always exist concrete actors with concrete demands. Laclau and Mouffe are forced to concede this, however implicitly, when sociologically ascribing the supposedly contingent emergence of new democratic subjects to modernization processes – i.e. they deem it a result of consumerism, bureaucratization and mass-media produced homogeneity. Not only are such explanations for the emergence of democratic movements unoriginal and already contained in the proceduralist approach of Radical Democracy I,[28] they also contradict the theoretical apparatus of discourse and hegemony by employing causal arguments and arguments borrowed from modernization sociology. Like Habermas, they explain democracy as a channel through which suffering can be voiced. Secondly, the constituted society is questioned by antagonism or argument. This argument revolves around the institution of a contentious commonality in which many experience the injustice of nothing being theirs. They are thrown back into the non-existence of those who have 'no part in anything'.[29] This begs the question of whether democratic conflicts contain only one binary antagonistic relationship – that is, only one world that is not part of another – or if there is a multitude of intertwined worlds. All of these conflicts have been manifest for several centuries. 'Society' is the concrete, permanently changing form in which they are contested. How these conflicts concur, how they openly erupt in specific conjunctures, and how they fade into the background for prolonged periods and yet remain effective requires explanation. Indeed, Laclau addresses this problem when elaborating his theory further: 'There is no future for the Left if it is unable to create an expansive universal discourse, constructed out of, not against, the proliferation of particularisms of the last few decades.'[30]

But by naming the problem, he also reveals that his theory of radical democracy has failed. After all, it was formulated precisely with the intention of asserting all the different movements and antagonisms that produce empty signifiers (in which all antagonistic demands concentrate) by contingently forming a chain of equivalence. What is more, before even attempting to analyze the discursive processes that lead up to the empty signifier, 'the left', Laclau already speaks of a 'left', its future, and its mission to produce a universalizing discourse; in light of his own theory, this seems astonishing. Nor is this plausible from the point of view of radical democratic theory: after all, universalism is to be constituted out of a non-identified 'constitutive externality'. Since a 'left' identity can only emerge as the contingent result of a discursive process, it is completely unclear why Laclau has such expectations of the 'left'.

What Laclau thus criticizes in his own theoretical terms is that the multitude of particularistic interests and lifestyles does not universalize itself by finding a common adversary. Within the framework of Laclau's theory, there are three possible explanations: 1) from a sociological point of view, one may claim that various lifeforms coexist differentially and pluralistically; 2) in terms of politics and power theory, it is possible to say that rulers prevent the pluralist differences from merging into a chain of equivalence in opposition to an adversary; 3) above all, however, one may point to the paradoxical demobilization by democratic theory itself. Although Laclau and Mouffe plead for antagonism,[31] Mouffe elsewhere softens this to mere 'agonism' – emphasizing positive aspects of certain forms of political conflict – thus preserving pluralism. Put differently, instead of being solved at all, the social and political problem that has led to antagonistic polarization in the first place is channelled into some constitutional pluralism. Strictly speaking, from the point of view of this theory, a radical democratic movement is not actually desirable. The theory offers no terms that could help constitute the left as an effective force with a view to overcoming the aforementioned problems. According to Radical Democracy II, democracy requires that a particularistic actor restructure the entire space by speaking up. A redistribution of the sensible (Rancière) or new hegemonic totalization (Laclau/Mouffe) occurs. Hence, it is possible for Miguel Abensour to write that democracy 'installs itself paradoxically in a place which defies any installation, the very place of the caesura between two forms of state, one past, the other to come'.[32] Democracy, then, consists of this act of instituting and constituting a new order. Every form of democracy implies that something is established. Therefore, it necessarily also implies a new exclusion: 'Every social order is political in nature and is based on a form of exclusion.'[33] Contrary to what Habermas implies in his analysis of the women's movement, this exclusion does not necessarily concern an already existing identity or interest. Rather, a new arrangement and new distribution of the sensible produces a disadvantage; it creates a group that has no part in anything, a group that previously did not exist and did not know that a politically constitutive action would affect it negatively. Democracy is therefore not tantamount to some special arrangement of political institutions; it is synonymous with the permanent possibility of a constitutive action that allows an unexpected and unknown exclusion to be put up for consideration again.

The essential thesis of Radical Democracy II is that there is no final form of democracy. Hence, it has been said that democracy always implied a kind of democracy that is yet to come (democratie à venir).[34] The democratic struggle cannot be concluded; new actors are repeatedly compelled to fight against a world shaped and distributed in a way that renders them nonexistent. Radical Democracy I bases democracy on universal moral standards; humans consistently, but always inadequately advance towards these standards, which they regard as their guiding regulative ideas. Radical Democracy II modifies this Kantian notion. Its impulse is not derived from the aspiration to live up to standards that can ultimately never be fulfilled. Rather, part of the logic that characterizes democracy is that it will always remain incomplete. No politically constitutive action can ever claim credit for constituting freedom, equality, and democracy in such way as to prevent people from demanding adequate democratic actions and a suitable conception of democracy in the future. Democracy is an internally incomplete project – it is always yet to come. The process of political argument never ends; antagonism is inextinguishable and constitutive for human society.[35]

It is possible to reformulate this as a criticism. Democracy is formalist and passive. It is based on the suffering of the excluded: new actors appear – the working class, women, victims of racist discrimination, refugees – and change the respective constellation, only to be replaced by other excluded groups. Society does not advance by an ever-increasing degree of emancipation – rather, one argument or antagonism replaces another. Democracy is not a form of shaping society; it fights against the results of instituted democracy. Put differently, in the name of democracy, conflicts never solve existing problems, they merely overtake them and brush them aside. It remains unclear if these problems continue to exist and determine social relations in the background, even if those who had no part manage to win a share.[36] Thus it is also possible to formulate this as a paradox: it is a constitutive necessity of democracy that there exist people who are excluded, who suffer, who have no part in anything – and that the struggles will endlessly go on and on.

This is indeed incompatible with socialism. Socialism, after all, aims to shape consciously social relation and to abolish forms of exclusion, suffering, indifference, oppression, exploitation, and destruction of humans and nature that are historically concrete. This must be understood in radical terms. Radical democracy is concerned with making visible excluded identities and uncharted experiences of suffering in accordance with existing norms. Beyond this, it has no defined objective. The socialist perspective, in contrast, aims to overcome historical relations and forms of existence that result from domination, such as the class of wage labourers, racialized individuals, and modes of subjectivation tied to the gender dichotomy.

THE SOCIALIST PERSPECTIVE

Reflections on open democracy and democracy to come (démocratie à venir) should not be read merely as a reaction to the proceeding erosion and closure of representative democracy. They are also a critical reaction to authoritarian processes in the socialist tradition, especially to the extent the latter has failed to develop an understanding how to shape socialist living conditions consciously and democratically. As early as after the American Revolution, the question emerged of whether future generations should simply accept the inherited freedom or if they should have the right to realize their own ideas of freedom through another revolution.[37] The socialist tradition indeed expected that once capitalist property relations were overcome through revolution, the immediate consequences would be the demise of class antagonisms, a rational management of nature, and the end of racism, sexism, and of the division of labour. Correspondingly, there would no longer be any political conflict nor need for democratic coordination mediated by the state. From this, it was possible to further conclude that any residue of conflict was down to historical vestiges (e.g. the petty bourgeoisie, experts), confused and pathological individuals, or provoked by external forces. Both versions of radical democratic theory reject the notion of such a harmonic and transparent society. Both accuse the left, particularly the Marxist tradition, of reducing politics to a superstructural phenomenon of the economy and therefore lacking any political or democratic theory. Radical democratic and socialist perspectives are not easily reconciled. Radical Democracy I is critical of socialism because it contains the notion that society as a whole creates itself through politics. Politics, according to this theory, is merely a subsystem of society; it would therefore be overburdened if it were to manage society as a whole. The positions of Radical Democracy II contain arguments for socialism, although they subordinate socialism to democracy. I want to reverse this perspective and make clear that democracy is an aspect of socialism.

The Marxist and socialist traditions continued the Rousseauian position according to which the working class embodies the general will of society; this is because workers do all the socially necessary labour that is a prerequisite for the material existence of society.[38] The bourgeois class, in contrast, only represents a corporate interest. However, it is evident that the working-class movement contains a number of different interests and political trends, as well as numerous conflicts. From a materialist point of view, this is not surprising: after all, the socially combined working class is heterogeneous in age, gender, regional and national origins, and experience in politics and struggle. Historically, great political efforts were required to unite all these diverse groups into one 'class'. Indeed, from a Rousseauian point of view conflicts between different sections of the class resulted from insufficient insight into the common class position or the influence of hostile class forces aiming to split the workers' movement. Consequently, ranks were closed, while critical positions and emerging trends or factions were quickly interpreted as deviations, weakness, or betrayal and correspondingly denounced.

Positions of this type necessarily assume that such differences can be overcome in struggle against the common foe, through scientific insight, or – in the last instance – when class divisions cease to exist. We must concede to Laclau and Mouffe that Antonio Gramsci's reflections on hegemony completely changed that perspective. In his view, the multitude of nuanced positions and conflicting trends were more than just empirical fact. Nor did they testify to a fragmented 'class'. Rather, he considered them organic differences rooted in diverse lifestyles and perspectives, which must not be disregarded. In this sense, Gramsci argued that even though ruling classes are capable of strategically exploiting such differences, it is just these differences that allow us to assume that many different emancipatory paths are possible:

It is a serious error to adopt a 'single' progressive strategy according to which each new gain accumulates and becomes the premise of further gains. Not only are the strategies multiple, but even in the 'most progressive' ones there are retrogressive moments.[39]

This means that the attempt to create unity on the basis of class interest as a common denominator is wrong and, as experience shows, leads to authoritarian results. When Gramsci speaks of hegemony, he means a process during which specific sections of the ruling or the working class universalize themselves and form a bloc. When organizing the apparatus of production, this bloc contains a concrete relationship to nature, a concrete articulation of manual and intellectual labour, and a specific alliance of various social groups. The historical bloc does not put an end to conflicts between the groups it contains – rather, it develops its own forms through which these processes are carried out. The organization of social labour is always at the centre of such historical blocs. The form that Gramsci envisions for the historical bloc, the form of councils, deals with numerous conflicts: those between different sections of production and services, town and country, immediate producers and consumers. A fundamental change in the social division of labour must overcome the relations of domination between manual and intellectual workers.

It is not my intention to use these insights as arguments against radical democratic approaches and the concept of democratic pluralism.[40] Rather, one might say that under bourgeois conditions, pluralism and the free development of individuals are only ever rudimentary. As Adorno once said:

> Through the word pluralism, it is suggested that utopia were already here; it serves as consolation. That is why, however, dialectical theory, which critically reflects on itself, may not for its part install itself domestic-style in the medium of the generality.[41]

Capital relations subject individuals to an abstract universality and create a specific equivalence between them by reducing different types of work to abstract labour. Wage labourers are disciplined, normalized, and rated according to the same criterion, namely socially necessary labour time – an average value that follows from competition between individual capitals and its productive forces. The possibilities to assert divergent interests are extraordinarily limited as they are consistently subordinated to social labour, which is organized, homogenized, and pluralized according to the principle of capital valorization. The general thus always dominates individuals while depriving them of the possibility to partake in defining the common. From this point of view, overcoming capitalist relations is not enough to solve all problems, but a necessary step to resolve some historical contradictions. Radical Democracy II strives to consider this aspect, even if it does not contain a systematic location for terms such as capitalist mode of production or socialism. Acccording to Laclau and Mouffe:

> Every struggle for radical democracy implies a socialist dimension, as it is necessary to put an end to capitalist relations of production, which are at the root of numerous relations of subordination; but socialism is *one* of the components of a project for radical democracy, not vice versa.[42]

The reason for this inversion of the relationship derives from radical democracy's critique of the classical conception of socialism, which assumes that 'the disappearance of private ownership of the means of production would set up a chain of effects which, over a whole historical epoch, would lead to the extinction of all forms of subordination'.[43]

Laclau and Mouffe's assumption is that there are no *necessary* links between capitalism, sexism, racism and the exploitation of nature is wrong – for them, there are only hegemonic articulations. Laclau and Mouffe's argument is untenable because it asserts that socialism is merely an economistic project, and furthermore that there can be a capitalist mode of production without sexism and racism. Capitalism historically emerged from the sixteenth century onward by internally linking multiple forms of domination such as racism, sexism, and the exploitation of nature with the exploitation of wage labour.[44] Emancipation needs to proceed in specific ways with respect to individual forms of domination, yet individual practices will not succeed if they fail jointly to blow apart the ties that link them together.

As shown above, radical democracy argues that conflicts may continue in new forms even in a hypothetical socialist society. Democracy is the formalism of revolution in permanence. However, democracy thus conceived fails to offer a solution to the aforementioned problems of modern capitalist society. Antagonisms are transformed into new agonisms while liberal democracy is accepted as a framework. To put it concretely and conceptually, it is not by accident that the concept of politics is at the centre of theory formation. This implies a notion of political action that logically precedes the social. One may conceive of Marx's theory as an alternative to this pre-modern, antiquity-oriented conception of the political. Aristotle's definition of man as a 'political animal' implies that humans are town citizens by nature. In this context, one could characterize humans under capitalism as toolmakers in

Benjamin Franklin's sense. Marx, in contrast, argues that humans are social and cooperative beings; they use their consciousness to coordinate labour and increase productivity in synchronized joint activities. [45]

Contrary to Laclau and Mouffe's claims, this does not imply that human cooperation is reduced to workers' interests. Rather, it encompasses all realms: discourse, knowledge, erotic relationships, familial forms, and social relations with nature (which no individual can facilitate on their own) are all part of what Marx considers the real community. The capitalist mode of production is characterized by a separation of economy and politics, which results in a paradoxical situation. In the economic realm, where humans produce material life, universal decisions concerning social development tendencies (products, investments, large-scale technological systems, standards, and so forth) are made by private individuals. Those who act in the name of the general public in the political realm do so professionally and are therefore particularist experts. The specific articulation of the capitalist mode of production implies that politics and the economy, the private and public sphere, and the individual and public realm are separated. With the specialization of the political sphere, there inevitably emerges the task of administering humans. There is not enough time to debate and make collective decisions – rather than being conceived as social labour, coordinated collective discussion assumes a separate existence. For that reason, the knowledge of the many about life conditions is missing. Ultimately, there is also a lack of competence with respect to decisions that affect long-term developments.

Under capitalist conditions, decisions that concern the ways in which humans work and live are essentially left to the owners of the means of production, whose profit-maximizing decisions bind common life for many decades if not centuries by the organization of labour, technologies, the separation of economy and politics, and the shape of the social and natural environment. Even the praxis of politics thus becomes a primordial rather than contingent form of social life, bearing consequences to which there is no alternative. Politics is a sphere in which particularistic groups argue to create a universality that will remain particularistic. After all, they are forced to assert themselves by means of special identities in order to pre-empt potential exclusion (which they simultaneously practice themselves). In contrast to this, the socialist perspective lays claim to a self-determined cooperation in the course of which supposedly constitutive disputes will be replaced by reconciled forms of coordination. When people leave prehistory behind and begin to shape their own living conditions, the tasks of coordination will be greater than is the case now. However, such tasks will be distributed widely so as to involve many people, and these tasks will be conceived as part of social labour. Consideration and knowledge will play a far greater role in debates than is the case today.

Translated by Maciej Zurowski.

NOTES

1   Colin Crouch, *Post-Democracy*, Malden: Polity, 2014; Giorgio Agamben, *Democracy, In What State?* New York, Chichester: Columbia University Press, 2012; Alex Demirović, 'Kehrt der Staat zurück? Wirtschaftskrise und Demokratie', *Prokla* 157(39/4), 2009; Wendy Brown, *Undoing the Demos: Neoliberalism's Stealth Revolution*, New York: Zone Books, 2015.

2   Regarding the EU, compare Mario Candeias and Alex Demirović, eds, *Europe – What's Left? Die Europäische Union zwischen Zerfall, Autoritarismus und demokratischer Erneuerung*, Berlin: Rosa Luxemburg Stiftung, 2017.

3   Compare Alex Demirović, *Demokratie und Herrschaft*, Münster: Verlag Westfälisches Dampfboot, 1997; Frank Fischer, *Climate Crisis and the Democratic Prospect*, Oxford: Oxford University Press, 2017.

4   Compare Dario Azzellini, 'Ein Epochenbruch. Die neuen globalen Proteste zwischen Organisation und Bewegung', *Prokla* 177(44/4), 2014.

5   Compare Ramón Espinar and Jacoba Abellán, 'Lo llaman democracia y no lo es. Eine demokratietheoretische Annäherung an die Bewegung des 15. Mai', *Prokla* 166(42/1), 2012; Mario Candeias and Eva Völpel, *Plätze Sichern! ReOrganisierung der Linken in der Krise. Zur Lernfähigkeit des Mosaiks in den USA, Spanien und Griechenland*, Hamburg: VSA, 2014; Jens Kastner, Isabell Lorey, Gerald Raunig and Tom Waibel, *Occupy! Die aktuellen Kämpfe um die Besetzung des Politischen*, Vienna: Turia + Kant, 2012.

6   Compare Brown, *Undoing the Demos*.'

7   See Jürgen Habermas, *Strukturwandel der Öffentlichkeit*, Frankfurt am Main: Suhrkamp, 1990, p. 20; Jürgen Habermas, *The Theory of Communicative Action Volume 2, Lifeworld and System: A Critique of Functionalist Reason*, Boston: Beacon Press, 1987, pp. 393-4.

8   See Jürgen Habermas, *Between Facts and Norms: Contributions to a Discourse Theory of Law and Democracy*, Cambridge, MA: MIT Press, 1996, pp. 305-6; Habermas, *Strukturwandel*, p. 41.

9   Habermas, *Strukturwandel*, p. 43; Habermas, *Between Facts and Norms*, pp. 371-2.

10   See Habermas, *Between Facts and Norms*, pp. 371-2, 305.

11   Habermas, *Strukturwandel*, p. 40.

12   See Alex Demirović, *Demokratisierung der Wirtschaft*, Münster: Verlag Westfälisches Dampfboot, 2007.

13   See Jacques Rancière, *Disagreement: Politics and Philosophy*, Minneapolis and London: University of Minnesota Press, 1999; Chantal Mouffe, *The Democratic Paradox*, London, New York: Verso, 2000.

14   See Habermas, *Between Facts and Norms*, p. 369.

15   See Habermas, *Theory of Communicative Action*, pp. 344-5; Habermas, *Strukturwandel*, p. 36.

16   Rancière, *Disagreement*, p. 29.

17   Rancière, *Disagreement*, pp. 22-3.

18   See Ernesto Laclau and Chantal Mouffe, *Hegemony & Socialist Strategy: Towards a Radical*

Democratic Politics, London: Verso, 1985, pp. 151, 155.

19   See Chantal Mouffe, *On the Political*, Abingdon and New York: Routledge, 2005, p. 14.

20   Compare critically Rancière, *Disagreement*, p. 100.

21   Laclau and Mouffe, *Hegemony & Socialist Strategy*, p. 153; compare Mouffe, *On the Political*, pp. 8-9.

22   '*Le commencement sans commencement, le commandement de ce qui ne commande pas.*' Jacques Rancière, 'Onze thèses sur la politique', *Filozofski Vestthik, Acta Philosofica* 18(2), 1997, p. 95.

23   Jacques Rancière, 'Ten Theses on Politics', *Theory & Event* 5(3), 2001, p. 5.

24   See Rancière, *Disagreement*, p. 17.

25   Laclau and Mouffe, *Hegemony & Socialist Strategy*, pp. 125-127.

26   Rancière, 'Ten Theses on Politics', pp. 12-13.

27   See Rancière, *Disagreement*, pp. 16-17; compare Alex Demirović, 'Herrschaft durch Kontingenz', in H.-J. Bieling, K. Dörre, J. Steinhilber and H.-J. Urban, eds, *Flexibler Kapitalismus*, Hamburg: VSA, 2001.

28   Compare Habermas, *Theory of Communicative Action*, pp. 374-403.

29   Rancière, *Disagreement*, p. 9.

30   Ernesto Laclau, 'Constructing Universality', in J. Butler, E. Laclau and S. Žižek, *Contingency, Hegemony, Universality: Contemporary Dialogues on the Left*, London: Verso, 2000, p. 306.

31   Mouffe, *On the Political*, pp. 16, 20.

32   Miguel Abensour, *Democracy Against the State*, translated by Max Blechman and Martin Breaugh, Cambridge: Polity Press, 2011, pp. xxxv, 16

33   Mouffe, *On the Political*, p. 18.

34   Jacques Derrida, *Spectres of Marx: The State of the Debt, the Work of Mourning and the New International*, London: Routledge Classics: 2006, p. 81; Jacques Derrida, *Rogues: Two Essays on Reason*, Stanford: Stanford University Press, 2005, pp. 80-93.

35   Compare Mouffe, *On the Political*, pp. 9, 16.

36   See Alex Demirović, 'Radikale Demokratie und der Verein freier Individuen', in *Indeterminate! Kommunismus. Texte zu Ökonomie, Politik und Kultur*, Berlin: Unrast Verlag, 2005.

37   Compare Hannah Arendt, *On Revolution*, London: Faber & Faber, 2016.

38   Compare Max Adler, 'Political or Social Democracy' [1926], in M. E. Blum and William Smaldone, eds, *Austro-Marxism, The Ideology of Unity Volume II: Changing the World: The Politics of Austro-Marxism*, Leiden: Brill, 2017.

39   Antonio Gramsci, 'Art and the Struggle for a New Civilization', in David Forgacs, ed., *The Gramsci Reader: Selected Writings 1916-1935*, New York: New York University Press, 2000, p. 397.

40   Compare Laclau and Mouffe, *Hegemony & Socialist Strategy*, pp. 179-88.

41   Theodor Adorno, 'Late Capitalism or Industrial Society?', 1968, available at www.marxists.org

42   Laclau and Mouffe, *Hegemony & Socialist Strategy*, p. 178.

43   Laclau and Mouffe, *Hegemony & Socialist Strategy*, p. 178.

44   Compare Karl Marx, *Grundrisse*, 1857, introduction. Available at marxists.org.

45   Compare Karl Marx 1894: *Capital* Volume 1, London: Penguin Classic, p. 444.